D0563756

BIGGER, BRIGHTER, LOUDER

To Amanda:
With best wishes

BIGGER,

150 YEARS OF CHICAGO THEATER

BRIGHTER,

AS SEEN BY *CHICAGO TRIBUNE* CRITICS

LOUDER

CHRIS JONES

THE UNIVERSITY OF CHICAGO PRESS • CHICAGO AND LONDON

CHRIS JONES is chief theater critic for the *Chicago Tribune* and adjunct professor at the Theatre School at DePaul University.

The University of Chicago Press, Chicago 60637
The University of Chicago Press, Ltd., London

Printed in the United States of America
22 21 20 19 18 17 16 15 14 13   1 2 3 4 5

ISBN-13: 978-0-226-05926-6 (cloth)
ISBN-13: 978-0-226-09071-9 (e-book)
DOI: 10.7208/chicago/9780226090719.001.0001

Library of Congress Cataloging-in-Publication Data

Jones, Chris, 1963–
Bigger, brighter, louder : 150 years of Chicago theater as seen by Chicago Tribune critics / Chris Jones.
pages ; cm
Includes bibliographical references and index.
ISBN 978-0-226-05926-6 (hardcover : alkaline paper) — ISBN 978-0-226-09071-9 (e-book)
1. Theater—Illinois—Chicago—Reviews. 2. Dramatic criticism—Illinois—Chicago.
3. Dramatic criticism—Illinois—Chicago—History. I. Title.
PN2277.C4J66 2013
792.09773'11—dc23

2013015593

♾ This paper meets the requirements of ANSI/NISO Z39.48-1992 (Permanence of Paper).

CONTENTS

CHICAGO TRIBUNE DRAMA CRITICS

In approximate order of tenure (some of which overlapped):

GEORGE PUTNAM UPTON (AKA PEREGINE PICKLE) (1834–1919)

WILLIAM LINES "W. L." HUBBARD (1867–1951)

PERCY HAMMOND (1873–1936)

SHEPPARD BUTLER (1893–1972)

FREDERICK DONAGHEY ("F. D.") (1869–1937)

CHARLES COLLINS (1880–1963)

CECIL SMITH (1906–1956)

CLAUDIA CASSIDY (1899–1996)

WILLIAM "WILL" LEONARD (1912–1977)

LINDA WINER (1946–)

ROGER DETTMER (1927–2011)

LAWRENCE "LARRY" KART (1942–)

RICHARD CHRISTIANSEN (1931–)

SIDNEY "SID" SMITH (1950–)

MICHAEL PHILLIPS (1961–)

CHRISTOPHER "CHRIS" JONES (1963–)

INTRODUCTION

1

THE THEATRE

Chicago Tribune

MARCH 25, 1853. Those who patronize the Theatre will be glad to learn that the indefatigable caterer for public amusement and instruction, Mr. Rice, has engaged the Misses Susan and Kate Denin, to appear on the Chicago board in a few days. During the time the Theatre has been opened for the present season, the house has generally been well filled with respectable audiences. The performances have given great satisfaction to play goers, and the selection of pieces, both for interest and moral, has been very judicious. The *corps dramatique* at the present time is more efficient and complete than on any former occasion. Mr. Perry, the leading actor, so well known in the theatrical world, and here in various characters he has played, has received much applause. McVicker, the comedian, an inimitable Yankee imitator, nightly convulses the audience with laughter; he is a decided favorite, and certainly deserves all the praise he receives. Mrs. Ryner, Mrs. Marble, Mrs. Banley and Mrs. Rice, in the various characters they sustain, win the approbation of all. Many new scenes have been painted and in a style that reflects the highest credit upon the artist, Mr. Smith. The "Landing of Columbus," the "City of Lyons," and other scenes have excited much admiration. The decoration and interior arrangement of the Theatre are as perfect as almost any out of New York. The bill of fare for to-night is an attractive one, the pieces for performance being "Speed the Plow," and "Sudden Thoughts."

And so it begins. This little notice appears to be the first, or at least the first extant, *Chicago Tribune* review of its city's theater, published about six years after the newspaper's founding in 1847 (when the population of Chicago numbered around 16,000). It would be followed by tens of thousands of *Tribune* evaluations of and pronouncements on the work produced on Chicago's stages—some boosterish, some witheringly critical, some informed and insightful, some depressingly ignorant. Thus this inauspicious little review—if we define a review as a report by someone who attended the show in question and offered some measure of critical evaluation for the reader—is the starting point for the long and sometimes strained relationship between the city's leading newspaper and its leading and most storied art form.

This book tells the story of the trajectory of Chicago and its theater through the eyes of *Chicago Tribune* critics who were there on various productions' opening nights. It focuses primarily on these first-performance reviews, although some feature stories and interviews are included when they appear to offer more perspective and analysis than the review itself.

The collection of reviews is intended to be representative rather than comprehensive. And it should be noted at the outset that there have been, for sure, many great and highly influential critics in Chicago who worked not for the *Tribune* but for the many competing publications in a city that saw scores of newspapers come and go. The first newspaper was the *Chicago Weekly Democrat*, which began in 1833, just a few months after Chicago's incorporation—as a village. The *Chicago Daily Tribune*, as it then was known, was the third newspaper to arrive, following also the *Chicago American*, which was first published in 1835. By 1860, the city already had 11 daily papers. In the ensuing years, many more famous names entered the journalistic fray; these included the *Chicago Daily News*, the *Chicago Sun*, the *Chicago Times* and the *Chicago Defender*, for many years the most powerful African American newspaper in America.

Many of these newspapers, and others, featured prominent critics and cultural coverage. Among the reviewers important to theater in Chicago: the famous Ashton Stevens of the *Herald-American*, a fierce proponent of Tennessee Williams; Glenna Syse of the *Chicago Sun-Times*, an important critic for more than 30 years; Hedy Weiss, also a long-tenured critic at the *Sun-Times*; Albert Williams and many others at the *Chicago Reader*; and a variety of other writers covering Chicago theater in daily, weekly, monthly and, eventually, on-line publications. Out-of-town critics from the *New York Times* (especially Frank Rich and Charles Isherwood), the *Wall Street Journal* (especially Terry Teachout) and others have been reviewing Chicago theater for decades. It is hard to imagine, for example, that "Grease" would have made it to Broadway without the support of Michael Feingold of the *Village Voice*, who came to Chicago to review that musical.

But this is the story of one newspaper's theatrical coverage—a newspaper that long has been the city's biggest and most durable, and that has reviewed Chicago theater since 1853, when Chicago was barely Chicago. The *Tribune* changed its political and aesthetic face over the years, and, of course, its critics changed as well. Although critics may or may not reflect the editorial views of their bosses, their theater reviews surely reflect the paper's identity of the moment: sometimes the *Tribune* was an impediment to the arts, sometimes a reactionary force, sometimes a scold, often a fervent booster.

This book does not, of course, tell about the shows that the *Tribune* chose not to review, choices that create a counternarrative of their own. The newspaper's criteria for what to cover and what to ignore varied over the years, as did the decision makers, but egregious omissions occurred. For example, the Skyloft Players, an important African American theater company in the Chicago of the 1940s that was founded by Langston Hughes, was virtually ignored by the *Tribune* throughout its history, at least insofar as sending a critic to its shows. Indeed, coverage of African American theater was scant in the newspaper throughout the first half of the 20th century—and arguably well beyond.

Some of the reviews that appear in this collection are of great Chicago shows, many of them famously so. Some are entertaining or perceptive assessments of weak shows. Some are both. And a few are fascinating for entirely different reasons that have more to do with the city, the moment and/or the newspaper than the theater. They have been selected mostly for their import. Given that the *Tribune* has published many thousands of theater reviews in its history, innumerable significant nights and notices are, of necessity, not included in this book.

But the 101 reviews gathered here reflect a remarkable body of work nonetheless. Very few of them have been republished, or widely read, since their initial publication with the news of their day. They appear here with their original headlines, most of their original typographical errors (with minor adjustments for clarity) and with the *Tribune* style—at times an eccentric style of the newspaper's own invention—of their original moment.

As for this first review, we cannot be entirely certain that the unnamed critic (anonymity was a common practice in the newspaper's early years) actually went to the show at John B. Rice's theater, located near the corner of Randolph and Dearborn Streets, but we get the sense he or she did.

The reference to McVicker, that "inimitable Yankee impersonator" who "nightly convulses the audience with laughter," is interesting. James H.

McVicker would go on to have his own famous Chicago theater–and John B. Rice, after selling his theater, would go on to become mayor of Chicago. Rice's theater, like the *Tribune* itself, was founded in 1847, though by the time this review appeared, he was already on to his second building–he built this one out of brick rather than wood.

Initially printed by a press that was powered by the movement of a pony, the *Tribune* would go on to own the Canadian source of the lumber that was fed into its printing plant. But the paper was a small enterprise at this juncture: the potential readers for this review, which was printed in the *Tribune*'s offices at 51 N. Clark St., likely numbered only around 1,000. The legendary *Tribune* editor and publisher Joseph Medill, who would revolutionize the newspaper and cement its reputation, had yet to arrive in Chicago.

Tellingly, this notice appeared in the paper that day in 1853 below two more prominent reports: one, that Messrs. Clybourne and Ellis were planning on slaughtering two hogs, each more than 1,000 pounds (a weight exceeding all the *Tribune* printed copies); and the other, that the largest load of lumber ever to leave the City of Chicago had just left for the town of La Salle, Illinois.

And thus Chicago's priorities were starkly laid out right there on that page: hog butcher for the world and windy self-promoter, specializing in commerce-driven superlatives. The arts came in a poor third. Critics, and the artists they covered, would rail against that perceived set of civic priorities for years. They still do.

But perhaps the most revealing remark of all is the second-to-last sentence of the review: "The decoration and interior arrangement of the Theatre are as perfect as almost any out of New York."

In the following years, *Tribune* critics would almost daily compare their city's theatrical productions with those in, or out of, New York. Many of those allusions were defiant assertions of superiority, or demands for respect, but many contained the same whiff of inferiority that we can sense here. The Second City syndrome has afflicted Chicago critics as much as its artists, then as now.

But the reviews should be telling the story.

2

JEFFERSON'S "RIP VAN WINKLE."

THE NATURAL SCHOOL OF ACTION. / PECULIARITIES OF MR. JEFFERSON'S PERSONATION. / THE DOG SNYDER

September 6, 1868

BY PEREGRINE PICKLE

Chicago, Sept. 5.
To the Editor of the Chicago Tribune:
In this world of amusement in which we dwell, palpably the finest piece of dramatic art is the *Rip Van Winkle* of Mr. Joseph Jefferson. We are accustomed to compare the personations of other actors. We establish degrees of merit in the efforts of Booth, Adams, Couldock, and Forrest, in tragedy, and Warren, Hackett, Owens, and Brougham, in comedy. But when we come to Mr. Jefferson's *Rip*, comparisons cease. It stands by itself, as sharply defined, as superbly drawn, as the Venus di Medici in statuary, one of Raphael's cartoons in painting, or Jenny Lind's Bird Song in music, and if we ransack the records of the stage, we find nothing to which we can compare it.

For the reason that his personation belongs to an entirely new school. It is the commencement of that dramatic era which Shakespeare foreshadowed in his advice to the players. It is the dissolution of that system against which Charles Lamb and Addison wrote so powerfully in *Elia* and the *Spectator*. I verily believe if Charles Lamb had seen Jefferson's Rip Van Winkle, although he was denouncing such great artists as Garrick and Mrs. Siddons, he would never have written that essay on the plays of Shakespeare, and that, if Addison had seen it, the *Spectator* would have been minus some of those sketchy papers on the playhouses. I believe that gentle soul, Charles Lamb, would have taken his sister to see *Rip*, and that they would have talked to each other as no two ever talked before; that great hearted Addison would have taken off his hat and made his best bow to him, that watery Sterne would have shed a Niagara of tears over the simple narrative, and Steele would have gone and got drunk out of sheer inability to do justice to the subject in any other way.

Mr. Jefferson's personation is totally unlike anything on the modern stage. Matilda Heron's *Camille*, in her younger days, approximated to it somewhat, but at present there is nothing that resembles it on the stage. Mr. Jefferson has quietly ignored all the rules, regulations and precedents of the stage. The stereotyped stage-walk—a sort of comico-heroic strut, which has been pressed into service for all sorts of characters, from *Harlequin* to *Hamlet*; the stage gestures; the stage attitudes which *Mrs. Toodles*, curtain-lecturing her intoxicated spouse, and *Lucrezia Borgia*, shielding *Genarro* from the *Duke*, both assume; the rolling of the eyes in a fine frenzy; the mouthing of phrase in a set manner to catch the phrase of the groundlings; the hackneyed entrances and exits; the rant and the making of points, are all foreign to Mr. Jefferson. With him the stage is merely an accident, no more essential to his personation than it was to Irving's conception.

This school of acting which Mr. Jefferson has adopted is the very highest form of dramatic art. In it he realizes the truth of the old adage, that it is the province of art to conceal art. *He completely identifies himself with the character*. That is the secret of his success—of his potent sway over the emotions of his auditors. It is this faculty which enables him so to blend humor with pathos that smiles follow tears in as quick succession as light follows shadow over a field on a summer afternoon. It is, perhaps, impossible for any person who has seen Booth to form any original conception of *Hamlet*. He invariably connects *Hamlet* with Booth, and the result is a theatrical *Hamlet*, and the poor *Ghost* always walks into our memories with a theatrical stride, and smells of the calcium. So with Couldock's *Luke Fielding*, Charlotte Cushman's *Meg Merriles*, Forrest's *Coriolanus*, or Burton's *Toodles*. All these personations were unmistakably fine, but the actors could not always merge themselves in the characters, because there was always the partition of theatrical necessities and precedents in the way. This is not the case with Mr. Jefferson. We do not connect *Rip Van Winkle* with Jefferson, but Jefferson with *Rip Van Winkle*. The transformation is complete. He acts, talks, walks, laughs, rejoices and mourns just as *Rip Van Winkle* would have done, just as any human being would do in *Rip Van Winkle*'s place. In looking at this personation—and I own to having laughed and cried over it many times—I never think of Jefferson. I never think of his art. I never get "enthused" enough to even applaud, for I should never think of applauding *Rip* were he alive and walking today the streets of the village of Falling Waters. To me there is no Jefferson on the stage, but the magnificent creation of Irving moving before me. And all this is done without the show of art. Mr. Jefferson never talks above the ordinary conversational tone of voice, uses only a few gestures and those of the simplest description, attempts no tricks of facial expression, and makes less fuss than the veriest supernumerary on the stage; and yet I question whether any living artist has such an instantaneous command of the smiles and tears of an audience as he.

In fact, I confess, I should be afraid of that man or woman who was not affected by this personation. It has been my good or bad luck, as the case may be, for many years past to have written on every actor and actress who have come to this city, and to have witnessed thousands of dramatic performances. Constant dropping of water wears away the rock, and I confess until I saw Mr. Jefferson, I have looked upon stage murders and all sorts of villainies with a large degree of composure; have even smiled at the lachrymose Mrs. Haller, beloved of young women, and have studied with all my might to discover the fun in the stage situation at which the audience was laughing; and instances are on record where I have slept the sleep of the just all through a five-act tragedy overrunning with murders, suicides, rapes, burglaries, divorces and *crim. con.* enough to have started a second Boston in business. And when I first went to see Mr. Jefferson, I went all calloused with dramatic labor. But if that man didn't have me laughing and crying alternately the whole evening, then I'm a sinner.

The entire personation is so complete and individualized that it is very difficult to select any particular scenes as better than others, for Mr. Jefferson is so thorough an artist that he neglects not even the smallest detail. But there are two or three scenes which seem to me to stand out more prominently than the rest. One in particular is the episode where he is ordered to leave the house of his wife. Most actors would have torn passion to tatters at this point, ranted and rushed round the stage, delivered mock heroics and dashed off in an ecstacy of blue fire with their arms flourished in the air, utterly forgetful of unities or properties. How different Jefferson! He is sitting upon a chair partially turned from the audience, in a maudlin state. His wife orders him to leave her house and never return. Perhaps she has ordered him that way before, for he pays little heed to it. She repeats the order in a louder tone of voice, but still he pays no heed to it. He has stretched out his arm and raised his head as if to speak, when she again issues her order in an unmistakable manner. (And right here let me credit Mrs. Cowell with some very handsome acting in this scene.) It strikes him like a thunderbolt. Without changing the position of a limb he sits as if that instant petrified. He is dumb with amazement as the terrible truth gradually becomes clear in his muddled brains. The silence, the motionlessness, the fixed look of the face, are literally terrible. And when he rises slowly, quietly tells the wife he shall never return, for he has been driven away, stoops and kisses the little one, and so easily passes from the doorstep to the outer darkness that it might have been the flitting of a shadow, you inevitably draw a breath of relief that the scene is over, and indulge in a genuine feeling of the most hearty sympathy for this good-for-nothing, lazy, drunken, good-hearted vagabond.

Equally can there be anything more affecting than the scene when, after his sleep, he returns to his native village to find that no one remembers him? [O]r anything more sadly eloquent than the simple phrase, "Are we then so soon forgotten when we are gone?" pronounced so simply and quietly, and with such a gentle vein of sadness running though it? This appeal, which any other actor would have thrust into the face of his audience as the place for "a point," Mr. Jefferson delivers so simply that you hardly at first catch the full force of its meaning, or become aware how much of life is summed up in the few simple words. It is a page out of real life, only another proof of the folly of supposing that you or I are at all essential to the rest of the world. We pass through life, and some of us kick up a great dust about our chariot wheels, enveloped in which we ride as divinities. We make a great stir upon our individual ant-hills, and try to convince ourselves and our fellow-ants struggling along with their burdens, that there never was such an ant as we, but somehow, when some bright day we go out of sight under the hill we have piled up, the other ants don't mind it much, but go trudging along over us just as usual. When we drop out of the world, so frail has been our hold upon it, that with the exception here and there of some friend to whom we have attached ourselves through a brief space of sunny days, we are not missed, except by the flowers and the animals we have tended, and the busy world goes on buying and selling, cursing and praying, loving and hating, just as if we had never played our little farce on its stage. As the waters part and meet again when a child throws a stone into them, so the waves of the world close up immediately when we leave, and the surface is just as smooth and as perfect as if we were still there.

Mr. Jefferson's make up is very remarkable. He must have studied the character with remarkable earnestness and closeness to draw it so perfectly. Before the sleep, his face is a thorough picture of the good-for-nothing vagabond who exists in every village and is remarkable for nothing but his big heart, which draws to him all the children and dogs of the neighborhood—a sure proof of the humanity of the dog. In general I think that big dogs and small children are the most perfect instances of thorough humanity in the world. A man who has a big heart will always be recognized by a dog quicker than by the two-legged humans. Equally dogs and small children always recognize each other. But of this I may speak at some other time. "To our muttons." After the sleep, the picture of the old man is just as perfect. In every detail of age, the pains in the joints, the shambling gait, the wrinkled face, the childish expression, he presents a counterpart of old age. In neither phase of character does he ever forget himself. He is always *Rip Van Winkle*. His forgetfulness of the audience amounts almost to impudence, and they tell me who are associated with him on the stage that he is equally forgetful of the actors. Off the stage, Jefferson is the most genial of men; like Yorick, full of jest and humor. On the stage, he never forgets that he is playing a character. He is *Rip Van Winkle* in front of the audience, behind the scenes, in the dressing room, and in the *entr'actes* even. He never lets himself down for an instance from the necessities of the *role* until the curtain falls on the last act. He believes that an actor can never become too familiar with a part, never study it too much, and the result is that he plays just as conscientiously now as he did when he commenced, and is constantly making the personation better.

Another singular feature of Mr. Jefferson's acting is that he not only makes *Rip Van Winkle* an actual living personage but the dog *Snyder* also. Although *Snyder* never puts in an appearance upon the stage, he is as important a *dramatis persona* as any on the stage. I think I have formed a perfect conception of that dog *Snyder*—a long, lank, shaggy, ill-favored, yellow cur, loving *Rip* with all his heart, hating *Mrs. Rip*, a sworn friend of all the children in the village, in a continual brawl and fight with the other dogs in the village, one ear bitten off in an unpleasantness with *Nick Vedder's* mean bull dog, but with a big heart after all in his carcass, and a dog who would always take the part of a small dog in a quarrel with a bigger one. Jefferson succeeds in making *Snyder* an actual canine, although he is never visible to the eye; and when *Snyder* goes rattling down the hill, scared out of his senses by *Hendrick Hudson's* phantom crew, I acknowledge to a feeling of sadness for the poor beast who is *Rip's* only friend.

Although Mr. Jefferson never makes a point of theatrical attitudes for mere effect, some of his poses are remarkably beautiful and artistic, especially that one as he stands shading his eyes with his hands, looking with amazement at the village of Falling Waters, after waking up from his sleep; also the careless way in which he sits upon the table in the first act, and the peculiar attitude in the chair when he is ordered from the house, to which I have already alluded. They are just such attitudes as a painter would choose to paint or a sculptor to chisel. They are thoroughly artistic, and much of this is undoubtedly due to the fact that Mr. Jefferson has very excellent talent in, and knowledge of, the sculptor's art, and had he followed it as a profession he would undoubtedly have achieved an eminence quite as elevated as that which he enjoys in the dramatic world.

If I have devoted considerable of this letter's space to Mr. Jefferson, it is because his *Rip Van Winkle* is a production of art worthy more than passing notice, in the presence of which, the gauze and tinsel of the spectacular drama seem very tawdry, and mock heroics of the sensational and romantic schools of action very false. He stands the only embodiment of the natural school of action—the only true school. Who will be the next to follow him and assist to reform and restore the stage to its proper place as a great educator of the people and exponent of art?

If the first *Tribune* theater review emphasized the rise of a new cultural venue in a frontier city, this pseudonymous piece by Peregrine Pickle was the first ever to focus with any depth on a Chicago actor. Published some five years after the Emancipation Proclamation, and for a circulation of around 50,000, the review is the work of George Putnam Upton (1834–1919), a prolific author and former *Tribune* war correspondent who would become one of the first arts critics in Chicago (he was known primarily as a music critic), with a tenure at such early city publications as the *Daily Native Citizen* and the *Evening Journal* as well as the *Tribune*. Putnam became the *Tribune*'s drama critic in 1868, the year of this review.

By this point, more than 250,000 people called Chicago home. Moreover, the American Civil War had come to an end, and Chicago's lakefront and parks were beginning to attract visitors from throughout the Midwest; these tourists were tempted as well by nights at the theater, among other urban amusements. Sensing this trend, the *Tribune* and its competitors began to write more about the arts and other leisure activities in its thriving metropolis.

For sure, the hero of an 18th-century Scottish novel by Tobias Smollett is an esoteric pseudonym for a critic on the edge of the frontier (Upton was a Brown University graduate who, according to *The Rise of a Great American Newspaper*, Lloyd Wendt's definitive history of the *Tribune*, had been hired on his second day in Chicago). But that curiosity aside, this is an amazingly prescient piece of writing for its time, an era well before experiments in realism and naturalism had permeated American theater in any kind of broad sense.

Joseph Jefferson, famous for his role in "Rip Van Winkle" and the man for whom Chicago's local theater awards would later be named, was inarguably the first true Chicago stage star: an actor who lived in the city some of his life, but whose reputation was international.

Aside from its length—this is one of the longest reviews in this collection and massive by *Tribune* standards of the era—Upton outdoes himself in the precision of his expression, the amount of context he provides for his analyses (he leads us gently into Venus de Medici and Raphael), the eloquence of his expression and the level of his detail on exactly what made Jefferson such a remarkable actor.

Here, clearly, was a man who had been to a lot of very good theater (Upton was very well traveled). Upton certainly was a Jefferson fan, as were many ordinary Chicagoans, suggesting here that Jefferson's Rip was superior to any Shakespearean performance we could name—apparently a dubious assertion, given the limitations of that hoary melodramatic play. We must view these assertions of naturalistic scope in the context of the era. Nonetheless, Upton makes a powerful case that Jefferson deserves his ongoing historical reputation as the first great Chicago star.

This is, according to the archive, the first *Chicago Tribune* review to really analyze in detail for the reader what one of its namesake city's performers actually did; yet more notably, it also places a premium on the importance of the realism of his performance. In 1868, few were using phrases like "the natural school of action," even if Upton's conception of what could be considered natural sounds colorful by today's standards. Still, he clearly saw Rip's dog Snyder in his mind's eye, even though the canine never set a paw onstage. Jefferson, apparently, took care of that.

This review surely would suggest that Chicago's, and the *Tribune*'s, interest in truth from its theater artists, as distinct from melodramatic excess, was established earlier than is generally thought. Jefferson, Upton asserts, adopting an Emile Zola–like fervor, realized "that it is the province of art to conceal art." He also saves one of the critic's most perennially powerful weapons, italics, for that phrase about how well Jefferson identified with his character—a skill that would, over time, become generally associated with Chicago actors.

Upton even seems to have a prescient understanding that Jefferson was potentially the first in a long line of actors who might reform the stage from its unrefined dramatic abilities, for the benefit of the citizens of a young American city still searching for its identity.

Upton enjoyed considerable notoriety. The *Tribune* began publishing the work of Peregrine Pickle in booklet form at Christmastime. And Chicago began to see the first stirrings of some lively interchanges between artists and critics, mostly involving Lydia Thompson, a British actress, producer and provocateur.

3

THE BLONDES

SOME PLAIN WORDS ABOUT THEM

The Opera House

February 20, 1870

BY PEREGRINE PICKLE

Chicago, Feb. 10.

To the Editor of The Chicago Tribune:

I shall write to you to day of amusements only, for I have much to say.

There is no rest for the wicked in this world, which reminds me to say that, as Miss Lydia Thompson did herself the pleasure to assail me personally at the Opera House on Friday evening, it may be expected that I have something to say to Miss Lydia Thompson in return.

And I have got something to say.

As the great Daniel remarked, "I still live." And what is more, I propose, as long as my penholder lasts, to stick my pen into Lydia Thompson's balloon until the thing collapses. And it is a very long pen-holder.

Now, do not imagine that I have anything against Lydia Thompson personally. She may be a gem of purest ray serene. She may be a flower wasting her sweetness on the desert air. She may be a thing of beauty and joy forever. She may be a pink of propriety and a pattern in respect to all the female virtues. I presume she is, for I know nothing to the contrary. I shall, therefore, assume that she is the model woman of the period, and not be led into the foolish mistake of imitating the gross personalities of her Friday evening speech. My battle is with Lydia Thompson herself; and I propose to fight it out on this line if it takes all summer and runs over into the fall.

Miss Lydia Thompson is the manager and the proprietor of the troupe of so-called blondes now performing so-called burlesques at the Opera House, and is therefore responsible for every word and action upon the stage. The remaining people on the stage are merely her puppets, moving as she pulls the strings, and the performances which these people give are as far removed from the domain of legitimate burlesque as the sun is from the earth.

In the first place, there is not one of the so-called blondes who can lay any claim to dramatic ability. They condition their success upon their personal charms alone, and, of course, they are lavish in the display of those charms, and omit no advantage of posturing and dancing which shall set them off. How those charms are obtained every novice knows. Stage charms are very cheap. The blonde is a compound manufactured from the resources of the dye-bottle, the rouge-pot, the enamel-box, the hair-dresser, padding, stuffing, pencilling, and semi-nudity. Without the aid of these artifices of the toilet, there is not one of the blondes who would be tolerated five minutes by an audience. Gross animalism is the effect produced. If there were anything to support it—if there were anything vivacious, sprightly, or in the remotest degree intellectual to relieve it,—it might be more endurable, if not more excusable. There is sometimes a refinement even to indecency; but here the appeal lies, pure and simple, to pruriency. There have been many artists who have appeared here in male costume, as, for instance, Kellogg, Morenal, Casiri, Mrs. Seguin and others, but they were modest, refined ladies in any costumes, and there was no hint of pruriency or immodesty about their appearance.

Now, the result of this appeal is susceptible of proof. What is the character of the audiences which go to see the so-called blondes? Are they made up of the opera-goers? No. Are they made up of the regular patrons of the drama? No. In the pursuance of my duties as a critic in this city I have been an attendant upon the drama and opera, well-nigh nightly, for fifteen years, and am, therefore, familiar with the audiences. The gallery is filled with men who belong to the ruff-scruff, and with half-grown boys. The rest of the audience is composed of old men who ought to know better, of jockeys and sporting men, and fast young men about town, who throng as thickly about the footlights as possible. Here and there a woman, who looks ashamed of herself, as she ought to be! The proportion of men to women is as 20 to 1, and a great many of these men sport diamond clusters, and large watch-chains, and otherwise proclaim their character in the most unmistakable manner. The broadest allusions bring out the heartiest guffaws, and the most vulgar displays the most enthusiastic applause. No woman who would preserve her self-respect can go to these performances. No man who has any self-respect can keep it long if he makes a practice of visiting them. What elicited the most enthusiastic applause and laughter on the opening night of the so-called burlesque of Aladdin? A remark too indelicate and gross for publication. It should, on the other hand, have been hissed, and this troupe of blondes should have been taught upon the instant that there are bounds of decency beyond which they cannot go. But it was the vulgar joke of the concert saloon, perpetrated upon a stage, which was consecrated to art, now degraded from its high purposes, for the edification of a concert saloon audience.

But the artificiality and semi-nudity and doubtful dialogue of these so-called blondes are not the only arguments against them. Not one of them displays a spark of dramatic ability. We have had actors of burlesque here before, who were more or less liable to the same charges of vulgarity; but they were actors. Furthermore, in this form of art, they were artists, I refer to the leading people in the *Opera Bouffe* troupes of Moeure, Bateman and Gian. Teatee, Desciauzas, and Rose-Bell were undeniably vulgar, but they were undeniably dramatic; also, Duchesne, Lagriebul, and Leduc were not always chaste, but they were always superb burlesque artists, and the admirable character of their section blunted the edge of their indelicacy. Now, these blondes have got nothing of the kind to fall back upon. They are either indelicate or nothing. Their business is simply the business of the concert saloon and nothing else. They are not performing burlesque ever. Of all the plays which they produce, not one can be called a burlesque. They were so originally, but they have been cut down, revised, remodelled, and adapted for this peculiar blonde business. A burlesque presupposes well-defined characters which are caricatures of the realities, and are intended to show the ridiculous side of human nature; a clearness and unity of plot, which must be dramatically constructed; scope for dramatic action; an always apparent contrast between the real and the caricature; music and dance which are appropriate to the general tone of the burlesque, and—unity.

And what do these capering, chattering blondes give us for burlesque? The thinnest thread of a story, which never calls to mind the original. Will any one kindly point out to me in "Aladdin," "Sinbad," or "Ixion" the slightest resemblance in a cry to the original themes which they purport to burlesque? Any other name would serve just as well. Upon this thin thread is strung the stuff which makes up the real business of these blondes, and that stuff is a compound of personal [——]; of advertisements for hotel and saloon-keepers; of stale, worn-out, threadbare jokes; of doubtful innuendos; of personal appeals to the audience; of slang songs of the period, with which Lingard flooded the community some time since, which were born in the concert saloons and have no more to do with burlesque than cannibalism has with Christianity; of the low slang of the street which fast young men bandy back and forth at saloon bars; of plays upon words which are so bad as to be almost nauseating; of dancing which never rises above the dignity of a double shuffle or the artistic merit of a break-down; and of wit which would make Planche, Byron, and John Brougham turn out their noses in ineffable disgust.

This is the compound which the blondes ask us to swallow and suppose it to be burlesque. It won't do.

My advice to the blondes, therefore, is to quit this business; to dress themselves, get their hair back to its original color, drop the name blonde, and take their places upon the dramatic stage. Where, by patient labor and honest study, they may succeed in accomplishing something. Miss Thompson, herself, is a bright, smart, intelligent little woman. She has some dramatic instincts and perceptions, which, under proper training, might be enveloped so that she could take a prominent position. Miss Weathersby, also, if she would give the matter more attention and herself less, would also make a good dramatic soubrette. Miss Pauline Markham, notwithstanding Mr. Richard Grant White's fulsome endorsement, has apparently no qualifications whatever for the dramatic stage, although her voice might be turned to good account upon the lyric stage. The other blondes are good for nothing anywhere. But, in the name of all that is decent, do not, after your present engagement is over, ever come here again as blondes. Stay in New York, go back to England, say good-bye to us and God bless you, go anywhere; but don't come here any more. We don't appreciate you; we are tired of you. It might all have been very pretty once, but the charm of novelty has gone, and there is nothing attractive left. It is all silly, very silly; stupid, very stupid; degrading, very degrading.

This puckish Upton classic, which rather blurs the lines between the troupe of "blondes" under review and blondes in general, caused a massive reaction after it appeared in the *Tribune* the year before the Great Chicago Fire rendered such disputes trivial. In its aftermath, the *Tribune* ran a series of sexist articles riffing on Upton's assertions about blondes and the lack of dramatic ability thereof.

Lydia Thompson, born Eliza Hodges Thompson, had made her name in the London burlesque scene. The troupe of "British Blondes" that had so offended Upton were the stateside introduction of the form of Victorian burlesque that had become popular in Britain. Thompson had arrived in America in 1868, and as Upton's review reports, her troupe was popular with males at the box office. "The Black Crook" was the first of the so-called leg shows to arrive in Chicago.

Upton was not the only Chicago critic to take offense. Wilbur F. Storey, the editor of the city's *Times* and an editor and writer known for courting notoriety, wrote a piece published four days later, criticizing the morality of these "British Blondes." On that day, February 24, the women hit back by posting notices attacking Storey. That evening, things got really nasty: the women caught Storey in the streets of Chicago (at the corner of Wabash Avenue and Peck Court) and horsewhipped him at gunpoint. Reportedly, Thompson had concealed the whip in her skirts.

The "Black Crook blondes," as they were sometimes called, ended up standing trial, an event that the *Tribune* greeted with six columns of salacious detail (Upton, presumably, was glad to avoid similar physical attack). Thompson, her husband (the manager of the troupe) and her colleague Pauline Markham all were obliged to pay a fine for their treatment of the critic, but had no trouble whatsoever selling tickets thereafter. That night, the *Tribune* reported, more than 3,000 curious Chicagoans, most of them men, packed into the Crosby Opera House to judge for themselves whether blondes had any dramatic ability.

4

A DOLL'S HOUSE

Columbia Theatre

MARCH 9, 1890. "Indeed, my Lord, but this is wondrous strange," exclaims one of Hamlet's attendants after the episode of the ghost; and Hamlet answers, "Therefore as stranger give it welcome."

Such generosity should we show toward foreign authors; for we are not insular like the English, nor self-absorbed like the French. We are more complex than the older nations, and therefore should be more broad-minded.

The fine audience which welcomed Ibsen's "A Doll's House" (improperly called "Nora") at the Columbia last week is a gratifying evidence of American liberality and wide sympathy. The plays of the Norwegian dramatist have been read and appreciated by many thoughtful people, whose intellectual hospitality has extended to the realistic school of Russian novelists.

If we had a free theater like that in Paris we might become better acquainted with other Scandinavian dramatists of the present day, notably

Björnson, who is as genial as Ibsen is severe. These two authors, by the way, have given the world the only dramas that are worthy to be placed on the same plane of literature with the great realistic novels of our era. Both these men have been directors of theaters in Christiania, and it was there that they acquired that technical skill which once proved useful to Moliere and Shakespeare. It is to be hoped that Mr. William Archer, Mr. Havelock Ellis, or some of the other translators of Ibsen will perform a similar office for Björnson, and at the same time for Kielland, the novelist. In this period of depression in the English drama and decay in the French it is grateful to turn to Norway and find a fresh, vigorous band of writers marching abreast in the foremost ranks of liberal thought.

It is amusing to notice the irritation occasioned among the Philistines everywhere by the production of one of Ibsen's social dramas. The author is now 62 years old, and he has fought for a long time in his own country against the same opposition which he encounters in America. That opposition comes from the fearful, conservative class; the good, prosaic people who can see nothing but the obvious aspects of morality, and put a literal and mean interpretation on everything that has a spiritual significance. These are the many. The admirers of Ibsen, on the other hand, are the few—those who know in the words of an American poet that "new occasions make new duties." and that "they must upward still and onward who would keep abreast of truth." The spirit which works in his plays is in the words of Mr. Havelock Ellis, "an eager insistence that the social environment shall not cramp the reasonable freedom of the individual, together with a passionately intense hatred of all those conventional lies which are commonly regarded as the pillars of society."

The aim of Henrick Ibsen in writing his social dramas may be clearly perceived in the works themselves; but more clearly, perhaps, in a speech which he made to a club of working men when he revisited his native land in 1885. Though he had been practically exiled years before he was received everywhere with enthusiasm. "Mere democracy," he said, "cannot solve the social question. An element of aristocracy must be introduced into our life. Of course I do not mean the aristocracy of birth, or of the purse, or even the aristocracy of intellect. I mean the aristocracy of character, of will, of mind. That only can free us. From two groups will this aristocracy I hope for come to our people—from our women and our workmen. The revolution in the social condition now preparing in Europe is chiefly concerned with the future of the workers and the women. In this I place all my hopes and expectations; for this I will work all my life and with all my might."

And grandly he has worked, especially to give a greater individual freedom to women. It is with justice that he has been called the "woman's poet." Study not only Nora in a "Doll's House," but Lona in "The Pillars of Society" and Mrs. Alive in "Dreams," and you will wonder how a man with so much love for humanity has been called a cynic—how a poet with such ardent hopes has been termed a pessimist.

His creation of Nora in "A Doll's House" would alone have been sufficient to prove him the most sympathetic and clear-sighted critic of woman's nature and her mission. His pity for his little heroine is great; his understanding of her profound; his truthfulness in portraying her as he finds her is undeviating and unrelenting. There she is, a child-wife with all the faults of inexperience and all the sweetness of a loving, womanly heart. She has been the pet of a father and is now the pet of a husband; and she has been protected from all badness, but has not learned the worldly prudence which is equivalent to hypocrisy. It is intention which makes the crime, and she is guilty of no crime when she commits a forgery. Rather than agitate her dying father she writes his name to a promissory note; and rather than inform her sick husband of the danger he is in she keeps from him the secret of the borrowed money. When she learns that her conduct, which to her was a sacred duty, is to the world a crime, and when she discovers that the atmosphere of that crime is already corrupting the natures of her children, she has still firm faith in the protection of her husband. He whose life she saved will at least be her protector; he will take on himself the crime, if necessary, to shield her from shame.

Her discovery, when she makes it, transforms her from a loving girl into a woman of shattered illusions—one who for the first time sees human nature stripped of its conventional garb. The husband for whom she had striven so desperately and so unwisely can see nothing but his own impending social disgrace. In his craven fear of exposure he overwhelms her with reproaches. Suddenly he discovers that there is no reason to fear—that he is safe. Then he forgives her; she will be once more his doll wife, his plaything. "I am saved!" he exclaims; "Nora, I am saved!"

(Is it not exquisitely masculine?)

And in the midst of his ecstasy of selfishness she asks simply, "And I?"

He does not understand her. Neither do those good people in an audience who cannot understand how a heart may be stabbed without a material knife, or how a life may be sacrificed without vulgar bloodshed.

It is for the benefit of such persons that Ibsen adds to the play the only touch that is inartistic—the pausing of Nora before her departure to explain that she has been living with a stranger and has borne children to one whom until that moment she had never truly known.

She goes at last, as she should have gone at once, calmly and determinedly, and the end of the play is an interrogation point, "What did she do afterward?"

It matters little what she did. The tragedy of her marriage, with which the play deals, is certainly complete. There is nothing to add to that.

It will not do to call her bad names. Those who indulge in this practice are simply accomplices of her husband—made of the same base earth. She has been a liar—yes, but she has loved truly and made sacrifices for the man she loved.

And she flirted. This is what makes the prudes condemn her. But this, according to the writer's idea, is the finest and loveliest stroke in the whole drama. Nothing so illustrative of a woman's essential purity has ever been written since Shakespeare put those infinitely pathetic phrases into the mouth of the mad Ophelia.

Nora has given Dr. Rank provocation; she has almost challenged him by her audacity, her imprudence; and he makes the crowning mistake of his whole miserable life when he puts the wrong interpretation to her action. He is better than her husband, however, in one respect. He no sooner makes the mistake than he sees it. There is no apology possible and he knows it. He goes away simply and untheatrically, and it is not surprising when it is learned a little later that he has gone to his death.

Some things, the Philistines argue, such as the marital relations, are not proper subjects for stage treatment. It may be true; but one leans to the opinion of Goethe that "no real circumstance is unpoetic so long as the poet knows how to use it."

Nora Helmer is not an ideal woman. This is practically the complaint of those who do not like her. There are more lovable women in romances, and even in every-day life. But there is no woman more real than she in fiction or in the actual world. And her sex has never received a higher tribute from any artist than it has in her character as drawn by Henrik Ibsen, cynic, pessimist, what you will—but above all things, poet of womanhood and lover of humanity.

By 1890, Chicago's population exceeded 1 million, and the *Tribune*'s circulation had risen to more than 80,000 daily copies of a newspaper that on some days could run as large as 32 pages. In this era, Chicago was in the midst of a cultural revolution of sorts, with such local architects as Dankmar Adler, Louis Sullivan and Daniel H. Burnham hard at work. For the first time in its history, the city could now claim an indigenous artistic culture, distinct from that on the other side of the Atlantic, although it also was frequently attacked by visiting literary figures–from Oscar Wilde to Robert Louis Stevenson–who reported at length on its ugliness and brutality, even if Wilde found a perverse beauty therein. "I have always wished to believe that the line of strength and the line of beauty are one," Wilde had written of Chicago in 1888, following a visit on one of his American tours of duty. "It was not until I had seen the water-works at Chicago that I realized the wonders of machinery, the rise and fall of the steel rods, the symmetrical motion of the great wheels is the most beautifully rhythmic thing I have ever seen."

But the newly massive labor force was also the scene of considerable unrest. Through the International Working People's Association, which published seven newspapers of its own during the 1880s, anarchists had begun a movement in the city, which was frequently roiled in disputes about working conditions and other socioeconomic issues. Four years before this review, violence had exploded in Haymarket Square, resulting in several deaths. The *Tribune* had covered the so-called Haymarket Riots, and the subsequent hanging of the alleged perpetrators, at exhaustive length. It had met the 1887 punishment with glee: "Dropped to Eternity," declared its headline the day after the notorious carriage (or miscarriage) of justice.

No wonder, then, that there was such local interest in Henrik Ibsen's famously radical play. Ibsen's best-known drama had its first American production in the unlikely locale of Louisville, Kentucky, in 1883. This first Chicago production, anonymously reviewed here, came about three months after the play's

Broadway's premiere. The Columbia Theatre, incidentally, was at 57 W. Monroe St. It had opened in 1881 and was gone by 1900, having burned to the ground. The Columbia, which had 2,000 seats, was no little theater. Ibsen was a big draw.

Although the *Tribune* was generally no friend of the anarchists, the review is strikingly welcoming to such a controversial play, although it's certainly self-congratulatory in tone, differentiating America from the "insular" English and the "self-absorbed" French. Chicago was gaining confidence. A case is made for work by Bjørnstjerne Martinius Bjørnson to be seen there; indeed, the critic is quite the advocate for all things Norwegian, posting the nation as the bastion of progressive thought, an indicator of the huge influence of Scandinavian culture in the Chicago of 1890. Moreover, this snarky anonymous writer mounts an overt attack on the anti-Ibsen forces, even calling them Philistines. In later years, as the *Tribune* became far more culturally conservative, readers would not easily find in its pages such a sentence as "That opposition comes from the fearful, conservative class; the good, prosaic people who can see nothing but the obvious aspects of morality."

Written about a year after Jane Addams established her Hull House, this review really doesn't tell us much about the production. But it is a very spirited, authoritative and eloquent defense of Ibsen, even of latent feminism, in an unexpected place. And read from today's perspective, when the reputation of this drama has been cemented, it feels astute about the play in very many ways. The critic, seemingly a radical, even mocks Torvald's manhood. "Is it not exquisitely masculine?" he or she says of his whining—which, given the pervasive stereotype of turn of-the-century Chicago as a relentlessly macho city, suggests that the actual gestalt of the growing metropolis was considerably more complex.

5

THE WIZARD OF OZ

Grand Opera House

CAST

The Wizard of Oz .... John Slavin
The Scarecrow .... Fred Stone
Nick Chopper, the tin woodman .... Dave Montgomery
Pastoria II .... Neil McNeil

Sir Dashemoff Daily	Bessie Wynn
Sir Wiley Gyle	Steve Maley
Timothy Alfalfa	Joseph Schrode
Bardo	May McKenzie
Tommie Toq	Ida Doerge
Peter Boq	Grace Kimball
Dorothy	Anna Laughlin
Cynthia Cynch	Helen Byron
Trixie Tryfle	Mabel Barrison
The Witch of the North	Aileen May
Glinda the Good	Dorris Mitchell

JUNE 17, 1902. It was after midnight when the final curtain fell on "The Wizard of Oz," but the audience that crowded the Grand last evening pronounced the new production a success, and the opinion was general that only reduction to proper time limits and the elimination of needless material which this reduction brings were necessary to make the performance of exceptional attractiveness, interest, and effectiveness.

The piece used is out of the usual run of musical comedies, extravaganzas, or comic operas. It has in it something of the fairy character of the London pantomime of holiday time, and yet in its abundance of vocal music and its absence of magical transformations does not conform entirely to the celebrated English model. Of plot there is only the faintest suggestion and of spoken dialogue there is an unusually small amount. It is, in fact, but little different from a concert given in costume, amid gorgeous scenery, and accompanied by dancing and gesture.

◠ ◠ ◠

But it is enjoyable, satisfying to both eye and ear, and in every respect an attractive summer season entertainment. The scenery is of exceptional beauty in both coloring and design, and the setting, "The Poppy Field," merits place [——] the loveliest in every way that has ever been seen on the stage of any theater in this city. The "Domain of the Sorceress [——] the splendor and glitter of the [——] the Henderson extravaganza scene [——] the "Poppy Field" has in it nothing of the tinseled show of those settings. Seen, as it is, through the softening haze of the gauze curtain,

L. FRANK BAUM, A CHICAGO JOURNALIST WHO BECAME FAMOUS FOR CHARTING THE ADVENTURES OF DOROTHY IN THE LAND OF OZ.

it possesses the qualities and exerts the charm of a fine picture. The tornado and the snow scene are effectively accomplished by a skillful employment of magic lantern effects on the gauze drop.

As for the performers, the honors of the evening were carried off by David Montgomery and Fred Stone, who as the Tin Woodman and the Scarecrow not only introduced two characters virtually new to the comic stage, but by their irresistibly funny presentment of them scored an immediate and pronounced "hit." Their dancing, singing, and funmaking gave the chief life to the performance and reached culmination in the "Cockney Negro Song," which they interpolated in the last act.

Next to Montgomery and Stone in the gaining of public favor was Anna Laughlin, who as Dorothy Gale, the maid from Kansas whom the tornado bore away to Oz, displayed not only a winsome face and trim, petite figure but proved her ability to dance gracefully and well, and sing acceptably. Helen Byron as the Lady Lunatic was fair to look upon, her singing was agreeable, and she made all that was possible of a rather useless and ineffective part. Bessie Wynn was a shapely poet laureate, and sang her one solo satisfactorily; Aileen May was a throaty voiced but good looking Witch of the North; Mabel Barrison an attractive Trixie, and Leona Thurber a sufficiently imposing Weenietoots. John Slavin had in the title role a part furnishing comparatively few opportunities for funmaking, but he made the most of such as were offered, and with his singing of "Mr. Dooley" earned hearty applause. His topical song in the last act proved inane, however, and fell so flat that its omission hereafter doubtless will prove advisable.

Stephen Maley, in the role of the ranting inventor, Gyle, accomplished all that was possible. Neil McNeil achieved the same praise-meriting results with Pastoria, a part almost as thankless as is that of Gyle; Edwin J. Stone was capital as The Cow, and Arthur Bill was an excellent Cowardly Lion.

The chorus and minor singers do good work in both dancing and singing and the feminine members among them are comely. The music of the piece is largely interpointed—especially that in the last two acts—but there are numbers in the first act—"Carry Barry," "When You Love," and the Poppy Chorus—that are by Mr. Tietjens, and show that he has the knack of writing catchy melodies such as are in favor at the present time.

At the close of the second act there were calls for both Mr. Baum and Mr. Tietjens. Bows from the proscenium box would not satisfy, and Mr. Baum finally coming before the curtain, expressed in a few phrases his thanks and those of all concerned in the production for the applause and favor accorded by the audience.

By the dawn of the 20th century, Chicago had been transformed. The World's Columbian Exposition of 1893 had made it far more confident and optimistic, and its culture bolder. Writers–including Upton Sinclair, Theodore Dreiser and L. Frank Baum–were increasingly attracted to the city, whose architects were boosted by the international attention that came from the success of the world's fair. By now, the Art Institute of Chicago had opened, as had the Field Museum, although Chicago still was riddled with vice and crime. And it still had its fervent detractors, who saw its rapidly expanding borders as barely containing a city of unspeakable crudity. "It holds rather more than a million of people with bodies," a visiting Rudyard Kipling had written of Chicago in 1899, "and stands on the same sort of soil as Calcutta. Having seen it, I urgently desire never to see it again. It is inhabited by savages. Its water is the water of the Hooghly, and its air is dirt. Also it says that it is the 'boss' town of America." Kipling clearly was on to something early with that last remark.

This is the first review of any performance, anywhere, of "The Wizard of Oz." The musical's author, L. Frank Baum, was himself a newspaper reporter in Chicago: he arrived from Chittenango, New York, in 1891 and worked at the *Chicago Evening Post* until he founded a magazine, *The Snow Window*, in 1897. In his spare time, Baum wrote books for children. This anonymous review is of the first stage version of Baum's original book, adapted by Baum himself with the aim of goosing sales of his story, and first staged at Fred R. Hamlin's Grand Opera House. The production's costume design was patterned after the original work by William W. Denslow, with whom Baum had spent time in Denslow's studio in the city's Fine Arts Building and whose illustrations had appeared in the *Tribune*.

Before opening night, Hamlin pumped up his show in the *Tribune*, modestly saying that it "will be recognized as a spectacular achievement of surpassing magnitude." There would be, he noted, over 100 performers on the stage, including "a ballet of twenty-four dancers." Small wonder, then, that the show lasted until midnight. At this point, the Wicked Witch of the West came from the North and characters by the names of Trixie and the Lady Lunatic were featured. The feminine members of the chorus, the critic allows, were suitably "comely." "Tietjens" is a reference to Paul Tietjens, a young Chicago composer.

Dave Montgomery, who played Nick Chopper, the Tin Woodman, and Fred Stone, who played the Scarecrow, were British comics who had come to Chicago directly from a pantomime in Liverpool. The pair became big American stars overnight, with Chicagoans, this review tells us, especially thrilling to their "Cockney Negro Song," which apparently was a feature of the final act; the inclusion of comic songs was typical of the era. Shortly after this review, the *Tribune* published their photos and said, "The *Tribune* awards the honors of pioneers in original comedy." Notably, the show was a musical revue aimed at adults (Toto was replaced by a cow), even though Baum's original book had been focused on children. The show moved to Broadway in 1903, where it thrived. Thereafter, a movie version rather exceeded expectations.

A *Tribune* writer named Russell McFarlane wrote about Baum during the 1950s, in a piece celebrating the 100th anniversary of his birth. McFarlane hit on something interesting about "The Wizard of Oz," the Chicago roots of which are often overlooked. If we could see past all the clutter and excess in Hamlin's 1902 extravaganza, we could perhaps discern a piece of work very much in the Chicago tradition of heartland realism—a kind of Brothers Grimm yarn of the tornado-plagued prairie. "Here," McFarlane declares, "was something new. A fairy story for boys and girls rooted deep in the American soil."

6

MR. BLUE BEARD

Iroquois Theater

BY W. L. HUBBARD

CAST

Mr. Blue Beard .... Harry Gilfoil
Sister Anne .... Eddie Foy
Fatima .... Miss Blanche Adams
Selim .... Adele Rafter
Imer Dasher .... Bonnie Maginn
Abdallah .... Nora Cecil
Mustapha .... Robert E. Evans
Irish Patshaw .... Herbert Cawthorne
Abaddin.. Sam Reed
Abumun .... Frank Young
Stella, queen of the fairies.................... Miss Anabelle Whitford

NOVEMBER 24, 1903. Wonder and unqualified admiration were the willing tribute paid to the new Iroquois theater last evening by the pronouncedly fashionable audience that assisted at its formal opening and dedication. A playhouse so splendid in its every appointment, so beautiful in its every part, so magnificent and yet so comfortable, Chicago has heretofore not been able to call its own. Only the Auditorium equals it in impressiveness and beauty, and the Auditorium is of course a thing apart, and not to be classed among the theater of the city.

The Iroquois is certainly unrivaled in perfection among the regular amusement places of the west, and it is doubtful if the east can boast more than one or two houses that are its equal. The enterprise which made the erection of the new theater possible has given the Chicago playgoers a virtual temple of beauty—a place where the noblest and highest in dramatic art could fittingly find a worthy home. That the noblest and highest in dramatic art may, perhaps, not find its home there, does not alter the fact that the theater is a place of rare and impressive dignity—a theater about as near ideal in nearly every respect as could be desired.

After the second act of "Mr. Blue Beard" last evening there were vigorous calls for Mr. Davis and Mr. Powers, the two managers who have the Iroquois in charge and who are chiefly responsible for its erection. Mr. Davis appeared before the curtain, bringing with him Mr. B. H. Marshall, the designer and architect, and in his speech of thanks for the approval expressed he announced that the Iroquois was the creation of western talent, abilities, and enthusiasm, and that western appreciation and encouragement were all that were desired, and that these were good enough for any man.

Mr. Powers was finally forced from the retirement into which he had fled, and after a cheery salutation from the gallery gave to the Chicago public the credit for the building of the new house—the liberality shown by the public in its patronage of the theaters already existent had made possible the planning and realizing of this splendid new one. Mr. Nixon of the firm of Nixon and Zimmerman was brought forward, and Mr. Davis proved the correctness of all the western claim by assuring the audience that Mr. Nixon was also from the west, being a Hoosier. There were loud and insistent cries from the gallery for Mr. Foy—he whom we call "Eddie"—but the orchestra struck up "America"—which the audience almost forgot to applaud—and the speechmaking was at an end.

◠ ◠ ◠

Whatever be the incentive which led to the erecting of the Iroquois, and whether all the talent and material engaged in its fashioning be exclusively western or not, the audience present last evening pronounced the new house a marvel of attractiveness, and only the most lavish praise was heard on all sides. The entrance itself is impressive, with its white marble panels, its wide doors of glass and mahogany, and its frieze of electric lights. But when the visitor enters the foyer he is almost overpowered by the spaciousness and magnificence of the view. Full sixty feet high is this splendid hall, for such it seems to be. The tinted marble pillars which rise on either side lend both solidity and beauty, while the skillful employment of mirrors in the walls and doors gives a sense of lightness and spaciousness. Great, wide staircases lead up from this foyer on either side, and meet at the back of a broad landing, from which other stairs rise to the gallery, thus affording entrance to all parts of the auditorium directly from the foyer.

The white of the marble, the rich Indian red of the panels in the walls, and the upholstered seats placed at each of the landings on the staircases, and the soft dull gold of the arched ceiling, all combine in a harmony that is grateful to the eye and a fitting preparation for the beauty of the auditorium itself.

For the auditorium is in truth admirable and satisfying in the highest degree. There is, in the first place, not a seat in the house which does not afford a view of the entire stage, and every seat is comfortable, the space between the rows ample, and the aisles wide and agreeably inclined. The auditorium is shallow, the balcony and gallery being brought close to the stage, but the absence of pillars and the graceful curve of the balcony and gallery remove all hint of stuffiness or crowding. The decorations are in dull red and soft neutral greens, with brighter red used in the boxes. The lights have been arranged so that there is a soft radiance everywhere, but no glare.

A curtain of deep red velour is used between scenes, a brilliantly colored autumn landscape decorates the act drop, and a woodland scene is on the fireproof curtain. All in all, a theater of surpassing beauty, comfort, and completeness.

⁂

The attraction chosen for the opening of the new theater was "Mr. Blue Beard," the Drury Lane extravaganza which was brought to this country from London last year to follow up the success achieved by its predecessor, "The Sleeping Beauty and the Beast." It is a lavish spectacle so far as costumes and scenery are concerned, but the amusement seeker who goes to the Iroquois expecting to find as stunning a production as was "The Sleeping Beauty"—to say nothing of "The Wizard of Oz" or "Babes in Toyland"—will be apt to be disappointed. It is not the equal in attractiveness of its predecessor, the coloring of both costumes and scenery being dull and generally ineffective. Materials in seemingly unlimited quantities have been used and there has clearly been no sparing of expense or labor in the fitting out of the piece, but the good taste in color combination and the fine sense for effective contrast and harmonies shown in "The Sleeping Beauty" appear to have been wanting when "Mr. Blue Beard" was prepared. It is, of course, a brilliant spectacle, but it is not the equal of those we have already enjoyed and possibly, we are spoiled.

Of story there is little or none—nobody expected there would be any, and nobody cared because there was none. There is the usual loving couple who have hard times getting their love affairs to running smoothly, there is the usual wicked persecutor of the maiden in this enamored couple—in this case he is Mr. Blue Beard—and there is, of course, the regulation good fairy and the magic horn which calls her to the hero's aid when matters get a bit too complicated.

The music of the piece is hopelessly common, save bits here and there which are filched from the classics, but the spirited manner in which chorus and principals sing the tunes and the vigorous style in which they dance to them, when the musical director, Herbert Dillea, keeps every performer admirably in hand, causes even such music to tickle the ears of the public and applause is generous, and whistling lips ready to make popular.

⁂

Of the company, Eddie Foy is the chief and ablest performer. He has little that is really amusing to do, but his personality is in itself so good natured, his humor so infectious, and his cleverness at funmaking so great that he cannot fail to win the tribute of applause and laughter from his auditors. He has two solos to sing, the character of which may be judged from their titles—"I'm a Poor Unhappy Maid" and "Hamlet Was a Melancholy Dane," the latter being given in connection with a Foyesque impersonation of Ophelia.

The hit of the performance was made by one of the chorus girls, who in the ensemble number, "Songbirds of Melody Lane," captured the audience's fancy by some remarkably clever and expressive eccentric dancing.

Harry Gilfoil as Mr. Blue Beard introduced nearly all the specialties in the way of animal and instrument imitation that he has at his command, and he has many of them. The audience received him and all he offered with approval. Herbert Cawthorne was mildly amusing as Irish Patshaw, Adele Rafter was a stately and good looking Selim, although her vocal abilities proved not remarkable; Blanche Adams was a pretty Fatima, and Bonnie Maginn a saucy and vocally acceptable Imer Dasher. The chorus is admirable for its physical comeliness, and is capable of singing quite well. The ballets are attractive and the aerial work of the Grigolatis effective as ever.

As is expressed here with such excitement, the Iroquois Theater, located on Randolph Street between State and Dearborn Streets, was a huge leap forward for Chicago theater. Only the Auditorium Theatre, here deemed in a class of its own, could compare. And this debut production of "Mr. Blue Beard," which had come from London, was clearly an enormous show, replete with a cast of some 200 performers and starring noted vaudevillian and drag artist Eddie Foy, Sr.

The Iroquois did not stand for very long. On December 30, barely a month after this highly self-congratulatory review appeared and while "Mr. Blue Beard' still was running, the theater burned down. The tragedy occurred as a consequence of what the *Tribune* would later report, in an early example of the paper's tradition of investigative reporting, was shoddy construction that disregarded even the most basic safety considerations. Even the asbestos fire curtain had jammed on the way down. Clearly, Chicago's entertainment venues were hardly immune from the city's early habit of moving too fast when it came to new buildings and developments. 600 people died, many of them children, in the Iroquois inferno—a couple of victims were from the show's company, but most came from the audience enjoying the very show that *Tribune* critic William Lines "W. L." Hubbard is discussing here, in one of the paper's first signed reviews.

Hubbard (1867–1951) was a fascinating figure, and was regarded, a successor observed, as "a gentle critic." He was born in New York, although his family (both his parents were spiritualists) moved to Kinmundy, Illinois, while he still was young. They then moved to Chicago in 1880. By 1890, following a stint of writing unpaid reviews for the *Tribune*, Hubbard was the music critic at the *Daily Journal*. He quit that post in 1893 to study piano in Dresden, and then moved in and out of Chicago over the next several years, eventually landing as music editor and then literary editor of the *Tribune*. He became the paper's drama critic in 1902 and remained in that job until 1907—so that explains why he was at the Iroquois Theater on this particular night.

Other than that five-year stand, Hubbard stuck with music. Thereafter, he became a music lecturer and, between 1912 and 1915, was the publicity manager and "official lecturer" of the Boston Opera House. While in Boston, Hubbard became known for the "Operalogue," a kind of lecture-performance hybrid wherein he would offer dramatic tellings of operas, replete with a piano accompaniment. According to Mary Patricia Rickert, who analyzed the Hubbard papers for Johns Hopkins University (where they reside) in 1913, the critic changed his first name to Havrah, reflecting his interest in the practice of theosophy. After the First World War and a brief return to the *Tribune*, he headed west for good.

Hubbard's death in 1951, by which time he was living in retirement in California, was reported in a *Tribune* column.

Many children were present at the fateful performance covered here by Hubbard, which took place on a Wednesday afternoon. Foy, the star of both this show and this review, would figure prominently in the events of that night, as the next piece reveals. But on this night in November, Hubbard could have no idea what would so soon befall this "temple of beauty." This was a triumphant night for Chicago and a time to heap praise on the very people who were, presumably, going to read this review and be delighted to hear about their own sophistication and "liberality." The show? Well, that was less important to the critic and clearly not that great. At least Foy's impersonation of Ophelia could be enjoyed.

New theater buildings, and the excitement they created in an insecure city, have been a part of the *Tribune*'s theater coverage since that coverage began, and have tended to show the paper's critics at their most boosterish. Euphoria and admiration on such nights of civic pride have been pervasive; it takes a strong stomach to write otherwise. But all the other theaters lasted longer than the Iroquois—soon to be revealed as a death trap in a city that, evidence was starting to show, was developing without sufficient regard for safety.

7

IROQUOIS THEATER FIRE

ACTORS IN PLAY ESCAPE ALIVE. / EDDIE FOY TELLS OF SCENES ON STAGE AND HIS FUTILE EFFORT TO STOP PANIC. / ORCHESTRA IS FAITHFUL. / ORDERS TO DROP THE CURTAIN ARE SHOUTED, BUT MECHANISM IS DEFECTIVE.

DECEMBER 31, 1903. All the 348 members of the "Bluebeard" company escaped, according to reports received by the stage manager, although many had close calls for their lives. Some of the chorus girls displayed great coolness in the face of grave peril. Eddie Foy, who had a thrilling experience, said:

"I was up in my dressing room preparing to come on for my turn in the middle of the second act when I heard an unusual commotion on the stage that I knew could not be caused by anything that was a part of the show. I hurried out of my dressing room, and as I looked I saw that the big drop curtain was on fire.

"The fire had caught from the calcium and the paint and muslin on the drop caused the flames to travel with great rapidity. Everything was excitement. Everybody was running from the stage. My 6 year old son, Bryan, stood in the first entrance to the stage, and my first thought naturally was to get him out. They would not let me go out over the footlights, so I picked up the boy and gave him to a man and told him to rush the boy out into the alley.

"I then rushed out to the footlights and called out to the audience, 'Keep very quiet. It is all right. Don't get excited and don't stampede. It is all right.'

"I then shouted an order into the flies, 'Drop the curtain,' and called

THIS SHOCKING *TRIBUNE* PHOTO FROM 1903 REFLECTS THE DEVASTATION OF THE INTERIOR OF THE IROQUOIS THEATER.

out to the leader of the orchestra to 'play an overture.' Some of the musicians had left, but those that remained began to play. The leader sat there, white as a ghost, but beating his baton in the air.

"As the music started I shouted out to the audience, 'Go out slowly. Leave the theater slowly.' The audience had not yet become panic stricken, and as I shouted to them they applauded me. The next minute the whole stage seemed to be afire, and what wood there was began to crackle with a sound like a series of explosions.

"When I first came out to the footlights about 300 persons had left the theater or were leaving it. They were those who were nearest the door. Then the policemen came rushing in and tried to stem the tide towards the door.

"All this happened in fifteen seconds. Up in the flies were the young women who compose the aerial ballet. They were up there waiting to do their turn, and as I stood at the front of the stage they came rushing out. I think they all got out safely.

“The fire seemed to spread with a serious of explosions. The paint on the curtains and scenery came in touch with the flames and in a second scenery was sputtering and blazing up on all sides. The smoke was fearful and it was a case of run quickly or be smothered.”

STAGE DIRECTOR’S STORY. Stage Director William Carleton, who was one of the last to leave the stage when the flames and smoke drove the members of the company out, said he was confident that every one of the 348 players had escaped. He said:

“I was on the stage when the flames shot out from the switchboard on the left side. It seemed that some part of the scenery must have touched the sparks and set the fire. Soon the octet which was singing “In the Pale Moonlight” discovered the fire over their heads and in a few moments we had the curtain run down. It would not go down the full length, however, leaving an opening of about five feet from the floor. Then the crowd out in front began to stampede and the lights went out. Eddie Foy, who was in his dressing room, heard the commotion and, rushing to the front of the stage, shouted to the spectators to be calm. The warning was useless and the panic was under way before any one realized what was going on.

MEMBERS NOT IN PANIC. “Only sixteen members of the company were on the stage at the time. They remained until the flames were all about them and several had their hair singed and faces burned. Almost every one of these went out through the stage entrance on Dearborn street. In the meantime all of those who were in the dressing room had been warned and rushed out through the front entrance on Randolph street. There was no panic among the members of the company, every one seeming to know that care would result in the saving of life. Most of the members were preparing for the next number in their dressing rooms when the fire broke out, and they hurriedly secured what wraps they could and all dashed up to the stage, making their exit in safety.

“The elevator which has been used for the members of the company, in going from the upper dressing rooms to the stage, was one of the first things to go wrong, and attempts to use it were futile.

"It seems that the panic could not be averted, as the great crowd which filled the theater was unable to control itself. Two of the women fainted."

FOUND DOORS LOCKED. "When the fire broke out," said Lou Shean, a member of the chorus, "I was in the dressing room underneath the stage. When I reached the top of the stairs the scenery nearby was all in flames and the heat was so fierce that I could not reach the stage door, leading toward Dearborn street. I returned to the basement and ran down the long corridor leading toward the engine room, near which doors led to the smoking room and buffet. Both doors were locked. I began to break down the doors, assisted by other members of the company, while about seventy or eighty other members crowded against us. I succeeded in bursting open the door to the smoking room, when all made a wild rush. I was knocked down and trampled on and received painful bruises all over my body.

"Some of the members of the chorus were slightly injured, but none of them seriously. Miss Dot Marlowe of the pony ballet was reported missing, but she turned up safe and sound."

"I was just straightening up things in our dressing room upstairs," said Harry Meehan, a member of the chorus, who also acted as dresser for Eddie Foy and Harry Gilfoil, "when the fire started. Both Mr. Foy and Mr. Gilfoil were on the stage at the time. I opened Mr. Foy's trunk and took out his watch and chain and rushed out, leaving my own clothes behind. I was so scantily dressed that I had to borrow clothes to get back to the hotel. Mr. Gilfoil saved nothing but his overcoat."

BLAMES STAGE FIREMAN. Herbert Cawthorn, the Irish comedian who took the part of Pat Shaw in the play "Bluebeard," assisted many of the chorus girls from the stage exits in the panic.

"While the stage fireman was working in an endeavor to use the chemicals the flames suddenly swooped down and out. Eddie Foy shouted something about the asbestos curtain and the fireman attempted to use it, and the stage hands ran to his assistance, but the curtain refused to work.

"In my opinion the stage fireman might have averted the whole terrible affair if he had not become so excited. The chorus girls and everybody, to my mind, were less excited than he. There were at least 500 people behind the scenes when the fire started. I assisted many of the chorus girls from the theater."

MANY NARROW ESCAPES. "I do not believe that any member of the company was killed," said C. W. Northrup, who took the part of one of Bluebeard's old wives, "although many of them had narrow escapes. Those who were in the dressing rooms underneath the stage at the time had more difficulty in getting out. I was in the dressing room under the stage when the fire broke out, and when I found that I could not reach the stage I tried to get out through the door connecting the extreme north end of the C shaped corridor with the smoking room. I joined other members of the company in their rush for safety, but when we reached the door we found it closed. Some of the members crawled out through a coal hole, while others broke down the locked door, through which the others made their way out."

DANCER SAVES COMPANION. Lolla Quinlan, one of Bluebeard's eight dancers, saved the life of one of her companions, Violet Sidney, at the peril of her own. The two girls, with five others, were in a dressing room on the fifth floor when the alarm was raised. In their haste Miss Sidney caught her foot and sank to the floor with a cry of pain. She had sprained her ankle. The others, with the exception of Miss Quinlan, fled down the stairs.

Grasping her companion around the waist Miss Quinlan dragged her down the stairs to the stage and crossed the boards during a rain of fiery brands. These two were the last to leave the stage. Miss Quinlan's right arm and hand were painfully burned and her face was scorched. Miss Sidney's face was slightly burned. Both were taken to the Continental hotel.

MUSICAL DIRECTOR USES AX. Herbert Dillon, musical director, at the height of the panic broke through the stage door from the orchestra side, hastily cleared away obstructions with an ax, and assisted in the escape of about eighty chorus girls who occupied ten dressing rooms under the stage.

"We were getting ready for the honey and fan scene," said Miss Nina

Wood, "talking and laughing, and not thinking of the danger. We were so far back of the orchestra that we did not hear sounds of the panic for several moments. Then the tramping of feet came to our ears. We made our way though the smoking room and one of the narrow exits of the theater."

SAVES MUFF AND BOA. Miss Adele Rafter, a member of the company, was in her dressing room when the fire broke out.

"I did not wait an instant," said Miss Rafter. "I caught up a muff and boa and rushed down the stairs in my stage costume and was the first of the company to get out the back entrance. Some man kindly loaned me his overcoat and I hurried to my apartments at the Sherman house. Several of the girls followed, and we had a good crying spell together."

Miss Rafter's mother called at the hotel and spent the evening with her. Telegrams were sent to her father, who is rector of a church at Dunkirk, N.Y. Among Miss Rafter's callers was W. H. MacDonald of the Bostonians, which company Miss Rafter was with for two seasons.

MANAGER PRICE'S EXPERIENCE. Edwin H. Price, manager of the "Mr. Bluebeard" company, was not in the building when the fire started. He said:

"I stepped out of the theater for a minute, and when I got back I saw the people rushing out and knew the stage was on fire. I helped some of the girls out of the rear entrance. With but one or two exceptions all left in stage costume.

"One young woman in the chorus, Miss McDonald, displayed unusual coolness. She remained in her dressing room and donned her entire street costume, and also carried out as much of her stage clothing as she could carry."

Quite a number of the chorus girls live in Chicago, and Mr. Price furnished cabs and sent them all to their homes.

Mr. Price believes he will be able to save some of the effects of the company.

MISS WHITFORD NOT HURT. Through some mistake it was reported that Miss Anabel Whitford, the fairy queen of the company, was dying at one of the hospitals. She was not even injured, having safely made her way out through the stage door.

Miss Nellie Reed, the principal of the flying ballet, which was in place for its appearance near the top part of the stage, was slightly singed by the flames before she was able to escape. The other members of the flying ballet were not injured.

Robert Evans, one of the principals of the Bluebeard company, was in his dressing room on the fourth floor. He dived through a mass of flame and landed three stairways below. He helped a number of chorus girls to escape through the lower basement. His hands and face are burned severely. He lost all his wardrobe and personal effects.

Though not strictly a review in the usual sense, this riveting account of one of the most notorious events in Chicago history (and still the worst theater fire in American history) was published the following morning. It was the very first entry in what would be weeks of *Tribune* coverage about this terrible night, which led to all manner of legal charges and, more usefully, the building of safer theaters.

On this day, the *Tribune* devoted six full pages and two partial pages to the Iroquois tragedy. The paper also ran most of the names and addresses of the dead, a formidable feat of reporting in this era that became famous. No other newspaper in Chicago had that list of names, which had taken the resources of the entire editorial staff to procure.

The piece, which still is harrowing to read, is notable for many things, but not least for its revelation of the role that Eddie Foy, Sr., the star of "Mr. Blue Beard," would go on to play on that fateful night.

Foy was, to be sure, a big star with a keen sense of the personal benefits to be derived from explaining his deeds to a *Tribune* reporter (for his pains, he got to see his actions re-created by Bob Hope in the movie "The Seven Little Foys"). And he would go on to write his own eyewitness account, expanding on what first was published here. Still, if we take Foy at his word, these were heroic acts.

We can see some questionable assumptions in this report, including the implication that chorus girls could not escape the theater without male aid. But this is nonetheless a vivid retelling of a night in the Chicago theater like no other. The reporter focuses intently on the company of actors, almost all of whom got out alive (most reports refer to no more than five actors dying, although the precise numbers remain hazy). Actually, it was the audience of ordinary, working-class Chicagoans that suffered the most: 70 percent of the 600 or so deaths were patrons seated in the gallery. Notably, showbiz people were already fascinating, even at this of all times; and the company of "Mr. Blue Beard" had quite the collective tale to tell as they described squeezing out of coal chutes and other such deeds of daring.

The shell of the ill-fated Iroquois survived, and was rebuilt as the Colonial Theatre, which was itself torn down in 1926. The Oriental Theatre, still a premiere venue, arose in its place, albeit with more attention paid to fire codes.

Of course, the Chicago theater scene was not just buildings. In 1908, the city of immigrants was roiling with political debate that spilled into its theatrical productions.

8

THE MELTING POT

NOVEL PLEA FOR RUDOWITZ. / SPEECHES IN REFUGEE'S BEHALF ARE MADE BETWEEN ACTS OF DRAMA. / PASTORS IN THE AUDIENCE. / PERSONS OF DIFFERENT RELIGIOUS BELIEF SEE "THE MELTING POT."

Chicago Opera House

DECEMBER 16, 1908. The cause of Christian Rudowitz, the Russian refugee, whose return to Russia in response to the request of the Russian government is to be passed upon by the authorities at Washington, was pleaded in a novel manner yesterday afternoon in the Chicago Opera house.

Upward of 200 preachers and several hundred settlement workers and members of university faculties attended a special presentation of Israel Zangwill's play, "The Melting Pot." Between the acts there was a curtain speech by Walker Whiteside, who enacts the role of David Quixano, and Jenkin Lloyd Jones, pastor of All Souls' church, spoke from a box.

The matinée was strictly by invitation, no seats being sold.

Although the play deals with the persecution of Jews in Russia, Rudowitz is a Lutheran from the north of Russia. Nevertheless the teaching of the play is universal religious tolerance.

In the audience were Catholic priests, Protestant ministers, Greek Catholics, and negro ministers. A delegation of thirty-five was present from Chicago Commons and Jane Addams headed a large delegation from Hull house.

PLEADS FOR THE IMMIGRANTS. Following the third act Jenkin Lloyd Jones stood up in the lower left box and addressed the audience:

"When asked on behalf of friends of liberty to put in a sentiment in defense of that hospitality which makes America American, I did not dare refuse," he said. "As an immigrant child I came to this country on an immigrant ship and landed at Castle garden. I followed the flag of this liberty loving country.

"We should stand as one man in the interests of that hospitality which makes America the asylum of the oppressed of our earth. Cruel Russia asks that we return one who has fought in the high and holy light of revolution. That government asks opportunity to oppress that man caught in the mangles of an inspiring revolution.

"Our flag must not be dropped in humiliation. Let the government at Washington see its duty clearly in this particular case."

ACTOR WHITESIDE IS CHEERED. Mr. Whiteside evoked repeated cheering when he responded to demands for a curtain speech.

"I had been told that the American people would not accept a serious message when hurled over the footlights in the guise of drama," said the actor, maintaining his character of the persecuted Jewish musician. "Mr. Zangwill declined to alter his play with the exception of a single line relating to the divorce question which was criticised by President Roosevelt as giving an unfair impression. He took out the line not in deference to President Roosevelt or the American people, but in deference to truth."

Back in those early days of Chicago theater, all kinds of unusual evenings were to be had. In this instance, a *Tribune* writer was attending a special performance of a play by Anglo-Jewish writer Israel Zangwill, "The Melting Pot," about a Russian-Jewish immigrant family. The show got interrupted by a politicized curtain speech delivered by one of its actors, who apparently maintained his character while doing so, only to be joined by an audience member opining from one of the boxes.

The cause of the day was that of a Russian refugee, Christian Rudowitz, who was living in Chicago. The city's Russian consul, acting for the czar, had asked that Rudowitz be extradited so he could be tried for his alleged involvement in the murder of several men.

Zangwill's play chronicles the persecution of Jews in Russia but, the critic found, is also a plea for religious tolerance in general. Overall, we get a real and vivid picture here of a progressive Chicago coming to a matinee for a good dose of left-leaning political drama—the town clearly wasn't all "Mr. Blue Beard." On this particular afternoon, the audience featured members of the Jane Addams Hull House, not to mention ministers of all faiths and, strikingly, races, although it is not known who sat where. There was speechifying and pronouncements and a defiant statement of independence, even if president Theodore Roosevelt apparently had already intervened, and with some success. The *Tribune* covered all this with apparent sympathy.

The Chicago production of "The Melting Pot" came a year before it opened in New York and Washington, DC. Chicago was in the political vanguard.

And Rudowitz? He got a good lawyer in Clarence Darrow, and on January 26, 1909, the U.S. government decided that his crimes were political, and thus allowed him to stay in his adopted home.

This matinee turned out quite well for everyone who showed up to see a play, and talk up another one.

9

"MAKE IT LOUD FOR CHICAGO," MANAGERS TELL THEIR PLAYERS.

BY PERCY HAMMOND

JANUARY 16, 1910. One evening last season the writer chanced to drop into one of the theaters within the loop an hour or so after the final performance of an entertainment that had been active in Chicago for a long time. The company was at the actor's gate of glory, ready to embark for New York, where an engagement was to begin the following week, and preparatory to that adventure the stage director and producer was giving counsel as to the artistic deportment necessary for success in the metropolis. He gathered the players all about him in the darkened auditorium and from the leader's chair in the orchestra pit urged them to subtler behavior in their appearances before the audiences of New York.

CRITIC PERCY HAMMOND, IN AN UNDATED PHOTO FROM THE *TRIBUNE* ARCHIVES.

The stage director was one of the most eminent of his craft, his annual product being larger perhaps than that of any of his fellows. So we attended to his remarks with diligence, and his advice is herewith reproduced in all its humiliating details. "You have been playing in Chicago for many months," said he, "and as a consequence everything you do and say is broad, overdrawn, exaggerated. This is the inevitable penalty that every artist must pay for appearing any length of time outside of New York. The audience you have been entertaining is crude, uncultivated, and unappreciative of anything except the most obvious methods. The west does not understand the niceties of the art of acting. The things that made your audience laugh this evening would cause a New Yorker to shudder. On Broadway you must be different. You must approach your points subtly, with finesse. You must be deft, quiet, inferential, suave, and artistic, else the engagement will be a failure. My last word to you is to leave your Chicago ways behind you, for Broadway will not tolerate them for an instant."

This utterance made such an impression upon us that we are able to quote it with stenographic accuracy. It impressed the company, also, for the members stated on their way to the train, chastened and meditative, sorry for their artistic sins, and determined to be good in New York. Of course, it proves little to record the fact that on the following Monday evening the suave, reticent, finished, subtle, and artistic performance of the play on Broadway initiated one of the most disastrous failures of the season. The result, however, was not without its elements of satisfaction to the sensitive Chicago observers, who watched the delicate points of the performance fall unnoticed at the feet of the fastidious New Yorkers.

BELIEVE NEW YORK MORE INTELLIGENT. A theatrical manager of experience informs us that most producers hold similar opinions in regard to the relative intelligence of playgoers in New York and in the west, and that when a play changes its base from New York to Chicago the actors are as a rule instructed to alter their performance to fit the more elemental taste believed to prevail in the hinterland. Though we have no great amount of faith in the intellect of the average American stage director, we are not prepared to assert that this lack of confidence in us is a manifestation of provincialism without foundation in actual conditions. Perhaps we are a trifle dull of comprehension. It may be that we cannot hear unless we are shouted at; that we cannot see without the aid of spotlight. Doubtless we are low of brow and lack the facilities of discernment and discrimination so acutely in evidence in other sections. We are not to be penetrated; we must be swatted else we do not understand. The managers must have made a study of us in comparison with others, and have some foundation for the conclusion that we are lacking in the cognoscence necessary to the enjoyment of artistic things in the theater.

But how are we ever to improve if we are subjected to such exhibitions of sheer sound and fury, as the performance of "Seven Days" at the Illinois last Sunday evening? Here is a brisk little play, full of easily comprehended situations, with no obfuscating complexities of plot or character to baffle the spectator of average sagacity. Acted nimbly as we are told it is acted in New York, it should be a cheering affair, stimulating if not important, and quite worthy [of] the attention of those who like their evenings in the theater freighted with no significance heavier than mere amusement. We like to think of Mr. Colin Kemper, the stage director of this play, as one of those who trust us, for he gave us performances of "Paid in Full" much quieter and more intelligent than those in New York. However, the nature of the proceedings at the Illinois Sunday night, carried on under his supervision, fills us with fear that he, too, suspects us. The vociferation of that occasion "outvociferized even sound itself," so dire was the noise made by most of the actors. They seemed to be turbulent even when they were still. Nearly every point was like a bludgeon, and when the evening was over one felt as if he had been beaten to a mental pulp.

There were pleasant exceptions to the general clamorousness of the affair, however, the chief among these was Mr. Roy Atwell, whose demeanor in one of the less essential roles, was that of a skillful farceur, certain, unforced, and serious. Miss Grace Griswold, too, acted with some semblance of sanity as the conventional stage spinster, conventionally angular and corkscrewed. The superabundance of Mr. Harry Tighe's impersonation of one of the leading characters was particularly regrettable, for he is a handsome and magnetic fellow, with the sort of personality that ought to fit well into farce. But he seemed to think he was in a gymnasium instead of a play and his performance was exclusively athletic. In case the management decides to put on a subdued version of "Seven Days" that entertainment will be permitted to enjoy the inestimable pleasure of our approval as a clean, alert, shrewd little farce with a commendable infrequency of banged doors and tarnished with no smut whatever.

TOO MANY THEATERS, SAY THE MAGNATES. Mr. Hayman, the New York manager, and Mr. Singer, the Chicago manager, diagnose the current commercial ailment of the drama and agree in the conclusion that we suffer from an overproduction of theaters. More people are interested in the play than ever before, they believe, and the output of worthy entertainment is heavier than it has been for years. Yet disaster follows disaster until the store houses bulge with discarded scenery, and the enterprise that not long ago would have been a prosperous success, must now be content with the shallow dividends which follow moderate attendance.

The four or five theaters of the first class which Chicago boasted ten or twelve years ago have increased to seventeen. In New York City there are forty "standard" price houses which must have plays and audiences. Neither those who write for the theater nor those who go to it have grown in sufficient number to keep pace with this wholesale extension; as a consequence managers are forced to produce mediocrities and worse to keep the theaters open, and audiences are distributed through so large a territory that their presence in any one place is apt to be scant. Mr. Will J. Davis of the Illinois attributes the activity in theater building to the traditional vanity of many of those associated with the business. "The other day," says Mr. Davis, "I read in THE TRIBUNE that a New York manager planned an excursion to Chicago to see a performance of one of his plays. He was to travel by special train at an extravagant rate per mile, the trip costing $3,000, an expenditure which he regarded as a mere detail of his everyday operations. Many ill informed men with money to invest are impressed with spectacular manifestations of that kind and are led to believe that the theatrical business and the mint are institutions with coordinate functions. So they decide they will build theaters and get some of this easy money. It is this general practice of boasting of inflated profits in amusements that entices men who know no better to enter and overcrowd the field."

Some of our correspondents have ideas as to the nature of the affliction that has befallen the theaters. One of them asserts that the avaricious spectator discourages many playgoers and causes them to depend on bridge whist and other diversions, though that evil is as nothing here when compared to the operations elsewhere. Another believes that the motor engrosses the preponderance of playgoers, and another writes that the moving picture entertainments are fulfilling the office of the drama for a vast majority of the public. Still another believes that the discomforts of transportation are responsible for sparse attendance. The opinion which we are disposed to regard as most accurate is one from a candid manager who says that the reason people are not going in great numbers to the theater is that there are not many things in the theater that the people care to see.

To be a Chicago theater critic, the evidence would suggest, is to constantly rail against poor treatment from the theatrical sophisticates of New York. Of the very many *Tribune* columns on this very theme, Percy Hammond's 1910 screed—written at a time when the newspaper was growing at an explosive rate—is one of the best and perhaps also the first.

Hammond (1873–1936) was both a music and a drama critic, as was common throughout the *Tribune*'s history. He was among the first of the newspaper's critics whom readers actually followed by name. An eclectic and internally well-regarded journalist, he held a number of different jobs at the *Tribune*, including time spent at its Paris bureau. Hammond, who joined the paper in 1908 from the *Saturday Evening Post*, was from a small town in Ohio, a conservative background that some saw in his writing, which (as we will see) tended to suggest that the critic was resistant to change. But he was also an interesting and very distinctive mix of hominess and literary pretension, inarguably an apt match for Chicago in the early 20th century.

In 1921, Hammond moved to New York, becoming the drama critic for the *New York Tribune* (later the *Herald Tribune*) until his death in 1934. After this move, he became well known–not least for infamously savaging Orson Welles's "Voodoo Macbeth"–and was a founding member of the New York Drama Critics' Circle.

This grandly defensive and sarcastic column is based on Hammond's having overheard a New York director lecturing his cast on how much smarter New York audiences were than the ones in Chicago, thus confirming all Chicago's self-doubts about how the East Coast culture mavens perceived it as lacking sophistication. Clearly, Hammond was deeply insulted. And he unleashes his venom on a topic that has preoccupied Chicago theater artists ever since.

One wonders how Hammond possibly remembered all this, seemingly months later. Was he frantically writing and storing notes (there were no tape recorders in 1910)? Or, as he claims, did what he overheard really upset him so much that he was able to recall all these quotations later with "stenographic accuracy"? Did the director know he was there? Or did he just not care? Did Hammond talk to the actors on their way to the train, or was that artistic license? Did he make this whole thing up?

We could see Hammond's piece as paving the way for Claudia Cassidy, a successor who would rage on this topic frequently. We can regard the column (with a review buried therein) as an indicator of a moment when theater in Chicago was growing fast, with standards slipping. But surely, this great classic of Chicago journalism also shows how the city was fighting back against the hegemony of the East Coast, standing up for its crude, frontier self and attempting to mount a defense against those who would condescend to its citizens. Hammond is praising New York shows that treated Chicago with respect, and serving notice on those that did not give his readers the sophistication he thought they deserved.

Almost everything in this piece could be written today, including Hammond's concluding assertion that the reason the theater was not doing so well is that there are "not many things in the theater that the people care to see."

This was by no means his only review on this theme.

10

MUSIC AND THE DRAMA: STILL THE "RURAL DRAMA."

BY PERCY HAMMOND

MAY 7, 1910. The "rural drama" persists. Its vitality successfully defies all the forces that in other classifications of the play prove lethal—critical disapproval, popular indifference, the comic weeklies, the variety theaters, indorsement of pedagogic bodies, and even the pretty wit of actors themselves. The least imaginative of plays may be depended on at all times for a bon-mot at the expense of "rural drama." Making the rounds of the newspapers that maintain a column devoted to clipped humor is a duologue between a playwright and a friend. The latter expresses wonder that the former's play was withdrawn from performance at the end of a single week. "Yes," sadly replies the playwright; "you see, it was indorsed by every clergyman in town!"

𝄐 𝄐 𝄐

Our pen is directed toward the theme by the impending production here of another play of the species. It is called by the press agent in his "ads" a "pomonic comedy," the adjective finding explanation in a descriptive line to the effect that it is an "idyl of the apple lands." Peter Pan expresses the truism that almost everybody is a descendant; and in that vein we would record our observation that almost every play of rural life [is] an idyl. We are, as a Column, not fond of press agents: when they do not mislead us into misstatement of fact they try to, which is far, far worse. But we are not finding fault with the one who unearths "pomonic" for use in advertising of the theater: he is, at least, performing the public service of sending a great many persons to the dictionary. Nor are we captious because of the correlation in this case of comedy and apples; for the apple has been too, too long the symbol of tragedy, from Genesis through the stressful Helen of Troy period down to the days of the core-de-ballet of modern musical comedy.

𝄐 𝄐 𝄐

Our thoughts concerning "Go West, Young Woman!" the impending play in question, have to do with finding a reason why playwrights continue to write and managers to produce "rural drama." Its survival in a day when Ibsen [has] become commonplace and "The Easiest Way" and "The Fourth Estate" thrive as examples of what native authors can do is something more than merely baffling: it is discouraging.

Playwrights—and among them have been our foremost—have literally boxed the compass of rural United States in seeking to give a touch of novelty or variety to this classification of the minor drama. Nearly every state in the union has been called upon to provide a scenic background for these plays of simplicity supposed to be sylvan, and of agony alleged to be agricultural. Indeed, the only state that has escaped, so far as we can recall, is New Jersey, which for a century or more has been the professional humorist's notion of a background for jokes and jests based on rurality of mind and matter. The new play lays Oregon under tribute; and we may reasonably expect to find Mount Hood looming on the backdrop, just as Brooklyn bridge is well nigh invariably the rural indication of outdoors, all night New York city, and the Lions of St. Mark the scenic "tip" that the action takes place in Venice.

Augustus Thomas and Clyde Fitch were not immune to the appeal of rusticity on the stage; for the former was animated by no high ambition to dramatize a mere neighborhood when he wrote "Alabama," while Fitch's "Lovers' Lane" was never intended to be anything more than it seemed to be. The late Joseph Arthur, who was in the van[guard] of literary Indianians, successfully footlighted the interior regions of his native state twenty years ago in "Blue Jeans" and died while working on his sixth or seventh effort to duplicate the achievement. Two decades of theatergoing have been marked by an unending procession of hardheaded old farmers, shrewish, elderly spinsters, salt-of-the-earth plowboys, low comedy oafs, and malign city chaps. So far we have been unable to detect any psychic difference as between those stamped "New England" and those bearing one of the numerous other geographical brands.

It may be that we are obtuse. But it just as well may be that the reason why playwrights and managers continue to pursue the "rural drama" is not unlike the reason why our foremost playwrights have, to date, not been represented in the offering of movements and institutions of which the New theater of New York may be regarded as the dernier-cri. The astute Mr. Brady, who is sponsor for "Go West," has taken down, we understand, something more than $1,700,000 in profits in the thirteen years of "Way Down East"; the sponsors for "In Old Kentucky" have been similarly fortunate in their dividends; and not even his hired eulogists venture to suggest in figures the increment that is the veteran Denman Thompson's.

Hammond's railing against what he calls "the rural drama" is a kind of companion piece to the previous column, written about four months earlier. He does not intend the moniker "rural drama" to be a compliment: he is attacking romanticism, melodrama and the faked bucolic nature of so-called Yankee dramas.

This is a very lively piece and a concisely expressed argument that, in the age of Ibsen, American playwrights were not treating the nation's flyover territory with the dignity it deserved. If Hammond's previous column is about the mode of theatrical production in Chicago and the way the city's audiences were perceived, this one is pleading for more serious dramas about small-town America (Hammond had not forgotten his roots in Cadiz, Ohio). Reading this screed today, we're struck by how most of the stereotypes Hammond identified in 1910 remain current (although the rural conception of New Jersey has shifted a little).

These were still early days for American drama, and Hammond was eloquently fighting for better homegrown plays in a world that had yet to see the great dramas of Eugene O'Neill and beyond, let alone the likes of Sam Shepard or Horton Foote. Hammond clearly was weary of real American places, and real American people, being used merely as interchangeably rustic backdrops; that's not changed so much, either. How fitting that he was making this argument in Chicago, which would, later that century, make its name specializing in the very kind of dramas Hammond clearly wanted in 1910, when Europeans were already writing about the seedy underbelly of ordinary burgs while Americans were still in the thrall of stereotype.

11

THE LITTLE THEATER BEGINS ITS ADVENTURE.

BY PERCY HAMMOND

NOVEMBER 13, 1912. Trustfully Mr. Maurice Browne's Little Theater set out upon its adventures last evening in a nook in the Fine Arts building, the plays experiencing performance being "Womenkind," by Wilfred Wilson Gibson, and "On Baile's Strand," by W. B. Yeats.

The ninety-and-nine were in attendance, occupying the ninety-and-nine chairs in the auditorium, which, architecturally, resembles a corridor in the Hotel Brevoort. It is rather long, slender, and dim and heavily carpeted—comfortable, certainly, but not quite cozy. At one side there is a sort of aisle, containing a stage box, and at the other an apartment where, it is inferred from the playbill, tea may be had at 25 cents the person. An air of austerity, if not rigor, pervades the place, though lenient here and there in its luxurious simplicity. It is easy of approach—that is, if one is not tardy. My endeavor, rather late, to intrude without being unsandaled, last evening was unsuccessful, despite mild beseechment, and I was forced with others to resort to one of the other numerous theaters in the building, there to await the conclusion of the first part of the ritual. Without commending "My Little Friend" to the Studebaker, I should say that it is a very good rule, indeed.

The play missed was that of Mr. Gibson, a minor poet of renown, and it was about a selfish man who, betrothed to one girl, had loved another with results. It was said on the authority of expert observers to have been a bit of bitter life, skillfully sliced. The stage of the Little Theater, one imagines, is more fit for the representation of this kind of simple "hut drama," as "Mme. X" calls it, than for one of Mr. Yeats' epic Irish friezes in miniature. "On Baile's Strand," the second play, was of this sort, with Irish kings galore, talking and battling, with and against one another for no reason whatever except a poetic one. Conchobar (pronounced Connaha) and Cuchulain, the high king of Ulster and the king of Muirthemne respectively, engaged in rhythmic controversy, and the play's plot ended with Cuchulain slaughtering, in a vagrant

Irish duel, his own son by a pale and amorous queen encountered by him in a trip to another province years before.

These episodes were recited and depicted with much more skill and assurance than is usually to be found in the amateur. For Mr. Browne's players are amateur, appearing without recompense, and even without the compliment of their names in the cast. Acting becomes a difficult art, not a mere knack, when its environment is architecturally hostile; and conventionality in the relation of the stage to the auditorium is the one commonplace which the "advanced" drama should not ignore, but usually does. The Little theater is just a step from a charade in a drawing room. Its impersonations are "pretending," not acting. They are make-believe, not histrionism. No illusion is probable. If the ninety-and-nine can forget the seams in King Conchobar's beard and the gaunt, un-Reinhardtian kitchen, posing as an assembly hall of the Irish kings; if their imagination can stem the fatal propinquity of actor and spectator, then they may have pleasure in the Little theater's attempt to realize Mr. Yeats' lovely resurrection of Irish myth. It is pleasant to report that they seemed to do so last evening. One presumes that in other circumstances Mr. Browne's players would be as generally effective as were the Abbey theater players in more favorable circumstances.

It would have been easy for one of ribald attitude toward the toy drama to make sport of the playing of the Little theater. For instance, the congregation of kings in Mr. Yeats' play was easily comparable to the second degree in the initiatory rites of the Knights of Pythias or the Modern Woodmen of America. The costumes were so obviously costumes, and the attitudes so obviously attitudes. Yet the ninety-and-nine, sophisticated as they are, dramatically seemed to look beyond and into the spirit, not the presentation of the play. Mr. Maurice Browne was, no doubt, happy at the outcome. For it was he who put the "y" in "drayma" hereabouts.

Percy Hammond wrote this review at the very beginning of the Chicago Little Theatre, an operation housed in the back of the fourth floor of the Fine Arts Building, 410 S. Michigan Ave., that was highly influential given that it lasted only for five years. Part of a national movement of "little theaters," it was founded by Maurice Browne, who was British, and his wife, Ellen Van Volkenburg. They wanted to make art and create a civic institution using local actors. Mme. X, a *Tribune* gossip columnist at the time, also covered

Browne's enterprise and the couple's desire for a new building, which never came to pass. The Chicago Little Theatre staged many plays by Henrik Ibsen, August Strindberg (one double bill was presented in honor of the playwright's birthday) and William Butler Yeats, and even a few by Chicagoans. Hammond makes much here of the "amateur" status of the actors, a peculiar concept for him, it seems. In later years, actors not getting paid much in Chicago would hardly be worthy of special note.

Hammond's piece offers a fascinating little description of what the 99-seat theater was like. In many ways, this was a prototype Chicago storefront. It seems that Hammond showed up late for the first show—perhaps an indication of where the institution sat on his list of priorities. Apparently, Browne did not let him into the theater, but made him wait for intermission. As things would go in Chicago, where little theaters slowly gained power and control, "just a step from a charade in a drawing room" would summarize a lot of the city's most famous productions. This was merely the first. In essence, Hammond seems to have viewed the whole Browne enterprise as amateurish—but he was clearly struck by the sophistication of "the ninety-nine" and their ability to look past what he, the professional critic, saw.

As time went on, Hammond did not soften much on Browne. "The note of the ingenue is in his personality," he later wrote. That's a bizarre turn of phrase, and, inarguably, offensive.

12

ROOSEVELT SKIPS BANQUET TO SEE HULL HOUSE PLAY.

VISITS FINE ARTS THEATER BETWEEN SOUP AND CHEESE—"DELIGHTED" WITH AMATEUR ARTISTS

DECEMBER 10, 1912. There was a banquet at the University club last night. Col. Theodore Roosevelt was the chief guest. Reporters were not permitted to attend. But between the consommé and the coffee the colonel was interviewed. The colonel sneaked away while the olives were being munched. He stepped into an automobile and sped to the Fine Arts theater to keep an engagement with Miss Jane Addams.

As Miss Addams' guest he reviewed the second act of "Justice," being presented by the Hull House players. His interview and probably his first work as dramatic critic is as follows:

"Impressive—most impressive. I must have the book. The act is excellently written and surprisingly well acted. I am most interested in it. I wish that I could remain for the entire performance. I enjoyed it immensely."

With characteristic brusqueness he stepped into the waiting motor and was whirled back to the interrupted dinner.

This piece is a rather delicious little curiosity–a piece of dramatic criticism published in the *Tribune* and coming from the mouth of the 26th president of the United States. It's also indicative of the huge national clout of Jane Addams, the progressive reformer, social worker, suffragist and peace advocate, whose Hull House Players apparently were enough to get Theodore Roosevelt to duck out of a banquet and see at least one act of a show, performed by amateur actors, at the Fine Arts Theatre.

From its beginnings in 1889, theater was a big part of Addams's work at Hull House, the famous settlement house on the Near West Side of Chicago. Her company of actors performed in all kinds of works, from classical Greek to Restoration comedy, mostly in the theater inside Hull House. In this instance, the Hull House Players (which at this moment had been around for 11 years) were performing downtown under the direction of Laura Dainty Pelham, a move that the *Tribune* suggested should be "encouraged" by a form of "enlightened provincialism" (whatever that means), since the Hull House Players was a "meritorious company."

"Justice," for the record, is a play by the English writer John Galsworthy, best known for writing "The Forsyte Saga." The piece advocates for better conditions in prison, and the Hull House Players were offering its debut in the United States. Roosevelt was not the only politician to see it: a very young Winston Churchill attended a performance in London in 1910 and, immediately and famously thereafter, set about changing English prisons from the House of Commons. Addams doubtless hoped for the same effect on Theodore Roosevelt, although it sounds like he did not delay in getting back to his dinner at the University Club.

According to her biographer, James Weber Linn, Addams had no illusions about the president, who called her "the most useful citizen in Chicago." He was emotional and peripatetic; she "never wavered" in her goals. Each found use in the other. In this instance, Roosevelt was so impressed with the show, he bought up as many of Galsworthy's works as he could find in Chicago, and read them on the train back to New York.

In a piece published just before this one, the *Tribune* said of the Hull House Players, after duly noting its amateur status, that "the latent talent of our people is a resource Chicago cannot afford to neglect."

13

UNDER FALSE PRETENSES

BEN HECHT'S EVENING: "UNDER FALSE PRETENSES."

La Salle Theatre

BY SHEPPARD BUTLER

CAST

Sally Jenkins	Maidl Turner
Mr. Smart	Gustav Bowman
Manny Epstein	Clyde Veaux
Helen Tarbell	Maude Hannaford
Margaret Schmidt	Catherine Carter
Mr. Gorman	Earle Mitchell
Felix Tarbell	Leo Ditrichstein
Edward (Bud) Jenkins	Albert Morrison
Norma Ramon	Mary Duncan
Sing	Alexis Polianov
Toy	Young Leo
Virginia Hansen	Carlotta Irwin
Murphy	M. Kelly
Richard Collins	Lee Millar

OCTOBER 3, 1922. Comes now Ben Hecht, Chicagoan, feuilletonist, and maker of novels, to confront the footlighting of his first full length play. The event was consummated under happy auspices at the La Salle last evening, with the deft and sparkling Mr. Leo Ditrichstein to speak the lines and an eager houseful to laugh at and applaud them.

Not often does a playwright fall, at the start, into hands as skillful as those of Mr. Ditrichstein. He knows his theater, and to "Under False Pretenses" he has given most entertaining presentation. I am told that it was he who, having read "Erik Dorn," proposed that its author join him in doing a play. Thus it was, perhaps, a task approached con amore. In any event both actor and dramatist seemed hugely pleased with the results. They took their curtain calls in impartial alternation, Mr. Hecht appearing jovially after each act and doing all the speech-making. This consisted of an admonition to note how moral the play is and to observe that it "gets moraler and moraler as it goes on."

Thus warned, we eyed the proceedings carefully, and Mr. Hecht probably will be chagrined to learn that some of us did not find anything so very immoral. True, there are perilous moments, but they are addressed in so whimsical a vein that they are occasions for mirth rather than perturbation.

Hecht is none of your playwrights who deal with people you know. He seeks out oddments of the human race, holds them up for your detached contemplation, and pokes fun at them. His characters enlist no sympathy, and seek none. They are there as material for jest, the subtler the better. "Clever" is a devastating word, but it is the word for "Under False Pretenses."

Thus, as might be expected, it is an uneven play, its first and third acts much given to talk and scattered action, though spotted amusingly with *mots* that would make it, I should think, a beguiling thing to read. Here and there is a sly line that—perhaps fortunately for the moralists—doesn't register.

◠ ◠ ◠

It is at its best in its frankly farcical second act, one of the gayest travesties I ever say of the so-called artistic temperament. Here is Ditrichstein as Felix Tarbell, dramatist and phrasemonger, in the apartment of a lovely lady with whom he is having a reluctant affair. He is a slave to sentiment in the abstract; when he confronts the reality it bores him.

He has talked loftily of backgrounds, and the lady has supplied one according to her lights—cushions, incense, and a riot of Japanese flummery. The cushions are uncomfortable, the incense chokes him, the beat of a gong makes him jump. He clings to illusion as best he may until the radiator begins to bang. Then he plunges down a fire escape as the beauteous one enters to complete her conquest with a lascivious dance.

◠ ◠ ◠

This is riotously funny; the rest has to do merely with developing the picture of Tarbell—an amiably impossible person, no farther abandoned in sin than the business of talking about it, but unable to make any one believe this, and abandoned in the end not only by his wife but by all his lights of love in the bargain.

An amusing trifle, and amusingly played, with Ditrichstein precisely the same quizzical, sententious, and imperturbable philanderer he has been in any of his half dozen most recent plays. The dark beauty named Mary Duncan makes a lovely figure of the second-act temptress, playing the part perhaps with more spirit than intelligence, but playing it well enough, and the others conduct themselves approximately as they should in a variety of roles.

Sheppard Butler probably did not know it at the time, but "comes now Ben Hecht" is an extremely prescient opening line for the first play by a writer who would become one of the most famous to emerge from Chicago. By the time of this review, the *Tribune* had increased its interest in literature and was part of a growing movement of local writing. Around 1915–1920, the paper was publishing the work of the likes of H. L. Mencken, H. G. Wells, George Jean Nathan, Joseph Conrad and even George Bernard Shaw. By 1920, the *Tribune* was selling over 400,000 copies a day, with nearly 600,000 on Sundays, far eclipsing its main rivals, the *Daily News* and the *Herald and Examiner*.

By 1921, Percy Hammond had left Chicago for the *New York Tribune*, later the *Herald Tribune*. His replacement at the *Tribune* in Chicago was Butler (1893–1972), who served as its drama critic from 1921 to 1924. Butler started working at the paper in 1905, first staying until 1909 and then returning from 1915 to 1924. He was both a writer and, at various points in his tenure, an editor. In the 1940s, he would go on to become managing editor of *Redbook* magazine, where he stayed until his retirement. He died in Florida at the age of 79.

Butler was an erudite writer, though certainly a critic with a less forceful personality and point of view than Hammond. A "feuilletonist," for the record, is a writer of light fiction and literary or satirical essays, which is a pretty good early description of Hecht, a man who would go on to do many things. Hecht, this review suggests, was far from a shrinking violet–he apparently appeared onstage at the end of each act of "Under False Pretenses" and made curtain speeches. Read deep into the review and you get a pretty fair and concise appraisal of Hecht's style: "he seeks out oddments of the human race, holds them up for your detached contemplation, and pokes fun at them."

You won't find many references to "Under False Pretenses" in the Hecht literature; by the time this show opened on Broadway on December 25, 1922, it was retitled as "The Egotist," perhaps in response to all those curtain speeches Hecht gave in Chicago. Hecht, of course, went on to cowrite, in 1928, "The Front Page," a great American play and a collaboration with the former *Tribune* reporter Charles MacArthur, whom he had met in Chicago and with whom he forged a remarkably fruitful creative partnership. Interestingly,

Hecht was one of several Chicago journalists who turned their careers as newspaper people into gigs as playwrights and screenwriters (another famous one follows here shortly).

Born in New York City and raised in Wisconsin, Hecht did well in Chicago, writing in many different arenas before moving to Los Angeles to become a hugely well-paid scribe; he even snagged an Academy Award for *Underworld*. Among many other fascinating aspects of a dramatic writing career that began with this review, Hecht also turned in some uncredited work on "Gone with the Wind." His screenplays include "A Star Is Born" (1937), "His Girl Friday" (the 1940 movie adaptation of "The Front Page") and "Strangers on a Train" (1957), among scores of others.

At the time of this review, Hecht was living in Hyde Park and working for the *Chicago Daily News*, where he was famous for his columns about ordinary Chicagoans, later published together as "1001 Afternoons in Chicago" (many years later, the city's Lookingglass Theatre Company would turn those sketches into a show). Alas, Hecht's sketches of struggling Chicagoans were fiction, not journalism; he did the right thing in changing professions. In his 1954 autobiography, he confessed to having made all these characters up. In today's journalistic world, that would have been a scandalous, career-destroying admission. But Hecht operated in a different era, and for the most part the admission merely added to his color. By 1924, he was gone from Chicago. Like so many of the city's writers, he headed off to a coast in search of money and fame: "1001 Afternoons in Chicago" became "1001 Afternoons in New York."

Meanwhile in Chicago, another *Tribune* reporter was getting her material at work.

14

BEULAH ANNAN AWAITS STORK, MURDER TRIAL

JAIL WOMEN WONDER "WHAT JURORS THINK ABOUT."

BY MAURINE WATKINS

MAY 9, 1924. What counts with a jury when a woman is on trial for murder?

Youth? Beauty? And if to these she adds approaching motherhood—?

CHICAGO REPORTER AND PLAYWRIGHT MAURINE DALLAS WATKINS, PHOTOGRAPHED AUGUST 27, 1927. PHOTOGRAPH BY FLORENCE VANDAMM FOR THE *CHICAGO TRIBUNE*.

For pretty Mrs. Beulah Annan, who shot her lover, Harry Kohlstedt, to the tune of her husband's phonograph, is expecting a visit from the stork early this fall. This 23 year old murderess, now waiting trial, is making this the basis for a further appeal to clemency.

COULDN'T TAKE TWO LIVES. Because of the "four-term" rule, Mrs. Annan's case cannot be continued for more than four terms of court without her consent. If she is brought to trial before autumn her condition can be considered by the jury, since it has the right to pass sentence. If the jury should give her death—

"There is no direct statute covering such a contingency," said a former state's attorney, "but the state would have to delay execution till after the birth of the child, since it would be taking two lives instead of one."

"Her condition has no bearing upon the legality of the case," said her attorney, William Scott Stewart. "It would be a matter of executive clemency, once the sentence was passed. Or it might affect the jury."

WHAT INFLUENCES A JURY? Will a jury give death—will a jury send to prison—a mother-to-be?

What affects a jury anyway? That's what they asked themselves, the seven inmates of "Murderess' Row," yesterday afternoon, for the conviction of one of their number broke the monotony of their life and startled them into a worried analysis. And Elizabeth Unkafer, the "queer" one, who received "life" for the leap-year murder of her lover, Sam Boltschoff, held the spotlight for a few brief hours.

"They gave her 'life' because she killed a man! I have killed a man; will they—" then they gamely shake their heads—no, it can't be life for them! "What counts most with a jury after all?"

Sex.

"A woman never swung in Illinois," said one triumphantly.

Looks. (Elizabeth Unkafer was not cursed with fatal beauty!)

JURORS HAVE EYESIGHT. "A jury isn't blind," said another, "and a pretty woman's never been convicted in Cook county!" Gallant old Cook county!

Youth. (Elizabeth was 43.)

Kitty Malm, who received life for shooting a watchman last November, is said to be the only [——] young woman who's ever gone over the road, and Kitty wasn't—well—quite "refined."

Of the four awaiting trial, the cases of Mrs. Annan and Mrs. Belva Gaertner would seem most similar to Elizabeth Unkafer's; each is accused of shooting a man, not her husband, with whom her relations were at least questioned; each is supposed to be "a woman scorned" who shot the man "rather than lose him." But neither was at all disconcerted by Mrs. Unkafer's sentence.

"I can't see that it's anything at all like my case," said Mrs. Gaertner, the sophisticated divorcée indicted for shooting Law, the young auto salesman, as she twirled about in her red dancing slippers.

"The cases are entirely different," said Mrs. Annan, quite the ingenue in her girlish checked flannel frock.

LIZZIE WAS NO BEAUTY. No, Elizabeth, with her straggly mop of red hair, pale eyes, and flabby cheeks, remembers it all too well. She paused in her scrubbing the jail floors yesterday afternoon to live it all over again.

Her attorney had pleaded "insanity."

"Think I'm goin' to say I'm crazy?" she asked indignantly. "Not much! They'd lock me up then with some that are worse than I am—and no tellin' then what would happen! I wanted 'em to shoot me—why not?—at State and Madison—make a big day of it, and given every one a front seat, but they gave me life instead."

Although not a theater review, this particular story is too interesting and theatrically compelling to be omitted from any book about the *Tribune*'s relationship with Chicago theater. Penned in the midst of a tumultuous time in Chicago when Al Capone and his rivals battled on the city's streets, this is a news story by a reporter named Maurine Dallas Watkins that would form the basis for the play, and then the musical, "Chicago." The singularly successful theatrical property, which did much to popularize the image of Chicago as a corrupt den of vice, would define the city to the world for years to come (the *Tribune*'s coverage of the show that resulted follows next).

Was Watkins a playwright masquerading as a *Tribune* reporter? Or was the originator of "Chicago" an ink-stained wretch who sold out her reporter's soul to showbiz? Most assume the latter, but it's still an interesting question. An ambitious woman, Watkins was born in Louisville in 1896, attended high school in Crawfordsville, Ind., studied at Butler University and went on to graduate school at Radcliffe College. While at Radcliffe, she signed up for a playwriting class, the "47 Workshop," that was taught at Harvard University by George Pierce Baker and included Eugene O'Neill and Philip Barry among its famous students. Many American theater historians regard Baker as the spiritual founder of the first generation of U.S. playwrights.

By 1924, Watkins had moved to Chicago. In February, she showed up at the *Tribune* looking for work as a reporter. Whether she was looking to beef up her grit to be a better writer—or merely attempting a career change—is unclear. But she was hired to write about crime from a "feminine" perspective, for $50 a week.

She made her mark on page one very fast, thanks to a couple of Chicago's nastier brands of killer women. The subject of this story, the glamorous flapper Beulah Annan, had shot her lover, Harry Kohlstedt, and then took a few moments to play "Hula Lou" on the phonograph as the poor fellow expired in a pool of blood (an episode that made it, pretty closely to reality, into the show). Kohlstedt had made the mistake of telling Annan he was leaving her. Annan had a fast-talking lawyer named W. W. O'Brien and gave many press conferences. She got offers of marriage. Six days later, she announced she was "pregnant," but the trial went ahead anyway, with Annan dressed to the nines in front of the all-male jury. According to Watkins's page-one story (containing another line that made it into the play), her defense was "we both grabbed for the gun."

Annan was found not guilty and walked away. Nobody talked about any "baby" again. But by then, Watkins was already following another crime. Belva Gaertner was a stylish divorced woman with an inconveniently dead boyfriend named Walter Law—a young and married automobile salesman. As Watkins's prose relayed with aplomb, Gaertner was found with the gun that shot the guy, and his blood on her body. In her defense, she said she had drunk too much gin to remember what came down. She got off as well.

With those colorful crimes in her notebook, Watkins quit the *Tribune* and renewed her relationship with Baker. The results are in the next piece.

15

CHICAGO

Harris Theater

BY F. D.

CAST

Roxie Hart .... Francine Larrimore
Amos, her husband .... Charles Halton
Fred, her man .... James Coyle
Flynn, her attorney .... Jack Roseleigh
Sergeant Murdock............................... William Crimane
Jake, a reporter.................................... Norval Keedwell
Mary Sunshine, another...................... Eda Heineman
Velma, an assassin .... Dorothy Stickney

Maggie, another	Caroline Morrison
Prosecutor Harrison	Griffin Crafts
Mrs. Morton, matron	Isabelle Winlocke
Babe	William Gargan
Slats	George Cowell

SEPTEMBER 12, 1927. All you may have heard in praise of "Chicago" as fun is quite true: It is as rich a reason for laughter as has in many years been proffered to those of us who think we are civilized, educated, adult, responsive, transilient, literate, something more than half-witted, what used to be called "aware," and what is now miscalled "sophisticated." If you be or if you think you are in possession of one or more of the qualities indicated, your rightful place is a seat in the Harris for at least one performance of Miss Watkins' gorgeous travesty on what happens to good-looking murderesses in the larger communities of this United States. It were silly for the most devoted of us, as Chicagoans, to be resentful because the piece is called "Chicago": that is, after all, the best of titles for it. And I hope the play is so much of a success here that it will run and run and run: this I hope for the good of the community's soul, and for the gratification I should take from thus learning there is a market here for fun like this is.

The tale is of what happened to Roxie in the eight weeks from the night she shot Fred in her bedroom to the afternoon of her acquittal. Its value resides in its being, in its essentials, like the tale of every lovable husband-killer in the criminal annals of the town. The play is, indeed, a screaming apostrophe to what Jake, the reporter, calls "gallant old Cook County." Told that publicity will save her from hanging, Roxie goes to it, and is saved; and she becomes in eight weeks such an addict that she is ready, if not eager, for another killing by the time the jury of fellow citizens files in to impart the information that she is an innocent woman.

Miss Larrimore, without anything bearing semblance to a good role since "Nice People," has in Roxie one that might have been designed with her in mind, although she was not called to it until the play was otherwise ready for its premiere. She acts it *con amore*: she gives to it immense gusto, humor, and understanding, enriches it with countless touches of perfect pantomime, and so identifies herself with it that I, for one, am unable to fancy in it any other actress with whose gamut I have acquaintance. She completely realizes the pin-headed little mattoid from the first oath in the dark until the final tableau as Roxie takes her place before the cameras with a new murderess in order that she may have one more day on the first page.

And a good general performance has its special merits in the acting of Miss Heineman, as a sob-sister of the yellows, and Mr. Roseleigh, who might be Mr. Darrow or any one of twenty other cash-down celebrities in criminal practice in Cook County.

This is the play that resulted from Maurine Watkins's story. Belva and Beulah had become Velma and Roxie. But aside from the change in names (Roxie Hart came from an old murder case in Indiana), the crimes were pretty much the same. From then on, Watkins had a spluttering Hollywood career as a screenwriter, never again reaching the heights of "Chicago." She routinely denied permission to anyone who wanted to buy the rights to her play. Some reports say she had developed belated remorse over treating murder with such a light touch. Only after Watkins's death in 1969 did "Chicago" get sold—and turned into a musical. When producer Barry Weissler revived the show in 1996, he declared that Watkins's commentary on crime, media and the legal profession finally had "found its time." Watkins, one imagines, would have disagreed.

Interestingly, F. D.'s *Tribune* review of the first national tour, following the original Broadway run, makes no mention of Watkins's time as a reporter in its own newsroom.

"F. D." was Frederick Donaghey (1869–1937), a dapper Philadelphia native and graduate of Princeton University, who became the *Tribune*'s drama critic in 1923 after several years as the paper's music critic and a stint in London as the European manager of the Wolfsohn Music Bureau, which arranged concert tours.

Donaghey combined a career in criticism with that of an arts manager. By 1930, he'd left the paper and become director of the Dramatic League of Chicago. Thereafter, he was publicity director for the city's Federal Theatre Project. On the side, he penned musical comedies, a couple of which were produced at the La Salle Theatre, where he also was a manager.

Alas, the 68-year-old Donaghey died of a heart attack in 1937 while sitting in his State Street dentist's chair, awaiting the extraction of a tooth.

16

TOBACCO ROAD

"TOBACCO ROAD" A STAGE RECORD FOR CUSSWORDS / DEPICTS POOR WHITE TRASH AT THEIR WORST.

Selwyn Theatre

BY CHARLES COLLINS

CAST

Dude Lester	Donald Barry
Ada Lester	Mary Servoss
Jeeter Lester	Henry Hull
Ellie May	Pauline Drake
Grandma Lester	Hallene Hilt
Lov Bensey	Leon Ames
Henry Penbody	Herbert A. Pratt
Sister Bessie Rice	Bonita Des Londes
Pearl	Haila Stoddard
Capt. Tim	Howard Banks
George Payne	Fisk[e] O'Hara

SEPTEMBER 3, 1935. Labor day brought into Chicago, at the Selwyn theater, the longest-lived play of the last five years and also, to use its own dialect, the cussingest play that has ever been staged in this profane era. It is the well-known and much talked-of "Tobacco Road," which has been in steady performance in New York for two years and is still active there, headed toward the long-run records of "Abie's Irish Rose" and "Lightnin'."

The Chicago cast for this earthy and grotesque study of Georgia white trash, in their most degraded and no-account form, is headed by Henry Hull, the actor who originated the remarkable character study of Jeeter Lester, often spoken of as a masterpiece. This is, indeed, a notable example of portraiture in a vein that has won fame for the Abbey theater company of Dublin and the Moscow Art theater of the Stanislavsky period.

Jeeter as acted by Mr. Hull is a foul-mouthed, gabbling, droll specimen of the degenerate peasantry of the south—strange, humorous, sinister and almost subhuman. The character is enriched with many strokes of faithful, sometimes loathsome, realism. An old man, he has much of the spryness of his youth, and he moves through the play doing nothing, chattering with simian vigor, like a satiric symbol of everything that is ornery, low-down and yet biologically persistent in the white-trash stock.

Dapper young leading men were Mr. Hull's specialty for many years until he found this rôle and proved himself to be a "character actor"—a phrase that usually implies whiskers and eccentric attire—of high distinction. His Jeeter is a perfect incarnation of the central figure in Erskine Caldwell's novel, of which this play is an effective dramatization.

The play follows the book faithfully for one-half of its course, utilizing only the incidents that are found in the text and following the vivid and natural dialog closely. Then, to endow itself with a plot in conventional form, and also to develop the theme of spiritual union with the land in Jeeter's grubby soul, it introduces an eviction scene, with a grasping bank as the mortgage-holding villain. At this point "Tobacco Road" begins to show a resemblance to the old melodramas of the Irish land troubles, and oddly enough Fiske O'Hara, once a follower of Chauncey Olcott in lyric Hibernian romances, acts the rôle of the heartless financier.

Jeeter and his drab wife, Ada—finely acted by Mary Servoss—are not burned to death in their tumbledown shack, as in the novel. She becomes a victim of the crazy son's automobile driving, but Jeeter survives as the curtain falls, still mouthing about his passion for the fields which his ancestors have tilled.

The cast is excellent, and the types of Georgia white trash that surround Jeeter and Ada are vividly portrayed. The play was received with enthusiasm. It is, indeed, a theatrical production of decided novelty.

This is arguably one of the most influential theater reviews ever published in the *Tribune*, given what happened in Chicago with "Tobacco Road," Jack Kirkland's adaptation of Erskine Caldwell's famous story of Georgia sharecroppers.

Charles Collins (1880–1963), a member of the *Tribune*'s editorial staff for 33 years and a newsman for 60, had become the paper's drama critic in 1930 and remained in that post until 1938 (previously, he was a critic for both the *Chicago Interocean* and the *Chicago Evening Post*). A University of Chicago graduate, Collins was a Civil War buff and, variously, a writer of short stories and librettos and the coauthor of an adventure novel set in the South Seas. His criticism for the *Tribune* was without question conservative in its nature, as his pieces included here reveal.

In this first instance, Collins reviews the Chicago version of a play that had already been running in New York for two years. He offers a fairly balanced review–admiring of Henry Hull's acting–but leads with his chin at what he felt was the huge amount of profanity in the show: perhaps the adjective "cussingest" required a wholesale invention, but it makes Collins's point. He now was writing for a newspaper that under its proprietor, Col. Robert R. McCormick, had hardened its attitudes, especially toward president Franklin D. Roosevelt and his New Deal. Three months after this review, the *Tribune* ran an editorial with a banner headline aimed at Roosevelt and his cabinet: "TURN THE RASCALS OUT."

Edward J. Kelly, then the mayor of Chicago, was a longtime friend and associate of McCormick, Collins's boss. Kelly also was a man anxious to prove his morality and separation from such notoriously corrupt predecessors as "Big" Bill Thompson, who had presided over Chicago's years as a capital of vice. Taking Collins's cue, Kelly showed up at the theater some nights later and attacked the show as "a mass of outrageous obscenity" that should be closed down. When the owners of the Selwyn Theatre refused the mayor's request that they go back to New York, he took action against them. By October 22, Kelly had revoked the license of the Selwyn, meaning that "Tobacco Road" would no longer be legal to present. He told the *Tribune* that while Chicago had always been "a liberal city with regard to the stage and other forms of entertainment," such "liberalism does not condone filth."

Quite the amateur critic himself, Kelly did not stop there, arguing, in essence, that the force of Hull's performance, which Collins so admired in this review, only made the show dirtier yet.

Those who made the show, including Caldwell, who was hanging around in Chicago, and the Shuberts, who were its producers, lawyered up fast. Caldwell swung back at Kelly, arguing that the show had played in many other cities without being closed down. Even Boston. "Tobacco Road," he said, "is no more profane than everyday life." Even the actor Hull weighed in, saying he'd heard from churchmen who supported the show. In a bizarre coincidence, Kelly and Hull even appeared together in the middle of the controversy on a "radio traffic drama." They stayed off the topic of "Tobacco Road."

Collins did not do the same. He wrote about the production in the pages of the newspaper time and time again, even at one point writing an entire article in the dialect of the play ("you never saw such an ornery lot of trash in y'r life as these people in 'Tobacco Road' ") and attacking Caldwell on the grounds that he had exaggerated the character of Jeeter, thus making Caldwell "a propagandist rather than a literary artist." This was common, Collins huffed, when it came to works "written with the fanatic zeal of the reformer."

On September 22, Collins really let fly, decrying "Tobacco Road" as little more than Marxist propaganda. "This is New Deal rhetoric," he fumed. "The play is an eddy in the current of sociological and literary propaganda, now running in the wake of political NewDealism (*sic*) to depict the American folkways as in dire need of reform, perhaps of revolution. It is a part of a movement to which many punk-headed young writing fellows are contributing, with a Marxian twist in their none-too-stable minds–a movement to deride and destabilize American civilization, particularly as represented by the old racial elements in the population, to cry calamity, to conjure up economic bugaboos such as 'the machine' (a mythical monster supposed to be devouring us) and to behave generally, in print, like a brood of cuckoos befouling their own nests."

This clearly was a very different *Tribune* from the newspaper offering such sympathetic pictures and reviews of the artistic reformers and progressive agitators of just a decade earlier. Alas, the *Tribune* drama critic was making no case for artistic freedom.

By October 30, a federal judge had lifted Kelly's ban and ordered that performances of "Tobacco Road" reopen at the Selwyn. But an appeal kept the show shuttered. On November 22, the *Tribune* announced that the federal appeals court had upheld the mayoral ban, and so the show must remain shuttered. The company departed for St. Louis without ever reopening its doors in Chicago.

The producer, the Shuberts' Sam Grisman, declared to the *Tribune* that his company would now tell every first-class producer in New York to stay away from Chicago, just as long as Kelly was in office. That is exactly what he did. All of a sudden, Chicago was a backwater in the New York mind.

In 2010, the city's American Blues Theater revived the show. "Had Mayor Kelly walked through the doors of the Richard Christiansen Theatre," the *Tribune* wrote, "and seen actors trying to find the truth in all the filth, he might have felt differently." But Kelly, who was forced out of office by Chicago voters in 1947, had been dead for sixty years by then.

But after putting a nail in "Tobacco Road," Collins was only emboldened. The *Tribune*'s attacks against New Deal and leftist policies had grown only more extreme. Clifford Odets was next to feel the collective wrath of critic and newspaper.

17

WAITING FOR LEFTY

PLAY BY ODETS LADEN WITH RED PROPAGANDA / "WAITING FOR LEFTY" GIVEN PROFESSIONAL PREMIERE

Selwyn Theatre

CHARLES COLLINS

CAST

Harry Fatt .... Morris Carnovsky
Joe .... Art Smith
Edna .... Ruth Nelson
Miller .... Tony Kraber
Irv .... Lewis Leverett
Florrie .... Phoebe Brand
Sid .... Jules Garfield
Clayton .... Bob Lewis
Keller .... Elia Kazan
Two Henchmen .... Sanford Meisner, Maury Miller
Dr. Barnes .... Roman Bolmen
Dr. Benjamin .... Luther Adler
A Man .... William Challee

MAY 18, 1936. Clifford Odets' "Waiting for Lefty," an example of vehement radicalism in drama which has been much acted by amateurs, was given its first professional performance in Chicago yesterday afternoon by the Group Theater company, now regularly occupied with the same playwright's "Awake and Sing." The occasion was another display of this organization's skill in acting and trend toward themes of social discontent.

The play is a heavily loaded piece of propaganda for a drastic change in the social order which will terminate the alleged conspiracy of the rich against the poor, the capitalist against the working classes. It bears all the familiar stencils of economic and political thought along these lines, which may be called communism or socialism, or I.W.W.-ism, as one prefers his labels. It is written in vivid and forceful dialog, strongly colored with the Bronxian idiom—the "nize baby" vernacular well advanced toward Americanism—in which Odets seems to specialize. He has a gift for the emotionalization of the speech of the New York masses and an oratorical sense which branches from the eloquence of proletarian speakers.

A labor union scene (taxicab drivers of the depression discussing a strike) is the foreground of "Waiting for Lefty." Its central portion, however, contains four episodes in the "cut-back" or "black-out" technique which are intended to offer object lessons from life outside of the play's frame. Only two of these episodes are relevant—taxi driver Joe's argument with his wife, who threatens to become a harlot to relieve the family's poverty, and taxi driver Sid's scene with his girl, whom he can't marry because they are too poor. They illustrate the thumping on the sexual bass drum which is characteristic of propaganda in a state of fever.

The other two interior episodes are dragged into the structure of the play so obviously that they injure Odets' position as a literary artist. One of them deals with the manufacture of poison gas; the other is an argument in favor of socialized medicine which also touches on the menace of anti-Semitism. All four episodes are dull little tracts, rubber stamped by demagogery.

To make a full length program the Group also gave a bill of sketches and recitations, characteristic of their amusements and exercises when they are rusticating between seasons. These were: A clever adaptation of the grave digger's scene from "Hamlet" into a modern teacher-and-pupil dialog; cowboy songs by Tony Kraber, to guitar accompaniment; a monolog called "I Can't Sleep," by Morris Carnovsky, of Odets' authorship; and recitations and impersonations in comic vein by Bob Lewis, in which a satire on the Barrymores was marked by a lapse of taste. Stella Adler, leading woman of the "Awake and Sing" company, was an effective mistress of ceremonies.

Perhaps Charles Collins's attacks on "Tobacco Road" had emboldened the critic, but the *Tribune* review of the Group Theatre's production of "Waiting for Lefty" has the air of a screed. Indeed, the very headline to the review—"Play by Odets Laden with Red Propaganda"—pretty much says it all. Collins, it would seem, had become very much a creature of Robert McCormick's anti–New Deal *Tribune*.

This was not the first production of "Waiting for Lefty" to play in Chicago: a local group called the Chicago Workers' Theatre had been granted the rights to the piece the previous year and had already performed it, albeit with scant notice from the *Tribune*. But on this night, the famous New York company known as the Group Theatre had brought its A-team to the Selwyn Theatre, replete with Stella Adler as, in Collins's words, "mistress of ceremonies." The cast of the show under review here included the famous acting teacher Sanford Meisner (as a henchman) and Elia Kazan as Keller. The *Tribune* had been obliged to show up for this one.

But Collins spits political venom at Odets' politics, becoming especially exercised at the sections involving women—that phrase about the "sexual bass drum" and "propaganda in a state of fever" takes some unpacking. We can see Collins's reporting instincts kick in now and again—he does, at least, offer the reader a sense of what went on—but this is as overtly politically partisan a review as the *Tribune* ever published.

Actually, Collins started raging against this show even before it opened. On the day before this review, he wrote a story announcing that the Group Theatre would present "special matinees" of "Waiting for Lefty," or, as Collins liked to call it, "an Odetsian tantrum." Here's how the news brief went: "This afternoon in the Harris Theatre the Group Theatre Company will offer a single performance of the play that gave hundreds of radical amateur actors an opportunity to foam at the mouth with pseudo-psychological importance." After reading that, the Group must have expected pretty much exactly what it got.

18

VOODOO MACBETH

'MACBETH' AS NEGRO PLAY COMES TO GREAT NORTHERN THEATER / WPA PRESENTS SHAKESPEARE IN HAITIAN STYLE / ORSON WELLES ARRANGES ALL-COLORED VERSION OF DRAMATIC CLASSIC.

Great Northern Theatre

CHARLES COLLINS

AUGUST 30, 1936. The ending of August brings a sudden, a completely unexpected, première to the Chicago stage. It happens to be a contribution from the federal theatrical projects, but it seems to wear its WPA badge with a difference and to possess an appeal for the playgoer who is not primarily interested in 40 cents worth of social relief. The production aroused keen interest in New York, and the WPA administration is so proud of it that the company has been sent on tour.

This novelty, scheduled to open in the Great Northern theater tomorrow night for a two weeks' engagement, is a Shakespearean tragedy—"Macbeth"—in terms of Negro character. The principal players and mob scene auxiliaries, 150 in number, are Negroes from the theaters and music halls of Harlem.

VOODOO MAGIC FOR SCOTCH WITCHES. The characters, although bearing their Shakespearean names, are intended to be Negroes; the scene of the action is Haiti, in the period of the "black empire" which followed the French revolution. The ambitious and bloodthirsty Scottish thane of Shakespeare's story becomes an Emperor Dessalines (assassinated in 1806) or a King Henri Christophe, the fantastic tyrant of La Ferrière (died 1820). The witchcraft of medieval Scotland becomes the voodooism of African savages. The text, however, remains Shakespearean.

In general, I deprecate the adaptation of classic works of dramatic literature into alien forms for the purpose of offering freakish exhibitions of so-called "modernism," or for giving groups of Negro actors an opportunity to parade in romantic costumes and chant spirituals. The result is usually a grotesque hodgepodge of hybridism. In the case of this "Macbeth," however, I feel fairly confident that the Shakespearean mood will be communicated without travesty. The director of this production and inventor of the Haitian version was Orson Welles, a young man of great talent in the theater arts and a loyal zest for Shakespeare.

BRIGHT TALENT OF ORSON WELLES. The story of Orson Welles has been often written in Chicago during the last few years. He is the Chicago lad who went to Ireland on a sketching tour and scored a hit as actor in Dublin; who was the leading spirit of the Woodstock Drama festival of two summers ago; who published a work of Shakespearean prompt books for use in schools and colleges, illustrated by his own stage and costume designs; who acted the rôle of Mercutio in

Katharine Cornell's first production of "Romeo and Juliet." I would trust him with any kind of a Shakespearean production, traditional or otherwise. He has given proof of a true genius for stagecraft.

Another ex-Chicagoan, now active in the theatrical life of New York, designed the stage settings and costumes—Nat Karson. The rôle of Macbeth is acted by Maurice Ellis; the Lady Macbeth is Edna Thomas. This is beleved to be the first time that an all-Negro company has interpreted Shakespeare on a formal tour. The Chicago engagement will be the fifth in the itinerary. The play was first staged in the Lafayette theater, in the Harlem region of New York, last winter, and then was moved into the Adelphi theater in the Broadway district.

By 1936, issues of race were impacting *Tribune* reviews. Collins, fresh from his outrage at "Tobacco Road" and "Waiting for Lefty," now found himself confronting Orson Welles's famous "Voodoo Macbeth" (sometimes called the "Negro Macbeth"), which the Federal Theatre Project, an outgrowth of Roosevelt's New Deal, had sent out on tour. This was a production by the FTP's Negro Theatre Project; it already had been a success in New York. Welles was just 20 years old; reportedly, he appeared in full blackface in Indianapolis after one of his actors was taken ill, but that was not necessary in Chicago.

In his *Tribune* review, Collins is generally positive, admiring the way the show gave "the colored interpreters of Shakespeare the right to remain within their own racial frame" (a coded phrase if ever there was one), although he also accuses Welles of "going on a mumbo-jumbo rampage" during the voodoo sections of the show. But this article, published on the day of the show's arrival, actually is more indicative of how much Welles's piece was a radical notion, even in Chicago. Collins justifies some of his racial attitudes with a most imaginative bogeyman: "a grotesque hodgepodge of hybridism," whatever that means. Welles, however, Collins clearly admired. For one thing, although born in Kenosha, Wisconsin, Welles had cut his creative teeth in Chicago.

Collins, though, was far from done with his racial anxieties.

19

MULATTO

"MULATTO" A DISMAL TRAGEDY OF WOES OF RACIAL PROBLEMS

Studebaker Theatre

BY CHARLES COLLINS

CAST

Cora Lewis .... Mercedes Gilbert
William Lewis .... Morris McKenney
Col. Thomas Norwood .... James Kirkwood
Sally Lewis .... Evelyn St[r]eich
Talbot .... Richard S. Bishop
Fred Higgins .... Frank Jacquet
Henry Richards .... J. J. Dillon
Robert Lewis .... Glen Boles
Store Keeper .... Francis Hallaran
Undertaker .... Dillon Deasy
Jed Tomkins .... Allan Moore

DECEMBER 28, 1936. The Studebaker theater has been restored to dramatic activity with a play called "Mulatto" which may appeal to people who like to wallow in the woes of racial problems. There are many such in this over-excited period which is clamorous with appeals for the righting of every social maladjustment; and perhaps the easily indignant will take this dismal tragedy to their bruised hearts, as they did in New York for months, and sob and sob and sob. If they choose to shatter their nervous systems in this manner, they will find a fairly well written play of the propaganda type, acted with skill.

This work deals with miscegenation from the Negro's point of view; in particular, it is concerned with the tragic position of mulatto children whose father, a white planter, has displayed a certain amount of parental concern about their education. This situation has had no painful results until the youngest son, who can pass as white, comes home from a school in the north with a headful of caste-breaking notions and the attitude of a collegiate liberal. In other words, he is so "fresh" that his own blacker brother would like to smack him down, for the improvement of his manners. The lad is not intelligent enough, however, to understand the perils of his rebellion against the customs of the environment in which he was born—Polk county, Georgia—and his conduct brings on an appalling catastrophe.

Here is a list of "Mulatto's" quietly arranged horrors.

White father threatens mulatto boy with a revolver and is strangled to death by his offspring.

The young murderer takes to the woods and is pursued (off stage) by the customary hounds and posse with a rope.

The dead planter, in his coffin, with candles at his feet, occupies the center of the stage during the last act, while some of the sherif[f]'s men, the coroner, and the overseer of the plantation hold a drunken orgy over the remains.

A pretty mulatto girl, sister of the murderer, is raped (off stage) by the white overseer in whose cabin she seeks refuge from the mob.

The mother of the mulatto family, faithful housekeeper for Massa Norwood for years, goes mad over the coffin as the hounds are chasing her boy, and recites long, loony speeches in a fine old melodramatic fashion.

The fugitive comes back to the house, with one shot left in his revolver, and after a touching scene with his demented mother goes to his bedroom of childhood, where he commits suicide just as the avengers charge in with their ropes, their guns, and their gasoline cans.

All this might cause one to despair of the future of a land where such things are invented by playwrights, but for one consoling line in the text. This is a statement that Col. Tom Norwood is the only man in Polk county, Georgia, who was so tactless about the upbringing of his illegitimate children.

James Kirkwood, a fine veteran character actor of the stage and screen, appears as the planter with admirable fidelity to type. Mercedes Gilbert has some touching passages as the mother of the unhappy brood. The unfortunate daughter is gracefully played by Evelyn Streich.

The senior author of "Mulatto" is Langston Hughes, a Negro poet. His collaborator is Martin Jones, producer of the play and present holder of the lease to the Studebaker, where he will probably present other and, one hopes, less depressing plays.

Just a few weeks after Orson Welles's "Macbeth," Charles Collins found himself at the Studebaker reviewing a touring production of "Mulatto," a play by Langston Hughes and Martin Jones, which had closed the previous September on Broadway after a run of 373 performances. Collins was not sympathetic to the piece, suggesting that its appeal was limited to those "who like to wallow in the woes of racial problems." In essence, he continues his attack on the New Deal era ("this over-excited period" is how Collins describes it, but we can see through his code). It's a pretty ugly piece of dramatic criticism, all in all. As will be evident, Hughes's name meant nothing to Collins. Nor, it seemed, did the entire Harlem Renaissance.

It's interesting that producer Martin Jones is credited here as coauthor; that was not the case on Broadway. According to Hughes's autobiography, the play was actually optioned by Jones for a Broadway production without Hughes's knowledge (the play had been written in 1930), and the producer inserted a rape scene into the text along with many other changes, also without Hughes's knowledge. Hughes noted that the piece "came darn near to being banned in Chicago," thanks to the rape scene that he had not even wanted to be in the show. For all that, "Mulatto" was a very popular play; it was the highest-grossing drama by an African American author until "A Raisin in the Sun" came along.

Collins reported the Philadelphia banning a few weeks later, and in an admiring tone, but the *Tribune* made no mention of any such controversy in Chicago.

For the record, "Mulatto" is Hughes's second play, penned long before he wrote the lyrics to Kurt Weill's "Street Scene" and the text to "Black Nativity," which, many years later, would become a staple of the Chicago Christmas.

20

WILDER'S "A DOLL'S HOUSE"

FOUR-STAR "DOLL'S HOUSE" BRINGS IBSEN TO LIFE: "DOLL'S HOUSE" WITH 4 STARS REVIVES IBSEN

The Grand Opera House

BY CHARLES COLLINS

DECEMBER 5, 1937. The current revival of "A Doll's House," famous for half a century but unacted in recent years except by students, serves as a happy means of passing the torch of Ibsenism from the old generation of playgoers to the new. The veterans of this form of dramatic idolatry have emerged from their lairs in honor of the occasion, roaring cheerfully, and the neophytes seem to be keen to learn the ritual. This production, admirable in its staging, contains four stars (Ruth Gordon, Dennis King, Paul Lukas, Sam Jaffe) whose acting, modern in its point of view, conforms to the tradition of brilliance in the play's theatrical history. There may have been better Noras, Thorvalds, Dr. Ranks, and Krogstads in the past, but I cannot remember them clearly enough to make any invidious comparisons.

The last Nora who slammed the door upon husband and children for me was one of the stage's greatest actresses—Eleanora Duse—but she was then a frail old woman, ready to die. That was in 1924. Miss Gordon, our present Nora, looks as young, as childlike and as kittenish as the character that Ibsen drew in his first act. She is, physically, the most nearly ideal Nora of my experience; but with this slightness of figure and appearance of youth she has the mature technique that the rôle demands.

Twenty years of an active stage career are behind this Nora. The part requires the spirit, face, and body of an ingénue, and also the insight and emotional range that come to an actress only in middle age. Miss Gordon has these qualities, and thus the American stage is seeing a Nora Helmer who expresses the full intention of the author. She has a few tricks to which Mrs. Fiske might say "Tsk, tsk," such as too frequent

THORNTON WILDER, WITH HIS SISTER, ISABEL, AT THE PARK ROW STATION IN THE MID-1930S.

use of the index finger in a pointing gesture, but these minor flaws do not mar the general interpretation.

⁂

The question of the new version of the text deserves full discussion. When it was announced that Thornton Wilder had rewritten the dialog for this production, many ancient Ibsenites who had grown up on William Archer's translation began to mutter in their beards and to ask why the standard English version, which had given so much faithful service, had been tampered with by a young sprig of modern literature? Archer himself has answered that question in the preface to his translation of Ibsen's prose dramas, which introduced "A Doll's House" and its kindred to the Anglo-American stage. He said:

"Henrik Ibsen's prose plays are in one sense very easy to translate, in another very difficult. His meaning is almost always as clear as daylight; the difficulty lies in reproducing the nervous conciseness, the vernacular simplicity, and, at the same time, something of the subtle rhythm of his phrases. How is one to escape stiff literalism on the one hand, lax paraphrase on the other? I cannot hope that I have always steered clear of the former danger; the latter I have done my best to avoid. *Had I been preparing the plays for the stage, I should have felt justified in omitting any inessential phrases that could not be rendered into easy and natural English.* As it is, I have allowed myself no such liberty, preferring to reproduce the poet's intention with all possible accuracy, even at the cost of a certain uncouthness or angularity of expression."

The italicized sentence above is a complete defense for Wilder if accused of any lack of reverence. He prepared a new acting version in the "easy and natural English" of our time without getting too far away from his source. Archer's version remains the better Ibsen; Wilder's is the happier medium for a revival of the play in this period. Archer translated directly from the original Danish; Wilder used a literal translation, prepared by a Danish linguist, as the basis of his new phrasing.

Helmer's pet names for his wife, "lark" and "squirrel," have been omitted in favor of the casual "darling" except in one line. The Scandinavian flavor of speech has disappeared; the dialog runs smoothly and briskly in standard Anglo-American stage idioms. The pattern of Ibsen's thought, however, has been followed closely. This is not a work of scholarship, since Wilder approached Ibsen at second hand, but it has literary merit and stage values. If "A Doll's House" were in general use today as a test piece for stars and an item in stock company repertories I believe that Wilder's version would replace Archer's.

PARALLEL PASSAGES FROM ARCHER AND WILDER. The similarity of the two versions may be illustrated by quotation of a passage in the third act, where Nora tells Thorvald that she intends to leave him. Here is Archer—Henrik Ibsen's Prose Dramas (Scribner's, New York, 1905), volume I., page 386:

Nora: I have waited so patiently all these eight years, for, of course, I saw clearly that miracles don't happen every day. When this crushing blow threatened me I said to myself confidently, "Now comes the miracle!" When Krogstad's letter lay in the box, it never occurred to me that you would think of submitting to that man's conditions. I was convinced that you would say to him, "Make it known to all the world," and that then—

Thorvald: Well? When I had given my own wife's name up to disgrace and shame—?

Nora: Then I firmly believed that you would come forward, take everything upon yourself, and say, "I am the guilty one."

A few lines of dialog then lead up to this passage:

Helmer: Oh, you think and talk like a silly child.

Nora: Very likely. But you neither think nor talk like the man I can share my life with. When your terror was over—not for me, but for yourself—when there was nothing more to fear—then it was to you as if nothing had happened. I was your lark again, your doll, whom you would take twice as much care of in future, because she was so weak and fragile. Thorvald, in that moment it burst upon me that I had been living here these eight years with a strange man, and had borne him three children. Oh, I can't bear to think of it—I could tear myself to pieces.

Wilder's version of the above passage runs in this fashion:

Nora: For eight years now I've been waiting for a certain wonderful thing to happen between you and me. I've been waiting patiently because I know that one can't expect really wonderful things to happen every day, and then when I saw this—this catastrophe—was hanging over me, I said to myself, "It's coming—the miracle is coming!"

Helmer: When was this?

Nora: Thorvald, when Krogstad's letter was lying in the box, it never occurred to me that you would think for a minute of submitting to that man's conditions. I was certain that you would say to him, "All right, tell everybody; publish it to the whole world." And I was certain that after that—

Helmer: After that, what? When I'd covered my wife's name with disgrace and shame?

Nora: Then I was sure that you'd come forward and take the whole thing on yourself. You'd say, "I'm the guilty one!"

Then, skipping a few lines, as in the Archer quotation:

Helmer: You talk like a child. You think like a child.

Nora: When you got over being frightened—not for me, but for yourself—and you knew there was nothing more to fear—then it was as if nothing had happened. I was your doll again—and you would take twice as much care of it in the future, because I was so weak and fragile. Thorvald, in that moment it burst on me that I had been living here these eight years with a strange man and had borne him two children. O, I can't bear to think of it—I could tear myself to pieces!

This Chicago run of Thornton Wilder's adaptation of "A Doll's House" came at the end of a pre–New York tour of the show, which opened later that month on Broadway. Wilder had penned the adaption for his friend Ruth Gordon, and as noted in *The Selected Letters of Thornton Wilder* (published in 2008), he wrote about attending one of the performances and finding it "packed with people." Collins makes much here of the deviations between the Wilder version and the William Archer translation, then the standard translation of the play.

Since 1930, Wilder had been living mostly in Chicago, where he was teaching at the University of Chicago. In her 2012 biography, Penelope Niven argues that he felt closer to that city than any other town in which he had resided. "He felt at home in certain German cities, especially Munich and Berlin, and the Swiss-German city of Zurich," Niven writes. "There were towns and villages he loved—New Haven and Hamden, Peterborough, Juan-les-Pins, Martha's Vineyard, Monhegan Island. But all in all, there was probably no city he loved more than he loved Chicago."

Wilder's letters reveal a variety of friends in Chicago, ranging from Fanny Butcher, the literary editor at the *Tribune*, to Jack McGurn, the "chief representative and lieutenant" of Al Capone. He was something of a celebrity, showing up in the *Tribune* gossip columns of the 1930s. He also was a popular speaker in the city. When he lectured at the University of Chicago's downtown outpost at the Art Institute of Chicago, Niven writes, "his topic—'Sophocles for English readers'—was advertised on billboards all over the city." One suspects it was Wilder, rather than Sophocles, who was pulling in the crowd.

21

THE SWING MIKADO

NEGRO PLAYERS STAGE 'MIKADO' IN SWING STYLE

Presented by the Federal Theatre at the Great Northern Theatre

CECIL SMITH

CAST

Nanki-Poo .... Maurice Cooper
Pish-Tush .... Lewis White
Ko-Ko .... Herman Greene
Pooh-Bah .... William Franklin
Yum-Yum .... Gladys Boucree
Pitti-Sing .... Frankie Fambro
Peep-Bo .... Mabel Carter
Katisha .... Mabel Walker
The Mikado .... Edward Fraction

SEPTEMBER 26, 1938. How the Japanese town of Titipu has changed since Gilbert and Sullivan first brought its doings to the attention of the English speaking world a half century ago! On extremely slight provocation the subjects of the Mikado nowadays toss off a tap dance or engage in a spree of the most authentic Harlem trucking. The Mikado himself, wearing garments of state consisting of a flowing robe of red and yellow awning stripes and a tall silk hat studded with weary feathers, explains his object all sublime in spicy swing rhythm.

These developments in the manners and mores of the Japanese people, and many others equally unprecedented, were revealed to an audience at the Great Northern theater last night as the Federal theater presented the premiere of its all-Negro version of "The Mikado."

◓◓◓

The scene of the action, it must be confessed, has been changed from Japan to an unspecified coral island in the Pacific. Clive Rickabaugh has designed two imaginative sets—the first with a background of mountain peaks, from which Fujiyama is conspicuously absent, and the second a striking South Sea locale with a moon and undulating waves in the middle distance. John Pratt has solved what must have been a knotty problem of costuming by finding a striking meeting ground of African and Japanese motifs.

The performance could easily have been a sorry mess, but it is not. The swing and jitterbug element, titillating though it is, has not been allowed to break out of the comic moments of the opera into the serious or sentimental parts. The dialog is spoken straight at all times.

◓◓◓

The principals have been schooled in many of the traditions of Gilbert and Sullivan behavior, and even employ a great deal of the conventional business. The singing is startlingly good a great deal of the time, and the choral climaxes sound almost as big as the triumphal scene in "Aïda."

Herman Greene, as Ko-Ko, the Lord High Executioner, is the one member of the cast who acts his rôle wholly in a vein of low comedy. Yet he is so direct, so intelligent in his unorthodox reading of his lines, and often so heartily funny in his antics, that he is actually the star of the performance. William Franklin and Lewis White, as Pooh-Bah and Pish-Tush, discover a higher plane of gentility, and Mr. Franklin in particular sings cleanly and forcefully in a good baritone voice.

On the musical side Maurice Cooper, a strikingly handsome tenor with a light, pleasing lyric voice, sings with exquisite taste and choice musicianship. He is the best Nanki-Poo I have ever heard, bar none. His vis-à-vis, Gladys Boucree, likewise sings Yum-Yum's music delightfully.

When all is said and done, this modernized "Mikado" is momentarily amusing for its iconoclasms of treatment, but much more permanently satisfying for the honest competence with which the enduring beauties of the opera are respectfully projected.

Cecil Smith (1906–1956), author of this review and successor in the *Tribune* drama chair to Collins, who left the beat in 1938 to write the paper's "A Line O'Type or Two" column, was among the more scholarly of the newspaper's critics. After leaving his post at the *Tribune* in 1943, he became the chairman of the School of Music at the University of Chicago.

Before his exit into academe, Smith penned a "valedictory article" as a drama critic after telling his readers that after a long internal battle between "the conflicting claims of journalism and education, education had won the day." That final article lamented the state of the arts in Chicago: "The leaders in these arts apparently have lost their idealism, their sense of functioning for the best welfare of their community." That sense of mission, and a palpable ease with educating the reader from the mountaintop, permeates Smith's writing for the paper.

Yet Smith was not easily pigeonholed. He is probably best known for writing a 1950 history of musical comedy in an era when few took the art form seriously. He wrote both music and drama reviews for the *Tribune* and other publications (in later years, he wrote music reviews for both the *New Republic* and—presumably after he once again felt the claim of journalism—the *Daily Express* in London).

This particular Smith piece is the first review of a notion that would be repeated several times in Chicago in the years to follow: making the music of the British composer Arthur Sullivan swing. The review is a tad dry, for sure, but Smith's enthusiastic notice offers a striking contrast to the way Collins greeted Welles's "Macbeth," a previous endeavor of the Federal Theatre Project.

"The Swing Mikado" was very much a Chicago project, conceived by the Chicago Federal Theatre's Negro Unit run by Harry Minturn, the director of this production, and populated by Chicago actors. The show ran at the Great Northern Theatre for five months before moving to Broadway, where it would inspire Michael Todd's "The Hot Mikado" the following year. Indeed, both of these "black Mikados" would end up duking it out on Broadway in 1939. Minturn had proceeded cautiously with his conceit—there was, really, more "Mikado" here than swing—and we can see that while Smith was open to the whole idea, he seems anxious to tell his readers that the titillating "swing and jitterbug element" had been kept in check. Smith was a populist, but a man of his time. This was a project that certainly exploited the interest of mainstream white America in exotic-seeming black performers; yet Smith, for all his erudition, did not point any of that out.

22

OUR TOWN

CHICAGO SEES WILDER'S NEW STAGE METHOD

Selwyn Theatre

BY CECIL SMITH

CAST

Stage manager .... Frank Craven
Dr. Gibbs... James Spottswood
Mrs. Gibbs .... Evelyn Varden
Mr. Webb... Thomas W. Ross
Mrs. Webb .... Helen Carew
George Gibbs .... John Craven
Emily Webb .... Dorothy McGuire
Rebecca Gibbs .... Patricia Ro[e]

Also Raymond Roe, Tom Fadden, Charles Wiley Jr., Walter O. Hill, Milton Parsons, Dora Merande, E. Irving Locke, Billy Redfield, William Wadsworth, Edward P. Goodnow and many others.

JANUARY 24, 1939. The bare stage of the Selwyn theatre, with its own white-washed rear wall as backdrop and scarcely more than a few chairs and tables as properties, is now the scene of one of the important theatrical experiences of this generation. In a series of prismatic reflections the simple realities of life and death in Grover's Corners, N. H., are transplanted into our midst.

"Our Town" is no ordinary three act play. Actually the narrative is a neatly organized series of vignettes, in which we meet some of the typical citizens of Grover's Corners and come to know a few of them extremely well. With genial adroitness Frank Craven, labeled the "stage manager," provides a framework of continuity. When the audience comes into the theater the curtain is already up. At the appointed moment Mr. Craven begins to explain things. He describes the village, identifies the characters, and generally prepares us for the freedom of Thornton Wilder's dramatic method.

◠ ◠ ◠

Once the action is under way it becomes apparent that Mr. Wilder has obeyed no rule of thumb laws of play construction. Snatches of conversation, sometimes from two places at once, flashbacks, glimpses into the future—all these are part of one of the most unconventional experiments in drama the American stage has seen.

And yet, somehow these fragments of New England daily life soon begin imperceptibly to add up into an impressive totality. From the daily living of Dr. Gibbs and his family and of Editor Webb and his family Mr. Wilder has selected just the incidents and the exchanges of ideas that make us know them best. Through the whole continuity Mr. Craven moves, adding wryly humorous footnotes, or simply helping us to keep our bearings in the story when we might get lost without him.

◠ ◠ ◠

The simplicities and commonplaces of life have always fascinated Mr. Wilder. The folk in "Our Town" are the stuff of which the solid New England population is made. Even at their most bromidic, they are real, flesh and blood people, living daily lives of the most complete usualness and normality. And at their best they express themselves with the wonderfully dry humor of New England, in which the obvious is understated with a brusqueness that verges on genius.

Of course two youngsters fall in love and are married. John Craven, the bright son of the "stage manager," and wistful Dorothy McGuire, represent the couple with completely engaging honesty. Their wedding so completely captures the essence of a million tearful weddings back home that there was audible sniffling during its progress last night.

Thomas W. Ross as Editor Webb, and James Spottswood as Dr Gibbs, are two salty veterans who do not know what it is to let a play down. Helen Carew and Evelyn Varden as their wives, are just the kind to cook three meals a day and make them something worth talking about.

A neatly articulated cast, dotted [with] such endearing youngsters as Patricia and Raymond Roe, maintain a mood of unabashed sentimentality. This sentimentality is really the most important thing about "Our Town." For Mr. Wilder has uncovered the one basic fact about New Englanders that they would give anything to hide—the fact that a crusty, matter-of-fact exterior is only a blind to hide some of the softest hearts in the world.

Smith's generally astute and thoughtful review of "Our Town" is of the first national tour of the original Broadway production. Given that Wilder's papers and correspondence reveal that he was making notes on the play as early as 1935, when still living in Chicago, a case could be made for "Our Town" being a Chicago play.

Some 70 years later, a Chicago production of this play, directed by David Cromer and staged originally by the Hypocrites, would move from Chicago to New York, where it would run longer than this original production.

23

ROMEO AND JULIET

VIVIEN LEIGH IS LOVELY JULIET TO OLIVIER'S ROMEO

Auditorium Theatre

CECIL SMITH

CAST

Romeo .... Laurence Olivier
Juliet .... Vivien Leigh
Nurse .... Dame May Whitty
Prince Escalus .... Wilton Graff
Tybalt .... Cornel Wilde
Benvolio .... Wesley Addy
Capulet .... Halliwell Hobbes
Lady Capulet .... Katharine Warren
Montague .... Ben Webster
Lady Montague .... Barbara Horder
Mercutio .... Edmond O'Brien
Paris .... Frank Downing
Friar Laurence .... Alexander Knox
Old Capulet .... Morton L. Stevens
Friar John .... Morton L. Stevens

And many others.

APRIL 18, 1940. Laurence Olivier's production of "Romeo and Juliet," fresh upon our stage after an initial week in San Francisco, is a revelation of the remarkable scope and vigor of this young artist's imagination. It is unreasonable to suppose, at this late date, that any staging of "Romeo and Juliet" can ever realize all of the preconceptions of any single spectator. But for all that its accomplishment is uneven, Mr. Olivier's version often attains to high beauty, and, when Shakespeare's youthful poetic involvements permit, to dramatic fire.

The play is luxuriously mounted in a handsome early Italian Renaissance period style, with no attempt to abstract the drama from the locale prescribed by Shakespeare. A revolving stage permits the story to unfold without the punctuation of tiresome intervals during scene changes.

Beautifully lighted, with careful attention to the differing qualities of light at different times of day and night, the settings are impressive. The street scene is excellently laid out, Friar Laurence's cell, which is not a cell at all but a charming pavilion, creates a remarkable sense of intimacy even in so large a theater.

Capulet's orchard, with Juliet's overhanging balcony, is less successful, for it comes to seem a little cloying and sentimental whenever it returns.

In designing the action of the play Mr. Olivier has been intent upon achieving the greatest possible sense of movement and pace. The entire plot, from Romeo's meeting of Juliet to the tomb scene, takes place between Sunday and Thursday. By maintaining an urgent restlessness much of the time this feeling of the tragic rush of events is projected with unusual force.

This point of view, however, sometimes exacts its toll from the individual actors. I bow to nobody in my intense admiration for the directness and honesty of Mr. Olivier's acting. Yet in the earlier scenes he embellishes his characterization with such constant nervous physical detail that the purely poetic aspect of Romeo's nature tends to be snowed under. Toward the middle of the play, as he begins to husband his resources for the impending climax, his acting takes on impressive stature. The scene in Friar Laurence's cell after his banishment he plays magnificently.

Vivien Leigh's Juliet is a figure of breathtaking outward loveliness. She does not have to resort to artifice to produce an impression of youth, and her entire interpretation is imbued with beguiling fresh simplicity. She reads her lines well, tho not penetratingly. In her performance, too, I miss the evocation of pure poetry, even in the balcony scene. This is less a matter of declamatory style, I suspect, than the inevitable result of her visible movement, which is always either staccato or accented, and never develops a flowing lyrical line. But one cannot ask the unattainable, and it will be many a long year before another Juliet so choice appears upon the Chicago stage.

Dame May Whitty, one of those unbelievable veterans of the English stage who apparently finds the exact note upon which to pitch any rôle, rounds out the character of the nurse to its full dimensions without resorting to exaggeration or affectation.

Of the others in the cast, too numerous to mention in detail, Wesley Addy as Benvolio, Alexander Knox as Friar Laurence, and Halliwell Hobbes as Capulet are especially excellent. Edmond O'Brien's Mercutio was too heavily conceived to bring the Queen Mab speech into its proper scherzo-like vein.

In the spring of 1940, Cecil Smith found himself reviewing what must have been a rather remarkable Chicago occasion and pre-Broadway tryout: Vivien Leigh, then 26 years old, playing Juliet opposite Laurence Olivier's 33-year-old Romeo at the acoustically rich Auditorium Theatre.

Leigh was fresh from "Gone with the Wind." The pair of young stars was in the midst of a torrid real-life love affair, complicated by their both being married to someone else. A little more than three months after the night of this review, the two were married to each other. In interviews published in Chicago, Olivier waxed lyrical on how well his leading lady understood her director.

This production did not do well financially once it arrived on Broadway the following month—and, unfortunately for them, both Olivier and Leigh had put their own money into the $60,000 show, causing them to lose a good portion of their savings. They would recover.

Smith gave the show, which was crossing the country by train and had already played San Francisco to lukewarm reviews, a far more favorable notice than Brooks Atkinson would in the *New York Times* a few weeks later. Indeed, Chicago seems to have been the only place where the show was admired at all, and even Smith laments the absence of the "poetry" of the play.

Notably, the production included a revolving stage, trucked into the Auditorium at great expense. The huge size of the show, which Smith seems to admire, and that surely would not have been out of place on the huge Auditorium stage, would be resoundingly attacked in New York. Atkinson began his harshly negative review with "Much scenery: no play." And, as Alexander Walker, Leigh's biographer, notes, Olivier was to be accused in the *New York Times* (although not by Atkinson) of "gulping down his lines as if they were so many bad oysters."

Did Smith not see this? Or did he see something in these young stars that others did not? Perhaps Olivier's famous insistence on realism just felt like a better match in Chicago, or it could be that the perfect sound in the Auditorium prevented the complaints of remoteness that plagued the production in New York. Then again, maybe Chicago and the *Tribune* critic were just starstruck (a common weakness throughout many of the reviews in this book). Walker points out that the show had been advertised in movie theaters with the tagline "See the great lovers in person." That perhaps caused a backlash in snobby New York; but Chicago and the *Tribune* took it more at face value.

We certainly get the sense from Smith's interesting notice that Olivier's show had the same kind of restless energy that would typify so much of his later work, both as a director and as an actor. The phrase "a figure of breathtaking outward loveliness" is surely paternalistic (indeed, the gushing Smith seems to have fallen wholly in love with Leigh), but also an apt description of the future Lady Olivier.

Still, once Olivier and his bride headed off to New York, Smith turned his attention back to weighty and controversial matters of music and race.

24

PORGY AND BESS

DISCUSSES 'FOLK OPERA' MERITS OF 'PORGY AND BESS' / CRITIC TERMS IT FORERUNNER OF U. S. TREND

Studebaker Theatre

BY CECIL SMITH

NOVEMBER 29, 1942. The late George Gershwin described "Porgy and Bess" as a "folk opera." But does it really justify this description? Does it give as true a representation of the spirit of Negro folk music as "The Bartered Bride" gives of the Czech spirit or "Halka" of the Polish? These latter accepted classics of folk opera were written by composers born within the social and racial group they sought to immortalize; while Gershwin, by birth at least, was an outsider to the culture he borrowed from.

In the course of the most authoritative survey of Negro music I have ever read, R. Nathaniel Dett offers a penetrating analysis of the difference between a serious Negro composer and a white composer who, like Dvorak in the "New World" symphony, turns Negro thematic materials to his own purposes: "The Negro composer," Dr. Dett writes, "rich in his heritage of song, reaches up for the canons of form, by which all music has been advanced; the white composer, schooled in the traditions of artistic development, reaches down for the inspiration which has ever sprung from the soul of those close to the soil."

𝄐 𝄐 𝄐

Because of the inadequate education that has been available, no Negro composer has yet been able to command the high degree of technical craftsmanship with which Dvorak, Smetana, and even Moniuszko were able to manipulate the folk materials they had known from childhood. A gifted Czech or Pole might have been expected to combine instinctive understanding of folk materials with mature workmanship, for he was fortunate in possessing both the "heritage of song" and schooling in the "traditions of artistic development" of which Dr. Dett speaks.

At the halfway point Negro artistic education has reached in our own generation (a point marking a happy advance over earlier conditions) probably no Negro composer could have made an entirely objective and presentable work out of an opera on the subject of Catfish Row. A lack of knowledge of the canons of operatic structure, of the needs of the stage, and of the temper of the white public which must support the opera, would probably have doomed such a work to lack of success.

𝄐𝄐𝄐

When George Gershwin began to interest himself in a Negro theme, he possessed two initial advantages over the Negro composers who might have liked to write "Porgy and Bess": He knew—in a rather schoolboy way, to be sure—the basic conventions and traditions of operatic composition; and he knew—as few have ever known it—the formula for commercial success on the American stage. So while it is true that "Porgy and Bess," as Claudia Cassidy has said, is "more Harlem than deep south," I am inclined to think that this is probably the only kind of "Porgy and Bess" that would have been likely to discover an audience.

Certainly the score of "Porgy and Bess" frequently lapses from characteristically Negro musical expression into straight Broadway, 1935. Many of the basic rhythmic formulas are not Negro at all; and if you listen analytically to the score you will be amazed to see how largely Gershwin overlooked the potentialities of the five-tone scale which colors so much Negro folk music, and which provided Dvorak with the essential melodic structure of much of the "New World" symphony. Jerome Kern's "Ol' Man River" in this regard is more of a Negro tune than most of those in "Porgy and Bess," altho the middle section of Kern's song is unpardonably labored, a fault Gershwin usually escapes.

𝄐𝄐𝄐

While Gershwin's ineradicably New York style does reduce the validity of "Porgy and Bess" as folk art, his defense lies in the fact that nearly all folk operas tend to employ fashionable styles that are at variance with the simple folk materials. In both "The Bartered Bride" and "Halka," which I have chosen for comparison because nobody has ever doubted their authenticity, the influence of highbrow music is constantly in evidence. The arias in "Halka" lean heavily on the cantilena style of

Donizetti and other early 19th century Italian opera composers. In "The Bartered Bride" Smetana forgets to be Bohemian for long stretches at a time, and employs a run-of-the-mine German romantic style.

Actually I think we owe Gershwin a considerable debt of gratitude, whether he has distorted and Harlemized Negro folk song or not. For in "Porgy and Bess" he has shown the way, and the only healthy way, in which American operas can successfully be written. Musical comedy is in a sense the folk art of the American legitimate theater, commercial tho its origins are. And Gershwin, having had sense enough to conceive his opera in terms which are understandable to patrons of the American musical theater, was able to write the first—and up to now the only—really popular American opera.

Altho it is a vital and admirable show, I do not believe "Porgy and Bess" should be judged in terms of ultimates of musical taste. Rather it should be studied and admired as the possible forerunner of a whole school of American operatic composition, a school which can come into existence whenever our serious composers desert their magnificent isolation and come to terms with the popular theater.

"Porgy and Bess" was first performed on Broadway in 1935. Here, Smith riffs (if that's the word) on the national tour of the 1942 revival (which made heavy cuts in Gershwin's score), as directed by Cheryl Crawford. This revival was far more successful than the original, running on Broadway for 9 months. It landed in Chicago at the Studebaker.

Smith's strikingly scholarly piece in the *Tribune* is really a fascinating read, probing the validity of the term *folk opera* and leading with the assertion that since Gershwin was, in fact, an outsider to Catfish Row–along with most everyone else involved in the writing of this opera, but Smith does not get into that–then it was questionable whether it would be fair to call his work a folk opera, since the composer was not of those folk, so to speak.

Then Smith turns to R. Nathaniel Dett, himself a black composer, born in Canada. Dett, he asserts, argues that the "negro" composer reaches "up" for "the canons of form," while the white composer reaches "down" for "the inspiration which has ever sprung from the soul of those close to the soil." Smith does seem to be advocating for better musical education of African American composers, although his argument that no black composer could have written an opera at this juncture is tough to swallow. Gershwin, he says, knew the basic conventions and traditions of operatic composition "in a rather schoolboy way," but apparently that still was enough to eclipse any possible black composer.

It's also clear, as this piece weaves on, that Smith cannot imagine anything but a white audience for the American opera. He was quite the advocate for the seriousness of musical theater; he did much in the pages of the *Tribune*, and beyond, to advance its cause. In many ways, his last paragraph here is an eloquent plea for the serious American musical, which would certainly come into vogue in the years that followed.

Smith had a good healthy streak of Chicago populism; his views on music and race are more complicated.

True folk opera or not, "Porgy and Bess" would be performed frequently in Chicago over the next decades, including a 1952 touring production starring William Warfield, Leontyne Price and Cab Calloway, which played the Civic Opera House for four weeks, and a stirring, stripped-down, 2011 revival at the Court Theatre in Hyde Park.

By 1943, Smith had moved on; the *Tribune*'s publisher, Robert McCormick, had personally recruited a new star for his newspaper, which was by now printing a million copies a day, more than twice that of any other newspaper in Chicago. Claudia Cassidy's so-called reign of terror would last for decades.

25

CARMEN

CRITIC TERRIFIED BY 'CARMEN' AT POPULAR PRICES / BUT SINGING ATONES FOR VISUAL DISASTERS.

Soldier Field

BY CLAUDIA CASSIDY

CAST

Carmen .... Bruna Castagna
Don José .... Kurt Baum
Escamillo .... Alexander Sved
Micaela .... Licia Albanese
Bermendado .... Michael Signorelli
Daneaire .... Giuseppe Cavadore
Morales .... Algerd Brazis
Zuniga .... Reinhold Schmidt
Frasquita .... Janet Fairbank

Mercedes .... Elizabeth Brown
Ballet with Ruth Page and Walter Camryn.
Conductor .... Paul Breisach
Stage Director .... Louis Raybaut

AUGUST 1, 1943. "Carmen," a popular opera at popular prices drew about 25,000 people to Soldiers' field last night, and the most important result was not the performance itself but the fact that several

THIS PHOTOGRAPH OF CLAUDIA CASSIDY IN 1951 WAS ONE OF THE VERY FEW IMAGES OF HERSELF THAT THE NOTORIOUSLY PRIVATE CRITIC ALLOWED TO BE RELEASED. PHOTOGRAPH BY G. NELIDOFF FOR THE *CHICAGO TRIBUNE*.

willing impresarios and some Chicago park board officials were in a kind of football huddle at the rear of the field, talking over possible plans for next summer.

These involve five or six weeks of opera and operetta, with improved amplification, a better stage, possibly one of those decorative water curtains that hide the prosaic business of scene changing, and a semi-circle of seats build on a ramp to the bleachers so that every one can see.

IMPROVED BY DISTANCE. Last night's "Carmen" lacked most of these charms, but it was a show that improved with distance. I recklessly saw the first act from the third row of chairs placed in the field, and from that vantage point the opera was truly a terrifying sight.

It began in broad daylight, with the singers catching the glow of the setting sun on facial color schemes aimed at operatic footlights, and showing all too plainly that Miss Albanese's wig and her makeup missed meeting by an anguished inch. This dolorous daylight also disclosed an unrehearsed performance in makeshift settings, observed over the heads of the Chicago Opera orchestra, which was doing some good work for Paul Breisach.

The fact that the singing was good, too, seemed not quite enough to atone for this welter of visual disasters, so with the growing dusk I walked to the back of the field and discovered another, and far better, show. The ugly things were blurred by distance, so that only the swirl of the stage picture carried, and the amplification scorned the echo that had accosted the ear down front.

GOOD CAST GETS CHANCE. From the rear, if you were lucky enough to be there, the good cast had a chance to display what it could do. Bruna Castagna seemed no more than a plump and jolly Carmen with a throaty laugh and a big contralto better in the lower regions than on high. Licia Albanese, her hapless wig blurred by distance, was again the best Micaela in the business, a lyric soprano with a voice that soars superbly, indoors or out. Kurt Baum, a new Jose, sang beautifully, particularly in the Flower Song, and Alexander Sved, a new Escamillo, made up in picturesque authority a good deal of what he lacked in the lyric line.

Seen from the rear, Ruth Page was a twirl of turquoise and violet, heading her ballet, and seen from the front, Algerd Brazis, a competent Morales, was a single newcomer among familiar faces in lesser roles. Oldtimers at the opera at once recognized Herman Tappo, once the captain of the chorus, again at the head of many of his contemporaries. It was a veteran chorus.

Here begins what many would consider the golden age of theater criticism at the *Tribune*: the Claudia Cassidy era. Although known by all her readers as Claudia, Cassidy (1899–1996) was, and is, unquestionably the most notorious critic in the history of the newspaper. She was known for high standards and a particular disdain for any producer intending to send a substandard touring production though her town. As we will see in these next reviews, her sharp-edged writing was unfailingly to the point; frequently witty; perennially unforgiving; often beautiful; occasionally cruel. Whether history has validated her passionately held opinions is very much open to question. Many of Cassidy's reviews sparked outrage; many changed lives; many made or broke careers. She terrified the most powerful of New York producers: those with touring shows headed for Chicago would spring for special rehearsals, lest they find themselves facing her wrath.

Indeed, it's hard to think of another critic in Chicago who had anything close to the influence of "Acidy Cassidy," to use one of her many nicknames. (She was often addressed by New York producers as "that woman at the *Tribune*.")

Cassidy presided over arts reviewing at the *Tribune* from 1942 to 1965. Much of her writing was produced for her famous column, "On the Aisle."

"Her sentences set off violent storms and she sits serenely as they rage around her," Bernard Asbell wrote of Cassidy in a fascinating, and generally withering, 1956 *Chicago* magazine article, mostly arguing that she did not have the musical training or technical knowledge to back up her opinions. Asbell, a sometime rival, was a harsh critic of the critic, regarding her work as in essence a triumph of style over substance and accusing her of shrewdly avoiding any forum where her ignorance might get called into question. In this truly dismissive piece, for which Cassidy refused to cooperate, perhaps to her detriment, Asbell quoted the actress and author Cornelia Otis Skinner on Cassidy's style: "pure bitchery."

Unlike most of the writers here, Cassidy has been studied at some length. There are at least two doctoral dissertations analyzing her influence on Chicago theater, and her papers reside in the city's Newberry Library. But her actual reviews have not been often read since their initial publication. And Cassidy generally avoided publicity, often demurring with variations on the theme of "I like to write but I don't like to be written about." Relatively few photographs of her exist, even though she was one of Chicago's most famous writers.

When in 1975 she accepted a Joseph Jefferson Award in her retirement from the actress Carol Channing, the *Tribune* reported that its critic had ascended to a stage, "something she never did in the 24 years she reigned."

Cassidy was born in 1899 in Shawneetown, Illinois, where she first started seeing shows on Ohio River show boats. She was a University of Illinois graduate in drama and journalism, became a secretary at the *Chicago Journal of Commerce* and arrived at arts criticism in the classic old-school way: an editor needed someone in a hurry to write a review. After she attracted attention at the *Chicago Sun* in 1941, McCormick wooed her to the *Tribune* in 1942; she was one of the colonel's best hires, and one of the very few leading women in a newspaper era relentlessly dominated by men.

Not only was Cassidy talented, she was astonishingly prolific, with her byline appearing in the newspaper almost every day of the week. Upon her retirement in 1965, *Time* magazine reported her departure under the headline "Exit the Executioner." "She walked like a queen," Asbell wrote of her demeanor, "and the world curtsied."

Cassidy was married to William J. Crawford for 57 years. After her husband died in 1986, she moved into the Drake Hotel, where she lived alone until her death in 1996, at the age of 96. The headline of her obituary in the *New York Times* read: "Claudia Cassidy, 96, Arts Critic: Did Not Mince Words in Chicago."

Indeed she did not, as will be evident in many Cassidy gems that are to follow here. Most of these reviews are of theater, since that's the focus of this book. And they are taken from Cassidy's heyday, running roughly from the mid-1940s through the mid-1960s, although she continued as a freelance critic in Chicago even after her retirement from the *Tribune*.

Cassidy was the *Tribune*'s performing arts critic, as adept at reviewing opera and classical music as the theater that gained her all her notoriety. She was highly influential in changing the directions–and, occasionally, the personnel–of both the Lyric Opera of Chicago, of which she was generally a powerful fan, and the Chicago Symphony Orchestra, with which she had a more complicated relationship. Some Symphony conductors (such as Rafael Kubelik, on whom she waged all-out war) were forced out of town by Cassidy, never to return. She wrote of Kubelik, "The symphony was as shapeless as his curious beat, being distorted by arms stiff as driving pistons or limp as boiled spaghetti."

Cassidy had many other enemies. After writing a negative review of "The Anniversary Waltz" in 1957, she was sued for $100,000 in damages by the show's producers (Cassidy won). Theatrical director Tyrone Guthrie called her "that bitch." At least one scorned soprano threatened publicly to punch her in the nose. Still, among discerning patrons of the arts in Chicago, the pervasive view was that Cassidy was most often right. And, as she pointed out on several occasions: "the only power a critic receives comes from the readers who trust him or her." And, as *Tribune* columnist Bill Granger wrote in a 1983 *Tribune* piece, "She [had] a reputation for integrity that would make Gandhi check his bona fides."

Cassidy was famous for writing very quickly–often unspooling her reviews in less than an hour. Thanks to her publisher's love of the controversy she generated, her clout at the Tribune Tower was unmatched. "Miss Cassidy's copy–and only hers of all the writers on the Tribune, is immune from editing at the copy desk," Asbell wrote. However, he proffered no evidence for that assertion, and may well have not known what he was talking about.

Our exploration of the Cassidy years begins with this review from 1943 (just two years into her long *Tribune* career). It is of a notable event–a performance of "Carmen" at Soldier Field, in front of 25,000 spectators, no less (it is hard to imagine an opera being performed in that football stadium today). Herein we can see the dichotomy that haunted much of Cassidy's writing: an enthusiastic embrace of populism coupled with a deeply felt anxiety that such an embrace would somehow reduce standards. Sarcasm was one of the most useful weapons in the Cassidy arsenal, and she is already brandishing its barbs here.

Read this funny, carefully observed and slightly frenetic review and you get a potent picture of a young and energetic Cassidy, running around Soldier Field, trying to get her head around what this all meant for her beloved adopted city.

Incidentally, "Carmen" was not the only opera staged at Soldier Field by the producers Fortune Gallo and Henry Zelzer that wartime summer. "Aida" was performed there one week earlier.

Cassidy, though, was most famous for her disdain for what she perceived to be second-rate populism. It did not take long for "that woman at the *Tribune*" to hit her poisonous stride.

26

ABIE'S IRISH ROSE

AGING 'ABIE'S IRISH ROSE' IS BAD (?) AS EVER

Studebaker Theatre

CLAUDIA CASSIDY

Isaac Cohen	Abe Gore
Mrs. Isaac Cohen	Bertha Walden
Rabbi Samuels	James O'Neill
Solomon Levy	Robert Leonard
Abe	Vincent Gardner
Rosemary	Jean Pearce
Patrick Murphy	Donald Brian
Father Whalen	Herbert Huffy
Maid of Honor	Joyce Siroln
Bridesmaids	Rue Tennigkeit, Nan Sargent, Janet Duffy, Madonna Manning
Flower Girl	Rosalie Mininni
Train Bearer	Mary Anne Frapolly

"It's the play the people choose,
Loves the Irish and the Jews."

MARCH 20, 1944. Maybe Ira Gershwin won't mind my juggling his immortal lyric that elected Wintergreen for president in "Of Thee I Sing." It's the only way I can hope to explain the rival immortality of "Abie's Irish Rose," which came back to the Studebaker last night after 20 years, several million dollars richer, and just as bad as ever, if not worse.

They tell me not a line has been altered, and I should hope not. There is something downright classic about the horrors of "Abie," not to be lightly improved. Its every drooling sentiment is festooned with a cliché and nailed up with a ponderous pun. Its people are comic strips who speak in the kind of dialogue usually lettered in balloons emanating from caricatured mouths, while the rabbi and the priest look on indulgently and shake their heads gently over the sententious kindliness Miss Nichols has wished upon them. It's all the same, even the borrowed bridesmaids who help Abie and Rosemary at their Jewish and

Irish weddings, tho, regrettably, they were not on hand to decorate the affair at the Methodist parsonage.

◠ ◠ ◠

Out of all this Miss Nichols has reaped an estimated $10,000,000, and is still reaping the harvest of revival and radio. It is all hers, the reward of faith in platitudes when nobody else would touch her saccharine saga of the Jewish boy who marries the Irish girl while their fathers spar all over the stage, spouting dialect, Irish fisticuffs, and Hebrew lamentation.

And I can't find it in my heart to blame them, or that earlier generation of critics who took one look at "Abie" and departed with the weary shrug of another wasted evening. Even as a classic of the curiosities of public taste, "Abie" is still a wasted evening, unless you happen to be one of the millions who find it hilarious.

◠ ◠ ◠

Its acting is as horrendous as its writing, which reminds me that a Moscow Art production of "Abie" would be something to contemplate. Donald Brian acts the father in pugilistic mood, while Robert Leonard lavishes upon Solomon Levy more acting to the square inch than the stage has seen since the visit of the Yiddish theater. Bertha Walden makes Mrs. Cohen a vast ruin of a woman, and Vincent Gardner is a handsome Abie to the pretty blonde who can't remember her accent who is Jean Pearce.

It's still the play the people choose, only, of course, not all the people. Not even, I promise you, all the Irish.

No Cassidy reviews are more fun to read than her vicious pans of bad touring shows, such as the review here of "Abie's Irish Rose." This play by Anne Nichols—the story of the love between a nice Jewish boy and a sweet Irish girl, requiring them to overcome the objections of their parents—was never a favorite of critics, but was very much a favorite of actual paying customers, running for a whopping 2,327 Broadway performances between 1922 and 1927.

By the time Cassidy attacked the play on the pages of the *Tribune*, it was already some 20 years old and, she here declares, "just as bad as ever." Note that this production was directed, and presented, by its author.

Cassidy savages the whole enterprise at the Studebaker Theatre with delicious viciousness, even using Ira Gershwin to turn her knife. By now, *Tribune* readers knew that the paper had a fearless critic. This review positively drips with sarcasm as Cassidy reveals how and why the play offended. For all her tart prose, we can see that she was mostly offended by its inauthenticity; Cassidy rarely liked anything that did not ring true to her. She also saw that this is a play that became popular by its seemingly daring portrayal of a controversial topic, but actually does so almost entirely by trafficking in stereotypes.

Was she envious of this cash cow? Cassidy certainly points out that Nichols had, at this point, made $10 million from her silly little farce; the critic clearly resented every last penny.

Cassidy was, of course, of Irish heritage herself—a background that comes up quite frequently in the reviews that follow and that, it seems, only made her hate "Abie's Irish Rose" all the more.

27

EARLY TO BED

'EARLY TO BED' BIT LATE, AND IS BAWDY BORE

Blackstone Theatre

BY CLAUDIA CASSIDY

El Magnifico .... Joseph Macaulay
Madame Rowena .... Doris Patston
Eileen .... Amy Arnell
Coach .... Mervyn Nelson
Pablo .... James Starbuck
Lois .... Janis Andre
Pooch .... Harold Cromer
Opal .... Helen Bennett
Lilly Ann .... Nickie O'Daniel
Jessica .... Ann Parker

AUGUST 29, 1944. "Early to Bed" was late to rise last night. A curtain scheduled for 8:30 went up at 10, and a good natured audience waited more or less patiently while the stage crew hung the delayed scenery, which reciprocated by being one of the show's major assets. There's something about a mishap like this that makes you so sympathetic nothing would please you more than to say the show, when you finally saw it, was a triumph. But I kept thinking that New York was getting even. Because in the last few weeks New York has been pretty mad at Chicago for sending it the tough turkey called "School for Brides." I think it retaliated. "Early to Bed" isn't precisely a turkey—well, not precisely—but brother, it certainly is tough.

A glimpse of the plot will tell you whether or not it is your show. Down Martinique way there is a brothel, a bordello, or what have you, called the Angry Pigeon. It is mistaken by El Magnifico, a moulting bull fighter, for a finishing school for young ladies, and into the annex he trundles an American track team making a good will tour. The double entendre flourishes, tho perhaps not quite so much as you might think. A good deal of the time the book doesn't bother with the second meaning. This sort of thing either is risqué, if you like it, or bawdy, if you don't. I thought it a bawdy bore.

But there are those Martinique settings by George Jenkins, which had style and charm even amid the perils of hasty hanging. There are a dozen or more striking girls, including the beautiful deadpan, Helen Bennett, who looks so haughtily from the pages of fashion magazines, putting emeralds and platinum mink disdainfully in their place. There are some modulations in the music that suggest the real and lamented "Fats" Waller, but only the Negroes of the cast seemed able to pluck their sly idiom from the clumsy brambles of the lyrics.

George Marlon's book has a one track mind without much on the track, while Robert Alton's routine dances fail to show how they could entice talented James Starbuck from the Ballet Russe. Doris Patston and Joseph Macaulay keep busy without having much that is entertaining to do, a Titian top named Ann Parker sings briskly, Janis Andre dances prettily, and Amy Arnell gets some shrill whistles, which may be a form of applause.

Maybe it all got better after I left. While I was there it was the kind of show a comedian named Mervyn Nelson could steal just by walking out and doing a specialty act about a school teacher and her charges entertaining the P.T.A. It wasn't that he was so funny—just funnier.

This choice Cassidy pan was the result of the tart critic being forced to cool her heels for 90 minutes after a show went up very late, apparently because the scenery was delayed on the road. "Early to Bed," for the record, was a touring musical comedy that featured the music of Fats Waller and had run for 380 performances on Broadway. Here, Cassidy serves up notice that this turkey was not good enough for her Chicago, a theme to which she would constantly return. As was her wont on these occasions, she doesn't spend too much time on details, instead riffing and punning to hilariously sarcastic effect–it is rather as if the reader were stuck in the theater with Cassidy herself, waiting for the show to start.

Unlike most of today's critics, Cassidy felt no obligation to remain in the theater until the end of the show (she once called sleep "a legitimate form of criticism"). She left before the end here; it was by no means the first time she'd headed early to the exits, sharpening her barbs on the way.

"Early to Bed" turned out to be Waller's last Broadway score. That previous December, he had taken the Santa Fe train from Los Angeles to New York and died as the train neared Kansas City. Mo. Self-evidently, that did not make Cassidy feel any need to go easier on Waller's final show.

The next show here, though, Cassidy loved more than any other. She would return to it throughout her career.

28

THE GLASS MENAGERIE

FRAGILE DRAMA HOLDS THEATER IN TIGHT SPELL

Civic Theatre

CLAUDIA CASSIDY

CAST

The Mother .... Laurette Taylor
Her Son .... Eddie Dowling
Her Daughter .... Julie Haydon
The Gentleman Caller .... Anthony Ross

DECEMBER 27, 1944. Too many theatrical bubbles burst in the blowing, but "The Glass Menagerie" holds in its shadowed fragility the stamina of success. This brand new play, which turned the Civic theater into a place of steadily increasing enchantment last night, is still fluid with change, bit it is vividly written, and in the main superbly acted. Paradoxically, it is a dream in the dusk and a tough little play that knows people and how they tick. Etched in the shadows of a man's memory, it comes alive in theater terms of words, motion, lighting, and music. If it is your play, as it is mine, it reaches out tentacles, first tentative, then gripping, and you are caught in its spell.

Tennessee Williams, who wrote it, has been unbelievably lucky. His play, which might have been smashed by the insensitive or botched by the fatuous, has fallen into expert hands. He found Eddie Dowling, who liked it enough to fight for it, Jo Mielziner, who devoted his first time out of army service to lighting it magnificently, and Laurette Taylor, who chose it for her return to the stage. He found other people, too, but ah, that Laurette Taylor!

I never saw Miss Taylor as Peg, but if that was the role of her youth, this is the role of her maturity. As a draggled southern belle who married the wrong man, living in a near-tenement, alienating her children by her nagging fight to shove them up to her pathetically remembered gentility, she gives a magnificent performance. The crest of her career in the delta was the simultaneous arrival of 17 gentlemen callers, and her pitiful quest in this play—as often funny as sad—is the acquisition of just one gentleman caller for her neurotically shy daughter, the crippled girl played by Julie Haydon. Her preparations for that creature, once she has heckled her son into inviting him, his arrival in the hilarious extrovert played by Anthony Ross, and the aftermath of frustration—these are not things quickly told in their true terms. They are theater, and they take seeing.

Fortunately, I have been able to hang around the Civic at previews and I have seen "The Glass Menagerie" twice. Mr. Dowling was good last night in the double role of the son and narrator (who says the first narrator was the angel of the annunciation), but he is twice as good as that when he is relaxed and easy. He had strokes of brilliance last night, but the long easy stride of his earlier performance is on a plane with Miss Taylor's playing and gives the play greater strength.

Mr. Ross enters late, but leaves an impression as unforgettable as his green coat and his face, which is perilously close to being a mug. Late of "Winged Victory," this stalwart actor does a superb job as the gentleman caller who finds his visit a little more than he bargained for. Which leaves only Julie Haydon and there, frankly, I'm puzzled. At times she has the frailty of the glass animals of the title which are her refuge from reality. But I couldn't quite believe her, and my sympathy went to her nagging mother and her frustrated brother—because whatever the writing, acting is the final word, and they acted circles around her.

It is hard to overstate Claudia Cassidy's role in rescuing this great and celebrated play and its now-iconic writer. Before this review, the most famous in this book, Tennessee Williams had been under pressure from his commercial producers to provide a new, happy ending, in which Laura finally gets lucky with her gentleman caller. As the play, which had been touring, approached its Chicago opening, interest from audiences was thin and the producers were thinking about closing the show the day after opening. The cast was in disarray. The weather in Chicago was terrible; the company had arrived at Union Station in the middle of a frigid blizzard. Laurette Taylor, according to her biographer, had not worked in quite a while; everyone was worried she would start drinking again. There are various accounts in Williams's diaries of her stumbling over her lines in rehearsal, fighting with the panic-stricken playwright and barely doing any acting at all. The dress rehearsal was a disaster. Chicago felt like the cold end of the entire project.

On opening night, Cassidy had to fight her way through ice and snow to get to the theater. She was surrounded by empty seats–various contemporary accounts recall a howling wind. Williams's mother also showed up, at that point mostly oblivious to the biographical nature of her son's play, which deals with her daughter's lobotomy. Then, just a few minutes before curtain, Taylor suddenly disappeared from her dressing room, only to be found by her panicked compatriots inexplicably in the basement of the theater, washing her costume.

After the show, Williams wanted to go to a church to await the reviews coming out (there was, apparently, a midnight service being held down the street). But the weather was too bad. He had to wait for Cassidy's verdict without the help of a priest.

The heavens opened when this review came out. Along with Ashton Stevens, who wrote for the *Herald-American* and called this play "both eerie and earthy in the same brush," Cassidy fell hard for "The Glass Menagerie," going back to see it on three successive nights (unimaginable today). Clearly, she understood how personal this play was to its writer. Clearly, she understood that she'd witnessed the birth of a masterpiece. And this review is by no means her last word on the play. She wrote about the "The Glass Menagerie" in various guises so many times and with such enthusiasm, a large group of theater people eventually made their way to Chicago from New York to see what had made the famously terrifying critic gush.

A year after this review, which was a turning point in Williams's life and career, the play was on Broadway, and Taylor's performance was being widely praised as one of the best pieces of acting of its era; its reputation has lived on. History has venerated Cassidy in this instance, at least: the struggling play she championed in a Chicago blizzard is now regarded as a masterpiece of American literature.

Williams wrote about the Chicago experience in his diaries: "It was an event which terminated one part of my life and began another about as different in all external circumstances as could well be imagined. I was snatched out of virtual oblivion and thrust into sudden prominence, and from the precarious tenancy of furnished rooms about the country I was removed to a suite in a first-class Manhattan hotel."

He never went back to "precarious tenancy," thanks in no small part to Cassidy, Chicago and this review.

29

FOLLOW THE GIRLS

GERTRUDE NIESEN'S "FOLLOW THE GIRLS" MAY BE THAT TURKEY TO END ALL TURKEYS

Shubert Theater

BY CLAUDIA CASSIDY

OCTOBER 23, 1946. "Follow the Girls," the Gertrude Niesen musical which creaked into the Shubert last night after two years in New York and a fling at travel, may be a blessing in disguise, tho the disguise was perfect while it confronted me. Later I wondered if this might be the turkey to end all turkeys, the draggled tail of the tawdry parade that marched in the war time boom, confident that if you just shoveled in enough dirt you could dispense with talent. Perhaps if that Bulova clock so handsomely displayed in scene one were a sundial it would tell Albert Borde, the producer, that it's later than he thinks. For I never saw a theater empty faster than the Shubert when "Follow the Girls" approached intermission, and not all the reprieved customers went back for more.

How Miss Niesen got caught in this one, beyond the bait of a song or two, I can't tell you, but once caught, she plays Mae West shrunk for size, wired for sound, and occasionally pickled in the vinegar of what she presumably considers comedy. Only when she is glimpsed in a dimmed spot, her swoosh of feathery bang as palely blonde as ever, does she look or sound like the girl of the night clubs who knows how to carry a torch. Her sultry song is "Twelve O'clock and All Is Well," if you have forgotten, and of course her saucy one, if that is the correct condimental description, is "I Wanna Get Married," which lurks late in the second half of the show.

Altho Miss Niesen, who plays Bubbles La Marr, a striptease with assorted suitors, has little enough material, no one else has any, and it's cruelty to actors to ask them to struggle with those inanimate objects called jokes. A pessimist would be discouraged from the start when a sailor at the Spotlight Canteen looks at the list of stars politely taking second billing to Bubbles, and asks, "What's a Lunt, and what's a Fontanny?" An optimist deserves what he gets.

The subplot involves a naval officer in love with a sinewy Russian dancer with a thick accent, falsely accused of spying by spies even a junior member of the F.B.I. might reasonably recognize. There are a good many people involved, most of them unfortunate, and Catherine Littlefield's dances are so extraordinary they drive Buster West into entrechats in self defense, until he briefly resembles Buster Youskevitch. In fact, things get so bad the audience actually chuckles a bit when Frank Krieg got tangled up in a girdle. Comparatively, it was hilarious.

By 1946, the *Tribune* had increased its arts coverage: a tabloid magazine called *Theater-Music* had been added during the war, aimed in no small part at boosting advertising revenue.

Since Cassidy went so far as to call "Follow the Girls" "that turkey to end all turkeys," its inclusion here seemed a necessity, given that she identified so many turkeys. This review is a truly spectacular reflection of her writing talent; there is no funnier first paragraph anywhere in her work (and it's a paragraph that accomplishes and contextualizes a great deal). Cassidy's attack on the star, Gertrude Niesen (a torch-song singer of some minor repute), is, to say the least, unstinting.

"Follow the Girls" had been a big wartime hit in both London and New York, where it starred Jackie Gleason alongside Niesen (who at one point was known as Gertrude Nissen) and played 888 performances. Luckily for Gleason, he bailed on the show before it came to Cassidy's Chicago.

Cassidy, though, was not so lucky for the great playwright Arthur Miller.

30

ALL MY SONS

MILLER'S PRIZE WINNER AN EARNEST EFFORT RATHER THAN A DISTINGUISHED AND ABSORBING PLAY

Erlanger Theater

BY CLAUDIA CASSIDY

CAST

Joe Keller	Sidney Blackmer
Dr. Jim Bayliss	Robert F. Simon
Frank Lubey	Dudley Sadler
Sue Bayliss	Ellen Mahar
Lydia Lubey	Hope Cameron
Chris Keller	John Forsythe
Bert	Bobby Martinez
Kate Keller	Beth Merrill
Ann Deever	Ann Shepherd
George Deever	James Gregory

NOVEMBER 18, 1947. In a world of regimentation perhaps the drama critics of Chicago are the last holdouts, and that is a great relief to me this morning. If we met in solemn conclave to hand out prizes for best plays I might find myself in the plight of those New York critics who incredulously saw their 1946–47 award voted to "All My Sons" over "The Iceman Cometh." That's all right if you think so, but I'll cling to my profound conviction that even from an aisle seat you ought to know a pygmy from a giant.

PLAYWRIGHT ARTHUR MILLER.

"All My Sons," which came into the Erlanger last night with the Theater Guild's blessing, is an earnest, not very competent play on the ancient theme, "Am I my brother's keeper?" The answer has always been yes, and Arthur Miller reiterates it with more fervor than clarity, with results more repetitious than absorbing. Few will argue with his thesis that it is [a] contemptible thing to have made blood money out of war, but it is difficult to find the dramatic focus of his fumbling efforts to make that fact more than three acts of not very convincing theater.

⌒⌒⌒

In the back yard of the Keller home, which is somehow a stage set despite painstaking efforts to make you believe it, you meet the Keller family and the girl who used to live next door, and who has returned in unusual circumstances. She hopes to marry Chris Keller, against the furious opposition of his mother, who demands that she remain faithful to his brother, a flier long since reported missing in action. The mother clings to the misty conviction that the boy is alive, and you soon see Mr. Miller's intent, for Joe Keller, her husband, by releasing inferior airplane parts during the war (and successfully shifting the blame to the girl's father) has caused the death of many pilots. In her mind, if the boy is dead, the father killed him. Actually, this is so, for it was a suicide death at word of his father's guilt.

Were this more effectively handled, it could be a powerfully moving play. To me, the best of it comes in the use of the title phrase. Joe Keller, who has in his own way tried to give everything to his two sons, says of the dead boy, who could not bear the knowledge of his father's guilt, "I guess he thought they were all my sons."

It is good for a playwright to have convictions, even tho some of Mr. Miller's are puzzling, notably his having the defeated Joe Keller say, "If my money's dirty there ain't a clean nickel in the United States," a credo with which Chris, the playwright's mouthpiece, flatly agrees. My objection to "All My Sons" is not to its ideas, but to its failure to make those ideas dramatically persuasive. It is perilously short on craftsmanship.

Its writing is not distinguished, its characters are commonplace, its invention is obviously manipulated. The Chicago company is almost entirely different from the original, and surely no improvement. I wouldn't have recognized gifted Shaindel Kalish in Ann Shepherd, who is just another actress. The best job last night was done by James Gregory as the girl's angry brother—perhaps because it is the kind of role Elia Kazan could have done superbly before he deserted acting for directing.

Cassidy's relationship with Tennessee Williams is well known; her relationship with the work of Arthur Miller has been discussed much less. She was, in general, much less sympathetic to Miller than to Williams or Eugene O'Neill. As late as 1984, long after she had retired from the *Tribune*, Cassidy even went after the much-praised Dustin Hoffman revival of "Death of a Salesman," starring Dustin Hoffman, calling the actor's performance "dwarfed and unimportant."

Here, though, Cassidy reviews Miller's "All My Sons," the wartime play about an Ohio manufacturer who had cut moral corners in the workplace, fresh from its New York triumph. She begins by comparing the piece unfavorably with O'Neill's "The Iceman Cometh," which it beat out on the awards circuit to Cassidy's chagrin. From that place of apparent pique, she crafts a possibly unreasonable but undeniably eloquent critique of the Miller play, essentially faulting it for what she considered a pedestrian kind of realism. It's hard to find another comparably well-crafted rebuttal to the play's many admirers.

As ever, Cassidy here was setting herself apart from her critical brethren (and they were men) in New York, whom she accuses of a lack of individualistic thinking (she had no problem criticizing members of her own profession).

She may have been prescient when it came to "The Glass Menagerie," but Cassidy was on the wrong end of history when it came to Miller. "All My Sons," which would be revived many times even after Cassidy was gone, is now regarded as a great American drama of the 20th century. Still, even fans of the work and the playwright will surely see something potent in Cassidy's essential argument for the play's mediocrity: it is impossible to disagree with its central assertion. In other words, Cassidy wasn't attacking Miller's politics so much as faulting him for what she considered a lack of craftsmanship and ideological complexity.

This is a stinging review; we might see it as the lesser-known antithesis to the famous "Glass Menagerie" review, which rescued an unknown play from potential oblivion. Here, Cassidy attempted the opposite: to prick the balloon of a play revered in New York. She did not like the Chicago production, directed, as was the original, by Elia Kazan. But her main objection was to the play itself.

Miller would have more than his share of subsequent flops. Nonetheless, few major American critics other than Cassidy dared to use the word *pygmy* in connection with him.

By now, the *Tribune* was 100 years old. Its circulation had reached 1.5 million copies on Sundays, and over 1 million on weekdays. Cassidy found herself with a very powerful megaphone for her criticism.

31

MILLER RESPONDS

'ALL MY SONS' IS CALLED MORE EARNEST THAN ABLE / PLAY'S AUTHOR DEFENDS HIS WRITING STYLE

BY CLAUDIA CASSIDY

NOVEMBER 23, 1947. I wish I had the roll call of New York critics who, according to temperament, were dismayed, disgusted or just sardonically amused when "All My Sons" won the 1946–'47 award of their tribe as the best play of the season, an unaccountable gesture by which it became a pygmy nudging its way past the giant that is Eugene O'Neill's "The Iceman Cometh." John Chapman was one of them, I know, and George Jean Nathan another, and I know, too, that the decision was possible because of a point system now discarded as unworkable.

But I still can't understand that voting. As it now stands at the Erlanger, "All My Sons" is considerably more earnest than able, and not all the difference can be due to cast changes, or such lines as the one which has a girl saying to a man who might be the Seven Sutherland Sisters' brother, "Why, Frank, you are losing your hair."

◠ ◠ ◠

Which is more important in the theater, ideas or craftsmanship? Myself, I don't see how you can be handing out prizes unless they go together. As craftsmanship, "All My Sons" does not rate very high. It is rather clumsily contrived and the one genuinely poignant home thrust of the dialog is the use of the title line in the final scene. Joe Keller, who has so loved his sons that he sent fliers to their death with faulty airplane parts rather than risk business failure by admitting those faults, learns that his pilot son has chosen suicide rather than the taint of such dishonor. As comprehension slowly comes, he says, "I think to him they were all my sons."

I would gladly give a prize—or, rather, absorbed attention, which is theatrically more valuable—to such a line in such a situation. But it doesn't make a play, tho it helps make a playwright's promise. As to ideas, who will question "All My Sons'" conviction that money so come by is blood money? Fewer will agree with Joe's outcry, "If my money's dirty there ain't a clean nickel in the United States." But Chris agrees, and Chris is the voice of the playwright.

⁂

That playwright, as you know, is Arthur Miller, also author of two books, "Situation Normal" and "Focus," the former an outgrowth of a search for material for the movie, "G.I. Joe." Obviously, his "All My Sons" has the warm, if not necessarily unqualified, admiration of many playgoers and of many professional critics, one of them Burns Mantle, who chooses it to head his season's list of ten best plays. Perhaps more interesting for our immediate purpose is what Mr. Miller himself has to say about it. The floor is his from now on:

"In the critics' comments on 'All My Sons,' he begins, "some notice has been taken of the play's structure, particularly the degree of complexity of its story. Because this question of complexity has been of prime interest to me since I began writing, I should like to say something about it in relation to 'All My Sons.'

⁂

"Soon after I started writing for the theater it became clear to me that my vision of what a drama ought to consist of was not widely shared, even by those writers, directors and critics for whom I had the greatest respect. The modern play, the three-act play, was supposed to deal with a single, small, slice of conflict—a 'conflict betw[e]en wills.' The story of a play must follow rather exclusively the career of one or two people, preferably one, with all other characters acting essentially as tributaries.

"I confess that some of the best plays I know do obey this pattern, but for better or worse I cannot feel it as the fullest possible reflection of life. It seemed to me then, and I think now, that the materials for a significant drama of contemporary life are very complex, and the problem for the dramatist is not solved by wiping out the complexity but by bringing order and form to it. I think, too, that in this question lies the answer to the decline of the contemporary drama as contrasted to the lively development of the novel. Playwrights have somehow assumed that an audience cannot follow a multiplicity of motivation, while the best novelists have fairly reveled in that singular fact of life.

For it seems to me that 'conflict of wills' is decidedly not the real stuff of which high drama is made. Human behaviour is not half as simple as that. The interesting thing in a human conflict, or more particularly in a character who is in conflict, is not only that he did what he did, or even what made him do it, but what nearly kept him from doing it. To understand a human action one must have a strong sense of the inner contradictions from which the action sprung. In those contradictions lies the significance of the action itself.

"So it should be obvious that to attempt more than a 'conflict of wills' means to create a denser play, a play with more 'thickness' than the stage usually deals with. It leads to a play with several interwoven stories rather than a unilinear sketch of conflict. Many people have asked whose play 'All My Sons' is—the mother's, the father's, or the son's. To me the central character is Chris, the son, if only because it is on the rock of his determination to obey his own decency that the catastrophe breaks. But I know that the women in the audience feel it is the mother's tragedy that is most important, some of the girls see Ann as the center, the young men are sure Chris is what I am talking about, and the fathers find Joe Heller closest to their hearts.

"And that's fine, because if this play were a story told around the table after the family dinner, or if it were something that had actually happened on the block, the neighbors or the listeners would identify themselves not with one of the participants as 'the hero,' but with whoever in the story they felt represented them. I don't see why a play must concentrate so fully on one individual as to wipe out this kind of conflicting allegiance in the audience."

Mr. Miller also believes that "the unwritten law of the theater requires the playwright to set his characters on one or the other side of the line of evil," and in refutation recalls that the night "All My Sons" opened in Boston an unwitting member of the audience gathered to view it was Mayor Curley, whose appeal to a high court on war fraud conviction was even then being denied in headlines.

I must say all this increases my interest in Mr. Miller as a playwright, but also makes me suspect he doesn't know much about theater. He ought to go more often. The irony of it is that he didn't write that play with multiplicity of motivation, complexity of characters, several interwoven stories, inner contradictions and conflicting audience allegiance. But Eugene O'Neill did—in "The Iceman Cometh."

Claudia Cassidy, we see here (and will see more of as we go), was willing on occasion to give those she criticized their say in the paper. At some length. So it went with Arthur Miller, whose theories on playwriting form a big part of this fascinating piece, published while "All My Sons" still was playing in Chicago.

That said, Cassidy gets to frame Miller's remarks the way she wants. We find her still harping on the slight she deemed paid to "The Iceman Cometh" by the "tribe" that was the New York Drama Critics' Circle and seeing "All My Sons" through that prism. By the way, the Miller scholar C. W. E. Bigsby points out that Miller was "always embarrassed about pipping 'The Iceman Cometh' to the prize, a prize, incidentally, which he swore he never got his hands on."

Cassidy, though, did not know that. And so she goes after "All My Sons" again, just in case the reader missed her attacks the first time.

Miller's comments are, of course, fascinating. It's not entirely clear if he wrote directly to Cassidy or if she found these comments from another source, but they don't appear to show up in any published collection of Miller's essays. In any case, the ideas he expresses herein, penned with a typical sense of detachment, are certainly consistent with the views he expressed elsewhere. And Miller was known for responding to critics.

Cassidy lets him have his say, but nonetheless suggests that the remarks merely prove that Miller "doesn't know much about theater." "He ought to go more often," she snarkily suggests, before getting in one more plug for why "The Iceman Cometh," not "All My Sons," should have won that prize. The next show, in Cassidy's telling, deserved no prizes whatsoever.

32

THE FIREFLY

THIS ONE IS A COLLECTOR'S ITEM—THAT IS, IF YOU COLLECT PREPOSTEROUS SHOWS

Blackstone Theatre

BY CLAUDIA CASSIDY

CAST

Nina	Grazia Aurelia or Beverly Shearer
Jack Travers	Frank Melton
Geraldine Van Dare	Gloria Ware
Mrs. Oglesby Van Dare	Kay Dealya
Jenkins	Jack Goode
Suzette	Gloria Evans
Pietro	Sparky Kaye
Herr Franz	Jack Baxley
Hugo Gessett	Hank Henry

DECEMBER 27, 1947. Santa Claus was wonderful to me up to 8:30 Christmas night. That was when the curtain rose on the Blackstone's revival of "The Firefly," which has had antiquarians digging desperately into the files to discover whether it played here some 30 years ago when it was new. By approximately 8:45 I had relinquished my shovel and changed my project. From now on I have no interest worth mentioning in "The Firefly's" past. My problem will be not to coincide with its future.

In its way, this shabby little theatrical horror is a collector's item. Rarely on one stage could you hope to encounter acting, singing, dancing, writing, staging, and direction on so preposterous a level. Friml's score is wasted, unless you want to hang around long enough to hear an arch baritone launch the lyric that opens what sounds like "Si-yimp-a-thy" with "Has someone been such a naughty boy?"

In holiday mood, I had other big moments. One in the first act when a Windsor tied singing teacher—in operetta always a kindly oldster with a German accent—was so enraptured with the voiceless heroine's one gesture (put those arms back in the boat) singing that he burst out with "You have the voice for which I have been waiting for." The other in act two not for anything that happened on the stage but simply that the playbill said it took place in "Mrs. Van Dare's Palatial Mansion, Bermuda." For third act gems you will have to do your own research. Santa Claus was obviously busy elsewhere, so I gave myself a Christmas present. I went home.

Here is another delicious Cassidy pan that reveals, among other things, that the holiday season did not make the critic any more inclined to spread goodwill. The object of Cassidy's ire this time is an aging operetta by Rudolph Friml—the operetta was a theatrical form that had been popular in Chicago and elsewhere earlier in the century but was, by 1947, viewed as the kind of thing that could ruin one's Christmas, as we gather from Cassidy's review. Even the 1937 film version, which starred Jeanette MacDonald, had ditched the original plot, which Cassidy had to sit through here. That plot concerns a young Italian girl who sings on the New York streets, but decides to disguise herself as a cabin boy on a ship headed for Bermuda. She falls in love, and things go (badly, apparently) from there. Poor Cassidy apparently had to work on Christmas night, but she exacted her revenge on "The Firefly" with an especially wicked and seasonally apt opening paragraph. This operetta had not lit up Broadway since 1931—so presumably this was a road-only confection that so annoyed Cassidy.

She had had enough by the end of Act 2, and so made an early exit (but as always, she fessed up to this). "I gave myself a Christmas present," she acidly wrote. "I went home." Just not when the playwright was Tennessee Williams.

33

A STREETCAR NAMED DESIRE

'STREETCAR' POWERFUL AND ABSORBING PLAY, WITH UTA HAGEN MAGNIFICENT IN A CRACK CAST

Harris Theater

BY CLAUDIA CASSIDY

CAST

Negro Woman .... Eulabelle Moore
Eunice Hubbel .... Peggy Rea
Stanley Kowlaski .... Anthony Quinn
Harold Mitchell (Mitch) .... Russell Hardie
Stella Kowalski .... Mary Welch

Steve Hubbel	Harry Kersey
Blanche Du Bois	Uta Hagen
Pablo Gonzales	Arny Freeman
A Young Collector	Wright King
Mexican Woman	Sidonia Kapero
A Strange Woman	Angela Jacobs
A Strange Man	Arthur Row

SEPTEMBER 23, 1948. You don't waste time with Dynamite, theatrical or otherwise, and the smoldering detonation at the Harris Tuesday night served notice that "A Streetcar Named Desire" is a powerful, violent, and absorbing play of wrenching impact and that Uta Hagen's performance in a first rate cast is the most pitiful, gallant, absurd and magical theater this town has seen since Laurette Taylor cast her spell in "The Glass Menagerie." There is a great deal of Taylor in it, for hers was the master key to the tragi-comedy of Tennessee Williams' haggard, haunted, and yet incomparably fragile women. But just as it is one thing to admire Toscanini and another to go and do likewise, so it is possible to know everything Laurette Taylor did except how she did it. Miss Hagen has a large share of the secret. I do not mean for an instant that her performance is a copy. I do mean it has to an exciting degree the same inner, unerring brilliance. It seems to bubble out of an inexhaustible well of inspiration.

When a superbly written role goes up in a blaze like that, Tennessee Williams is riding so swift a rocket to the moon no wonder some of the excitables expect every word he writes to dim the refulgence of its predecessor. He can write, he can write like a million dollars, and that what he writes is essentially dramatic is a godsend to the impoverished stage. But to insist that he has "developed" is more patronizing than perceptive, for all that he is was to be discovered in that earlier and, to me, finer play. Compared to the haunting perfection of "The Glass Menagerie," "Summer and Smoke" has still to prove itself in rewriting, and the prize laden "Streetcar" has a few purple touches and an excess of climaxes more incisive direction would have blotted out. But the fact remains that he can write like a fallen angel, this clinical poet of frustration. His "Streetcar" can reach out in the dim theater and catch you chokingly by the throat.

He has, among other things, a stabbing talent for titles. They are provocative, picturesque, and they make sense. If you saw "Summer and Smoke" you could say that this girl, too, found the obverse of death in desire, and that it was she, terrified, desperately pretentious, pitifully insecure, who took the street car named Desire to the squalor in which her sister dwelt with a brutish husband in the jungle of sex.

The husband is a realist and not so thick skinned as to miss the obvious implications. Relentlessly, he ferrets out the fastidious visitor's past. It is nothing to him that all her life she has fled the dusty answer of her first love, the suicide of her homosexual husband. In words of one syllable he tracks down the ugly story of the girl in the shrinking Mississippi plantation, surrounded by death, slipping out to desire until as a public figure she is asked to leave town.

He strips her of Mitch, the gentle, kindly man who might have been her salvation, and he takes her in callous cynicism, leaving his wife to accept the truth or hide behind the conviction that her sister is mad. Perhaps indeed she is mad, for she has nothing left when her veils of illusion vanish in the bald glare of brutal fact. It is a shocking thing to see that squat institutional female come to take her to the madhouse now her only refuge, but at this point the playwright makes a tender, chivalrous, superbly dramatic gesture. The doctor sizes up his patient, lifts his hat, and gallantly bends his arm. Terror fades from her face as she returns to illusion. "Whoever you are," says Blanche Du Bois, "I have always depended on the kindness of strangers."

There should be room left to speak of Jo Mielziner's frowzy yet somehow fascinating New Orleans setting, the violence and clarity of most of Elia Kazan's direction, the brute force impact of Anthony Quinn's playing, the conviction of Russell Hardie's Mitch, the warm, deep honesty of Mary Welch as the sister. But most of all there should be room to tell of the miasma of horror Williams has created, and how Uta Hagen brings its victim to terrifying life.

Claudia Cassidy was never more ecstatic than when reviewing her favorite playwright, Tennessee Williams. Most certainly, she was confronted here with a remarkable cast for "A Streetcar Named Desire," including Anthony Quinn as Stanley Kowalski and Uta Hagen as Blanche Du Bois. In the case of Hagen, Cassidy offers the most powerful compliment in her quiver: she compares her to Laurette Taylor in "A Glass Menagerie." This production was a tour (there were actually two national companies) of Elia Kazan's original Broadway production; Quinn and Hagen would go on to play these roles together on Broadway in 1950. "Streetcar" was already a massive hit when it arrived at the Harris Theater.

This review represented a huge breakthrough for Hagen. "It has always been assumed on Broadway, and resented in the hinterlands, that stars are born only on Broadway," *Life* magazine would write shortly afterward. "But Chicago, which has been having its best new season in years, has seen two new stars spring full-grown onto the stage." One was Richard Carlson; the other was the 29-year-old Hagen, who would become one of the most acclaimed actors of her generation.

Hagen taught acting classes in Chicago while she was in the city with "Streetcar," and, *Life* remarked admiringly, she "sew[ed] for her young daughter."

In his production history of "Streetcar," Philip Kolin reports that Harold Clurman was the real director of this tour, even though Elia Kazan's name remained on the playbill. Kolin says that Hagen had refused to watch Jessica Tandy's version of the role, preferring to craft her own performance, which by most accounts, including this one, was far more assertive and robust than that of Tandy, who had a much smaller frame and thus seemed far frailer to critics. Kolin observes that while Tandy's Blanche seemed in trouble from the start, Hagen figured out that the play worked better if Stanley's rough treatment more directly caused Blanche's breakdown.

As a Chicago critic, Cassidy clearly preferred the more powerful Hagen take on Blanche to Tandy's demure neurotic. Hagen was an actress more of the Chicago school.

The critic was capable of myriad ways of lauding Williams's gifts on the pages of the *Tribune*. "He can write like a fallen angel, this clinical poet of frustration," Cassidy writes here, perfectly capturing a man whose work she knew probably better than any other critic in the country. This "Streetcar" review also has a masterly ending—it feels to the reader as if Cassidy knows precisely how many column inches she has left. There is a slight note of frustration as she concludes in that she cannot pen more, and then a perfect marriage of content to space. This is Cassidy at her very best.

She was to return to Williams many more times—especially with his plays that needed her support far more than "Streetcar." But in the meantime, she had a more pressing question to answer.

34

WHEN AN AUDIENCE BOOS AND DEMANDS ITS MONEY BACK—JUST HOW BAD CAN OPERA GET?

BY CLAUDIA CASSIDY

MAY 3, 1949. How bad can opera get? In the days of its musical decline, Chicago has been confronted by many a questionable performance, some under its own dimming signature, some blandly presented by visitors of purportedly high and blatantly low degree. I have sometimes wished that a long suffering public, rather than accept less and less for its hard earned cash, would stop being polite about things no impresario, however cynical about public taste, would be caught dead presenting unless it fattened his pocketbook.

Yet Sunday afternoon when a Civic Opera house audience mocked, booed, and hooted Virginia Pemberton's Violetta in a shocking performance of "La Traviata" I was not too sure that such European candor is the American solution. I was rather on the side of those outraged customers who at the end of the first act demanded their money back, tho as one of them told me, she was still out the cab fare it cost her to get there in the rain. They were taking their revenge, not on a misguided singer, but on the primary source of injury, the management.

𝄐𝄐𝄐

This was not the first time that Fortune Gallo has executed a dubious maneuver to keep his San Carlo Opera troupe going. Furthermore, he had Pemberton precedent, for in the shabby Chicago days of the late Paul Longone Miss Pemberton accosted the startled Micaela and twice disposed of Mimi before her time. That was a good 10 years ago, and nothing had happened since to persuade the most optimistic that she could cope with Violetta.

It will not be news to Mr. Gallo that Miss Pemberton's so-called lyric song suggests the parrot coached cawing of the crow, or that her way with fioriture resembles that of the late Florence Foster Jenkins, who became a collector's item and made enough money out of catastrophic coloratura to make you wonder if the joke was on you.

𝄐 𝄐 𝄐

But I am afraid Miss Pemberton is in deadly earnest, which makes it sadder, and a more sadistic story. Not only was her performance vocally a disaster, but she became pitifully lost in the glittering arias of the first act, and wandered about the stage in search of clews, emitting two of Violetta's favorite but all too apt ejaculations, "It's strange!" and "Folly!" A frantic conductor and prompter finally extricated her, and she emerged for solo curtain calls, apparently under the delusion that a noisy reception is invariably a tribute.

Few things could be more ridiculous than to review such a fiasco, but it is safe to say that Stefan Ballarini and Mario Palermo were comparatively solid operatic citizens, and that Violetta's party has rarely had so many genuinely entertained guests. But Carlo Moresco, the conductor, must have decided there has to be an easier way to make a living. He stuck to his post long enough to conduct the evening's "Carmen" (which had a new and unobjectionable Micaela in Helen Clare Snow), but when the troupe headed for New York, Leo Kopp was its new maestro. I understand Mr. Moresco is heading for South America, and I can't say I blame him.

No producer of opera in Chicago wants to read "How bad can opera get?" No singer wishes her voice to be compared to "the parrot coached cawing of the crow." But both of those indignities were unloaded by Claudia Cassidy after an apparently horrific evening spent at the Civic Opera House in the spring of 1949. Luckily for the Lyric Opera (an institution that would suffer through some of Cassidy's wrath in later reviews), Cassidy had gone to the opera house that night to review not a Lyric production—this was about five years before the company's founding—but a work by the San Carlo Opera Troupe, a traveling opera company that specialized in visiting cities poorly served by better-known ones. Cassidy did not make this company welcome in Chicago, although she offered up for her readers one of her most hilarious reviews. She was, on this and other occasions, fully capable of attacks on individual performers that would, in today's world, be deemed cruel.

The San Carlo Opera Company, which frequently was on the brink of ruin, lasted until the mid-1950s, when it disbanded. Fortune Gallo was an Italian-born impresario known for keeping production costs low and, remarkably, making opera pay (he titled his autobiography *Lucky Rooster*). In its 1970 obituary, the *New York Times* said that Gallo, who had lived until the age of 91, had "done more to popularize grand opera in America than any other man." Intriguingly, the Broadway theater now known as Studio 54 was originally built by him as the Gallo Opera House.

Cassidy would have known Gallo pretty well; he had managed the Chicago Opera Company earlier that decade. (The company operated from 1940 to 1946, with Gallo at its helm until 1945.) As Cassidy notes nastily here, the unfortunate Virginia Pemberton was also a veteran of that company; she must have been delighted to get away from Cassidy's Chicago and back out on the road. Cassidy, Gallo and Pemberton surely must have discerned, had an agenda to lay out.

35

THEATER NEEDS A PRESENT AS WELL AS A PAST TO HAVE A FUTURE

GOOD NEW PLAYS WOULD COAX STARS FROM SO MANY REVIVALS

BY CLAUDIA CASSIDY

JUNE 12, 1949. Up to a point, nostalgia is brushed with glamour; beyond that, the dictionary is nearer the truth with its starker definition, "home-sickness causing severe melancholia." Altho some of our favorite stage folk are casting wistful glances over famous shoulders, a brilliant new play apiece would quickly coax them from cobwebbed contemplation of things past. It is a fine thing now and then to have a Katharine Cornell as Miss Browning or a Helen Hayes as Victoria, and undeniably the Lunts have an affinity for romantic reunion, especially in Vienna. As for classic theater, would we had more of it. But it is no secret to anyone who loves the stage that it needs a present as well as a past if it is to have a future.

Good new plays are always scarce, and perhaps of late they and our stellar players have been incompatible. You could work up a case by saying imagine the Lunts in "Death of a Salesman," or Cornell in "The Madwoman of Chaillot," or Judith Anderson as Blanche in "A Streetcar Named Desire," but you also could work up a case, and a more interesting one, by saying why not? The fact remains that nothing of the sort has happened, and that the theater's most valued stars are falling back on revivals and adaptations.

Of course, you rarely know how many of the younger playwrights have their wares turned down by established stars, and in turn make new stars, and you do know the elder playwrights have not been too fruitful of late. Furthermore, it isn't surprising that if Maxwell Anderson keeps reverting to that Tudor gesture signaling the headsman, he has to change his royal pawns. Rex Harrison's Henry is now sending Joyce Redman's Anne to her doom as Helen Menken's Elizabeth condemned Helen Hayes' Mary of Scotland and Lynn Fontanne's ageing Elizabeth accepted the bitter price of death for Alfred Lunt's Essex—tho I must say the gesture has not carried the same impact for me since the Lunts made it unforgettable.

But they have a way of making theater indelible, given half a chance, and for years they were rich in vivid plays. Perhaps when Robert Sherwood is rested from "Miss Liberty" he will write them another in the rich and varied Sherwood tradition. Or, perhaps, if S. N. Behrman must cling to adaptations, he can find another "Amphitryon." For "I Know My Love" is hard on everyone, but rather harder on him than on its stars. It makes him seem a dull writer and a clumsy craftsman, which he never was.

As for the Lunts, it merely indicates that deprived of a good play they will tackle what they can get. Friends who saw the Marcel Achard original in Paris tell me it was dull as "Aupres de ma Blonde," and theater folk instantly ask if the Lunts were playing it backwards or forwards when they shut up shop for the summer last week in Milwaukee. This is a serious question. When the play was due in Milwaukee last March its six scenes (transferred to Boston but not rooted there by such devices as affectionate mention of Koussevitzky's Mozart) were dated 1939, 1920, 1918, 1902, 1888. When the delayed engagement opened June 1 those scenes ran 1939, 1888, 1902, 1918, 1920. Juggling them could make little difference to the moribund plot, but it did give the Lunts the chance to shed half a century with one intermission change. This is a gala stunt, highly amusing. But it is scarcely enough for a play to tell us that at any age the Lunts are resourceful, decorative and delightful. We know our loves.

With Mother Hubbard in charge of the contemporary cupboard, there aren't even enough bones of plays to go around. After a season on radio, Helen Hayes will be trying out William McCleery's "Good Housekeeping." After a London season in "September Tide," Gertrude Lawrence may come back in Noel Coward's "South Sea Bubble." After a season of waiting, Katharine Cornell goes into September rehearsal with Kate O'Brien's "That Lady," adapted from "For One Sweet Grape," in which she plays a luckless lady at the court of Spain's Philip II., who not only wears a patch over one eye, but is immured in a castle because a king in those days could do quite a lot when he was jealous. The lady should have remembered the fate of Philip's son, Don Carlos, so remarkable it set Verdi to writing an opera.

𝄐 𝄐 𝄐

But Judith Anderson, after the blazing triumph of "Medea," has no play at all. "Salome" is out, on grounds of being a luxury no one can afford. She is thinking about Oscar Wilde's "A Woman of No Importance," played by Rose Coghlan in 1893. If you have forgotten, it is about a woman deserted by an Englishman of title as being of no importance, who finds she has the same opinion of him when he gets around to asking her hand in marriage, one grown son later.

This really comes under the head of searching in the archives, and reminds me of Ina Claire's talk a year or so ago about reviving Somerset Maugham's "Lady Frederick" at the behest of James Reynolds, who wanted to design the settings. I wrote a piece about it then, wondering how Miss Claire—or, for that matter, the Ethel Barrymore of 1908—could disillusion an importunate young man by letting him see her remove cold cream and appear without make-up. I would have forgotten it except that I got a bristling letter from a firebrand in Tipperary who was of the opinion that in one innocent item I had maligned his friend Reynolds, his cherished Ireland and his adored Miss Claire. Anyway, it was nice to have a letter come that long, long way from Tipperary.

Miss Barrymore, meanwhile, clings to Hollywood. Ruth Gordon, back from England, is quicksilver who might turn nostalgic with "Years Ago" or contemporary with "Over 21." Margaret Sullavan, Betty Field—I haven't heard a word about them, and Miss Field has a playwright husband, Elmer Rice. Maybe he has a play up his sleeve. Maybe Tennessee Williams will be back with his pockets crammed. Maybe something will come along by Harry Brown, who wrote "A Sound of Hunting." Maybe, as Mr. Hammerstein would put it, some enchanted evening will find the curtain going up on a stranger and coming down on a man who can really write plays. It doesn't happen often if you are hoping for it, but in the long view it happens all the time. If it didn't, the theater would be all past and no present, much less future.

This passionate *cri de coeur* about the need for new plays is the first of several interesting Cassidy commentaries. Here, she laments the way that established stars had been clinging to revivals; she argues, using a broad range of examples, that better new plays would better challenge these leading lights of the theater. It's a very sophisticated and eloquent piece of journalism, really, reflective of Cassidy's long-held ambivalence toward Alfred Lunt and Lynn Fontanne, big stars in Chicago at the time, and even finding room to poke a little fun at a correspondent from Tipperary. It's clear from this that Cassidy was anything but a nostalgist, her famously high standards notwithstanding. In this commentary she recognizes that new plays are the lifeblood of the theater–just as they would be at the heart of the Chicago renaissance that was to come, thanks to the likes of Studs Terkel.

36

DETECTIVE STORY

"DETECTIVE STORY" OPENS IN THE BLACKSTONE, A TOUGH, BOLD STENCIL OF A PLAY

Blackstone Theatre

BY CLAUDIA CASSIDY

CAST

Detective McLeod	Chester Morris
Mary McLeod	Lydia Clarke
Arthur Kindred	Walter Starkey
Susan Carmichael	Elinor Randel
First Burglar (Charlie)	Steve Gravers
Second Burglar (Lewis)	Alan Rich
Detective Dakis	Leonard Yorr
A Shoplifter	Marian Winters
Joe Feinson	Studs Terkel
Detective Brody	Paul Lipson
Dr. Schneider	Raoul De Leon
Lt. Monoghan	Kirk Brown
Crumb-Bum	Jerry Fritz
Mr. Gallantz	Pitt Herbert
Mr. Pritchett	William Phelps
Tami Giacoppetti	James Bender

NOVEMBER 2, 1949. "Detective Story" came to the Blackstone last night, a tough, bold stencil of a play sharply cut in the image of reality rather than created from the flesh and blood of reality itself. Which is perhaps just as well for its popularity, for if you believed in the grim executioner of a detective and the criminal abortion background of his young wife, it could be pretty hard to take. As things are, the stage is filled with puppets, manipulated on the obliging strings of plot. Sidney Kingsley has written from the outside in, not the inside out, and he makes a lively pattern with those pliable stagefolk who are types, not people. You won't necessarily be bored just because you don't believe it.

Mr. Kingsley is said to have spent months in research, and pictorially it paid off. His New York detective squad room looks authentic, at least to a drama critic. It is dingy inside and squalid outside, and thru it passes a parade of offenders, petty and otherwise, first timers and old hands. There are detectives on the make and on the square, and one of them, Paul Lipson's Detective Brody, seemed to me to have more than grease paint in his veins. He didn't bellow and he didn't put on an act. But you knew he was there, and felt a little safer, just in case you or your friends should get arrested.

For Detective McLeod is a hard man to believe, tho an interesting one to watch. Bitter, vindictive, grim jawed, a loud mouthed bully, he admits no compromise with the law. He can't see any difference between an habitual criminal and a boy who put his hand in the till the first time, and when he gets on the trail of an abortionist he is so enraged at subornation of witnesses he beats up the phony doctor in his own squad room. But he is at least consistent up to the next to last moment. When it turns out that his wife had been treated by that same abortionist before their marriage, he rejects her. And he walks into a gun because he is made that way. That last gasp change of heart—well, maybe. It's not sure even death would change what Kingsley made of McLeod. He is a tough customer, and a dangerous man to have even on the right side of the law.

Chester Morris plays him grimly, with outthrust jaw, and a good deal of competence. Lydia Clarke has a clearcut face and a good voice for the wife—she might easily turn out to be something more than an ordinary actress. Most of the others are cast and directed as types, which they play with no particular distinction. Studs Terkel does a capable job as one of those philosophical reporters you never meet around newspaper offices, tho I once knew a philosophical editorial writer, who gave it up and took to writing for the pulps.

Anyway, I want to know if Martha Graham really said the direction was like a ballet. In "Detective Story," when one part of the stage is alive, the rest of it stops living. Ballet isn't that way at all.

Here, perhaps, is one of the very plays Cassidy was hoping for in the previous piece: "Detective Story" by Sidney Kingsley. This review is of interest for many reasons–Cassidy's opening sentence is a magnificent way to start a review, and her final sentence offers quite the sting in the telling—but not least because of the presence of one Studs Terkel in the touring cast at the Blackstone Theatre. Cassidy reviews him as doing "a capable job as one of those philosophical reporters you never meet around newspaper offices," which would suggest that Terkel was pretty much playing himself.

Terkel, of course, would become one of Chicago's most beloved and long-lived cultural figures. Here in 1949, he was working as an actor some 26 years after his family first moved to Chicago. He had already acted a good deal with a company called the Chicago Repertory Group (it was at that time that Louis Terkel took the name Studs and met his wife), even appearing in "Waiting for Lefty." One year after this national tour of "Detective Story," which had gone out while the hit play was still doing well on Broadway, he would land his famous "Studs' Place" variety show back in Chicago, before he fell victim to McCarthyism and found himself blacklisted from commercial radio.

Meanwhile, few breathed a word of criticism about Tallulah Bankhead. Even Cassidy was charmed.

37

PRIVATE LIVES

SPRING, TALLULAH BACK IN TOWN WITH BAROMETER REPORTED ON WAY UP

Harris Theater

BY CLAUDIA CASSIDY

CAST

Sibyl Chase .... Barbara Baxley
Elyot Chase .... Donald Cook
Amanda Prynne .... Tallulah Bankhead
Victor Prynne .... William Langford
Louise .... Claudine Le Due

MARCH 21, 1950. Tallulah Bankhead, spring, and the indestructible "Private Lives" are with us again, so that familiar sultriness is in the air, with promise of squalls as well as jonquils. In the two and a half years since she quit the Harris to play Broadway and points deeply south, the remarkable Miss Bankhead has acquired a better performance, a shorter haircut, a slimmer figure, a square cut ruby for the first act, a rectangular emerald for the second, and no doubt the Kohinoor for the third, tho I wasn't around that long to check. She has clung, meanwhile, to Donald Cook as a crisp leading man who can cope, and to her fascinating salary arrangement, which is something like $3,000 a week, plus percentages.

As another remarkable woman with a head for figures seems to have said, "A ring on the hand may make you feel very nice, but a good performance lasts forever." And while Miss Bankhead can twist an audience around her impertinent little finger, there are more rings coming straight from the boxoffice. For this time the cyclonic temperament, the booming baritone, the snarls of rage, and the amorous dove sounds are just the amusing trimmings they should be. For when Miss Bankhead isn't too busy being a personality, she is also an actress. In that first act I believed her every inch of the way as the ever so faintly haggard beauty of the wide, shadowed eyes who could play hob with two honeymoons by running away with her ex-husband.

Frankly, that is about all I still believe when confronted with "Private Lives," for 20 years and half a dozen visits are more than even a Coward comedy of bad manners could hope to withstand. Miss Bankhead and Mr. Cook miss no tricks, and add plenty of their own, but you can't help wondering how they can play that deadly second act season after season without screaming in boredom. Come to think of it, perhaps that's why their rage sounds so real.

The other two roles should never be wished on human beings, but this time Barbara Baxley is playing Elyot's shrill little second wife, and William Langford is Amanda's handsome stuffed shirt of a second husband. The orchestra, you will note, investigates Noel Coward self-castigated music, "Strange how potent cheap music can be," then takes off into "Kiss Me, Kate's" "So in Love with You Am I." Someone noticed that we seem to like our love stories about divorced couples with smoke in their eyes from carrying a torch.

Claudia Cassidy was no fan of Noel Coward—here she takes on "Private Lives" and calls his music "self-castigated," whatever that means, and she also has a lot to say about the famous star of this particular night at the Harris Theater, Tallulah Bankhead. We can detect Cassidy's healthy disdain for those moments when an actress's celebrity persona eclipses her actual acting. Her opening line is, as so frequently was the case, delightfully wry.

Bankhead had previously done "Private Lives" in Chicago in 1947–in fact, this play gave the actress the longest run of her career. Bankhead, who was at her peak, toured with the piece for more than two years and made a good deal of money. At that earlier pre-Broadway engagement in Chicago, Cassidy had written admiringly of her (a redheaded actress who some people said Cassidy actually resembled), although she called the play a "repetitive exercise in trivia." But it was clear to Cassidy then, as here, that audiences were eating Bankhead up.

Bankhead and Cassidy were friends, an acquaintance that was widely commented on at the time. Bankhead, it seems, could take Cassidy at face value. Cassidy seems to have liked Bankhead's spark and outré personality, but set herself up as the actress's moral artistic guide. Read this review carefully, and you see much of the complexity of that relationship.

Cassidy went after Coward a good deal. "He has been disinclined to play Chicago since 'The Vortex,'" she wrote around the time of this review, "but he has no trouble collecting royalties here." Clearly, Cassidy was annoyed that Coward and his costar Gertrude Lawrence had bypassed Chicago when they did their own production of "Private Lives." Bankhead, it seems, was some recompense for a critic spurned.

But this critic was about to unleash one of the most famous reviews of all.

38

SOUTH PACIFIC

HERE'S THAT FABULOUS SHOW WITH A LESS THAN FABULOUS CAST

Shubert Theater

BY CLAUDIA CASSIDY

CAST

Ensign Nellie Forbush .... Janet Blair
Emilie de Becque .... Richard Eastham
Bloody Mary .... Diosa Costello
Luther Billis .... Ray Walston

Lt. Joseph Cable .... Robert Whitlow
Liat .... Norma Calderone
Capt. Geo. Brackett .... Robert Emmett Keane
Cmdr. William Harbison .... Alan Baxter
Musical Director .... Franz Allers

NOVEMBER 15, 1950. Well, it got here at last—the fabulous "South Pacific," which, even 19 months after the New York smash, was potent enough to pile up a $550,000 advance sale for the troupe that last night ended the Shubert's booking worries for a long time to come. I wish I could call it a fabulous troupe—that I could shoot the works and tell you Janet Blair and Richard Eastham have washed Mary Martin and Ezio Pinza right out of my hair. But maybe that doesn't matter too much, especially if you don't have the originals of "Some Enchanted Evening" too vividly in mind.

For except for the wistful perfectionist this must be a wonderful show. Not the best show ever staged, not even to all of us the best Rodgers and Hammerstein show. But the public as a whole seems mad about it, and even doubting Thomases admit it is a big, lusty item with some happy times to remember. For Richard Rodgers has dipped deep into his wealth of melody, which wells up higher the deeper he dips, and the second of the Oscar Hammersteins has poured the riches of his lyrics into a book more durable than inspired.

⁂

It always seemed to me that two of the men I most admire, Joshua Logan and Jo Mielziner, let them down in staging and designing the musical, for what they have done a good deal of the time is as artificial as Rodgers and Hammerstein are real. When Rodgers and Hammerstein really write a song it is no conventional hit for a lively show. It is a catch in the throat, a thrust in the mind, or a warmth in the heart.

A lot of this had spilled into "South Pacific," where sometimes it sparkles and sometimes it surges, and sometimes it just plainly speaks its mind. I like just about all of it except "You've Got To Be Taught," which to my ear is less convincing than the obvious truth it has to tell.

When you get right down to casting, which is the heart of the Chicago company matter, my medal goes to Ray Walston, whose Luther Billis is as real as that chiseling seabee come to life, as ruthless, as conniving and as charming. Diosa Costello is a reliable Bloody Mary except when it comes to making you want to set out for Bali Ha'i, which I confess I have never found irresistible. Robert Whitlow's Joe Cable and Norma Calderon's Liat are just figures on the stage, much as I love "Happy Talk."

◠ ◠ ◠

As for Miss Blair and Mr. Eastham, both with talent to spare, the trouble may be that they are impersonating Miss Martin and Mr. Pinza, and the essential characters should be just about reversed. That is, Miss Blair is no hick, however charming, and Mr. Eastham is no man of the world to sweep a girl off her feet. He is a pleasant man with a good rich voice, and his accent is close to Pinza's own; he is closer to a Hoosier farmer than an exiled French planter.

So the very essence of that strong attraction between the girl from Little Rock and the middle aged man is knocked galley west before the curtain rises, and Miss Blair didn't help it much by being scared out of her wits in the first scene. But neither could she put over "I'm Gonna Wash That Man Right Outa My Hair"—not with the Martin charm, tho in that scene she turned out to be a better dancer than singer. The trouble is, Mary Martin *is* Nellie Forbush, for Nellie takes that rarest of women, a born clown with more than one touch of Venus.

◠ ◠ ◠

So here we are with "South Pacific," and yet not "South Pacific" as it was in the original, even on the nights when the magnetic Pinza was happily loafing on the job.

This is one of Cassidy's most notorious reviews—and a piece that cemented her reputation as a critic who detested second-rate tours coming through her city. "South Pacific" was, of course, a massive hit in New York, and its arrival in Chicago had been eagerly anticipated. As Cassidy notes here, the show had a $500,000 advance in Chicago, a colossal sum in 1950. And then Cassidy washes the tour right out of her hair. In short, she did not consider the touring cast led by Richard Eastham and Janet Blair good enough, and had no trouble telling her readers what they were missing when she compared the show with its New York original.

This review—which certainly opens Cassidy to the charge that she could be closed-minded when anyone but the original New York cast took to the road—was covered extensively in *Time*, *Newsweek*, *Variety* and elsewhere. It had New York producers scheming to keep out-of-town critics away from Broadway openings, if only so they wouldn't be tempted to make unflattering comparisons with touring casts, but Cassidy had none of that. One of her central campaigns was that the Chicago company should be the equal of the Broadway original. She fought it over and over again.

Cassidy's comments about "You've Got to Be Carefully Taught," which would become one of the most widely admired numbers in the show, are especially interesting, and it's not at all clear what she means here. But it's very clear what she was missing.

One of the actors in this company, Robert Emmett Keane, fired back at the critic, calling her "one vitriolic woman . . . [who] pours sulphuric acid over every new show which is brought to Chicago." Keane apparently made at least one appearance at a ladies' luncheon club, opining that the only thing wrong with theater in Chicago was Claudia Cassidy.

That didn't stop Cassidy. At least she still had Tennessee Williams.

39

THE ROSE TATTOO

"ROSE TATTOO" A STIMULATING DRAMA IN BUD / NEW PLAY CALLED FRESH AND PROVOCATIVE

Erlanger Theater

BY CLAUDIA CASSIDY

CAST

Serafina Delle Rose .... Maureen Stapleton
Alvarro Mangiacavallo .... Eli Wallach
Rose Delle Rose .... Phyliss Love
Jack Hunter .... Don Murray
Assunta .... Ludmilla Toretzka
Estelle Hohengarten .... Sonia Sorel
The Salesman .... Eddie Hyans
The Doctor .... Andrew Duggan
Father De Leo .... Theo Goetz
The Strega .... Daisy Belmore

TENNESSEE WILLIAMS AT HIS TYPEWRITER

Guisepina .... Rossana San Marco
Flora.. Jane Hoffman
Bessie .... Florence Sundstrom
and others.

DECEMBER 29, 1950. It is not now the play he intends it to be, "The Rose Tattoo" Tennessee Williams is entrusting to us in the pangs of tryout, but in a town where too many warmed over bookings have dulled the edge of playgoing, it is a fresh, provocative, and stimulating thing to see. It has many rewarding scenes that draw luster from within, and some foolish ones over-decorated from without. It needs what Mr. Williams' plays always have needed, clairvoyant direction, and mesmeric power, in this case of volcanic origin, in the leading role. It needs sharpening of design, detonation of climax, and, if it is to end in affirmation, a luminous finale.

For Mr. Williams was never a playwright to reach for apples in a garden canopied with stars. His play, if he can pull it off, deals with the mystical and the earthy, the passionate and the ecstatic.

BLENDS SOUTH AND ITALY. This seems to me a natural reaction of an imaginative southerner to the impact of the Italy of the south. He has tried to pull them together. Down on the gulf coast, between New Orleans and Mobile, he imagines a village where live oaks drip their moss over a community of Sicilians. A ripe, dark woman is waiting for her husband as for a lover. In his name, Rosario Delle Rose, the scent of the oil in his hair, the tattoo on his breast, she cherishes the symbol of the rose, and in a kind of ecstatic stigmata she believes she glimpses the rose tattoo on her own breast as the symbol of conception.

But she loses husband, child, the conviction of having been greatly loved. She is tormented by flickers of gossip, mocking laughter, the memory of the carelessly raffish blonde who had ordered the rose colored shirt for a man so disturbingly familiar as she described him. Tortured by doubt she pleads for a sign from heaven, and in despair or desire, or both—the play is not very clear on the point—she settles for a clown with a good memory who puts rose oil on his hair and on his breast what she again feels burning on her own as the symbol of conception, the rose tattoo.

STRONG GRIP ON ATTENTION. This is the dominant theme, not yet fully developed. In sometimes effective, sometimes queasy, counterpoint is the story of the daughter whose Sicilian heritage is stronger than her deep south fragility implies, and what that heritage does to her when she meets a boy she loves—or perhaps loves the first boy she meets. There is a wonderfully amusing scene in which the mother warns the boy off, a potentially remarkable one now clumsily handled in which the boy keeps his word under harshly ironical circumstances. No doubt this and other awkward or puzzling scenes will be made clearer now that Mr. Williams has seen his play in audience action.

Even as it stands, incomplete, inconclusive, and at times exasperating, "The Rose Tattoo" has a strong grip on attention. The role of the mother is remarkable, with a direct candor Maureen Stapleton understands and projects, tho its furies are at the moment beyond her grasp. Eli Wallach is mercilessly honest and pungently amusing as the clown come wooing—sometimes, it seems, on the "Streetcar" that rode Marlon Brando to fame.

SAILOR ACTED REMARKABLY. Don Murray is remarkable as the sailor, Phyliss Love has the qualities for the daughter when she doesn't force, and there are interesting performances by Ludmilla Toretzka as herself, Eddie Hyans as a bully of a soft spoken salesman, Sonia Sorel as a predatory female, and Jane Hoffman and Florence Sundstrom as a couple of deep south floozies.

Boris Aronson's single setting is attractive and workable, and David Diamond's music lurks almost mournfully on the fringes of hearing. But Daniel Mann's job of direction, like Mr. Williams' job of rewriting, is only partly done. The stage is too cluttered, too noisy, too disturbed by the irrelevant. The cackling hag with the evil eye is all wrong—compare her with the haggard apparition of the flowers of death in "A Streetcar Named Desire." For tho Mr. Williams can write amusingly for the stage, he has an indelible talent for the macabre in despair. In the new play the woman who orders the rose silk shirt drops a black veil as she departs. In that veil, a double edged symbol of grief, a play-acting little girl wraps herself to mourn her father. You will find no more revealing gesture in "The Rose Tattoo."

By 1950, Tennessee Williams was back in Chicago, trying out another new play: "The Rose Tattoo," starring Maureen Stapleton as the play's central character, a hot-blooded widow. The role initially had been written for the Italian actress Anna Magnani, who turned it down; Stapleton was an unusual choice.

Invariably at her best when writing about Williams, Cassidy gave the work a mixed but affectionate review. There is here a great tenderness in her writing, belying her reputation. Clearly, she felt a palpable connection to Williams's poetry. "Mr. Williams," she writes, rather beautifully, "was never a playwright to reach for apples in a garden canopied with stars." That said, she further displays her innate understanding of the fragility and weaknesses of his plays: she calls this early version "incomplete, inconclusive, and at times exasperating." After Cassidy's review came out, Williams changed the ending of the play.

Over at the *Daily News*, Sydney Harris did not share Cassidy's enthusiasm for "The Rose Tattoo," arguing that comedy in the play did not gel with the more weighty themes. Williams did not appreciate that. "He did not seem to realize that *was* a serious play treated with humor," the playwright wrote in a letter penned to his mother and grandfather from the Sherman House. He also used that occasion to complain about Chicago's winter weather.

This review makes clear that Cassidy was no prude. After its premiere in Chicago, "The Rose Tattoo" would open in New York in February 1951, and many of that city's critics found Williams's intentions with the play prurient. George Jean Nathan called it Williams's "latest peepshow." Others were kinder. Back in Chicago, Cassidy saw, and wrote eloquently of, its flawed beauty.

Magnani would go on to win an Academy Award for the Stapleton role in the subsequent Daniel Mann movie.

40

ACTOR KEANE SPEAKS UP; ASSAILS TRIBUNE CRITIC

JANUARY 26, 1951. An actor turned the tables yesterday and hurled a few sharp barbs at a critic. His performance was so spirited that members of the Chicago Drama league found it almost as diverting as the show in which he appears—"South Pacific."

Robert Emmett Keane, who plays Capt. George Brackett in the Rodgers and Hammerstein musical, was the actor. His target was Claudia Cassidy, music and drama critic of THE TRIBUNE. The setting was a breakfast in the Blackstone hotel given by the Drama League for the cast of the play. Several hundred women members of the league overflowed the ballroom and filled the balcony.

Keane plunged into his heated and heartfelt criticism of Miss Cassidy as soon as he was introduced by Toastmaster William Montgomery McGovern, Northwestern university professor and writer.

"The reason there are so few plays running in Chicago now, where there used to be a dozen dramas and half a dozen musical comedies 20 years ago, is due entirely to one vitriolic woman," he declared.

"She pours sulphuric acid over every new show which is brought to Chicago, and she scares away from the city the management of every decent show which is produced in New York each season."

The actor now had one of the most attentive audiences he ever faced. There was some buzzing around the room from women who were saying, "He must mean Claudia," and there was applause. Then there was silence as ears were strained to hear what was coming next.

"I don't know exactly what the Drama league's purpose is," Keane went on, "but I'll tell you one thing you can do to help the theater. There is only one way to handle a woman like that and only a woman can do it."

◠◠◠

The way to "clip the wings of Claudia Cassidy," said Keane is to write to THE TRIBUNE and to have your "rich husbands with influence" write to protest her appraisal of theatrical and musical fare.

Keane paused for breath while his audience tittered and applauded his performance.

"Or, since you all love drama and drama connotes romance, why don't you make yourselves matchmakers and get Miss Cassidy married?"

This sally fell flat. A director of the league informed Keane that Miss Cassidy is married.

The actor recovered quickly. "Well, then," he said, "why not have her divorced and get her married to Westbrook Pegler?"

With an actor's sense of timing, Ke[a]ne sat down while the audience was still laughing. The women, it was plain, considered Keane's performance a great show, tho some who had read Miss Cassidy's review when the show opened last November might have been surprised by his bitterness.

◠◠◠

The critic had made some comments on the performances of some members of the cast, but Keane's had been neither praised nor condemned. His name was printed only among the cast of characters.

Richard Eastham, the star of the show, who had been described by The Tribune critic as "no man of the world to sweep a girl off her feet" and a "pleasant man with a good rich voice," also spoke.

"I am a milder man than my cohort, Mr. Keane," he said, "even tho I came off worse in the review of 'South Pacific' than he did. I am a firm believer that the reviewer is entitled to his opinion any time, anywhere, and any place, and that it should be published as such."

He was interrupted by applause, including some from the table where other members of the cast and their wives were seated.

ᴖᴖᴖ

"I just would like to say that some reviewers are unfortunate in the way they put things—and I am not referring to any specific reviewer. I simply meant that sometimes a critic will say a man is bad when perhaps they mean to say he is not good in the part the reviewer is referring to."

Many members of the league who have not seen the show will be making judgments of their own the evening of April 10 and the matinee of April 11, when the league has arranged to attend the show as a body.

In this fascinating little curiosity from the *Tribune* in 1951, we see the newspaper report on a public attack on its own famous critic. The attacker was stage and screen actor Robert Emmett Keane–Capt. Brackett in the touring company of "South Pacific" that Claudia Cassidy had so brutally savaged. He decided to hit back, hard.

Keane was giving a breakfast talk at the Blackstone Hotel to the members of the Chicago Drama League, comprising mostly female theater and education supporters (the league would last until 2012, when it disbanded). It sounds as though Keane tried to attack Cassidy without actually mentioning her name, but his audience quickly grasped his target (the notion of people whispering "Claudia" sounds dead-on; all of Cassidy's readers seemed to have referred to her by first name only).

Keane doesn't stop with his clearly sexist assault: as the unnamed *Tribune* reporter quotes him, "There is only one way to handle a woman like that and only a woman can do it." The mind boggles, but what Keane apparently meant was to encourage the assembled women to have their "rich husbands with influence" write to the *Tribune* in an effort to get rid of Cassidy. Yet more scandalously, he alternately suggests that they marry her off. Actually, Cassidy already was married–William J. Crawford was her husband for 57 years (he died in 1986).

Keane did not win out with these attacks tailored to a powerful woman critic. Cassidy didn't go anywhere for a long time. And Keane? Although he'd been in Laurel and Hardy movies in the 1940s (playing a con man, one of his regular movie types), he didn't do much on stage or screen after this date with the Chicago Drama League. Long married to actress Claire Whitney, he died in 1981.

Cassidy would outlast him. And she was unbowed in making her continual demands that Chicago deserved the best.

41

WILLIAMS AND MIELZINER MAKE SOME THEATER SUGGESTIONS

PLAYWRIGHT, DESIGNER SHARE AVERSION TO RUNDOWN SHOW

BY CLAUDIA CASSIDY

APRIL 22, 1951. For every fatuous bore or crude opportunist who clutters the theater scene by assuming that his lack of taste is your own, there is a crucified talent as well as an outraged audience. When I sat with mounting disgust thru as much as I could take of the debased version of "A Streetcar Named Desire" recently at the Harris, I felt less sorry for myself than for Tennessee Williams that his powerful and poignant play had been so cheaply distorted, and for Jo Mielziner that his wonderfully imaginative setting and lighting had been reduced to a mangy mess. I might not have been so generous had I known then that the whole distasteful muddle was parading praise I among others had chosen with care to do the blazing original credit.

Such a fiasco carries formidable repercussions. The more perceptive the audience, the more violent the revulsion. Admitting that this was a horrible example of the deterioration of once spellbinding theater, the fact remains that the exception today is the touring production that recreates and sustains the quality of the original. What to do about it is a major topic of serious theater conversation. Apropos of the "Streetcar" disaster, Mr. Mielziner and Mr. Williams have made their own suggestions. Read them and see what you think.

Discussing "the inadequacy of some New York productions playing Chicago," Mr. Mielziner writes, "This is a subject that has been as painful to me over a number of years as it has been to you. Since you have the courage to bring the subject to the country's attention, I would like to have you know that there are some managers, directors, and designers here in New York who are attempting to use constructive and creative methods of meeting the problems of touring.

"There is no question about the fact that road conditions make the touring of the average large productions economically impossible. The usual approach to preparing a production for a road tour, as you so well pointed out, is to literally put an axe to a delicate fabric with precious little discrimination. This technique is like buying a magnificent Christmas tree and finding that two feet must be eliminated in order to stand the tree up, so two feet are hacked off straight thru the trunk right at the top.

"I have always had the theory that it is not only truer to the tradition of good theater but in the end sounder economically to start from scratch and find a tree perhaps less tall and not so wide in its spread, but that can stand as a complete and beautiful tree to serve its purpose within the limitations of the ceiling height.

"This is not just a cry in the wilderness from a designer who has so often suffered from road amputations. I want you to know of a meeting called last week in New York by Kermit Bloomgarden. He invited the author, Arthur Miller, the director, Elia Kazan, and this designer. The subject of our conference was how can we send out a company of 'Death of a Salesman' which can not only play small towns (sometimes under woefully inadequate conditions) but even high school auditoriums and whistle stops where you have perhaps a maximum of four hours available to set up the production.

"There was no intention at this meeting of taking a complex and well thought out production scheme and putting an axe to any part of it. On the contrary, we started out with the following premise: What are the essential values in this play that must be protected if a vital scene or piece of business is impossible to carry out because of touring limitations? It was agreed that certain elements in the present script (such as the boys disappearing from the beds in the attic room) could only be solved with rewriting by the author, restaging by the director and redesigning by the scene designer.

“In other words, we started from scratch. It remains to be seen how successful we will be, but at least here is a management that is tackling the problem from a healthy point of view, yet determined to give the maximum effectiveness to this play despite road conditions. The same constructive attitude governed our thinking on the question of the most demanding and elaborate lighting problems.

“Please believe that I am not writing this in any spirit other than saying ‘Amen, I agree with you’ but here thank goodness are some serious people in the theater who are trying to meet this problem with taste and integrity.”

Tennessee Williams states his own point of view: “I am second to no one, not even to you, in my detestation and horror of bad road shows, particularly of my own plays. I haven’t seen the present touring company of ‘Streetcar,’ have been spared that. But I saw the Pauline Lord company of ‘Menagerie,’ and it was one of the nightmares of my professional life, which is, I suppose, my real life. It must have taken five years off her life, just as a failure in the theater takes five or probably 10 years off the life of a playwright. I can’t even stand to see first string companies doing my plays after a year or more, when the fire is gone and it has turned to habit.

“Long runs are a sort of artistic abomination. The only cure is a decentralized theater. So that plays can be done freshly, all over again, off Broadway, in place after place, each time created brand new. Why don’t you take the stump for it in Chicago? No better place on earth! Second companies, tired companies, underpaid and exhausted companies, cynically slipshod companies will debase and exhaust our American theater until the great cities can support their own fully professional legitimate theaters which they take at least as seriously as their museums, symphony orchestras, colleges or zoos. So far Dallas and Houston, with their highly successful theaters-in-the-round, have pointed the way, but the enterprise in those cities is still hardly more than semiprofessional and not yet important or influential enough to challenge the present system.

"Now as for second companies. One must be fair about them. Very often the players are gifted and they are nearly always sincere. It is their managements, usually, that are to blame. All they care about in some cases is scraping the bottom of the box office barrel. Furthermore, it is often these touring shows that keeps a playwright solvent between his new productions and after his taxes. And altho I am as unable as you to stomach bad performances of good plays, the patience, the forbearance and sympathy of audiences always amazes me. No matter how badly a play is performed, there are people who get something out of it if it has something to give.

"I hope and pray that you will take up the cause of a great new theater center in Chicago, passionately and eloquently . . ."

Not without eloquence and passion themselves, these spokesmen. Shall we see what we can do to help?

After the previous attack, Cassidy bided her time. But three months later, she published the letters of a couple of her famous defenders—Tennessee Williams and Jo Mielziner—who had applauded her stance on shoddy touring shows. Williams had good reason to return Cassidy's favor, of course, and a vested ongoing interest in doing so. Still, it's notable how many of these complaints about touring productions have remained current. It's also amusing to read about Williams going after tours of his own shows (he reveals he had not even seen the latest tour of "A Streetcar Named Desire" that sparked this piece).

But that's not the only reason this is perhaps the most important piece of writing in this book.

For Williams also tells Cassidy to "take the stump" for a decentralized theater—in other words, for Chicago to build its own theater and stage its own world-class productions ("a theater of our own," as Richard Christiansen, one of Cassidy's successors, would put it years later).

"No better place on earth," Williams writes of Chicago as a potential theater capital (he makes no mention of the weather, as was his wont). "I hope and pray that you will take up the cause of a great new theater center in Chicago, passionately and eloquently."

As we will see, Cassidy started doing precisely that in the years to follow, with tangible results. Here, she implies that Williams set her to the task.

So, behold a real find. Maybe it was Tennessee Williams, as much as anyone, whom the homegrown Chicago theater has to thank for its own existence. Cassidy just had to run a few more of the pretenders out of town.

42

THE FIG LEAF

SOME HAPLESS ACTORS BOOBYTRAPPED IN "THE FIG LEAF" AT THE SELWYN

Selwyn Theatre

BY CLAUDIA CASSIDY

CAST

Fred McCall .... Ernest Truex
Carrie McCall .... Sylvia Field
Carmen Cassidy .... Sally Moffet
Donald Duffy .... James Costigan
Harold Hillstover .... James Leo
Heidi McCall .... Barbara Bolton
George (Bink) Binkley .... Clifford Cothren

OCTOBER 9, 1952. Odd how some of the sillier shows pull themselves together long enough to write their own relatively trenchant obituaries. About midway of "The Fig Leaf's" opening in the Selwyn last night an athletic housemaid named Carmen Cassidy demanded, "Boy, O, Boy, how childish can you get?" This was a libel on children, except perhaps the kind that scrawl on the back fence, but at least it detected a grain of immaturity in a distasteful bore masquerading as domestic comedy.

The authors have put their faith and all their boorishness, which is considerable, into what is known in hack circles as "the twist." You can see them sitting in their little smoke filled room without an idea to their collaborating names, then one of them chortles, "I've got it! Usually it's the fellow who gets the girl in trouble and then won't marry her. Let's give it a twist and turn it the other way 'round."

One twist, of course, leads to another. It turns out the girl isn't going to have the baby, after all, the doctor just got mixed up—and here the medical profession gets a break, because in the summer theater tryout the clown was just having his little joke to get those nice young people together. The title comes from the idea that women are so forward nowadays you really need the fig leaf to tell men and women apart. What the authors forgot is that on the stage you have to know robots from people.

At such a fiasco I sympathize with the actors even more than with the audience, tho they get paid while the customers shell out hard cash. My theory is that audiences can leave if they like, letting off steam in transit, while hapless actors in such ineptitude are boobytrapped. In the case of "The Fig Leaf" at least three of them fought back and now and then made a point of their own. One, of course, was Ernest Truex. Mr. Truex is a person, an amusing, likable comedian, tho his so-called play crosses him at every turn. Mr. Cothren has a lean lankiness, a touch of Lincolnian rue, that might do the theater a good turn. As for Mr. Costigan's timing, it seems natural. It can almost keep you from noticing what he has to say.

Even as Cassidy took up the mantle for a homegrown Chicago theater, she still was professionally bound to review the New York (or New York–bound) flops. And she surely entertained along the way. Here's a witty pan for "The Fig Leaf," a tryout that Cassidy ensured never made it to Broadway. Here, she muses on who has it worse at such shows—the paying customers or the trapped actors. We can also see a fine example of one of Cassidy's frequent tricks: using a line or two from the show to hoist it on its own petard.

43

GIGI

AUDREY HEPBURN'S BEGUILING 'GIGI' HAS THE MILLER CACHET AT THE HARRIS

Harris Theater

BY CLAUDIA CASSIDY

CAST

Gigi	Audrey Hepburn
Mme. Alvarez	Josephine Brown
Andree	Doris Patston
Gaston Lachaille	Michael Evans
Victor	Ronald Telfer
Alicia de St. Ephiam	Margaret Bannerman
Sidonie	Bertha Belmore

NOVEMBER 6, 1952. Time was when the Gilbert Miller cachet meant something in Chicago playgoing. How nice for time to repeat itself. For Mr. Miller has sent, indeed, has brought us his "Gigi," a kind of Gallic Cinderella in reverse, a girl who, in a manner of speaking, prefers the pumpkin coach to the glass slipper of the not unreasonably confused Prince Charming, who is prepared to deal on Aunt Alicia's canny courtesan terms in a munificence of carats, only to find himself offering a wedding band. The play is Colette's "Gigi," adapted by Anita Loos, gaily staged in Raymond Sovey's amusing settings, the whole given a turn of the century whirl in a glimmer of painted gauze curtains and hurdy gurdy waltzes to set off Audrey Hepburn of the winged face and the great dark eyes.

"Gigi," please, is just for fun. It isn't above popping champagne corks for comedy, breaking eggs and dishes, showing a female of the period in her corsets, or another of slightly equine aspect being arch with that brand new instrument, the telephone. But it is at its shrewdest in comedy of character, and one of the funniest scenes in seasons is that in which Aunt Alicia instructs Gigi in the way a cocotte worth her keep should feather her jewel box. Does it have a moral? Well, I wouldn't be sure about it. Gigi, of course, gets more by refusing less, but then she is no trend, she is, quite uniquely and delectably, Gigi.

And there you have, in Miller terms, a Machiavellian maneuver. As I remember it, when the comedy opened in New York the Hepburn name was all ready to go up in lights, only it didn't until next morning when it seemed the public, not the producer, had made her a star. Such decry, such stardom. I just say that without her there might be no "Gigi." She gives it point and focus and heart. She is fresh and honest, but even in middy and cotton stockings she is undeniably alluring. When she tells her young man she loves him, you think, why how nice for him, she really does.

So that is why it ticks, this tale of Parisian cocottes of more or less renown—Grandma who fell discreetly in love, Mama who did it indiscreetly and so wound up singing bits at the Comique, and Aunt Alicia, who feathered her bijou nest—all teaching Gigi the way she should go in cajoling Gaston from games of piquet and gifts of licorice strings to jewels and cars and a house of her own. You have to believe that in their way they are eminently respectable, that Gigi is more strictly brought up than most girls, tho she knows more, too, and you have to believe that Gigi and her Gaston really fall in love. Because of this special Gigi, you do.

So it is a charmer, this light hearted little play with an undercurrent of rue and an edge of satire—and note how the settings act, from Grandma's bourgeois red plush to Aunt Alicia's pseudo elegance with no real place to sit down. Most of the cast is unchanged, the major change being Margaret Bannerman, not as clinically perfect as Cathleen Nesbitt's Aunt Alicia, but knowing her way around. Michael Evans' Gaston is as right as the Hepburn Gigi, Doris Patston and Bertha Belmore seemed to me to have improved, and Josephine Brown to be giving more than her usual bounce to an already bravura role.

Audrey Hepburn did not do many shows in Chicago. But she did come to Chicago with "Gigi,' which had opened (and closed) on Broadway the previous year. At the time of this review of the tour, Hepburn was just 23 (this was some nine years before the movie "Breakfast at Tiffany's."). According to Hepburn's biographer, Martin Gitlin, she spent this Chicago engagement with her fiancé James Hanson. By the time "Gigi" left town, the couple was kaput. At the end of this short tour, Hepburn made the movie "Roman Holiday."

"Audrey Hepburn of the winged face," Claudia Cassidy writes admiringly of a young woman on the very edge of colossal stardom with her "great dark eyes." And the great, dark J. J. Shubert? He was about to declare war on the *Tribune* critic.

44

PRODUCER TAKES ISSUE ON HOW PLAYS SHOULD BE WELCOMED

J. J. SHUBERT, OF SHOWS OF SAME NAME, VIEWS CHICAGO FUTURE GRIMLY

BY CLAUDIA CASSIDY

MARCH 29, 1953. Harbinger of a fresh outbreak in his personal war on critics is this letter from J. J. Shubert, who followed it with orders to his Chicago staff that reviewers were to attend the second, not the first, night of "Affairs of State," opening Wednesday at the Selwyn theater. Mr. Shubert begins the letter by saying that while on "one of the leading newspapers of the country" I have "unfavorably criticized all of the plays that have come to Chicago," and he continues:

"In reading the criticism of 'Paint Your Wagon,' I think it was very unfair because you do not seem to take into consideration the hardship of trying to get ready for a play in the very short amount of time that it takes to place it on the stage for presentation. The company arrived Sunday night, the equipment for the show arrived from the baggage cars on Monday, and to get ready for a performance with stagehands who have never seen the play makes it almost impossible to give performances without some unforeseen things that might happen to the scenery, lighting, and equipment. You find fault because they are not perfect as plays that are being given in New York where they prepare a play for a week or more to get everything ready for a performance. On a tour the unfortunate part is that they have to get ready for a performance without this preparation. We have to contend with all various trade unions that are now incorporated in the producing of a play. The producer has got to pay everybody from actors to all stagehands in every department so it is impossible for them to lay off unless some unforeseen accident would happen.

"I bring this forth because you only write what you see and hear. That might be true but at least a little consideration should be shown during a first-night performance where there has been so little time to get everything running smoothly. It has been very hard to get enough shows to keep the theaters open and besides we cannot get the producers to go to Chicago and produce new plays. Practically all the producers avoid Chicago until the very end of their tour in the Midwest for fear that you will do them such serious damage because of The Tribune's vast circulation in many of the surrounding states. 'Paint Your Wagon' bookings reflected this and they only played Chicago at our urging. We had to furnish the bond money for the actors and for all other trade unions in the theater to induce them to go to Chicago. And, what they feared took place—the show had to close there in one week.

"The producers' arguments are as follows: We cannot afford to go on and have our plays criticized by the leading newspaper in Chicago because it hurts the surrounding territory. People have gotten into the habit of looking at the criticism of shows that would open in Chicago, and it would hurt all the larger cities adjacent to Chicago, and it would hurt our tour in such cities as Columbus, Detroit, Toronto, Cleveland, Pittsburgh, Washington, Philadelphia, Boston, and all other smaller cities.

"I do not think it is your intention to close up plays and I know that you are not antagonistic, but the practice in Chicago has not helped having bad criticisms. We have tried very hard, giving the producers all sorts of arguments and in some cases having to guarantee them against a loss to come and play Chicago. You have not been very kind to plays. As a rule there is always something lacking in your criticism to make people go to the legitimate theater.

"As you know, we are not newcomers in Chicago. We have been there for over 50 years or more, and at one time or another we were in charge of practically all the legitimate theaters. We are not in the moving picture business. We have given everything we possibly could to Chicago in the way of entertainment in the legitimate theater, and I really think a little more consideration would help us get the plays for Chicago and might get them to open there. Your criticism affects the attendance and you cannot run any kind of a business without customers. The theater seems to be the only business that is attacked. This form should have been abolished many years ago, because no other business suffers as much as the theater. When the public is informed that a play is not of any value, naturally they will not go. There is hardly any criticism of any department store of what they sell, but I think that anything that smacks of artistry is always subject to attack. As I stated, I think the system is obsolete. Of any business of any kind, the theater is the only one picked out for praise or attack.

◠ ◠ ◠

"I would gladly be in favor of leaving it to the public themselves without having self-appointed specialists stating whether or not a play is worth seeing. We advertise in newspapers like any other shopkeeper and the only thing we sell is entertainment. It seems to have pleased practically every critic more or less but yourself.

"I can only see one thing that might alleviate the situation—openings in Chicago should be for the public, and the people writing for the newspapers should see the play on Tuesday nights instead of Monday nights. Monday should be for the opening—wherein anything happening could be rectified then, so the specialists of the theater who have to write for same should see that we do not have a repetition of 'Paint Your Wagon.'

◠ ◠ ◠

"Very few producers have large bankrolls and since you have criticized on various occasions about new plays not being produced in Chicago, a little kinder treatment to them might induce some to make Chicago their opening night. All the producers seem to fear your dislike of plays, and it is a risk they do not care to take. I think you should know the situation. They seem to fear the condemnation of a new play and it does not help the theatergoing public and the surrounding territories adjacent to Chicago.

"I hope you will take this letter in the spirit in which it is written because I know the reason for not getting plays produced in Chicago. If your interest lies within the spirit in which it is written, I think the theatergoing public will profit by same."

By 1953, no lesser personage than producer and theater owner J. J. Shubert was assailing Cassidy for her savage reviews of his touring shows. In this Cassidy piece, the unbowed critic uses Shubert's own letter to give him his say in print. She likely was delighted to do so; there is no better evidence anywhere of her own power.

Shubert's words here are a very telling indication of Cassidy's huge impact (for the worse, he thought) by the early 1950s—not just in Chicago but across the entire Midwest, where she was widely read, even in this pre-Internet age. He argues that her standards are hurting his ability to bring shows to Chicago, and that tours are now avoiding the city until the last possible moment, if only as a way to counter the likelihood of a Cassidy pan that could kill all business for miles around. Apparently, her damning review would end a show in Washington, DC, and Toronto as well as Chicago. So says the man who should know.

Shubert here talks as a booking agent and a landlord—he has to deal, he says, with legions of producers who were terrified of Cassidy and thus hated going anywhere near Chicago. This was clearly hurting Shubert's bottom line—he says that he basically has to cover producers' potential losses to get them to go anywhere near Chicago. In essence, he is asking Cassidy to be kinder. And he asks at great length, citing (as producers frequently did and do) his own advertising in the *Tribune*.

Interestingly, the practice of critics attending the second night of touring productions that Shubert was trying to (punitively?) put into place—and that Cassidy was apparently resisting with such fervor—is now commonplace in Chicago. Critics have given in. Or maybe they are just more reasonable.

Cassidy never says whether she asked Shubert for permission to print what seems to have been a personal letter. It's hard to imagine she bothered to ask. But increasingly, Chicago theater was becoming less dependent on the likes of Shubert.

THE COMING OF BILDAD

'BILDAD' YIELDS A GLEAM TO LOTS OF TIME AND PLENTY OF PATIENCE

Playwrights Theatre Club

BY CLAUDIA CASSIDY

CAST

Bildad .... Eugene Troobnick
Peleg .... Paul Sills
Jered .... Owen Canliffe
Friend .... Bob Michaels
Marta .... Joy Grodzins

Brother Thomas .... Edward Asner
Brother John .... Thomas Erhart
Brother Samuel .... Creighton Clarke
Street Vendors .... Zohra Alton, Estelle Luttrell
Anora .... Jean Mowry

AUGUST 20, 1953. Having cast himself as Peleg, the handy man to Bildad's holy man, the Sancho Panza to Don Quixote, the Leporello to Don Giovanni, Paul Sills has a lot of time these nights at the Playwrights Theater club to listen to his play, "The Coming of Bildad." He must have discovered at once that in performance it is discursive, diffuse, and, taken in a lump, dull. But he must have sensed in that lump the nugget of what he tried to create, for even the outsider with patience now and then caught its gleam.

In the little upstairs theater, whose audience is as deafening in response as the actors in attack, Mr. Sills has really shot the theatrical works. He has tried to write in one sweeping gesture a whimsical, satirical, poetical allegory, with his feet on the ground and his head in the stars, strewing the air with the casuistic, the equivocal, and the metaphorical with Roman candle redundance. But his play has an air of exuberance, tho it exhausts your indulgence, it has a streak of imagination, moments of wildly amusing nonsense, moments of coming out from behind that falseface with something touching and true to say.

⁂

Bildad and Peleg are hoboes on the make, with the take invariably jeopardized by Bildad's unfortunate talent for speaking the truth at the wrong time. At their newest stop he determines to reform, and does his best to be the town's moral adviser on true con man terms of joining the elders in their hypocritical alliance against the young. But Bildad is a schizophrenic, torn between love and love of glory, and when it comes time to prosecute the boy who says he did not unlock the gate to get to the girl, Bildad is at once prosecuting attorney, defense attorney, and the private citizen who unlocked the gate himself. You can't tear even a schizophrenic that many ways, so Bildad and Peleg go on their way, to figure out another racket.

⁂

Bildad, tho he talks more than mortal can bear, is an interesting fellow who can cozen the populace or beg a radish for his love from the Hogarthian troll played with gusto by Zohra Alton. The boy and girl (Owen Canliffe and Joy Grodzins) have the reality of the young in a dream, as if they never doubted what is true. The elders are caricatures in writing, direction and performance, the worst kind of amateur card stacking to destroy every scene they play.

Altogether, this is a queer hodgepodge, but it has those gleams of promise, and those outbursts of wild exuberance that spill over the edges and strain the theater's seams. It makes me wish Mr. Sills good luck.

Even though she railed against shoddy tours, Cassidy did not always do the best job of actually attending homegrown Chicago theater once it started cropping up. For one thing, her plate was full with opera, music and theater, especially since she spent several months of the year in Europe. For another, we can see in her writing some disdain for "amateur" (often a synonym for "local") artists; that prejudice would not disappear until the era of Richard Christiansen, when those local artists surely could not be called amateur anymore.

But here's a crucially important review by Cassidy of a pivotal local arts group—the Playwrights Theatre Club. The 25-year-old playwright, Paul Sills, was the son of Viola Spolin, known for her development of acting exercises she called Theater Games. He was also the founder of the Second City, an event that still was six years off. Few would do more for Chicago theater than Sills, who died in 2008 at the age of 80.

Sills had emerged at the University of Chicago in concert with such actors as Mike Nichols, Elaine May, Sheldon Patinkin and David Shepherd (the director of the show Cassidy reviews here), all pioneers in making Chicago the global center of improvisation and sketch comedy. But that was still many years away in 1953 (even the Compass Players did not emerge until 1955). This little theater at 1560 N. LaSalle St. (the former home of a Chinese restaurant) featured some formidable actors—Ed Asner is in the cast list printed here, along with Eugene Troobnick, another improv pioneer. Other shows featured Nichols and Barbara Harris, who would marry Sills. Bernie Sahlins also joined the group, which lasted only two years.

But by 1953, the Chicago theater revolution was under way. And what did Cassidy make of "The Coming of Bildad," which has receded now into history? Not much. She calls it "a queer hodgepodge." But there is encouragement in many of her other words. We can sense her excitement at being in an intimate theater where the audience really can be heard.

It would be overstating the subtext of this review to say that Cassidy saw a movement coming, the very movement that Tennessee Williams had encouraged her to champion, but it most surely was in the air. And she takes the time to wish Sills well. This review represents an endorsement of his future, at the very least.

By 1955, the Playwrights Theatre Club was gone, shut down by the Chicago Fire Department using tough regulations established in the aftermath of the Iroquois Theater fire. In the end, Chicago's theatrical past got in the way of its future.

Temporarily.

46

THE CHILDREN'S HOUR

HELLMAN'S STRONG, UNSPARING, ANGRY PLAY OPENS AT THE HARRIS

Harris Theater

BY CLAUDIA CASSIDY

CAST

Peggy Rogers.. Sandra March
Catherine .... Nancy Plehn
Lois Fisher .... Carol Sinclair
Mrs. Lily Mortar.................................... Mary Finney
Evelyn Munn .... Mary Lee Dearring
Helen Burton .... Carolyn Rosser
Rosalie Wells.. Lynn Thatcher
Mary Tilford .... Iris Mann
Karen Wright.. Priscilla Gillette
Martha Dobie.. Patricia Neal
Dr. Joseph Cardin .... Theodore Newton
Agatha.. Edna Courtleigh
Mrs. Amelia Tilford................................ Fay Bainter
A Grocery Boy.. Gordon Russell

NOVEMBER 10, 1953. It is hard to see how the censorial mind could hang the tags indecent or obscene on Lillian Hellman's "The Children's Hour," which moved into the Harris theater last night and held its audience in the grip of serious, undivided attention. This was true 20 years ago when the play was new, and that basic fact has not changed in Kermit Bloomgarden's revival. What has stirred up the most commotion in provincial minds is that the plot hinges on the accusation of unnatural affection between two women school teachers. But the point of this strong, unsparing, angry play is the effect of that lie on the lives within its orbit. Then why this particular lie? Because, I think Miss Hellman might tell you, the uglier the lie the more vicious its consequences. It was a fact in Scotland, this story. Here it is absorbing, tragic theater, and to say it is not for children is to be redundant.

In a highly respectable, more than a little snobbish, community Karen Wright and Martha Dobie have a school for girls. Karen is engaged to marry Dr. Cardin, whose aunt, Mrs. Tilford, is their patroness and has made them the dubious gift of her granddaughter, Mary, as a pupil. Mary is a horrible child, a congenital liar, wise beyond her years, cruel, cunning, unspeakably vicious. Out of a desire for revenge at fancied wrongs, the overheard remarks of Martha's malicious aunt, and her own hold over the other girls, including childish blackmail, she conjures from hints, innuendo, and the refuge of hysteria the story her grandmother takes as truth. By the time Mrs. Tilford tries to make amends, the school is closed, Karen is deserted, and Martha is dead by her own hand.

Cheaply handled, this could be the most lurid melodrama. But Miss Hellman is not a cheap playwright. What interests her is the motivation of the lie, the ease with which public opinion is manipulated on a hush hush subject, and the desert of doubt in which even the most loyal are left stranded. The frozen rejection with which Mrs. Tilford faces the accused women is one facet of public opinion, the prurient probing of the boy with the box of groceries is another. But the desert holds the doctor, who wants to go away with Karen and try to forget, because a grain of doubt chokes him, and it holds Martha, who destroys herself in the terror of self-doubt. The loneliness is like a room whose walls shrink. In the end there are two castoffs, Karen the destroyed and Mrs. Tilford the destroyer.

◠ ◠ ◠

This is not a pretty play, but it is an absorbing one, especially in the first act of motivation and the third act of consequences. The second act of accusation is oddly weak both in writing and performance, except for Iris Mann's feline cunning as the child and Lynn Thatcher's little girl terror as Rosalie, her victim. The others are just standing on the stage, saying lines as written. They are as unreal as the makeshift stage setting.

But this is the exception. In the schoolroom, a real room, these are real people. Patricia Neal of the striking, slightly gaunt, good looks, the deep voice, the streak of boyish humor. Priscilla Gillette, plumper than before, and touched with candor. Mary Finney as the silly, malicious Lily Mortar. Theodore Newton as the doctor. Fay Bainter as Mrs. Tilford, tho I don't think fond grandmamas simultaneously acknowledge audiences and the arrival of grandchildren. But Iris Mann is not to be defeated by a scene or a setting. From curtain to curtain, even when she has left the stage, this is the vixen child's play.

In 1936, The Theatre Guild announced plans to bring to Chicago "The Children's Hour," the scandalous lesbian-themed drama that had catapulted the 29-year-old Lillian Hellman to fame. But on September 4, 1936, the *Tribune* reported that the guild had told the paper that city officials had informed it that "the city administration would not sanction performances of the drama here." The paper also said that the movie version had been shown in Chicago, but with "the questionable aspects of the story removed," which must have left virtually nothing behind. Thereafter, the word was that "The Children's Hour" had been banned, as has been the case in Boston. The play was announced, but it never arrived. Its first production in Chicago did not take place until 1940, when it was produced by a local group, the Actors Company of Chicago.

The city had changed a lot in two decades—with Claudia Cassidy leading its growing cultural sophistication. But it's still a reasonable assumption that "The Children's Hour" remained controversial in 1953. Cassidy carefully prepared her readers for the play, writing in a preview article that its prior censorship had been "misguided," explaining how the play was based on a real court case, and pronouncing the work "a landmark in the American theater." And in this passionate opening-night review, one of her best, she throws her weight behind it.

Cassidy certainly dodges the word *lesbian*, substituting "unnatural affection" in her lead, so we could certainly argue that her support was muted, politically at least. Nonetheless, she calls the work's detractors "provincial minds," surely an attempt to remind her readers that they would never want such an insult ascribed to them.

Cassidy saw real people in the play—one of her key criteria for praise. Her support packed the theater. She had some more dreams to share, too.

47

AMPLIFYING THEATER FOR CHICAGO PIECE, WITH SIGHTS ON THE MOON

BY CLAUDIA CASSIDY

JANUARY 9, 1955. "Make no small plans. They have no power to stir imagination." A Chicagoan once said that. His name was Daniel Burnham and I wish I had known him. For that was about what I had in mind a month ago when I wrote a hopeful piece about putting Chicago back on the theater map before we all expire of theatrical malnutrition. By this I meant to do in theater what Fritz Reiner and Artur Rodzinski before him did to restore the Chicago Symphony orchestra. What the Lyric Theater did to Chicago opera. That is, put Chicago on a par with the best anywhere, and give it an edge if possible. Why shoot at a lamp post when that is why they hang out the moon?

You might be surprised at some of the responses. How about foundation sponsored arena theaters in strategic neighborhoods? Go right ahead, but that's not what I am talking about. How about a midwest syndicate of touring shows? What sort of shows? Well, say a duplication of a recent Broadway failure, "The Tender Trap," with a couple of Hollywood nobodies brought in for "names"? Go right ahead, but that's not what I am talking about. Then how about a batch of stars, each to appear in a play of his own choice? Hmm—do go ahead, tho that's still not what I am talking about.

◠◠◠

The telephone also wanted to know if I have the backing all lined up, and if so, will I please hand over the names of the backers? It inquired whether or not a certain newspaper would be interested in going all out for such a project, and if a certain adjacent radio and television station would lead the band wagon? I'll tell you a secret. I haven't asked them. O, yes, and one more thing. Tactfully, of course. But if (a) there is such a project, and (b) I have the backers in my pocket, (c) how much of a hand do I want in running things? I'll tell you three secrets: (a) there isn't, (b) I don't, and (c) none. As Hugh Marlowe used to say in "The Voice of the Turtle," "I just want to get around and appreciate things."

I would appreciate helping, tho. That would be fun. For to repeat myself on a favorite topic, what we could create more of here is that receptive climate in which exciting things happen. See how it pays off? I'm not sure that anywhere else in the world today you could duplicate Beethoven's Fourth Concerto as Rudolf Serkin recently played it with Reiner in Orchestra hall. I'm positive that because the time was ripe and the climate right Maria Meneghini Callas came into her own in our Civic Opera house. The cumulative sequence of her Norma, her Violetta and her Lucia brought her talents into supreme focus, and no one knew it better than she did.

◠◠◠

You can never count on such results, but neither can you call them happy accidents. Say, rather, that when conditions are right they have the opportunity to happen. Conditions were right because a few people with imagination, courage, and persistence refused to take no for a dusty answer. When the town let Rodzinski go in the face of his marvelous "Tristan" with Flagstad, some gave up in disgust. Others hung on, and in the long run they won. We now have two major musical assets. The Chicago Symphony orchestra is 64 years old, endowed with a rich heritage, some of it in seven figure cash. The Lyric Theater is a year old and not endowed at all. Except with talent, opportunity, and a backlog of 19 performances remarkable enough to stir up local excitement, echoes of international renown, and a surprising sensitivity in some venerable quarters suddenly on the defensive.

In all this, how does theater fit? In precisely the same fashion. Why should we make small plans when outsiders make so many of them for us? Why not shoot the moon, with that same imagination, courage, and persistence? What moon? Well, let's be specific.

In the concert hall and the opera house we cherish the classics. They are the backlog of the repertory from which all else develops, including talent and taste. Yet we keep the classic theater on the shelf and cheat ourselves out of our theatrical eyeteeth. For by classic theater I don't mean the academic approach. I mean theater of glamour, brilliance, and style, in which actors test their mettle against the great roles, in which audiences are swept out of themselves by the great plays. From such roots something live, stimulating, and exciting could grow. Inevitable sprouts would be new actors, new playwrights, new directors, and scenic artists, and not least, a new audience.

Ideally, we would have a superb new theater, or a fine old one superbly restored, and that would be the Auditorium. Big for plays, yes, but resonant enough to do the great plays justice. Ideally, too, such a stage could be hospitable to lyric theater. It could develop dancers and give musicians another door to something more rewarding than hack job frustration.

It would be a waste of time to consider any of this without certain flat stipulations. Ample endowment contributed as a long range investment in Chicago's future. First rate professionals who know their jobs to run it without amateur interference. No nonsense about "local talent" unless you can also say talent without saying local. Prices within reach of people not on expense accounts, and tickets at the box office (or on subscription) where they belong. Most of all, a magnetic stage. No other need apply.

If ever there was a manifesto for the creation of a vibrant theater in Chicago, this is that piece. Cassidy even begins with a quote from famed local architect and urban designer Daniel Burnham: "Make no small plans." And what are those plans? "Put Chicago on a par with the best anywhere, and give it an edge if possible." She draws here from her experience with the Lyric Opera, at this juncture just a year old, and with the Chicago Symphony Orchestra, which already had been playing for 64 years.

In 1955, when the regional-theater movement was still in its relative youth, Cassidy's inclination was toward a classic theater—this is just one of several pieces she wrote arguing that the Auditorium Theatre should be a home for the classics. By today's standards, the Auditorium would seem absurdly large for such a project, but Cassidy clearly just saw its size as increasing the scope of the event. She craved a "theater of glamour, brilliance and style," which is by no means the direction in which the local theater ultimately went, gritty Chicago never being quite the glamorous town that Cassidy, who spent a lot of time in European capitals, wished it would become. In this piece especially, we begin to discern the void between her tastes and the direction that the theater she covered was taking.

But even if her view of potentially great Chicago theater had a certain gilt-edged quality, Cassidy also wanted "new actors, new playwrights, new directors, and scenic artists, and not least, a new audience." Of course, she was in no way willing to compromise her famous standards, which is perhaps what she gave her city above all else.

"No nonsense about 'local talent,'" she writes here, "unless you can also say talent without saying local."

On April 1, 1955, Col. Robert McCormick, the man who had hired Cassidy and propelled her newspaper to its position of influence, died in his sleep. The *Tribune* dedicated seven and a half pages to recounting the life and times of its proprietor; it would never be able to replace the size or volume of his personality. A week later, Richard J. Daley was elected mayor of Chicago.

ANNIVERSARY WALTZ

NOT AS GOOD, OR EVEN WORSE, 'WALTZ' IS REVIVED AT THE BLACKSTONE

BY CLAUDIA CASSIDY

CAST

Millie .... Helen Martin
Okkie Walters.. Warren Berlinger
Alice Walters... Beverly Lawrence
Debbie Walters...................................... Mary Lee Dearring

Bud Walters	Jeffrey Lynn
Chris Steelman	Henry Beckman
Janice Revere	Charlene Lee
Harry	Sidney Mayer Jr.
Sam	Allen Herion
Mr. Gans	Steven Chase
Mrs. Gans	Virginia Morgan
Handyman	Jack Mathiesen

JANUARY 1, 1957. "Anniversary Waltz," a shoddy comedy with a vulgarly synthetic point of view, ran six weeks at the Harris last season under its original auspices, tho not with its original cast. New Years eve, a shoestring revival came to try its luck at the Blackstone. As I left the theater a young man at the door said, "I don't think it's as good as it was last year, do you?" That isn't precisely the way I would put it. I think it is even worse.

Moss Hart's casting and direction had at least a slick veneer of pace and farcical style. Despite Mr. Hart's startled repudiation of the Blackstone venture, its playbill carries the proud line, "Originally Directed by MOSS HART," and adds elsewhere, "Director of 'MY FAIR LADY.'"

This opens a whole new vista in billing. The Chicago Symphony orchestra can boast of certain symphonies, "Originally Directed by Beethoven." And "No Time for Sergeants" can brag, "Directed by Morton Da Costa," who had absolutely nothing to do with "Maid in the Ozarks."

If you missed "Anniversary Waltz" the first time, the plot need not detain you. At his 15th wedding anniversary a leering husband with too much to drink tells his horrible in-laws that it is in fact his 16th. He kicks in his second television set when his teen age daughter, a horror on her own account, telecasts the tidbit on Juvenile Jury. His wife is about to leave him when she finds out she is going to have a baby. Compound this with an intrusive maid and two leering delivery men from a local purveyor of television sets, duly plugged on each entrance. Call it repulsive domestic comedy, drably staged, with acting ranging from competent to embarrassing.

Perhaps the 9:30 show fared better than the one at 7, which was sparsely attended. But it isn't true that everyone there came on passes. I know for an incontrovertible fact that three tickets were sold, and at full, uncut boxoffice prices.

In this review, which sparked a lawsuit, we can positively feel the steam rising from the critic's pen. The main object of Cassidy's anger is the practice—then relatively new, now common—of directors handing off their work to associates and assistants, with the phrase "originally directed by" consequently going into the playbill. Cassidy condemns this practice as no more logical than the Chicago Symphony billing one of its performances as "originally directed by Beethoven." To some extent, this is just another of Cassidy's delicious pans. But there's also a note of increasing frustration creeping into her snark. Clearly, this was not the theater she wanted for Chicago. And for the record, a "a shoddy comedy with a vulgarly synthetic point of view" is a remarkably concise, terse and accurate way of condemning drivel, telling us all we need to know in ten words. It is vintage Cassidy.

The producers got no revenge in court. Judge Harry M. Fisher of the Circuit Court announced he was going to dismiss the suit with the words "I don't see how it is libel." The plaintiffs agreed to pay the defendants' costs.

49

LYSISTRATA

THIS MAY BE WORST 'LYSISTRATA' SINCE THE ATHENIAN PREMIERE

Studebaker Theatre

BY CLAUDIA CASSIDY

MARCH 13, 1957. Unlikely as it now seems, there may have been worse performances of "Lysistrata" than the Studebaker Theater company's last night. After all, much can happen in 2,368 or so years of even occasional performance, and a comedy about a sex strike to end war is bound to stir up trouble. The tale persists that Aristophanes had to leap into the title role at the Athenian premiere in 411 B.C. when his leading actor fled because he was afraid to play it. Women play women's roles now, and women are made of bolder stuff. Otherwise, Vicki Cummings would have fled that same title role well in advance of the Studebaker's 7 o'clock curtain.

Not, of course, for precisely the same reason. The Athenian presumably fled scandal. Miss Cummings might wisely have fled the monumental miscasting of a lifetime. In a sea of ineptitude she is a Gibraltar of disaster.

Handsomely clad in shades of pleated pink chiffon, with a large Greek knot tumbling from her blonde hair, her Lysistrata suggests a junior Mae West playing it straight. Her voice is nasal, her delivery has all the supple give and take of the steam roller, and her gestures are classic. That is, right arm out and down, left arm out and down, both arms out and down together. As the vaudeville boys said, "Put those oars back in the boat."

Where was Paul Sills, the director, all this time? Right in there directing on the same general level, which reduced a brilliantly bawdy farce to a deadly bore with a few sniggers. Some of the trouble was a wholesale lack of talent, which denied the play wit, charm, and style. Some was an outburst of director's ideas which introduced Pan as a goggle-eyed observer, sometimes in duplicate, turned types into caricatures, and made the old men's chorus a paunchy vaudeville turn bawling lyrics over the pit's "special music."

It was hard to hear the words, but as consolation consider this sample:

"It's your muni-CIP-al duty
To dance for peace."

Lost in the clumsy shuffle is an old and famous comedy, candid, audacious, amusing, and not without sense. It has more things to say about war and peace than Lysistrata's campaign to make women inaccessible until their men agree to stop fighting.

To see Lysistrata, Myrrhina, Lampito, and gay little Kalonika vividly acted, with a Kinesias to match and a production to set them off is know why Aristophanes has lasted for centuries. To see the Studebaker's "Lysistrata" is to realize that the old Playwrights Theater club has just moved downtown.

For all her enthusiasm about homegrown Chicago theater, Claudia Cassidy was not supportive of Paul Sills or his pals at the Playwrights Theatre Club. Not many of the group members' names made it into Cassidy's scathing review; but this infamous Studebaker Theatre "Lysistrata" actually featured Mike Nichols and Elaine May in the almighty bomb, not to mention such famous sketch-comedy names as Severn Darden, Barbara Harris and Andrew Duncan. In his book *Something Wonderful Right Away*, Jeffrey Sweet (who also was in this show) calls the production "the worst 'Lysistrata' ever seen by mortal man." Nichols headed the old man's chorus, Sweet reports, with Darden improbably heading up the women's chorus. Bernie Sahlins, the first producer of the Second City, directed along with Sills. Luckily for him, he escaped Cassidy's wrath.

In 1955, unmentioned by the *Tribune*, the Compass Players, featuring this very same group, had started in Hyde Park; this was the comedy ensemble (the inventers of improv, we might say) that formed the founding nucleus of the Second City. At the time of this review, Compass had just disbanded. But Sahlins had leased the Studebaker Theatre and created a new theater company by the same name with grand designs of being that long-awaited resident Chicago theater, long before the Steppenwolf days. Cassidy no doubt showed up to see if this was the great Chicago enterprise that Tennessee Williams had encouraged her to support. She found one of the very worst shows in Chicago history.

Incidentally, Cassidy wrote her own headlines—with Beckettian wit.

50

WAITING FOR GODOT

'WAITING FOR GODOT' ENDS STUDEBAKER SEASON FOR SUBSCRIBERS ONLY

Studebaker Theatre

BY CLAUDIA CASSIDY

CAST

Estragon .... Louis Zorich
Vladimir .... Harvey Korman
Pozzo .... Moultrie Patten
Lucky .... Mike Nichols
A Young Man .... Andrew Duncan

MAY 15, 1957. By a curious twitch of fate the Studebaker's "Waiting for Godot" is apt to be played in a void on both sides of the footlights. Samuel Beckett's tragicomedy concerns the infinite loneliness of the human soul constricted in the immensity of space. His stage has the mutations of a Nordic dusk which seems not to change at all, his sun is cold and cheerless, his stark stick of a tree is no less barren for sprouting the few stiff leaves that make a mockery of birth.

Because the Studebaker Theater company has reached the end of its frayed managerial rope and this last play of its season has shut down even the box office to save money, the void extends into the audience. Those who wanted to buy tickets were turned away, and subscription has shrunk sharply since the promising 16,000 who signed up for the first series. Yet opening night was played to an audience less unfortunate in size than in its fringe of titters and guffaws that constantly tore the mood and snagged the fabric of the play.

This was doubly a pity because it increased the tilt of the evening toward vaudeville, and there was from the start too sharp a suggestion of "There were once two tramps named Gogo and Didi." Yet the production has its points and the play is fascinating. An audience sensitive to its overtones can make it flower in its desert of despair. Some receptive observers find it profound, some amusing, some endearing. Perhaps the secret is a blend of all three, but to see that you need a virtuoso presentation of its spatter brush of styles. I miss, too, in this production the twanging, humming sounds that sometimes bring into reverberant focus the echoing immensity of space.

Perhaps really to see "Godot" you must have seen the incomparable Bert Lahr as Estragon called Gogo, for there was the incarnation of the dependent one's charm, his cruelty, his ecstatic sensitivity. Louis Zorich began as a vaudeville clown, which is not the same as the great clown of vaudeville. But before the play was over he was sensing the rough ground under Gogo's vulnerable feet. Without the titters and the guffaws he may yet make the journey.

Harvey Korman's Vladimir, the dependable yet no less vulnerable one, played in reverse. He began in a reassuring security of style, then embroidered simplicity. Moultrie Patten finds only the surface of the rich man, and Mike Nichols has the pitiful puppet look of the slave Lucky, but not his terrible outpouring of words jerking from a long jammed machine.

Yet this was a first performance under difficulties no outsider could quite know. It will improve and it will not bar you completely from a play whose hopeless tramps are waiting for the one who never comes, yet the possibility of whose coming must at all costs never be repudiated.

In her review of what would be the final production of the Studebaker Theatre Company, Claudia Cassidy is generous, even a little wistful for the failed artistic enterprise. She captures the mood of what sounds like a grim night, even if Mike Nichols, who was playing Lucky, came out reasonably well. That was it for the Studebaker Theatre Company.

Nichols would go on to many things, of course, including his own production of this same play, staged in 1988 at New York's Lincoln Center for the Performing Arts and starring F. Murray Abraham, Robin Williams, Bill Irwin and Steve Martin.

Meanwhile, Cassidy was still to persuade Chicago to create the kind of theater she wanted to see.

51

ARE BROADWAY'S LEFTOVERS ENOUGH OR SHALL WE TRY ROLLING OUR OWN?

BY CLAUDIA CASSIDY

JULY 4, 1957. Chicago finally revolted on the operatic and symphonic fronts, sweeping out the too long tolerated invasion of mediocrity with the young brilliance of the Lyric and the seasoned skill of Fritz Reiner. But what about the theater, whose cherished reputation as the fabulous invalid is more romantic than realistic? What's fabulous about theatrical invalidism when it consists for the most part of belated, rundown, miscast versions of Broadway shows, many of which were no great bargain when they were new? Our theater is less a romantic invalid than a broken down wreck.

We never lack for illustration, but two in particular are sizzling on my desk. One is the Chicago failure of "Cat on a Hot Tin Roof" for the simple reason that Chicago has returned with notable disinterest the contempt in which the whole abortive booking held Chicago. The other is the case of "Auntie Mame."

Hedging against Rosalind Russell's eventual departure from the New York cast, the management has scoured the land and has come up with Greer Garson as replacement. Miss Garson is a beauty and a spirited charmer. In her own way she could be worth seeing when Miss Russell's loping comedy and casual chic take leave of a personality show. But what about the touring company headed for Chicago? It is being farmed out to another management, with Constance Bennett named as Auntie Mame. This reverts to the oldest, most discredited kind of casting, or miscasting, which has made so much touring theater the disaster it is today. In the last 15 years or so Miss Bennett has several times indicated to Chicago that she has no flair for comedy. The last time was in 1952 in a piece of summer junk called "A Date with April." This horror was, or so it declared, on its way to Broadway. Broadway, which never knew its luck, was spared.

⁂

Getting back to "Cat on a Hot Tin Roof," it would be hard to see how a major producing company could more completely mishandle a valuable property. Chicago is a Tennessee Williams town—has been ever since it discovered the man's quality in "The Glass Menagerie." We got the first look at his "The Rose Tattoo," and a brilliant duplication of "A Streetcar Named Desire," with Uta Hagen and Anthony Quinn. A season or so later a shoddy distortion of "Streetcar" was trucked in by error and briefly exhibited downtown. When I wrote what I thought of the unsightly mess both Mr. Williams, the betrayed author, and Jo Mielziner, the frustrated designer, wrote in eloquent agreement. Their letters were printed in full April 22, 1951.

I wonder what these two think of "Cat" in Chicago, where an inferior troupe got off to a bad start, and where replacements had been constantly replacing replacements, while the box office slid slowly down from brilliant promise to red ink recognition of the theater facts. Mind you, this was no trucked in imposter. This was the first Chicago booking of Williams' biggest money maker, with the imprint of the Playwrights' company and Elia Kazan. You can guess what Mr. Kazan thought of it when he shook his head from left to right at the thought of returning the exhibition to New York as a two-for-one venture. Odd he had not noticed it was no better here, or perhaps not half as good, at full prices.

⌓⌓⌓

Producers will answer all this with the usual parade of tired facts. It is not easy to get actors to tour, or to stay in a show for a long run. Many a director loses all interest in a show once it has been geared to what he considers its sharpest focus to dazzle Broadway. Well, this is simply saying that we put our faith in show business, over which we have no control. The best solution I know is to put our faith in theater, which we can control, and which is in the long run infinitely more rewarding.

Some theater folk were astounded when the recent visit of London's Old Vic pulled $100,000 into the Shubert in the two week engagement of four plays. In the first place, it was a good company. More important, that company was playing superb plays—"Romeo and Juliet," "Macbeth," "Richard II," and "Troilus and Cressida." There are plenty more in the classic bin where they came from. The great plays never won their laurels in the library. They thrive best where they were born to thrive, on the living stage.

I thought of these things again when I went up to Stratford last week to help open the fifth season of Canada's Shakespeare theater. Stratford is not too easy to reach, and it is short on accommodations for visitors. We stayed in Canada's London and drove 100 miles each night to see the play—a gesture not regarded as unusual in our gadabout family. One indication of the interest that festival has stirred up in four busy seasons is that 37 newspapers covered the opening. That is quite a stream of copy cluttering up the nightscape.

What is good for Canada is not necessarily the solution for us except in the universal domain of supply and demand. The classic stage—and in the English language the incomparable classic is Shakespeare—supplies plays, trains actors, stimulates directors, and creates the best possible audience. It is in all ways the richest source of talent—creative, recreative, and receptive—in developing the contemporary stage.

Canada started its fifth season in a new $1,500,000 theater almost fully paid for, and it has its first grant from the new council of arts. That theater is altogether charming, curving the audience about two-thirds of the way around its apron stage, and its fluted parasol roof is saucily crested with a crown bearing pennants. Acoustics are not quite what they were under the old tent—Ravinia had that trouble, too, when it substituted a handsome roof for resonant canvas. But the fluidity of the Canadian stage is a joy, achieving swiftness of momentum without loss of focus. And if you like hearing an audience laugh, you should hear the continuous uproar at the Tyrone Guthrie "Twelfth Night."

We have no such theater, and, barring a miracle, no hope of getting one soon. But I keep going back to the Auditorium in such moments. The house has the resonance, the capacity, and the margin for splendor to give such a theater a home. It could project the apron stage the Old Vic did not bring to Chicago because the Shubert had no place to put it. It could be developed into one of the town's richest assets which could in time become a national treasure.

Talent is power. We all know that. Canada is developing its acting talent and tapping some rich lodes. If we had such a theater, run on the highest professional standards, what Broadway does or doesn't send us would be less important. If visiting orchestras are good, fine. If they aren't, it isn't disastrous. We have our own topflight Chicago Symphony orchestra for 28 downtown weeks. If visiting opera is brilliant, so much the better. Turkeys are less a sorrow, knowing that the Lyric is extending its realm of front rank opera, which has glitter and glamor among its assets. Who knows, if we had that theater on a similar basis, it might even develop that long desired resident ballet. All these things could travel. They should. But they would belong to us.

By the time this "On the Aisle" commentary appeared in 1957, well over two years had gone by since Cassidy's previous commentary "amplifying" the idea of a Chicago theater. Here, she touches on many of the same themes, comparing the homegrown theater with the local opera and symphony, which already had undergone what Cassidy saw as a kind of native revolution, throwing out the touring colonizers from New York.

The rhetoric now is more intense. "Our theater," Cassidy writes, "is less a romantic invalid than a broken down wreck."

As ever, she is railing about substandard touring productions, which lack the original stars or directors and thus hold her city in contempt. The horror of all horrors was a shoddy "Cat on a Hot Tin Roof," which upset Cassidy greatly, being as she saw Chicago and Tennessee Williams as symbiotic (and, by implication, herself as Williams's chief admirer).

Cassidy is also writing here of the Stratford Festival in Canada, then just five years old and with its famous Festival Theatre brand new. Stratford now is full of hotels and inns, but at this juncture Cassidy was forced to stay in London, Ontario, and drive 100 miles each night to see the show. What she saw in Guthrie's Stratford brings her back to Chicago's Auditorium Theatre, which she sees as the perfect place to put such a theater so that "what Broadway does or doesn't send us would be less important." She would get her wish to some extent—but the Auditorium would remain a touring house. Chicago theater would sprout in the neighborhoods, locales that did not hold much interest for Cassidy at this time. As for the "long desired resident ballet"? It would take until 1995 for the Joffrey Ballet to leave New York and provide Chicago with a world-class company. The Joffrey would take up residence at the Auditorium.

Meanwhile, Cassidy was about to encounter Eugene O'Neill at the Erlanger. She would fall hard.

52

LONG DAY'S JOURNEY INTO NIGHT

EUGENE O'NEILL'S LAST TESTAMENT IS POWERFUL, PITIFUL, AND MAGNIFICENT

Erlanger Theater

BY CLAUDIA CASSIDY

CAST

James Tyrone .... Anew McMaster
Mary Cavan Tyrone .... Fay Bainter
James Tyrone Jr. .... Roy Poole
Edmund Tyrone .... Chet Leaming
Cathleen .... Liz Thackston

JANUARY 7, 1958. One of the great plays of a lifetime came to the Erlanger last night and there were empty seats in the house. I don't attempt to explain this, or to say why this play of all plays lacks the support of Theater Guild-American Theater Society subscription, which underwrites almost everything that comes to town, including the junk.

I do say that if we let it die here we have only ourselves to blame that the town is turning into a theatrical desert. For this is Eugene O'Neill's last testament, "Long Day's Journey Into Night." A power house of a play, it has fallen into good hands. In Chicago as in New York it is magnificently acted, and so superbly staged it seems just to happen.

O'Neill wrote it as a form of exorcism, for he was the youngest of the haunted Tyrones, the consumptive boy haunted by love of the sea and love of words, living in this gaunt summer house with the stingy actor father, the dope ridden mother, the alcoholic brother, and the Irish aura of whisky, eloquence, recrimination, sentimentality, and despair—in the wild ups and downs of the Irish temperament brilliantly captured in what is probably the most fascinating card game never played.

That card game comes in the last and most powerful act of a play lasting almost four hours. It happens in the darkness of waiting night. The brother is carousing. Upstairs the mother whose last cure has failed is slipping deeper and deeper into the past, which is her drugged refuge. Downstairs the sick boy and the father whose stinginess is condemning him to a state institution attempt to pass the time. But on the table with the deck of cards are two whisky bottles, and in both men is a lifetime of talk, tho you can't say it was ever bottled up. When talk goes too far, as it always does with the Tyrones, they attempt to go back to the game never really begun.

It is a marvelously written scene, full of irony and tenderness and a kind of remembering compassion. You would swear nothing to come could match it. But in comes the drunken brother, with things on his mind, too. He matches it.

These people dig at each other with the jagged necks of the broken bottles from which they take the refuge of oblivion. That in the sharpest shards love and hate are often undistinguishable is the tragedy of mankind, not just of the Tyrones.

◠ ◠ ◠

If you asked me which town has the superior cast, New York or Chicago, I couldn't tell you. Each is complete in itself, or at least complete with the same limitation. I have not yet seen a Mary Cavan Tyrone who matched my image of the role, an image indelibly stamped as I read the play by memories of Laurette Taylor. How she would have held her own with that batch of Irishmen—what a curtain she would have given that last mesmeric scene.

Fay Bainter is remarkable in the part for most of its distance, especially in the addict's sly pretending, and in the pitiful withdrawal into a withered wraith. But like Florence Eldridge she makes some scenes seem to need cutting when acting is all they crave.

For all the Tyrones are talkers, and how the men talk. Anew McMaster as the father—a shell of a withering actor at the start, with a touch of ham—a mighty actor as the shell cracks and the man shows. Roy Poole as the elder brother, the map of Ireland on his face, the furies of the world hounding him. Chet Leaming as the younger brother with a face that says the black last testament is his own. These are actors. If you miss them, you cheat not them, but yourself.

This volume contains many of Cassidy's more withering reviews; yet here is one, for a touring production of Eugene O'Neill's "Long Day's Journey into Night," that stands in sharp contrast: in her entire career, there is none she wrote more ecstatically than this. Cassidy loved O'Neill as much as she did Tennessee Williams (she demonstrably did not feel that way about Arthur Miller). It's also worth noting that by no means is this her only positive review of a touring production.

Even though the cast here is different from the one Cassidy saw in New York, she finds the road company the equal of the Broadway production. This is a most eloquent celebration of a great American drama: "These people dig at each other with the jagged necks of the broken bottles from which they take the refuge of oblivion. That in the sharpest shards love and hate are often undistinguishable is the tragedy of mankind." Indeed.

Once again, the image of Laurette Taylor is back. When Cassidy gushed, as she does here, the comparison with her favorite actress was her biggest compliment.

To her readers, Cassidy must have seemed supremely self-confident by now. But was that really the case?

53

IBM CRITIC, OR HOW TO TALK YOURSELF OUT OF A PERFECTLY GOOD JOB

BY CLAUDIA CASSIDY

JANUARY 25, 1959. Are people necessary? Evidence in the conspiracy to eliminate them piles higher every day. An earnest conductor who may have been having personnel trouble once assured me that the orchestra of the future will consist of a few instruments electrified into tonal infinity—a prospect the musicians' union may be postponing longer than he thinks. The composer has no such security. Electronic composers not only maneuver recorded sound on magnetic tapes, they mix sounds from three signal generators, and I quote, "one producing pure tones, another producing impulses, the third producing 'white noise.'" Furthermore, Columbia and Princeton universities are acquiring what the man across the page dubs an Electronic Chair. That is, they share a Rockefeller foundation grant devoted to composition and research in electronic music.

On even more audacious ground, European opera houses, which are government endowed and so can afford to be experimental, are plainly trying to eliminate that ancient and honorable institution, the opera chorus. A serious example of this trend was the Scala's "Lucia di Lammermoor," staged and directed by Herbert Von Karajan for Maria Meneghini Callas. Instead of the kilted, knobby knees of tradition, Karajan had tried to hide his choristers by muffling them from chin to floor in great black cloaks rendered further inconspicuous by scenic blackout. This one I saw in 1956—it gives fair warning as to what may have happened since.

⁂

All this inhumanity to man is getting too close to home to be altogether comfortable. Time was when I could muse with equanimity on the prospect of an electronic opera whose music came from synthesized generators controlled from a robot switchboard and sung, say, by that electronic monster once recorded by RCA-Victor with the tongue in cheek claim that "It is capable of reproducing any sound which has ever been produced, or any sound which may be imagined by the human mind." At least I thought it would be something new to write about.

What made me think I was writing? Just the other day, in an outburst of optimism about sluffing off concerts I preferred not to cover, I suggested that my newspaper install an IBM machine at Ravinia into which I could feed the program, the name of the conductor, the temperature, assorted train and plane noises, and several mosquitoes, whereupon it would relay a neat review to THE TRIBUNE.

At best I hoped for an occasional chuckle, or scowl, as the concert case may be. So what happened? In came one of those beautifully (electronically?) typed letters on the letterhead of International Business Machine corporation, signed by James E. Kokie, applied science representative. Letter herewith:

"Dear Miss Cassidy—

"I read with interest your record review in last Sunday's TRIBUNE. In it you mention the possibility of having an IBM machine relieve the music critic of some of his chores.

"Actually, modern computer technology has advanced to the point where this is now feasible. We now have large-scale memory devices which are capable of storing the vast amounts of information which would have to be called upon in the problem. As you may know, a computer differs from a calculator inasmuch as a computer has the ability to make logical decisions and hence evaluations based on the date fed into it. Your analysis of the type of input data to be fed into the computer is surprisingly accurate. Not only would we have to feed in controllable factors (e.g., the program the conductor has chosen) but also the uncontrollable factors (e.g., train noises, temperature).

"Most computer programs have highly descriptive names—e.g., ASPIRIN and MOONSHINE. Others have descriptive names the letters of which stand for something—e.g., SOAP for Symbolic Optimum Assembly Program. It might be possible in our case to write a program called CLAUDIA. This would stand for Criticism and Laudations of Artists Under and During Interpretive Activities.

"However, since the days of CLAUDIA and the Ravinia IBM machine are still remote, you will (thankfully) continue to write your own reviews."

At best that's a reprieve. I am thinking of starting the SPHB or Society for the Preservation of Human Beings. Meanwhile, tho I may not be around to participate in humanity's comeback, I detect signs. Even now, some electronic music has a glint of personality—note Pierre Henry's in "Musique Concrete"—an eerie whiff of individuality, an oblique peering of something inimical, even a bit dangerous. Sooner or later a robot chorister, like a robot conductor, is bound to get ideas of his own.

𝄐 𝄐 𝄐

As for those IBM critics, tho at the start they might serve the detached business known in dull circles as "constructive, fair, and unprejudiced reviews," the night would come when some feeder-inner would be all worked up, either for or against, and some of it would creep into the review, setting us off on the start of an old cycle. Come to think of it, we might even wind up with electronic lawyers, for who else would sue, or defend, a machine?

By the early years of the 21st century, full-time arts critics were dropping like pesky gnats from newspaper staffs in America. But 1959 was still among the glory days of full complements of critics at major dailies such as the *Tribune*, and even at far smaller newspapers. Yet Claudia Cassidy, it seems, could sense the dark future.

In this fabulously prescient curiosity written long before bloggers, Yelp, websites and aggregation, she ponders whether her job could be done by a computer, even though this was far too early for any terminal to have been anywhere near her desk. There were no PCs in 1959. Yet not only does Cassidy smell automation coming for journalists, she also probes the changes in recorded music, although she had no idea of the scale of what was coming down the pike there, either. And she admits that electronic music was beginning to get "a glint of personality" (and she isn't talking rock'n'roll). So here's yet more evidence that Cassidy was no fool when it came to sensing what might be happening next in the world she inhabited.

Remarkably, what she clearly intended as satire–the idea of installing a computer at Ravinia, her plugging in the raw data that would produce her review copy automatically–was actually coming true by 2012, at least in data-rich reporting fields such as local sports, with computers actually doing the writing. In fact, the *Tribune* would find itself embroiled in a scandal with Journatic, a computerized reporting service (in which the newspaper had invested) that did pretty much what Cassidy lays out here for her readers.

Cassidy should have listened to her source from IBM, who rightly notes that what she was writing about was perfectly possible—in fact, just 53 years later, it was a reality in many areas of Cassidy's profession. The arts were holding out, however, presumably because the "feeder-inners" (as Cassidy puts it in her delightful final paragraph) were still deemed worthy by their bosses of processing a show better than a machine. For now, anyway.

But no computer could have appreciated the work of a young Chicagoan named Lorraine Hansberry as did Cassidy.

54

A RAISIN IN THE SUN

WARM HEART, BACKBONE, FUNNYBONE IN BLACKSTONE PLAY AND CAST

Blackstone Theatre

BY CLAUDIA CASSIDY

CAST

Ruth Younger.. Ruby Dee
Travis Younger....................................... Glynn Turman
Walter Lee Younger .... Sidney Poitier
Beneatha Younger .... Diana Sands
Lena Younger.. Claudia McNeil
Joseph Asagai... Ivan Dixon
George Murchison.................................. Louis Gossett
Bobo .... Lonne Elder III
Karl Lindner .... John Fiedler
Moving Men .... Douglas Turner, Ed Hall

FEBRUARY 11, 1959. "A Raisin in the Sun" is a remarkable play, acted to the Blackstone hilt of its warm heart, its proud backbone, and its quicksilver funnybone by a gifted cast headed by Sidney Poitier, Claudia McNeil, and Ruby Dee. It is a new play still in tryout, with time for the cutting and adjusting that can make a powerhouse of its potential strength. More important to Chicago is that it has the fresh impact

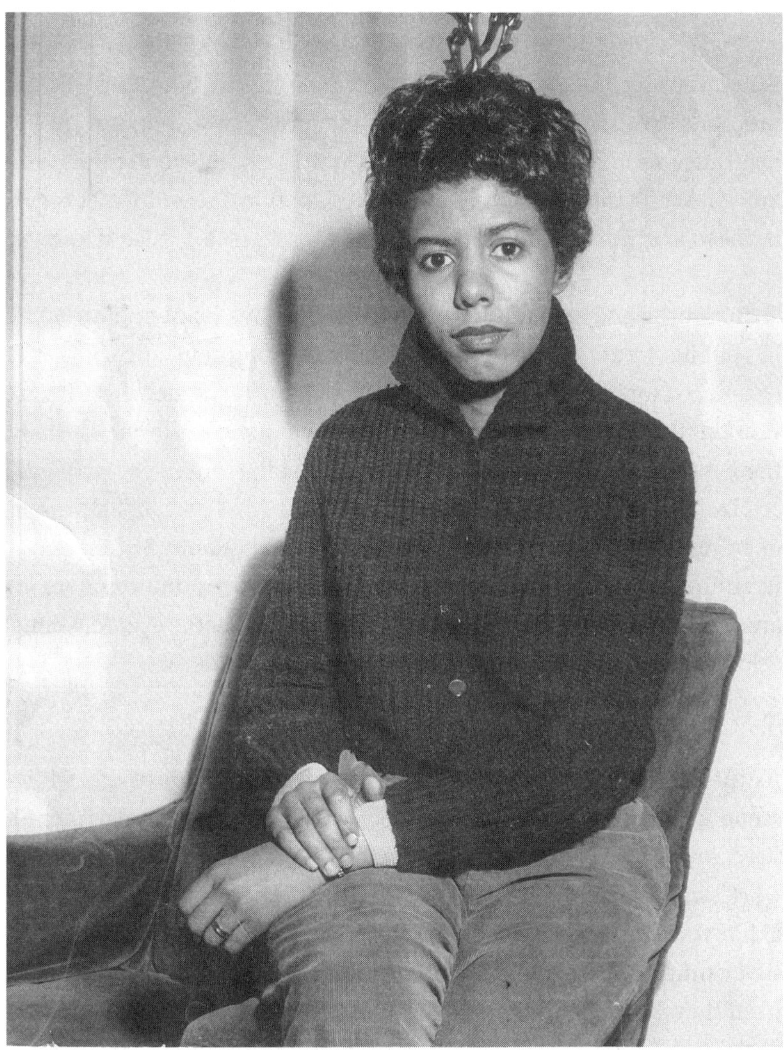

LORRAINE HANSBERRY, THE AUTHOR OF "A RAISIN IN THE SUN," AS PHOTOGRAPHED IN 1959.

of something urgently on its way. Lorraine Hansberry can be proud that she wrote it, and her friends, Philip Rose and David J. Cogan, that they brought it to the stage.

It was common knowledge in advance that the title comes from a poem by Langston Hughes, the one beginning, "What happens to a dream deferred?," but not all of us knew the poignant irony that gives the final curtain reverberations the second act climax now lacks.

◠◠◠

When that second act ends the sobbing son has all but destroyed his mother's dream of a decent home for the family by losing most of her insurance money to a fast talking fake. It is a scene you expect, you know it will happen, and it happens on schedule. But in theater terms it doesn't come off. You respect it, but you don't feel it, so it fails on stage.

But at the end, when the son has reclaimed his manhood, when he has put his dream of quick riches aside for the long haul, and the family has picked up its courage to try its luck in the new home where it isn't wanted, the mother, who has given every cent she has in the world to the new house is the last to go. And as she stands there you suddenly realize that this ratty apartment, without sun, or a private bathroom, or enough bedrooms, but with cockroaches, is her home. But she leaves it, smiling, taking her puny plant and her far from puny courage, for another stretch in a lifetime haul. This is theater with reverberations, echoes, and a tug at the remembering heart.

◠◠◠

As the play ends on that authentic note of nostalgia, it begins with a scene a veteran playwright might envy. In that scrubby apartment a tired woman is trying to get her son off to school, her husband off to work, when neither wants to go. She has in-laws, too. It is a scene of exhaustion, of frustration, of bickering—but also a scene of that quicksilver humor, that sudden shifting into grace, that ability to laugh at itself that makes good company. You care about these people from that first scene, which is half the battle of a play.

As the angry young man who happens to be a Negro, Sidney Poitier strides a wide range from the one who wants something for nothing to the man who will try it the hard way. Claudia McNeil is the matriarch with depth and humor except when the director has her turn coy for her daughter's beau. Ruby Dee is the one most touching, the young wife who almost loses. Diana Sands as the rebellious sister, Glynn Turman as the small boy of the house, Ivan Dixon and Louis Gossett as the callers—all hold their own, tho the two men suffer from scenes that try to stuff too much into the play. John Fiedler is the white man who comes from the new house community to pay the Negro family to stay away. The neutral "inoffensiveness" of his casting is as interesting as the scene in which Poitier tells him the payoff is rejected, and why.

In general, Lloyd Richards' direction is so right that the false spots are probably on their way out this morning.

One of the most important reviews in Chicago theater history, Claudia Cassidy's enthusiastic endorsement of "A Raisin in the Sun" and Lorraine Hansberry, its young Chicago playwright, would change the course of American theater. It helped bring to Broadway the first play by an African American female, and arguably did as much for black theater as any review in any newspaper ever did.

When Cassidy showed up to review the play, it was just starting out with the actors Ruby Dee, Glynn Turman and Sidney Poitier (not to mention one Louis Gossett in a small role). The company was just one month away from its Broadway opening, well before the show was fully on its feet. At the moment of this review, *Brown v. Board of Education* was less than five years old. And the *Tribune* remained a conservative newspaper, even if less flamboyantly so, following McCormick's death. As recently as 1955, it had argued in an editorial the absurd notion that Chicago was "without segregation."

In his memoir, "Raisin"'s producer, Philip Rose, says that the Chicago run of the play was scheduled right before it was to open on Broadway (it already had played New Haven and Philadelphia), and that Hansberry was not only terrified of taking the play to her hometown—especially since it portrayed her hometown—but especially scared of risking a Cassidy review. No New York critic held such apparent fear for her.

"Not Chicago. Not with my play," Rose reports Hansberry as saying, after she learned that the company would perform at the Blackstone Theatre while the play was still being rewritten.

"Cassidy," Rose writes, "was the most feared and often most vicious critic in the country." He was convinced she'd be angry about the production's start in New Haven instead of her own Chicago (though Cassidy was why they'd picked New Haven). He notes that he told Hansberry, "You don't know what she'll write," only for Hansberry to respond, "Yes I do, I'll show it to you." And with that Hansberry pulled out her own review of her own play, as if Cassidy had written it. Appearing in full in Rose's book, it is a hilarious satire of a Cassidy pan.

"The Blackstone Theatre has been regrettably dark for a goodly portion of the 1958–9 season," Hansberry's spot-on Cassidy-style review begins, "but at no point have the theater's prospects been murkier than they were last night for the premiere of 'A Raisin in the Sun.'" She goes on from there–at great length–in that critic's voice. "For if the current tenant of the Blackstone truly represents the negro dream for America then the KKK cannot be far behind. And I for one say God Bless them for that." Hansberry's apparent talents as a satirist have been insufficiently appreciated.

"Raisin" arrived in Chicago with no advance ticket sales, and according to Rose, it did no business at all for the first few days. The producers gave most of the tickets away. And then came this Cassidy review that would decide the company's fate–and whether it would even open on Broadway.

Actually, Hansberry need not have worried. With "A Raisin in the Sun," Cassidy was–crucially for the young playwright–on the right side of history. She notes that the play has "the fresh impact of something urgently on its way," even if we detect a certain delicacy in how she phrases all this racial change for publication in the *Tribune* (what she doesn't say here is as interesting as what she does). Yet by calling Poitier "the angry young man who happened to be a Negro," Cassidy crucially links "Raisin" to the movement of well-educated but working-class protagonists that was sweeping London in plays like John Osborne's seminal "Look Back in Anger." There is code at work here, but the intention of the review is clear: send this important Chicago play on its way.

When "Raisin" reached New York, it would be seen as an American story, but this was always a Chicago play. The character of Walter Lee Younger speaks of standing at the corner of 39th and South Park. Indeed, the entire story is based on Hansberry's family's decision to move into Washington Park on Chicago's South Side, a white neighborhood at the time, although the fictional neighborhood of Clybourne Park clearly was standing in for Lincoln Park. Hansberry's father had bought the Washington Park house in 1938 and his new neighbors tried to force the family out, resulting in a 1940 Supreme Court decision involving a covenant restricting blacks from purchasing or leasing land in a particular Chicago neighborhood. No play is more rooted in Chicago than this one.

Cassidy is very careful here not to talk about these matters too explicitly–she stays away from the city's precise racial history and frames the play very much in terms of its universals. In fact, we could read this entire review without ever knowing that "Raisin" is set in Chicago. Cassidy knew her readers, and what it would take (or not take) to get them to the theater.

Nonetheless, "A Raisin in the Sun" would turn out to be a drama that reverberated through Chicago theater history. "Clybourne Park," a play by Bruce Norris that riffed on its themes, would win the Pulitzer Prize for drama in 2012. Cassidy had no idea, of course, that "Raisin" would have the impact it did (not to mention Poitier's impact), but she was shrewd enough to see that this was a work to be reckoned with.

Hansberry would move to New York as this play opened on Broadway. By 1965, she had died at the age of 34 from pancreatic cancer.

Cassidy, meanwhile, was finding new lows.

55

A GLANCE AT THE PAST, PRESENT AND FUTURE OF CHICAGO CAFES

BY WILL LEONARD

DECEMBER 27, 1959. There have been complaints that this department hasn't served up a "think" piece for a long time, so we'll avail ourselves of the year's end to come up with weighty thoughts. What better time than New Year's eve to take a look into the past, the present, and the future?

THE PAST. Any review of 1959 in the cabarets would have to note that this was the year Lenny Bruce played the Cloister once and Mister Kelly's twice in eight months. . . . Carol Channing's staid satire of a strip tease was an Empire room shocker in May, Sophie Tucker's vulgarity packed the place in November. . . . Hans Brinker won the silver skates in the ice show at the Boulevard room, which was more than he ever was able to do in the book. . . . Lily St. Cyr took a bath twice a night at the Black Orchid. . . . Sally Rand packed the Brass Rail for 10 weeks, returned six months later and again is in her tenth week there.

Best cabaret show of the year: Will Holt's "All In Fun" at the Gate Horn.

Most improbable act of the year: The Edmond sisters at the Preview lounge, blonde triplets alleged to have won (separately) three beauty contests.

Shortest lived room of the year: The Pan American House at the Graemere, which opened and was changed into the Greentree Inn before you could get your napkin unfolded.

Noisiest spot of the year: The St. Louis Browns Fans room at Captain Chips' on Rush street.

Most frequently used cabaret theme of the year: "The 50th state." Space limits prevent listing of spots that used this gimmick.

Best waitress of the year: Ruthie Lieberman of the Cloister.

Most nostalgic triumph of the year: Maurice Chevalier at the Empire room.

Memorable hits of the year: Red Skelton at the Chez Paree, Bob Scobey at the Continental Cafe.

Most impressive newcomers of the year: Dave Gardner at Mister Kelly's, Al Hirt at the Empire room, Charlie Manna at the Cloister.

Most striking new décor of the year: Archie Schrom's mosaic murals in the Indian room of Don Roth's Blackhawk.

Mysteries of the year: What became of the Old Town Williamsburg Inn, announced to open in October? What became of Sarah Vaughan's 17th and 18th engagements at the Blue Note? Frank Holzfeind listed her June visit as No. 16, her November one as No. 19.

THE PRESENT. The Second City, new cabaret-theater-coffee house at 1842 N. Wells st., has a cleverly written, smoothly performed revue that sparkles excepting when it becomes too precious. Improvisations in response to audience requests are skillful and imaginative, as in the old Compass theater from which some of this company stems. "Business Man," a comic impression of TV's "Superman" translated into the Wall street idiom, is a brilliant sketch, and sidelong glances at automation and advertising are almost as good. The songs are weak. Severn Darden is a much better comic than at the Gate of Horn a few weeks ago, and Eugene Troobnick is a standout in an excellent cast of seven.

CABARET CALENDAR: Two performances of "Quick Changes" tonight at Way Off-Broadway, 1205 N. Dearborn, at 5 and 8 p.m. . . . Monday: The Blue Note will be open for its annual "college night," with Duke Ellington and band, and a new ice show will open in the Boulevard room. . . . Tuesday: Dorothy Dandridge opens in the Empire room, and Henny Youngman and Diana Trask open at the Cloister. . . . Wednesday: The Blue Angel opens in its new location on Michigan avenue, the Club Rouge opens on Randolph st. with Dick Haymes starred, and Jane Morgan opens in the Camellia House. . . . Thursday, New Year's eve: See page 11 and below for details.

THE FUTURE. Our forecast of cabaret things to come in 1960 indicates that this is the year when:

There will be more coffee houses, but after awhile there will be fewer. There will be more hypnotists in the hinterland clubs, but after awhile there will be fewer of them, too. . . . Monique van Vooren will become the first singer to have been starred in the Camellia House, the Chez Paree, and the Empire room. . . . Ruth Reinhardt, who took her first vacation in 12 years from Jazz Ltd. in 1959, will not take another one. . . . Duke Hazlett, who looks like Frank Sinatra with his hat on, will not take his hat off. . . . The happiest to all you cats! . . . End of think piece.

Sometimes—maybe often—*Tribune* critics missed the importance of huge events. Here's a case in point—the notice amid a lot of clutter, reprinted here, of the very first revue at the Second City, a Chicago institution in the making that would change the face of American comedy and survive well into the next century.

This is the first review by Will Leonard (1912–1977), who eventually would succeed Claudia Cassidy at the *Tribune*. Their careers were linked in many ways: when Cassidy had first moved to the newspaper, Leonard had taken over her job at the *Chicago Journal of Commerce*. Born in Chicago, he began his career in 1929 as a copy boy at the *Chicago Evening Post*. He then went to the financial department of the *Chicago American* and spent time at the *Chicago Herald-Examiner* before landing in Cassidy's post at the *Chicago Journal of Commerce*. Leonard joined the *Tribune* in 1951, hired to write its "Tower Ticker" column. He was, at the time of this review, the paper's nightlife columnist, so the Second City, being a cabaret, fell under his domain. In time, his portfolio was expanded.

In 1951 in his "Tower Ticker" column, Leonard wrote an amusing defense of the critic as a family man. "The citizen with the 9-to-5 working schedule, the participation in rush hour, the three meals a day, the theater ticket bought and paid for, and the time-and-a-half for overtime is smugly confident his is the definitive existence. The critic's life, he tells the appraiser to his face, isn't 'normal' because the reviewer rises and retires at hours that don't meet the non-critic's requirements."

Leonard went on to argue otherwise.

"Most of the critics we've known have fuller home lives than the 'normal' working stiffs on the 9-to-5 shift. The 'average' guy who snorts at the eccentricity of the reviewer's regimen rises at too early an hour, gulps little if any breakfast, dangles from a strap or contends with peak automotive traffic en route to the office, spends the beautiful daylight hours bent over his work, returns just in time to miss the sunset, sends his children to bed after a little more than a glimpse of them, and turns in because he's tired, not because he wouldn't prefer to watch a little more TV. The night-blooming opinion writer with the 'abnormal hours' rises with his youngsters (they'll see to that), breakfasts at leisure and spends the morning with them, runs down to the office while they're taking their naps, returns in time to renew acquaintance when they awake, leaves for his reviewing chores about the time they're getting into their pajamas—and owns a more thoro domestic routine than the fellow who scoffs at the critic's 'crazy' hours."

Aptly enough for one so happy in his job, Leonard would, as journalists like to say, die with his boots on. In 1977, as he was being carried from the newsroom after a heart attack that would prove fatal, he was heard to say of his most recent article, "I just realized the lead is in the second [para]graph." Editors made sure that the Sunday paper reflected his wishes. And that his obituary contained this story, just below the lead. The obituary also noted that Leonard sometimes wrote under a pseudonym: Eugenie Wells, combining two streets near his Old Town home.

But in 1959, Leonard was early in his career. He barely noticed the Second City, which had opened that December 16 in an old Chinese laundry on Wells Street. But, well, he'd shown up and given his two cents, ten days later. Leonard would turn into one of the Second City's biggest fans, but at this juncture it was just another Chicago café. End of think piece.

56

TOO MANY HATS

SPRIGHTLY REVUE AT SECOND CITY IS FIRST RATE

WILL LEONARD

FEBRUARY 21, 1960. The second show at the Second City is first rate. Perhaps the lads and lasses were just feeling their way with the revue that opened the place last December. The new one, "Too Many Hats," really has the sparkle and sauciness, the speed and the irreverence, the imagination and the buoyancy, that this intimate, topical, smart set show should have.

The missile lag? Don't worry about it. Great books? Let's get distracted from the subject with talk about the neighbors around 76th and Jeffery. Men? Hmph! Japanese movies? I'll never forget "I Was A Teen-Age Radioactive Tuna." The Archduke Franz Ferdinand at Sarajevo? Poor guy! Yellow jaundice? There are worse colors. Sigmund Freud? He made a nice buck. Sen. Harry Byrd? A minstrel show seems a strange place to find him.

"Too Many Hats" has a lot of assets and not too many of anything. The pace is sprightly, the touch light, the music less frequent and more effective. The excellently balanced cast includes, in alphabetical order, Howard Alk, Severn Darden, Andrew Duncan, Barbara Harris, Mina Kolb, Paul Sand, and Eugene Troobnick, not to forget Bill Mathieu, who wrote the songs and plays piano and trumpet, sometimes simultaneously. It is customary to state that some of these persons were once with the Compass Players, whence came Shelley Berman, Mike Nichols and Elaine May, but we'll never repeat that truism again. From now on, so far as we're concerned, the Mathieu-Troobnick-Sand-Kolb-Harris-Duncan-Darden-Alk group is plenty good enough to stand on its own reputation.

Where is this place, you ask? It's in Old Town, at 1842 N. Wells st., where Wells street faces Lincoln Park.

By its second revue, the Second City was attracting enough attention for Leonard to pay more attention himself. Here's his review of "Too Many Hats," that second show (in its early years, the Second City changed shows far more frequently than would later be the case). We can tell from the content of Leonard's review that the theater on Wells Street was, in its early days, very much interested in what now would be regarded as wonkish humor. Leonard points out how the company grew from the Compass Players, but it's already clear that Second City would be its own brand.

By this point, the improvisational group already had established many of the elements that would become enshrined in its identity: cheap tickets (those to "Too Many Hats" cost $2.50), plenty of booze, two acts, little or no advertising, an intellectually oriented clientele (many coming up from the University of Chicago) and very smart actors working at the top of their game. Leonard caught many of these things; he and the *Tribune* were catching on quickly.

Meanwhile, Cassidy was wrestling with the Goodman.

57

THE MILLIONAIRESS

GOODMAN BANKRUPTS 'MILLIONAIRESS' SHELVING SHAW FOR A CARTOON

BY CLAUDIA CASSIDY

OCTOBER 30, 1963. Aren't you, inquires the reproachful telephone, going to say something about the Goodman's "The Millionairess"? The trouble is that my Goodman misadventures are beginning to sound like a broken record—I go to openings, regret the indiscretion, and slip out the instant the lights go up at the first intermission. Yet the place is usually full, and at least in the sense that it makes no public protest, the audience is satisfied. Isn't that enough?

Of course not. The Goodman hangs out its shingle as a school of drama in the august premises of the Art Institute, and it sells a subscription season of what could be interesting plays, adding professional guests as lures. Then it makes an inexcusable botch of the plays. You could count the exceptions of less than one hand.

"The Millionairess" is belated Shaw and not the cream of Shaw, but in brilliant performance it has the Shavian glitter of thrust and parry, a cat and mouse pounce of ideas, a diverting sense of paradox. Its rampageous heroine is an amusing eccentric in the realm of the born boss, a human separator who rises as cream by depleting other people's milk. Shaw gave her one of his more outrageous names, Epifania Ognissanti di Parerga—nothing short of Epiphany All Saints' day—and for contrast plumped her first into the sedate but luxurious office of a barrister in Lincoln's Inn Fields. She promptly flounces into, and breaks the fragile back from "a Chippendale of the very latest fake."

All this is Shaw taking careful aim. But John Reich, the Goodman director, decides that the play is a cartoon comedy—Shaw specifically said Jonsonian—and Jacob Burck designed the first act in that image as a broad spoof on modern art. Yet when Patricia Jessel's Epifania, who has unaccountably turned into Madame X, sits on a squat and plainly indestructible chair, the back falls off.

The alleged British barrister says "amachoor." Shaw's Seedystockings, "a pleasant, quiet little woman of the self-supporting type," has turned into Betty Boop. Alastair the athlete is dumfounding.

This is a school of drama?

Even as young William Leonard was prowling the cabarets between kissing his children, the grand Claudia Cassidy still was on the legitimate theater beat. In this interesting piece, she tells her readers that she really does not like Goodman Theatre openings all that much, especially "The Millionairess," the one here under review.

Given how the Goodman would become the leading resident theater in Chicago–if not in America–this might seem a strange point of view to be coming from the city's leading critic. And since the company had been founded in 1922, it might seem even stranger that this is one of Cassidy's very first published reviews of its productions. But up until the 1950s, the Goodman had made a point of not inviting critics to its shows, which were essentially student productions.

In 1963, the Goodman Theatre was not what it is today. In fact, Cassidy's criticisms during its early years had a great deal to do with pushing the eventual professionalization of the company (she actually became an artistic consultant there after her retirement). Only in 1969 did it become a fully professional theater under John Reich; that still was six years away here. The Goodman may have existed during the first wave of the resident theater movement, but it had a very different identity from the regional-theater pioneers in such cities as Dallas or Washington, DC.

Reich, an Austrian, certainly had professional ambitions: he worked hard to put the Goodman more in the public eye, coming up with public lectures, marketing plans (created with Danny Newman) and the other elements of a successful regional theater. He wanted the theater to be regarded not merely as a school, but as "an art theater for the whole city." Eventually, he got his wish.

But at this point, Cassidy saw the Goodman as very much a student operation, part of the training programs at the School of the Art Institute. Reich had added professional guest artists to juice up his student casts, and his roster included Lillian Gish and James Earl Jones, but student casts still dominated productions. Eventually, the student programs would become the province of the Theatre School at DePaul University as the Goodman got out of the actor-training business altogether after the Art Institute found itself staring down a $200,000 deficit. But that would not happen until 1978. The Goodman would not become an entity independent from the Art Institute until 1977.

We get the sense from Cassidy's review of "The Millionairess" that she was being goaded by her readers into continually showing up at the Goodman, despite her being burned there so many times before. And Cassidy did not like to be told what to do. Provoked by a lousy production of a play by George Bernard Shaw, she goes after the Goodman hard here, arguing not only that it made a botch of this particular play but that it made a habit of such botches.

"This is a school of drama?" Cassidy sneers.

58

"CAMELOT" AND OTHER ROAD SHOWS

VAGARIES OF THEATER IN CHICAGO FROM THE BEST FOOT FORWARD SUCCESS TO THAT CYNICAL CHEAT, THE RUNDOWN 'ROAD SHOW'

BY CLAUDIA CASSIDY

DECEMBER 15, 1963. If you wanted to illustrate show business outside New York and how it affects Chicago you could scarcely find five shows better tailored to make some points than the ones here right now. "How to Succeed" represents the careful and crackling reproduction of a big Broadway musical, with the Shubert rosily done over to match. "Camelot" is the cynical road show version of a vastly expensive Broadway musical that even in the original laid a critical egg while cashing in on great expectations and a huge advance sale. "Never Too Late" exposes a poverty of resources to terrify anyone who cares about theater. "Seidman and Son" is an affectionate vehicle for Sam Levene, treated with amiable respect. "Black Nativity" is an enchanting show handicapped at the start by the bumblings of "road show" takeover.

Nothing in theater is more destructive, more inexcusable, or more short-sighted than the very term "road show." In older days the person who applied it to Chicago fare would have been an ignoramus scarcely worth correcting. Today the term is no less revolting, but it is more widespread. Junk is not only trundled into town by the carload, it has a captive subscription audience.

◠◠◠

Call "A Man For All Seasons" an honorable exception. It was an exceptional play admirably done, and my Christmas present came early when it suddenly prospered at the boxoffice, leaving all other non-musical plays far behind. "How to Succeed" is another, in totally different kind. "How"—I am getting lazier by the paragraph—is a big, lusty cartoon of a musical comedy with some rapier infighting. As a spoof on big business it is both uproarious and in a baffling kind of way endearing, because Dick Kallman has captured the cherubic charm of its non-hero, a barracuda who thrives on live bait. Willard Waterman is just the man for the uneasy tycoon who makes his last (in the show) and juiciest morsel.

"How" is what all the best big shows duplicated for us used to be, an expert job of re-creation. It was restaged for the Shubert opening, giving up a Monday night's revenue to have a run-thru without an audience, to pace the show. In other words, it treated Chicago as a valued customer given the best foot forward treatment.

◠◠◠

"Camelot," which reported a gross of about 8 million dollars during its 25 months in New York, did no such thing. It elected a "student preview" played to what had more the look of post-graduates. It also elected the Civic Opera house, which is approximately three times the suitable size, possibly because nothing smaller was available. The opera house seats about 3,750—Spectator's Guide figure—and has extra rows set in where the orchestra pit is cut from opera size.

That "Camelot" has been a woeful disappointment from its start three years ago is one of the hazards of show business. The Lerner and Loewe "My Fair Lady" had set up such expectations—I am talking of the crack productions, not the rundown horrors that came staggering in later—and the movie version of "Gigi" had underscored them. When people tell me they did not like "My Fair Lady" I assume they saw an inexcusable production and refer them hopefully to the impending movie with Rex Harrison and Audrey Hepburn. Cecil Beaton's fresh costumes rival the originals.

"Camelot" lacked the book and the music—it goes in for jokes like this one: "Where did the knights of the Round Table learn their chivalry? At knight school." But originally it had the best cast money could lure, and what many considered the most beautiful trappings yet lavished on a musical. It had above all else Richard Burton as King Arthur. Even the recording tells the value of that, wrapping it up in the finale with one word, "Camelot," spoken with the haunting, unaccented sadness of a fading dream.

Chicago's "Camelot" has with one or two exceptions a hopelessly inferior cast warbling hopefully into a bristling array of microphones. Kathryn Grayson, its Guinevere, and not a good one, but nonetheless the one people are told they will hear, has been out of the cast repeatedly, with no information given to newspapers, who have to find such things out for themselves.

I expected "Camelot" to be, if nothing else, a delectable eyeful. I find it rather gim-cracky. Knowing Oliver Smith's work, and its value, I wonder how much is left out, or if the local failure is primarily one of lighting. In any case, "Camelot," for all its heralding three years ago, is a dud. And I can't understand billing the late Moss Hart as director. He had a heart attack during the show's tryout, and died two years ago.

"Never Too Late" is the sort of thing that makes you cringe in your chair if you happen to think theater rather above the moron level. It is one of those suggestive, sniggering shows crammed with the desperate things a director does when he hopes you won't notice the lack of a play. George Abbott has gone considerably beyond the call of duty when he hauls bathroom fixtures on stage, and has Will Hutchins, who might as well have stayed on television, stick his head in the toilet bowl.

They tell me, not that I believe a word of it, that the original company disarms you with Paul Ford's performance as the irascible father-to-be of a belated baby. Unhappily, I will never know. It is never too late to know when you have had it.

"Black Nativity" was heralded by a young lady who submitted her photograph, along with information that she was to represent the producer (who took the show over for touring) on radio and television. By the time the show fell into sympathetic hands too much time had been lost. The last I heard it was fighting to survive the pre-Christmas lull, with sales piling up for futures.

Oddly and regrettably, "Black Nativity," a genuine joy-bringer, is the only show of the five not to have the four week backing of Theater Guild-American Theater Society subscription, money in the bank to nourish a slow start. It was briefly an optional attraction, which seldom amounts to a lot. What it needs right now is a conga line to the boxoffice, preferably led by Alex Bradford with Marion Williams.

Even as all sorts of changes were taking place in Chicago theater, the lousy road shows were still coming through town, and Cassidy, more acidic as she aged, was still attacking them. Here, in a piece that combines several observations on the matter of the shoddy tour, she goes after "Camelot," the touring version of which she clearly despised. Instead of Richard Burton, Cassidy got a road cast "warbling hopefully into a bristling array of microphones." Worse, she had caught wind that the lead, Kathryn Grayson (not that Cassidy liked her), was missing a lot of shows, a habit being covered up by the producers.

But increasingly, Chicago was presenting Cassidy with a different kind of theater. The question for her was whether it was the kind of theater she actually wanted.

59

THE BRIG

'THE BRIG' A BRUTAL, EAR-SPLITTING TRAP FOR ACTORS AND AUDIENCE

Hull House Theatre

BY CLAUDIA CASSIDY

JANUARY 13, 1965. Kenneth H. Brown's "The Brig" is rather like being sent to one, with intermission as reprieve if you can't take it. As played in Hull House's grim little box of a theater on Broadway near Belmont, it suggests that if the Marine Corps is being libeled, it should speak up; if it is not being libeled, it is horrifying, and that quite a case could be made for going permanently AWOL in this no man's land identified by the playbill as Japan in 1957.

The platform stage juts out into three surrounding rows of seats, so the shock treatment is shared. A wire stockade holds the stacked bunks of prisoners all Joseph K's in that you have no idea what their crime, where their trial, or why their punishment. They are quivering pulps of flesh and nerves deliberately made so by sadistic guards who might happily be shot at dusk—why wait for dawn?

Almost every step takes the prisoners to a white floor line they may not cross without permission, and the guards are sneeringly inattentive and contemptuously deaf. The screaming is formidable. So are the blows, the abuse, the cruel little tricks, the whole hideous uproar. It repeats itself into infinity until finally when one prisoner is released, there is no possible doubt as to the fate of the new one arriving.

Theater has long been a platform to expose and correct abuses. I have no idea if "The Brig" fails in that category. But even stranger than for an audience to expose itself to such screaming, ear-splitting brutality is for actors, professional or amateur, to subject themselves to such treatment. Blows can be faked. Interminable push-ups and screaming yourself hoarse can not.

Luckily, Bob Sickinger's company plays only week-end performances, with four days to recover. But as it plays in deadly earnest, I doubt that four are enough.

And so we arrive at the Claudia Cassidy review published shortly before her retirement from the *Tribune*, though she would continue to opine on the arts on WFMT-FM radio in Chicago, for *Chicago* magazine, and occasionally elsewhere. The piece is telling, for sure. It is a review wherein Cassidy was on the wrong side of history.

If the Chicago-style theater that now represents the brand of the city's culture to the world had any obvious beginning, any clear precursor, the work done by Bob Sickinger at the Hull House Theatre is certainly a candidate for that place in history. Sickinger, who died in 2013, worked in the Hull House settlement house, on the corner of Belmont and Broadway in the Lakeview neighborhood. He was, to say the least, an intense personality. Even David Mamet, who was working at Sickinger's theater as a teenager, recalls being cowed. This particularly famous production of "The Brig" was noted for its intensity, its hyperrealism, its in-your-face style. Cassidy lays out what it contained with her usual attention to detail.

Sickinger was, for the most part, working with amateurs, though these were hardly avocational folks looking for a leisurely diversion. More accurately, they were the first of Chicago's storefront, non-Equity actors. Sickinger was, in essence, redefining what was meant by community theater. In an essay written about his experience, Mamet recalls, "We were the community talking to itself."

As Albert Williams wrote in the alternative weekly the *Chicago Reader* many years later, Robert Sickinger's role in these early years of the formation of the Chicago aesthetic is hard to overestimate, but he certainly had his detractors. His theater at the Hull House has been much studied, and the general conclusion is that Sickinger was among the first, if not the first, to actually provide an alternative to the big downtown theaters and the traditional community operations. His tenure at the Hull House lasted for only six years, but it was profoundly influential. Those who worked with him include Warren Casey and Jim Jacobs (the authors of "Grease"), Mike Nussbaum, movie director William Friedkin, and, of course, Mamet himself. "The Brig" was among Sickinger's most successful shows; it was a piece of hypernaturalism. Its author, Kenneth H. Brown, was a former U.S. Marine, and his play, which was famously produced in New York by the Living Theatre in 1963, depicts a dehumanizing day in a U.S. Marine prison (Brown had had that experience himself). Sickinger's fans lapped it up.

So why did Cassidy so despise it? Well, as Williams noted, Sickinger was no fan of critics; he even juiced up his shows to get the reviews he wanted and then let his actors create a more organic kind of work after the opening night had passed. Many in the theater did not like Sickinger, regarding him as self-promoting, even if intermittently brilliant. But probably the most likely answer to that question is that although Cassidy so craved a native Chicago theater, as we have seen, the theater that actually sprouted in the city's neighborhoods so notably was not the kind of theater she herself wanted. In fact, it was a long way from her vision of classic drama at her beloved Auditorium Theatre or Tennessee Williams works at the Civic Theatre in productions worthy of the past greatness of Laurette Taylor. And so Cassidy couldn't recognize that the revolution was happening—the rebels were using different tactics. Chicago theater would grow up in "grim little box[es]" all over the city. And Cassidy had called for it brilliantly and articulated the need for it like no other critic, before or after.

But when it arrived, she was not cheering, because it was not what she wanted. Or maybe that's going too far. Maybe she just hated "The Brig." Either way, the Cassidy years were coming to a close at the *Tribune*.

Will Leonard, for one, knew that a giant was making her exit.

60

THE CASSIDY YEARS

CLAUDIA CASSIDY TALKS ON HER YEARS AS CRITIC

BY WILLIAM LEONARD

JANUARY 13, 1966. Claudia Cassidy, who has been writing reviews of others for more than 30 years, yesterday made her own debut as a public performer, speaking before a luncheon meeting of the Publicity Club of Chicago at the Sheraton-Chicago hotel. She spoke to an audience that packed the Crystal foyer of the hotel and hung on every word in hushed silence, and gave her an ovation at the conclusion of her remarks. Miss Cassidy retired last month as drama and music critic of THE TRIBUNE and now writes a critic-at-large column that appears every Monday.

Her memories ranged from Bruno Walter's: "Talent is power" (which is why Miss Cassidy herself is strong) to Joe E. Lewis' remark at the Chez Paree: "First time I ever saw three heels in one pair of shoes," from Bert Lahr as a men's room attendant in "Du Barry Was a Lady" to the time Walter Damrosch said to Serge Rachmaninoff after a piano concerto: "Maestro, during the slow movement you gazed so deeply into the distance. Do you mind if I ask you what you were thinking about?" Rachmaninoff replied: "I was told that no standees would be allowed in the balcony. There were 37."

Of such is the range of Claudia Cassidy.

She told how she became a drama critic (at the old Chicago Journal of Commerce) in the traditional manner—"by accident," in the era when an editor selected a new reviewer by calling out: "Hey, you!"

"When the boss was desperate," Miss Cassidy declared, "I was handy. He liked it and gave me the job. And I stuck to it, possibly because years before, a man named James Gibbons Huneker had blown off the dust. Pedantic criticism would bore me out of my wits. Huneker was no pedant. It was Henry Mencken who said that because of Huneker, 'Art is no longer, even by implication, a device for improving the mind. It is wholly a magnificent adventure.' It can be. It should be. And that is the whole point."

THIS PORTRAIT OF CASSIDY IN 1979 REVEALS BOTH THE CRITIC'S AGE AND HER UNBOWED PERSONALITY. PHOTOGRAPH BY CHARLES OSGOOD FOR THE *CHICAGO TRIBUNE*.

The late Eddie Johnson, who headed the CHICAGO TRIBUNE color studio, didn't get too excited about the ladies Claudia nominated for cover girl treatment before his cameras. "Eddie was partial to pretty young movie starlets," Miss Cassidy recalled. "He said my people had too much mileage. But the studio did miracles of retouching. Once we thought we had fixed up Gertrude Lawrence to look as ravishing as she was. She threatened to sue."

Visiting companies of Broadway hits and great music and dance organizations on tour are all very well, she asserted, "but, given my druthers, I would have our orchestra and our opera of such luster as to make the world visit us. . . . I know that some attempts are being made to help matters, and more power to them. But I am talking about the best, the very highest level. The day a critic settles for second best, the public will get the third rate."

And so the executioner made her official exit as the drama critic of the *Tribune*, though she would continue to write a column as its critic at large. William Leonard, the man about to take Claudia Cassidy's seat, here attempts to assess Cassidy's impact over more than 30 years, using a public talk she gave soon after her "retirement." His piece contains many grand remarks from her that demonstrate her unique combination of power, eloquence, attitude and unstinting honesty. These are good qualities in a critic.

With the benefit of almost 50 more years of history, it's easy to go further in assessing Cassidy's impact than either Leonard of Cassidy herself could. Cassidy made Chicago a theater town to be reckoned with. She stood proudly for quality. She insisted that Chicago audiences deserved everything that New York audiences got. She was tireless in her support of excellence. And, as we have seen, she was a selective champion of new work, helping bolster the reputations of such plays as "The Glass Menagerie" and "A Raisin in the Sun." She certainly could write the meanest, funniest pans any American critic has ever penned, and yet she was eloquent in her defense and analysis of work she admired. She has been under-studied and underexposed. And, most important of all, she was a magnificent writer.

Cassidy would live until 1996, residing in her later years at the Drake Hotel. She continued to contribute to the *Tribune*, to *Chicago* magazine and to the WFMT public radio station, a relationship that ended in 1983, when she went out in a widely covered blaze of controversy.

As reported by the *Tribune*'s classical music critic John von Rhein, Cassidy had a dustup with Norman Pellegrini, then WFMT's program director. Pellegrini contended that Cassidy's reviews of the Chicago Symphony Orchestra and the Lyric Opera were "biased" and forbade her from reviewing music for the station, though he allowed her to continue her theater and dance coverage. Faced with that edict, Cassidy quit.

According to von Rhein, Pellegrini also had been censoring Cassidy's tapes for some months prior, deleting references to the orchestra. At the time, various commentators (including von Rhein and *Tribune* columnist Bill Granger) wondered aloud whether WFMT was "muzzling" Cassidy because it had financial ties with both the Lyric and the Chicago Symphony as a broadcaster of their work; the station and those institutions issued vigorous denials. Pellegrini, who clearly did not relish being cast as a censor, nonetheless insisted that his reasons were valid. Yet he never was willing or able to go into any detail about the matter, even as his station was widely castigated for "restricting free speech and censoring critics," as Granger put it.

And Cassidy? "I just wasn't going to change, that's all," she said to von Rhein. "The whole thing has come as a total surprise. But I don't think the day will ever come when Norman can damage my reputation."

For good or ill, this late-career incident merely confirmed her tenacity.

After Cassidy's death, a theater in the Chicago Cultural Center would be named in her honor. Despite–or maybe because of–all the controversy surrounding her work, no Chicago arts critic has been, or surely will ever be, more feared, more admired or more influential. Claudia Cassidy helped convince Chicagoans that their city could support a theater, music and opera scene that was not dependent on out-of-town tours but would attract patrons in its own right. And a woman who became a critic "by accident" accomplished all this in an era when few women were in positions of power at the notoriously paternalistic *Tribune*, or indeed at any American newspaper.

Now came a new era. Nonetheless, back in 1966, Leonard clearly felt pressure to continue Cassidy's tradition of opining on the most desirable trajectory for Chicago theater. He thus headed to Hyde Park on the city's South Side.

61

TEARS FLOWING OVER THE STATE OF THE THEATER

BY WILLIAM LEONARD

NOVEMBER 13, 1966. One of the last three weeks, during which this commentary has been absent from these columns, this correspondent spent on the University of Chicago campus, participating in a conference on "The Arts and the Public," sponsored by the university's division of the humanities. While other groups discussed the status of fiction and art, a baker's half-dozen of show biz folk sat around a cluster of tables in the Center for Continuing Education, talking (and arguing) about the state of the theater.

◠ ◠ ◠

There was one playwright (William Gibson, author of "Two for the Seesaw" and "The Miracle Worker," among other things), one director (Alan Schneider, who has staged all of Edward Albee's plays), two producer-directors (John Reich of the Goodman theater and Robert Sickinger of the Hull House theater), one academician (Robert Corrigan, dean of the school of arts of New York university), one commentator (Studs Terkel, jack of numerous trades), and one "journalistic critic" (this reporter).

After nearly a week's backing and filling, there came the time to agree on summary statements. The one filed by the theater parley fearlessly declared that:

1. The audience for the Broadway theater is declining;
2. The public has abdicated its own critical function, and has delegated too much authority to a relatively small number of newspaper reviewers;
3. Social factors militate against theater-going in this country, with the group's opinion divided as to whether the current illness of the American theater is formal or social in origin;
4. The theater needs support or subsidy, yet such assistance, whether political or private, may entail dangers to the theater's freedom of artistic expression;
5. The university should develop its function as a patron of the theater by presenting those new plays which would stand little or no chance of being produced in the commercial, unsubsidized theater.

That was the gist of the official report. This correspondent subscribes to the first, fourth, and fifth of those arguments, would hesitate over the third, and reject the second. My personal report would include two points, developed during the lengthy discussions, that are not mentioned above. I would add these:

6. No one faction in the professional theater seems to know or care about the functions and troubles of the other factions;
7. The professional theater is wallowing in too much self-pity.

With the notable exception of Bill Gibson, a clear-thinking individual who declared he and other professional playwrights have only one duty—to write plays and let the audience take care of itself—the conferees opened their tear ducts all the way about the sorry state of Broadway and "the road." True, there aren't as many theatergoers as there were before the days of radio, balloon tires, the boob tube, night baseball, repeal, the discotheque, the lighted school house, the all-night gasoline station, and the drive-in hamburger stand complete will leggy car hops.

But two members of the panel, both from the allegedly benighted village of Chicago, testified that they had succeeded in finding ticket buyers for semi-professional and subprofessional theater. Reich noted that the Goodman's subscription list had grown, in seven years, from 1,800 to 12,600; Sickinger testified that Hull House subscribers, in three years, have zoomed from 1,700 to 4,500. Somewhere around Chicago, apparently, are a number of citizens who can be coaxed out to the theater of an evening, even if the product is not a "Broadway smash hit" with "the original New York cast."

◠ ◠ ◠

The academic critic, the campus' teacher of drama, came in for some discussion which concluded that he was the man to set a play in its historical perspective, whereas the journalistic critic has come to be seen ("improperly," it was agreed) merely as an arbiter of taste.

"The academic critic," the report surmised, "tends to write for other academic critics, and there is at the present almost no critical writing which bridges the gap between the esoteric utterances of the scholarly journals and the more immediate writings of the journalistic critics."

That was about as close to a kind word as the newspapers received at the conference on the public and the arts. Schneider, because not all the journalistic critics always have thought that all the plays of Edward Albee are wonderful, was willing, nay, eager, to wipe them from the face of the earth.

An otherwise keenly intelligent man, he was the most egregiously bitter man in the colloquia. He despised the average playgoer because he (according to Schneider) is going to the theater against his will. I don't understand this, but he repeated it, in variations, so often that I guess he believes it. He despises the Pulitzer Prize committee because it did not agree with him that "Who's Afraid of Virginia Woolf?" deserved the laurel.

◠ ◠ ◠

And, especially, he despises journalistic critics. He sneers spectacularly because they take notes. O, don't get him wrong. Some of his best friends are critics. But, drat it, they are not infallible. Of all the persons I met at the U. of C., I think Alan Schneider was one of the most provocative. He's a light year off base when he gets on the subject of critics, but he's a stimulating man.

It was his influence, I am sure, that caused the drama division's summary report, submitted on the final day, to start off: "The present state of the theater is not entirely the fault of the journalistic critic."

Entirely? That caused me to laugh and laugh and laugh.

William Leonard, now of course the *Tribune*'s chief theater critic, in the first few weeks of his new assignment went to the University of Chicago, where he attended an (apparently multiday) conference, "The Arts and The Public." His conclusions here are interesting, and so is the cast of theatrically oriented conference attendees: Studs Terkel, William Gibson, Robert Corrigan, John Reich, Robert Sickinger (who must have been glad to see that Cassidy was not there) and Alan Schneider. These men (and they were all men) came up with a lament for the declining Broadway audience and the power of too-few critics (they had no idea how much worse that was going to get), and kvetched over the difficulty of being artistically independent when reliant on someone else's money.

At least Leonard adds a few notes of dissent, arguing that the professionals in the group were factious, interested mostly in their own areas and inclined to self-indulgence. Leonard, it seems here, was his own man. He goes after Schneider, because Schneider, as was his wont, had gone after the whole tribe of newspaper theater critics. Leonard clearly was signaling to his readers that he still had their interests at heart, not those of these whiny theater makers.

But we can also see the facts here about the growth of Chicago's resident theaters, especially the Goodman Theatre, in the mid- to late 1960s. Something was brewing. Leonard would soon be able to follow a different world from the one explored by Cassidy. But next he would wrestle with Edward Albee's mother, who probably would have preferred to talk with Cassidy.

62

ALBEE AND HIS MOTHER DISCUSS HIS WRITING

BY WILLIAM LEONARD

MARCH 19, 1967. Edward Albee, who has been called "the most important American dramatist of his generation," has said of his writing that it is "a condemnation of complacency, cruelty, emasculation, and vacuity; it is a stand against the fiction that everything in this slipping land of ours is peachy-keen." His plays have been peopled by rapacious, merciless women, ugly caricatures of motherhood and wifedom, and downtrodden, ineffectual males who are too contemptible to be pitied.

In his "Who's Afraid of Virginia Woolf?" the male struck back at last, fighting a tooth and nail draw with the relentless wife who would destroy him. In his earlier "The American Dream," the mated antagonists weren't even dignified with given names. They were Mommy and Daddy, who adopted a son they called "the bumble," Mommy gouged the bumble's eyes out, cut off his sex organs, hands, and tongue, before he died. When the bumble's identical twin came on the scene, physically perfect, he was unable to see, to love, to touch, or to communicate.

Edward Albee who was adopted at the age of two weeks after his birth in 1928 by Reed Albee, wealthy owner of a chain of vaudeville theaters, and his second wife, Frances, fought continually with his mother, a dominating woman. It is no secret that he left home in 1948 after a particularly tempestuous quarrel with her, and went to live alone in New York City.

His writing, it has been agreed, is autobiographical. When pressed on that point, Albee has replied: "Your source material is the people you know. Ultimately, every character is an extension of the author's personality."

I called a Palm Beach phone number the other day to talk with Albee, whose latest play, "A Delicate Balance," opens tomorrow at the

Studebaker theater. A woman's voice told the long distance operator: "Edward is not here. This is his mother. Anyone who wishes to speak to him will have to talk with me."

I was delighted at the opportunity. She explained that her son had just left, after spending 10 days with her at her Florida home. As soon as an opportunity presented itself, I asked if she had experienced any embarrassment when "An American Dream," with its picturization of Mommy, was produced in New York.

Frances Albee replied pleasantly: "I never knew it had anything to do with me. I think it's very interesting of you to ask that question."

There were those, I explained, who had thought the play autobiographical. Mrs. Albee said, again pleasantly: "I never knew it had anything to do with me." And, quite cordially, she told me where to find Edward by phone.

◠ ◠ ◠

The playwright answered affably, ready, despite his professed antipathy toward drama critics in general, to talk about "A Delicate Balance" or anything else.

The play has been called not only his best to date, but a more mature, a more mellow variant on the wife-versus-husband theme of "Who's Afraid of Virginia Woolf?"

Albee said: "Critics WOULD use expressions like that. No, it's not more mellow. It has an easy compassion. It makes its points more quietly, almost surreptitiously. It's not really, as it has been called, a play about the antagonisms between people, but about the difficulty of making a choice."

I read aloud the wife's words in the final act: "Time happens, I suppose. To people. Everything becomes . . . too late, finally. You know it's going on . . . up on the hill; you can see the dust, and hear the cries, and the steel . . . but you wait; and time happens. When you do go, sword, shield . . . finally . . . there's nothing there . . . save rust; bones; and the wind."

"That," said Albee "is the key point of 'A Delicate Balance.' It isn't a play about one person's responsibility toward another. It's about time."

◠ ◠ ◠

When I commented that this play differed from its predecessors in giving the husband a voice and a choice, Albee quickly replied: "But he isn't able actually to make that choice. It's too late."

"Who's Afraid of Virginia Woolf?" was a sellout for a season on Broadway, and was made into a movie for which Albee got half a million dollars and 10 per cent of the kind of fantastic gross that can be taken in by those co-stars Elizabeth Taylor and Richard Burton. "A Delicate Balance," on the other hand, while generally rated a superior play, ran less than four months after it opened on Broadway last September, and the original New York cast now is touring it.

I recalled an occasion in Ypsilanti, Mich., last summer, when I heard drama critics from all over the United States discussing the "Who's Afraid of Virginia Woolf?" film, not in terms of the importance of its content on the screen, but in terms of what tremendous box office it would have because it included a few morsels naughtier than traditional movie fare.

Albee, as might be expected, chuckled: "That's what I would expect of drama critics. And as for that, people always go to plays for the wrong reasons."

"A Delicate Balance" his best play? Albee has written in too many directions, sometimes realistically, sometimes in the abstract, sometimes (as in "The Death of Bessie Smith") as a social commentator rather than a stylist. He has written one-act plays, full-length plays, one adaptation (of Carson McCullers' "The Ballad of the Sad Cafe"), and even had taken on the task of an emergency rewrite of the Truman Capote musical, "Breakfast at Tiffany's" before advising David Merrick to give up and pour the whole expensive thing down the drain.

◠ ◠ ◠

Naturally, Albee expects the new play on which he is now at work to be his best. "It's a very, very strange play," he admits. "It has only two humans, along with some underwater creatures, not all of whom will be mute. I'm hoping to combine the realistic and unrealistic this time. And although I don't even have a final title, I'm very optimistic about it."

All of Albee's nine plays excepting "Malcolm," a seven-performance flop on Broadway last November, have been produced in Chicago. Most of them, however, have been seen here in the hands of semi-professional or sub-professional companies. Only "Who's Afraid of Virginia Woolf?" has had an Equity presentation in the Loop, preceding "A Delicate Balance" to the same Studebaker stage in 1964 with Nancy Kelly and Shepherd Strudwick in the leads, and returning in 1965 with Vicki Cummings and Kendall Clark as the combatants.

The veteran team of Jessica Tandy and Hume Cronyn has been playing the roles of Agnes and Tobias in "A Delicate Balance" since last fall. This is the seventh Broadway show in which they have paired since their marriage in 1942. Chicago has seen them only in "The Fourposter," the two-character comedy at the Blackstone in 1952, and "The Man in the Dog Suit," at the Hinsdale Summer theater in 1957.

Co-starred with them, as Agnes' alcoholic sister, is Rosemary Murphy, who played the deceived wife in "Any Wednesday" for two years on Broadway.

"A Delicate Balance" will be at the Studebaker only until April 8.

This piece is not, of course, a review. William Leonard intended it as a preview article to his interview with Edward Albee. It ends up being a rather fascinating little interview with Albee's mother, who happened to answer the telephone when Leonard called the playwright in 1967. "Anyone who wishes to speak to him," she apparently said, "will have to talk with me." Leonard, not missing an unusual opportunity, asked her if she felt any embarrassment after the production of "American Dream." She apparently insisted that she did not know it had anything to do with her. She was not the first mother of a playwright to make such an assertion.

The woman on the other end of Leonard's phone line, it seems, was Frances Albee, who had formally adopted the playwright in 1929 in Larchmont, New York. The Albees were an old American family of great wealth, as evident in Albee's plays. Frances Albee was a very tall woman, as noted in her adopted son's "Three Tall Women." According to Mel Gussow's biography of Edward Albee, she had an unfaithful husband.

Frances Albee is regarded as the model for several Albee characters, including Mommy in "The Sandbox" and "The American Dream" and A in "Three Tall Women." She generally did not give interviews about the son from whom she was mostly estranged. She died in 1989.

The unnamed new play that Edward Albee was working on at the time of this piece was "Seascape." In 2012, Steppenwolf Theatre Company would take its hit production of "Who's Afraid of Virginia Woolf?"—much discussed here—to Broadway.

63

LOOP NO LONGER HAS MONOPOLY ON THEATER

BY WILLIAM LEONARD

JULY 2, 1967. It used to be a drama editor's traditional chore, at this time of year, to sum up the Chicago theater season just ended and compare it, statistically and qualitatively, with preceding seasons. There were many more theaters in the Loop, in those days, than there are today, but his task was simple.

The only theater that counted was the standard, Equity, touring shows that played downtown. There was nothing outside the Loop excepting rank amateurism beneath journalistic notice.

The drama editor simply counted up the productions that had stopped off in Chicago on their tours, and wrote: "In the season of 1946–47, there were 31 shows, at nine theaters, for a total of 281 playgoing weeks, compared with 37 shows at nine houses for 326 weeks in the season of 1945–46."

Twenty years later, an editor could write: "In the season of 1966–67, there were 17 shows, at six houses, for a total of 131 weeks."

If that makes it sound as if the playgoing possibilities in the Loop are about half as numerous as they were 20 years ago, the figures are not lying. But the Loop figures no longer have a great deal to do with what is going on in Chicago theatrically.

Twenty years ago, there were no professional stars in semi-professional productions at the Goodman, no Hull House putting on amateur presentations of near-professional caliber, no American

Conservatory theater filling Ravinia with excitement, no Second City, no Happy Medium, and none of the outlying resident companies which, tho they spend almost all their time on light, forgettable comedies, occasionally come up with a prestige item or a premiere.

Only 17 professional theatrical attractions came to the Loop last season, but they represented a mere fraction of the number of stage shows that entertained Chicagoans who have fallen out of the habit of going downtown after dark.

Let's consider the productions that were seen from June 1, 1966, to May 31, 1967, in the half dozen Loop playhouses that still seem to have survived the wreckers and the realtors.

Longest run, keeping the Blackstone lit for all 52 weeks, of course was "The Odd Couple." Second longest was "Hello, Dolly!," which [——] out a 47-week run at the Shubert in December. Then the Shubert went to nonmusicals, with "Philadelphia, Here I Come" and "Marat-Sade," and now has been dark since last March, one of the longest idle periods in its history since it opened on the site of the old Majestic in 1945. It will re-light five weeks from now, with Howard Keel in "On a Clear Day You Can See Forever."

The Studebaker kept busy with a succession of briefer engagements—"Any Wednesday" in a return trip with June Wilkinson, "Generation" with Robert Young being replaced by Barnard Hughes who was replaced with Don Porter, "Hostile Witness" with Ray Milland, the National Repertory theater with three plays ("The Imaginary Invalid," "A Touch of the Poet," and "Tonight at 8:30"), "The Fantasticks" in a fantastic return engagement, "A Delicate Balance" with Hume Cronyn and Jessica Tandy, "The Owl and the Pussycat" in another of those returns, and "Wait Until Dark."

McVickers, which had attempted musical comedies five years ago, then reverted to movies, returned to the fold of legitimate theaters with "Half a Sixpence," "The Royal Hunt of the Sun," and "Fiddler on the Roof," the latter now about midway in a nine-month run which will keep it on Madison street until October.

The Civic Opera house found time for the Bristol Old Vic, presenting "Hamlet," "Measure for Measure," and "Romeo and Juliet" in the course of one week, the D'Oyly Carte Opera company with three tried and true Gilbert and Sullivan works, and five performances of a revival of "Porgy and Bess."

The Civic was rumored for months as the new Chicago home of the A.C.T., but that dream vanished. It did house the world premiere of "That Summer—That Fall," Frank Gilroy's new play which failed to duplicate the success of his "The Subject Was Roses," and went on to a quick demise in New York.

And that was the entire season of 1966–67, according to the old method of including only the professional productions in the Loop. But those 17 touring efforts give slight indication of what went on in Chicago theater over the year.

There no longer is a simple method for adding up a season in these parts. The A.C.T. presented eight plays to sold-out houses in the Howell Murray theater at Ravinia. The Goodman brought Chicago its first, most exciting look at "Marat-Sade." It also brought Jerome Kilty in "Tartuffe," Dolores Sutton (and the author, Tennessee Williams) to town with "Eccentricities of a Nightingale," James Ray and Carrie Nye in "Much Ado About Nothing," Gloria Foster in Strindberg's "A Dream Play," and Terry Lomax in "Oh, What a Lovely War!"

The A.C.T., in a six-week season that set the town abuzz with a sudden realization that Chicago needed a repertory theater, filled the Howell Murray theater at Ravinia for "Six Characters in Search of an Author," "Charley's Aunt," "Uncle Vanya," "Tiny Alice," "Misalliance," "Endgame," Beyond the Fringe," and "Under Milk Wood."

Bob Sickinger's polished amateurs at Hull House introduced us to John Hersey's "The Child Buyer," Harold Pinter's "The Birthday Party," Venable Herndon's "Until the Monkey Comes," and John Whiting's "The Devils."

Second City presented four original satirical revues in the course of the year. The Happy Medium, before it turned into a rock 'n' roll parlor, had New York's "The Mad Show" for 19 weeks. The Harper housed a Chicago produced revival of Jean Anouilh's "Becket," a locally-produced revue, “Summer in the City,” two plays from off-Broadway, Douglas Turner Ward’s “Happy Ending,” and “Day of Absence,” and two presentations of Beverly Younger in her one-woman show, “Women in the Great Society.” John Gielgud and Irene Worth presented “Men and Women of Shakespeare” at the Goodman.

The old, established outlying theaters continued to bring “name” stars in vintage comedies to suburbia, and two brand new playhouses were opened within the city limits. In the Round Dinner playhouse, on the southwest side at Archer and Mayfield avenues, inaugurated a series of musical comedy revivals last September, without big name stars, but with a meal and a show in one package.

The Ivanhoe theater, an attractive arena theater adjoining the historic Ivanhoe restaurant on the north side, opened last June with Thelma Ritter in the aged “The Late Christopher Bean,” made a try at prestigious production with Mercedes McCambridge in “The Glass Menagerie,” and, as the new season opened, achieved nation-wide publicity by presenting Princess Lee Bouvier Radziwill in “The Philadelphia Story.”

How does one add up a theatrical season like the one of 1966–67? Certainly not simply by counting up what showed in the Loop alone, as we did back in 1946–47.

Those days have gone forever.

And so with Claudia Cassidy now reduced to being the *Tribune*’s critic at large, William Leonard got his chance to opine on what he thought should be the future direction of Chicago theater. He serves notice here that Cassidy’s long-established practice at year-end of summing up the offerings at the Loop theaters (almost all touring shows) was no longer a fair judge of what now constituted Chicago theater. It’s also notable, of course, that the beginnings of the homegrown Chicago theater coincided with the demise of the once-extensive slate of touring productions.

Leonard makes reference here to the attempt to bring the American Conservatory Theater to Chicago. ACT ended up going to San Francisco; had the various wealthy donors who wanted to bring it to Chicago succeeded, it seems unlikely that the Goodman would have found the way so clear to blossom as the city’s flagship theater.

This piece is a fascinating overview of what the Chicago theater scene—a scene very much in transition—looked like in 1967, when the Loop was receding as an artistic destination and the neighborhoods and their storefront theaters were very much on the rise. Yet we also see here the struggles Leonard and other *Tribune* critics had with defining what now constituted professional theater. That was a debate here to stay.

64

ANIMAL FARM

BALLET AND DIALOG; AN IMPERFECT MIX

Organic Theater at Holy Covenant Church

BY WILLIAM LEONARD

MARCH 15, 1970. Ballet and dialog mix like oil and water. The new version of George Orwell's "Animal Farm" on the north side is supposed to be an allegorical drama but it's about nine-tenths wonderfully imaginative choreography and one-tenth boring dialog. If the Organic theater only could have mimed the entire thing, in this production at the Holy Covenant church on Diversey avenue, instead of breaking into sporadic conversation, it would have been a much better show.

As it is, this is an interesting and frequently refreshing effort. The seven members of the cast enact not only pigs and cows and horses and chickens and occasional humans, but even rocks and plows and stones and windmills and growing crops. For the last, the audience is pressed into service, the playgoer raising an arm slowly to signify a sprouting plant of some kind or other.

The grunting, squealing, squawking actors effect wonders in projecting the animals' personalities, as they rebel against man's bestiality toward beasts, take over farmer Jones' farm to run it themselves, then find themselves in a fascist state with the pigs as tyrannical over the other animals as humans ever had been.

It is a sad story and a grim one, and it is unleavened by humor. There are oppression and death on every side, which is what Orwell was trying to say years ago. The young players do their work well, in the middle of the church floor, with the pews removed and a few rows of seats around the arena.

Tho the book is obvious and predictable and repetitious, the show is worth seeing, if only for that animalistic choreography. There are no credits listed for that or for the writing of the play, but Stuart Gordon directed.

The name is familiar? Yes, this company stems from the one that was busted on the Madison campus of the University of Wisconsin a year ago for putting on a "Peter Pan" with nudity. (That old thing!)

There are no such shenanigans at the Holy Covenant church.

By 1970, the Chicago theater renaissance was under way with the arrival of one of its most crucial companies—Stuart Gordon's Organic Theater. This group did mostly original work, relied on improv, was noted for its intensity and high failure rate and generally was one of the first manifestations of what would come to be thought of as the Chicago theater aesthetic. Gordon, who was Chicago born, had arrived in town from the University of Wisconsin–Madison. On that campus, he'd made a name for himself by founding a company called Screw Theatre and producing a version of "Peter Pan" that protested the war in Vietnam and cast Mayor Richard J. Daley as Captain Hook.

Along with wife Carolyn Purdy-Gordon, he founded the Organic in 1970, and in this piece Leonard reviews its very first production, of George Orwell's "Animal Farm." The critic would return, as will we, to the Organic. But Leonard was not fond of this first venture: he bluntly begins his less-than-nuanced review by asserting that "ballet and dialog mix like oil and water," which is rather an absurd general pronouncement, however they might have seemed at this particular show. Leonard was not a stylist even remotely akin to Cassidy. But he called the shows, the changing shows, as he saw them.

65

THE BODY POLITIC EXCITING, MAYBE REVOLUTIONARY

BY WILLIAM LEONARD

APRIL 19, 1970. Nobody else in the theatrical world is doing what they're doing—at least that's what the young players at the Body Politic, the "story theater" operation on Lincoln avenue, profess to believe. This is Paul Sills' latest venture, in which the actors narrate old, established stories, meanwhile miming the action they are describing. The technique may not sound exciting or revolutionary, but we know already that it certainly is the former, and it could prove to be the latter as well.

"What we'd like," said one of the players as the rehearsing cast sat around the otherwise deserted playhouse, converted unpretentiously from a deserted storefront, "is for some of the other satirical and improvisational companies around the country to steal the style from us, and improve on it, so we could steal it back again, and go from there."

Nothing ever moved a story along on a stage more rapidly than this "story theater" fashion of presenting one, and the classic tales are told with new nuances, as well as with speed.

◠ ◠ ◠

For instance, we wrote of "Ovid's Metamorphoses," the first production last October: "The fluidity is remarkable, and the imagery is beautifully effective. Jove hurling thunderbolts, Mercury descending to earth with a crash landing, goddesses swimming underwater, Pygmalion carving Galatea from a piece of stone—these and several other flights of fancy work stunningly in this technique."

The second production, "The Master Thief," comprised fairy stories by the Grimm brothers. They came off electrically, filled with talking animals, magic, invisible people, and wishes made to come true.

The third production, "The Parson in the Cupboard," which opened Wednesday in the barnlike former storefront at 2259 N. Lincoln av., includes eight scenes, based on Aesop's fables, on other Grimm brothers' stories, on an anonymous Russian story, and a scene based on a Scottish ballad.

◠ ◠ ◠

Sounds like children's theater, with all those fairy stories? Not any more than Aesop's is for kids! These stories of fools and felons and fiends and foolish feuding are timeless—and so, audiences find them filled with references that sound as if they were inspired by today's headlines.

Actually, the players were saying, nothing is added to or subtracted from the original story. It's all there. The actors go to it as if they were interested in nothing more than entertaining—and let the audience delightedly discover the message itself.

"We let the story tell itself," said Chuck Bartlett, "instead of trying to sell it. We don't try to do the Grimm brothers' work for them; they've done it already."

Del Close used to be one of the better players at the Second City a few years back. For the last few seasons he's been directing at the Committee, a satirical theater of the same kind in San Francisco. Now he has taken a leave, to join the Body Politic for what he expects will be about a year.

"Sometimes," he declared, "we don't know quite what the story is going to do when we start rehearsing. Sometimes, it seems, it's the audience that tells us what the point of the story is."

Do they start with some kind of a script?

No, Sills asks for suggestions as to stories they might play (but they always seem to wind up doing the ones of his choice). Then they read the story, put the book down, and start in telling it and acting it simultaneously, inventing their own dialog as they go along.

This is a little reminiscent of the Second City system, but the end product is entirely different.

"We don't tell the story in terms of an actor's lines," declared Gerritt Graham, "but in terms of events."

"And," added Cordis Fejer, the young actress who appeared at the Goodman recently in Harold Pinter's "The Basement," "this is a real community theater. It appeals to people who don't wait for the Broadway hits to come to the Loop. I don't mean just people from the neighborhood. About a third of our audiences come from suburbia."

That, of course, is what Paul Sills wanted, when he founded this unusual theater. That's why he called it the Body Politic. He wanted to reach the body politic.

Just about a month after encountering the Organic Theater in its early experiments, Leonard, who was famous for his straw hats, rolled in to see the work at another new venue that would become a famous part of the Chicago theater scene–the Body Politic, an operation associated with the Reverend James "Jim" Shiflett, a Presbyterian minister and social activist who was operating at 2257 N. Lincoln Ave. on Chicago's North Side. The Body Politic was, in its first instance, more of a community arts building. But Shiflett had sought out Paul Sills, who returned to the scene with this new company. Here, Leonard reviews one of its most famous productions.

Following the lead of Glenna Syse, by now the theater critic at the *Chicago Sun-Times*, Leonard got behind the Body Politic, using words like *revolutionary* to describe its innovations. Sills, never beloved by Cassidy, had found a friendlier critic.

This piece also contains some fascinating insights into the work of Del Close, who was involved with Body Politic. In many ways, what Close and Sills are discussing here would form the basis of the subsequent improvisational work that would be done at Improv Olympic, an improv theater and training school (later known as iO) that would be highly influential, along with the Second City, in American comedy.

Leonard, it seems, is grasping the similarities and the differences between the Second City aesthetic (improv used in the creation of original, scripted sketch comedy) and the harder-core improv being posited here by Sills and Close. This division, already evident in this piece, would congeal over the years into a kind of aesthetic rivalry between sketch advocates and improv purists. Body Politic, Leonard saw, was on the cusp of something different from what he'd reviewed in his cabaret and nightlife days.

66

GREASE

GREASY NOSTALGIA FULL OF LAUGHS

Kingston Mines Theatre

BY WILLIAM LEONARD

FEBRUARY 12, 1971. Nostalgia usually is sweet. When it's dished up with a reeking flavor of cynicism, that makes it funny instead.

Kingston Mines Theater, on Lincoln Avenue near Fullerton, has been so far out in its avant garde productions hitherto that few besides astronauts could stay with it. Now it has flipped its wig and is presenting an original musical comedy harking back to, of all things, the way it was in high schools around Chicago in the late '50s.

And this has to be one of the most screamingly funny shows in town.

JAMES CANNING (DOODY) AND SUE WILLIAMS (RIZZO) IN THE ORIGINAL PRODUCTION OF "GREASE" AT THE KINGSTON MINES THEATRE IN 1971.

Its name is "Grease," and its characters are the louts in plenty of that material in their pompadoured hair, and the tramp lasses who wore saddle shoes, bobby socks, skirts just below the knee and jackets with the name of their club (in this case the Pink Ladies) sewed on the back.

Music by Jim Jacobs and Warren Casey has the tang of the period, a prerock era in which the words were decipherable, usually sung by a well synchronized quartet accompanying the soloist, and often with maudlin sentiment.

A great portion of the spectators at the Kingston Mines could have been in high school about 10 years ago, and they scream in hilarious recognition, as the kids onstage discuss fan magazine articles about Fabian or Frankie Avalon or the roller coaster opening scene in "This Is Cinerama."

"Grease" opens with a 10th anniversary reunion of the Rydell High School Class of 1960, the school principal pontificating in banal and mealy-mouthed fashion of the good old days.

Then we go back to those days, when this group of seniors constituted a bunch of foul-mouthed, lazy, brawling, useless, cheating, disrespectful no-goods. Their combination of stupidity and arrogance, since the show tries to prove no moral, is funny. Against the background of the music from memory lane, its comedy value is enhanced.

Jacobs and Casey wrote the book and lyrics, as well as the score, which is played by a small band that flirts with rock tho it remembers that this was a teen-agers' world when rock was in its infancy.

Only a youthful cast could give "Grease" the heady spirit on which it soars, and these players work with energy and enthusiasm that are exciting, tho they are not the most polished performers in the business.

Polly Pen shines as the clean-cut, well-scrubbed square from the enemy camp, an "establishment" girl who is proud to be a cheerleader and tries unsuccessfully to coax one of the boy slobs into respectability. Leslie Goto shines as the wistful little square who tries to be good until she becomes too lonely, then switches to the Pink Ladies, as tough a bunch of broads as ever swaggered across a prep school campus.

Kingston Mines is an amateur theater with weak acoustics, but these amateurs are doing a show worth seeing (for those who don't mind dirty four-letter words and lots of them).

For a sense of just how much one of the most famous shows in Chicago history changed before going to Broadway, we just have to read the first sentence of William Leonard's review of "Grease": "a reeking flavor of cynicism." Not what most later fans of Danny, Sandy and the Pink Ladies would expect.

"Grease" began life at the old Kingston Mines Theatre in Lincoln Park (located in a former trolley barn at 2356 N. Lincoln Ave., where a parking garage now stands). The blues club, now nearby on Halsted Street, was in the front and the theater was in the back.

Penned by Jim Jacobs and Warren Casey, this racy, edgy musical was a huge hit in 1971. It belonged to the Northwest Side of Chicago, and to the real sons and daughters of the working-class men and women who raised their postwar kids in its rough-and-tumble boundaries. "Grease" was, in this original form, not much more structurally than a spoof of the old Alan Freed movies that would invariably end with the bad-boy hero reforming in the final reel. Jacobs and Casey merely decided to turn that narrative on its head. "We said to ourselves," Jacobs would later recall, "what if the girl changes instead?"

After this first production, as its refreshingly candid creator Jim Jacobs noted in a *Tribune* interview many years later, "Grease" was never the same. "When we went to New York," Jacobs said, "we were told it was necessary to make the characters lovable, instead of scaring everybody. The show went from about three-quarters book and one-quarter music to one-quarter book and three-quarters music." The show that Leonard reviews here did not have an opening number called "Summer Nights," but one called "Foster Beach." In addition, there was much colorful 1950s-era slang—phrases like "eat me" and "suck wind." There were references to Taft High School, the Palmer House, Lake Shore Drive and those accommodating Cook County Forest Preserves.

Songs were divided equally among an ensemble cast. In the place of "Born to Hand Jive," there was a number called "Boogie Man Boogie" (a "Monster Mash"–like affair). Sandy didn't warble "Hopelessly Devoted to You," but a song called "Kiss It." And there was a title number, but it sure wasn't written by Barry Gibb.

Jacobs also said in the same interview that he and Casey (who died in 1988) never resisted any of these changes. They were young Chicago guys writing their first show. They wanted to play by the rules. And thus Jacobs (who was an actor in the early days of Chicago theater and once worked for the *Tribune*) made enough money from "Grease," and its various movies and spinoffs, to last a lifetime. According to him, "The very first guy who saw the script in Chicago was Paul Sills," the late improv guru. "He asked us if we wanted him to direct it. We told him no, because we wanted to put it up in the next five years."

Leonard was not the only critic who championed the show (despite his misgiving about the "amateur" performers) and helped it move to New York. Michael Feingold of the *Village Voice* flew in to see it twice and also became an unlikely champion. Director Michael Bennett also came in to see it (but decided that he'd add feathers and ruin it). The 1978 movie version, produced by Robert Stigwood, added disco-era songs (now part of the live show) and the star power of John Travolta and Olivia Newton-John, forever tagging Sandy as, ideally, a blonde. The show was changed, but its title became a household name.

But the story doesn't end there. After a lousy national tour of "Grease" came through town in 2009, Jacobs would tell the *Tribune* that he missed the original. He would lament how much the show had changed when it moved to Broadway and later Hollywood: the deletion of songs, characters and local references; the sanitization of the real language of the neighborhood kids; the complete separation of a show about a community from the very community that had created the show. PJ Paparelli of the American Theater Company would read that *Tribune* story, and "The Original Grease" would return to Chicago in 2011 in its original form—before the palm trees, the Bee Gees, the reality shows, Frankie Avalon, the big production numbers, the PC police, the campy comedy, the big star with the Australian accent and the endless succession of musical tours—pretty much as Leonard reviews it first here. Once again, "Grease" was a piece of populist theater about ordinary Chicago teenagers.

Even as the greasers were still playing, Cassidy was returning to Tennessee Wililiams. For one last time in the *Tribune*.

67

TENNESSEE WILLIAMS—A THEATER ORPHEUS WHO LOOKED BACK

BY CLAUDIA CASSIDY

Claudia Cassidy, retired drama and music critic of The Tribune, draws on her vast theater experience, her admiration for Tennessee Williams and her recollections of his past successes for this article.

JULY 4, 1971. He now says, "Call me Tom." But I can't. Thomas Lanier Williams is Tennessee to me and always was, even in the days when he signed himself "Tenn" or, with that deceptive air of faintly indolent amusement, "10." Nor can I interview him, and never tried. It seems to me that Tennessee hides from interviews behind an impenetrable facade of candor.

At first it may have been shyness. Writers often are shy about the spoken word. Later? I sometimes think that some costly—in both senses—psychiatrist said to him, stop pretending. Your name is Thomas Lanier Williams, called Tom, not Tennessee, which you picked for yourself. And don't let anything really touch you any more, it hurts too much. Smile and laugh a bit wildly and admit everything, in a detached sort of way. Even insist on telling. If you tell everything, even too much, people can't pry because there is nothing left to find. So, they find nothing.

⁂

Tennessee called Tom, but not by me, ran away from a life he did not like and invented one of his own, but he took the old one along with him—as Thomas Wolfe did in "Look Homeward, Angel"—because he could not leave it behind. Pretending and hurting, denying and remembering, escaping and coming right back, he wrote his finest plays. Everybody pretends and hurts, denies and remembers, escapes and returns. We recognized truth—transcended, to be sure, but truth—when we saw it in Tennessee's first plays.

The secret Tennessee, the one I don't pretend to know in person, but see so clearly in his plays, has a strong kinship with Orpheus descending. He knows it. He has been writing his Orpheus play all his life, and it never quite succeeded, not even when his name blazed on the marquees of the world. He is haunted by his Orphic echo of the sweet singer who descends into the underworld, looks back, and is torn apart by the harpies—who to Tennessee are deep south bigots with bloodhounds and blowtorches on a lynching spree.

Bloodhounds are bad enough, but blowtorches? The searing, blasting symbol brings the myth too close? It was all right for Orpheus, son of Apollo and perhaps of Calliope, to go into Hades to rescue his dead wife, Eurydice. It was all right for his song, which made even Pluto weep, so to disarm the infernal spirits that they gave her back to him, on one condition. He was to walk ahead of her and not look back. But she implored him and he loved her and he looked back. So Orpheus returned to earth alone, he never again looked at a woman, and in Dionysiac orgy harpies tore him apart. A myth is all right, rather picturesque. Didn't even Gluck write an opera about it? But blowtorches?

⁂

The first Tennessee Orpheus I know about was the 1940 "Battle of Angels." The Theater Guild opened it in Boston and wound up apologizing to the appalled audience. It "closed in tryout," an ominous thing for a young playwright. But he did not back away. He rewrote the play as "Orpheus Descending." Cliff Robertson and Maureen Stapleton played it, and it failed. He rewrote the screen play, "The Fugitive Kind." Marlon Brando and Anna Magnani played it, and it horrified a lot of people.

Yet it would not surprise me if close at hand on Tennessee's work table there is a working script of Orpheus descending. Perhaps some day a searing, blasting composer will think of it as an opera, now that Lee Holby seems to have a success with "Summer and Smoke."

Odd, how many have forgotten that in 1955 the Lyric staged Tennessee's "Lord Byron's Love Letter," Raffaello de Banfield's lovely, lyrical soaring into the high tessitura of the supreme experience remembered. Astrid Varnay was the old woman remembering, and Carol Lawrence was the little dancer who met the poet for one magical moment on the windswept Acropolis.

"This is a memory play," says Tennessee in and of "The Glass Menagerie," and he could have said it of so many more. He does look back. It may have been his undoing, but once it was his strength. He looked back to his sensitive boyhood in that matriarchal household in Columbus, Miss., on the Tombigbee, which is a kind of life known to no household outside the deep south. He looked back in anguish to his sister Rose, who really did have a glass menagerie. Rose, given a frontal lobotomy by consent of her parents, but without Tennessee's, who did not even know until it was too late.

⌒ ⌒ ⌒

Out of all this and more came "The Glass Menagerie," a fragile, haunting, wonderfully funny play that grows stronger with the years. Out of Rose's tragedy came "Suddenly Last Summer," where the young girl who saw too much is rescued from lobotomy by a compassionate young surgeon. How often Tennessee must have wished he had been that man.

Two of my most potent theater nights came in Chicago's little Civic in those two plays. In that December blizzard of 1944 "The Glass Menagerie" introduced a playwright and restored Laurette Taylor. Tennessee wrote of Amanda Wingfield, "She is not paranoic, but her life has been paranoia." He wrote of Tom, "a poet with a job in a warehouse," who is Tennessee, who clerked in a shoe store, "His nature is not remorseless, but to escape he has to be without pity." Tennessee and Laurette understood each other. They were as unsparing as they were magical.

The other night was just as unexpected. Diana Barrymore, who had been a rather pitiful joke in the famed family of her brilliant, aberrant father, stepped out to play the girl in "Suddenly Last Summer," and seared the heart.

◠◠◠

If I could say just one thing about Tennessee Williams, it would be that he has an infinite compassion for women. A chivalric tenderness that sometimes betrays him. When he rewrote "Summer and Smoke" as "Eccentricities of a Nightingale," he gave the pitiful heroine a way out of rejection by turning the potent young doctor next door into an emasculated booby. It ruined the play, but I suspected that in some way Tennessee could not bear Miss Alma's desolation, especially when Geraldine Page was Miss Alma.

But that came later, when his work had run into trouble. At the beginning, the most powerful young playwright of our time could work in what Carl Sandburg called the priceless climate of loneliness. He knew that compassion strikes deepest when there is no way out.

A long time ago I wrote, "I am not one who can find in Mr. Williams' farewells the ray of light called hope. As 'The Glass Menagerie' dimmed its candles on desolation, so 'Streetcar' opens the doors of the madhouse to a woman who only by the grace of God will be mad when she enters them."

Has anyone who saw it forgotten that "Streetcar" curtain? There was that violent, brawling, hurting play that catapulted Marlon Brando into a fame of sheer, hypnotic brute force he could never quite escape. Everyone thought "Streetcar" a man's play. With Brando, it was.

◠◠◠

But "Streetcar" is a woman's play. It belongs to Blanche Du Bois and Uta Hagen took possession here in Chicago, with Anthony Quinn. I saw Jessica Tandy play Blanche beautifully, and Arletty play it badly in Cocteau's Paris production all live moss, naked Negroes and shrill searchlights, and fragile, frightened-eyed Vivien Leigh play it in London. But Uta Hagen tore you to tatters. I walked out of that performance to see Tennessee in the back row, tears pouring down his face.

Could anyone forget that last "Streetcar" scene? Pretentious, promiscuous Blanche of the pitiful airs and graces, who has found that the obverse of death is desire, is raped by her potent hulk of a brother in law, and her sex-obsessed sister has her committed rather than admit the truth.

When they come to take her away Blanche shrinks from the squat, institutionalized female. The man in charge takes over. He lifts his hat and offers his arm. Blanche takes it like a woman going in to dinner. She says, "Whoever you are, I have always depended on the kindness of strangers." It is a lovely, gallant exit, but an exit to the madhouse just the same.

Yet there is a vast difference between those two plays that first told us so much about Tennessee Williams. In "The Glass Menagerie" the outer dusk is a jungle where savage cats tear each other apart. In "Streetcar" the beasts have moved indoors, and the jungle is the heart.

It is no news that success has its problems. Tennessee had worked alone, as a man must. He began to have to collaborate, or think he had to. Elia Kazan, a brilliant director and money at the box office, wanted rewriting. The originals I have seen were finer.

I thought too that some stage direction, powerful in its own terms, destroyed Tennessee. Theater is an old hand at violence from without, which can be spectacular and which also can crush what is inside. Tennessee understood the more devastating shock of violence from within. Repeatedly he shattered the world of illusion in which alone he seemed to live, shattered it by unbearable inner tensions whose very explosion outward is a kind of release.

I felt that strongly about "Cat on a Hot Tin Roof," and was reassured when George Keathley's revival released the play's full power. I have always wondered what he did with the Miami tryout of "Sweet Bird of Youth" as a long, one-act play. Rewritten, recast and redirected, it never did have more than one act, but that act was indelible.

In the slatted shadows of that southern hotel room Chance Wayne was in mortal danger. When he walked out for the vengeance of castration it was tawdriness tacked on. But that first act of the once golden boy and the withered ex-movie star remains irresistible. Both Paul Newman and Rip Torn played the kept boy, Geraldine Page the heartbreakingly funny woman whose reaction to unexpected success was that of a wilting flower given fresh water.

Somewhere in all this was the compassionate understanding that we all need to be recognized, and that the artist's need is greatest of all. Thousands of writers must have said that. But Tennessee said it better than most. He could reach out in a dark theater and catch you by the throat.

Once in Spoleto, he did it to me again. I had gone to the high hill town to see the tryout of "The Milk Train Doesn't Stop Here Any More." There on that dreamlike little stage was another marvelous, terrible old woman, Flora Goforth, with a fierce passion for life, an uproarious voracity sprung from the same intuitive understanding that had created Amanda Wingfield.

The play blew up at the end, and the detonation was deafening when the Burtons turned it into "Boom." But on that little stage at Spoleto, with Hermione Baddeley as Flora Goforth and Mildred Dunnock as a vulture veiled in black and virtuosity, it was marvelous while it lasted.

Somehow, as Tennessee looked back, he was more and more Orpheus descending, the figure that has haunted his writing life. The harpies descended in their hideous guise as voracious bird-women with tearing talons. Flesh was ripped and cannibalism was not the word unspoken. Terrible birds struck on bleak sand spits with no place to hide.

It is not just Tennessee's triumphs that haunt me. I can still see the ravaged, half-blinded beauty of Margaret Leighton in "The Mutilated," the fierce refusal of Zoe Caldwell to go down with "Slapstick Tragedy." To me, the tryout "Night of the Iguana" was bankrupt. Bankrupt is the end of a road, not of the world.

For Tennessee is a playwright, unless in that terrible phrase Brooks Atkinson reluctantly applied to him, psychiatry has made him "consume his own insides." He knows that tragedy clings to the precipice of comedy, so that some of his saddest people are the most endearingly absurd. He knows the vulnerable ferocity of the heart. He has written powerful, brilliant, absorbing plays that took a rocket to the moon. He has been hag-ridden and haunted and away too long. Yet if he never wrote another line in his life, he has enriched theater beyond counting and we are forever in his debt.

Remember when Amanda said, look over your left shoulder and make a wish on that little silver slipper of a moon? There will be a full moon Thursday night when George Keathley introduces Tennessee's new play "Out Cry" at the Ivanhoe. Amanda's wish was "Happiness. Good fortune." But then all Tennessee's plays are a cry of the heart.

This is our last Claudia Cassidy piece, written after the great critic had semi-retired. It is about her favorite playwright, Tennessee Williams, and it is an extraordinarily moving piece of analysis that deserves rescuing from obscurity. Its headline is telling–Cassidy, of course, is looking back on her own career in this piece, albeit hiding behind Williams. No piece–not even the "Glass Menagerie" review–is more revealing of the closeness of their relationship.

You can't miss the change in tone here from all those previous Cassidy reviews. For a woman who hated giving interviews, hated being photographed, despised the very notion of being the subject of articles herself, she is remarkably personal here–and, frankly, pretty much *only* here. The more times one reads this piece, the more it seems that Cassidy saw herself in Williams's women, especially such characters as Blanche Du Bois. He touched her like no other writer, and she returned the favor with profound sympathy and understanding.

This piece hasn't been read much in the years since it first was published. That's a great shame. For it is a remarkable article on a great American writer penned by the Chicago critic who probably understood his work the very best of all.

68

TENNESSEE WILLIAMS'S "OUTCRY"

THE PLAYWRIGHT'S NOT FOR ROASTING / WHAT WAS IT THAT COMPELLED TENNESSEE WILLIAMS TO UNDERGO YET ANOTHER TRIAL BY FIRE AT THE HANDS OF CHICAGO'S DRAMA CRITICS?

BY CLIFFORD TERRY

AUGUST 22, 1971. As of March, 1962, Tennessee Williams had written a dozen major plays, including "The Glass Menagerie," "Summer and Smoke," "The Rose Tattoo," "Suddenly Last Summer," "Cat on a Hot Tin Roof," "Sweet Bird of Youth" and "The Night of the Iguana." He had won two Pulitzer Prizes and three New York Drama Critics awards.

In March, 1962, Tennessee Williams made the cover of Time Magazine—which some say is akin to running for office and having Harold Stassen manage your campaign. Usually, the "Time Jinx" applies to athletes—the 20-game-winner who suddenly comes up with a sore arm, the golf champion who develops the "yips" on the putting green, the star quarterback who, a week after the issue appears, completes one pass out of 45. Now, it seemed, Time had begun to plant its kiss of death upon the literary.

The facts, of course, are that the 1960s provided years of hell for Thomas Lanier Williams, brought about by his inner torment, his much-publicized penchant for booze and pills (culminating in a stay in the psychiatric division of Barnes Hospital in St. Louis)—and *not* by magazine-cover voodoo. Still, from March, 1962, on, Williams wrote:

"The Milk Train Doesn't Stop Here Any More" (1963), of which Robert Brustein said in The New Republic: "The writing is soft, the theme banal, the action sketchy, the play unfinished—and since there is no drama, why should there be a review . . . ?"

"Slapstick Tragedy" (1966). Newsweek Magazine (under the headline, "The Crass Menagerie"): "At present Williams seems in the sad position of an aging soprano who is forever straining to demonstrate that her cracked, expiring voice can still hit the high, pure notes that won her fame."

"The Two Character Play" (1967). Herbert Kretzmer, London Daily Express: "Seldom, even in the half-light of the theater, have I seen an audience as patently perplexed as this one. It would need a psychoanalyst—and preferably Tennessee Williams' own—to offer a rational interpretation of the enigmas that litter the stage like pieces of an elaborate jigsaw."

"The Seven Descents of Myrtle" (originally, "The Kingdom of Earth"), 1968. Wilfred Sheed, Life Magazine: "A play that some audiences can take straight and others with salt. Unfortunately, even with salt, the taste is bad. . . . As a comedy, Sid Caesar would have done it better and quicker in a television skit years ago. . . . You don't direct a play like this. You simply give it a whump on the tail and tell it to keep moving."

"In the Bar of a Tokyo Hotel" (1969). Time Magazine: "(It) seems more deserving of a coroner's report than a review. . . . There is an axiom of the race track that a thorobred will eventually revert to form. One must

never forget that, despite his present esthetic humiliation, Tennessee Williams is a thorobred."

In spite of such remarks from the theatrical touts, the thorobred, now 60, apparently couldn't care less that they shoot horses, don't they? Since the world premiere of "The Two Character Play" in London those four years ago, he has taken the original thru at least 10 major rewrites, including the one—under the new title, "Out Cry"—that closes tonight at the Ivanhoe Theater after a run of six weeks.

Two days after the Ivanhoe opening, Williams stated on a television talk show that he had little to say about the newspaper reviews (unanimous in their lack of enthusiasm). "There was some incomprehension present. . . . One critic said it was full of self-pity when it is really more like self-*laceration*. Of course they missed something. Weren't we asking a lot from them? I would hope they all come again. . . . This play should have had as much time in preparation as a musical. As of now, we're at the same stage as a Broadway show that's in New Haven."

George Keathley, the director-producer of "Out Cry," said he thought the print critics had a tendency to intellectualize too much. "It's a play they should *feel*. They cut themselves off from the emotional impact. . . . We had rave reviews from the radio critics—Claudia Cassidy . . . Jerry Landfield . . . Roy Leonard . . . Sig Sakowicz . . ."

"Claudia's review," Williams added, "was the best I've received in 15 years. *She's* not busy scratching down the lines incorrectly." (Miss Cassidy, THE TRIBUNE's retired music and drama critic, is credited with being highly instrumental in launching Williams' career with her enthusiastic review of "The Glass Menagerie" in 1944.)

Ten days later, the playwright was eating lunch in the Ivanhoe Restaurant, when suddenly a line of matinee-bound women swept across the dining room like a platoon of raging South American ants. "Mr. Williams! Mr. Williams!" one of them bubbled while simultaneously whacking him on the shoulder. "I'm going in to see your play!"

Momentarily stunned (what does one say in answer to that?), he told her, "Well, you behave yourself."

Keathley was saying that plans hadn't been formed yet whether the play would go to Broadway or an arena-style theater off Broadway, and whether it would stop off in Boston or New Haven or Washington. "The more interesting gigs we have, the better," Williams joined in. "George Keathley is one of the great creative directors in America today. Not just a great interpreter—but a great creator. (Kazan was, too, but sometimes in the wrong way.) So we're getting a good look at the play here in Chicago. However, with the exception of Claudia, I don't think we've faced the most sensitive critics that can be found in America."

⁂

This March, it was announced that the Ivanhoe would produce the American premiere of the then-named "Two Character Play"—in its "Bangkok version," so called because the author had made the revisions there. Keathley, who owns a house just a bicycle ride away from Williams' in Key West, pedaled over for dinner a year and a half ago, learned about the rewrite and told the playwright he wanted to put it on in Chicago—which would make it the fourth Williams' play to open here (following "The Glass Menagerie," "The Rose Tattoo," and "The Night of the Iguana").

"Tennessee was thinking of setting up a nonprofessional production at a college campus in Florida just to take a look at it," Keathley recalls. "I said to him, 'Bull——. I'll give you as first-class a production as you're ever going to get.' He said: 'Wellll . . . I like Chicago. I would like the opinion of a major city.' "

Keathley, who has been called one of the leading directors of Williams' work, had previously staged the world premiere of "Sweet Bird of Youth" (1956) in his Studio M Theater in Miami, as well as the 20th anniversary production of "Menagerie" on Broadway six years ago, and the Ivanhoe revivals of "Tattoo" and "Cat." His only Williams disaster, in fact, was the premiere performance of "Eccentricities of a Nightingale," a rewrite of "Summer and Smoke," produced at the Tappan Zee Playhouse in Nyack, N.Y.

"I made a mistake in casting," Keathley remembers. "A dreadful mistake. The producer wanted Edie Adams. Well, Edie Adams couldn't cut the mustard and Edie Adams doesn't look like Miss Alma by a long shot, but we did it anyway. The technical facilities were incredibly bad, the stage manager was new and an idiot, the set designer didn't know what he was doing. . . . And then, thank God, somebody dropped a cigaret and the whole backstage burned down and all the performances were canceled. I thought to myself, 'Somebody up there loves me.'"

It is the day before Williams is due to arrive in Chicago for rehearsals, and a month before opening night, and Keathley is sitting in his office at the Ivanhoe. "I feel a very . . . major . . . very large responsibility for what's about to happen. Because I know that the play will be more or less successful depending on what *I* do with it. It's a scary thing. In a way, I have the rest of his writing career . . . whether he stops now or goes on. The play is extraordinarily difficult to do, and very easy to kill. It's easy to make too hysterical, it's easy to make it too static. There are many, many pitfalls. Tennessee told me at the time of 'Suddenly Last Summer' in New York, about 1957, that he didn't want to write for Broadway again because of the pressures, the costs, the critics. I would think it has to be a very frightening thing."

Keathley says that if the play is a success, he will take it to New York himself—unlike "Sweet Bird," which fluttered away from him. "I wouldn't let that happen again. Before, I was 29 years old and very naive. Well I'm going to be 46 this month and I'm no longer naive. I'm raising the money right here in Chicago. When it gets to New York, it will get there in as good a condition as our imagination and energy will allow. I want to protect the play and I want to protect him more than anything else. And I'm ruthless about it. If it means going out on a national tour for 10 weeks in 10 different cities. Because I believe in him."

Keathley adds that he asked Williams to change the title to "Out Cry" to avoid confusion with the play-within-the-play, which is also "The Two Character Play," and that he also wanted to lead him into a more lyrical title.

The playwright has described "Out Cry" as being about the last 10 years of his life—a period of great difficulty, of steady deterioration. "If you must say what the play is 'about,' say it is a tragedy with laughter. It affirms nothing but gallantry in the face of defeat—but that, I think, is no small thing to affirm in the Pentagon's shadow." (Structurally, the play is about a 40-ish brother and sister who are actors, deserted by their entire company in some unnamed, boondocks theater, in which they eventually become trapped. They perform a play-within-the-play, which also features a brother and sister who are trapped, psychologically, within their house, where their father had killed their mother and himself. It is thus, of course, about one's confinement. It is also about fear and despair, and it is also intensely autobiographical—too much so, said some of the critics.)

The part of the sister is played by Eileen Herlie, appearing at the North Side theater for the fourth time. The brother is played by Donald Madden, who most recently appeared opposite Claire Bloom in two Ibsen revivals in New York, and who had been in three other Williams' works—the original cast of "In the Bar of a Tokyo Hotel," the London production of "Milk Train" and a TV version of "Camino Real."

◠◠◠

It is three weeks before the opening, and the cast is rehearsing in a onetime warehouse on North Clark, across the way from the Ivanhoe and, incidentally, one block west of a street named Broadway. Director Keathley has jogged over from his lakefront apartment, carrying a conch shell (one of the props)—which prompts all sorts of reactions from neighborhood Nosy Parkers. Donald Madden is exhibiting the astrological shirt he will wear in the play. ("The whole winter sky is on the back. There's Orion.") Eileen Herlie spots another prop, a statue of the Virgin Mary, and picks up its crown. "Actually," she tells Keathley, "what I wanted to do was twirl it around on my finger during the first act, but I was afraid I'd get a letter from the Church." Tennessee Williams walks in, says he is tired. "I've been living it up too much." He orders a take-out lunch from the Ivanhoe's restaurant. It is not your ordinary chicken-salad-on-whole-wheat-and-hold-the-mayo take-out. A dinner-jacketed waiter brings it (roast beef on rye) on a tray covered with a linen napkin; on the tray is a half bottle of St.-Emilion (Crin Noir '66). The most extraordinary thing, however, is that in this age of tab-signing, Tennessee Williams pays for it himself. Donald Madden takes a look at the tray, says, "I still think I make a better sandwich," and washes down his home-constructed one with a gulp of Coke right from the bottle.

A photographer is given a few minutes, and Williams patiently agrees to different poses. ("Want a shot of me eating here?") A small man with a beard and black-frame glasses, he appears to be quite gracious, but never really at ease; he is quick to laugh, altho sometimes at unexpected moments, like Al Capp.

"Tennessee is incredibly shy and honest," says Keathley. "He's embarrassed about his honesty, which makes him all the more shy."

"He's completely unpretentious and puts everyone at ease," adds Aaron Gold, the Ivanhoe's PR man, at the outset of rehearsals. "I was very nervous when I first met him. I kept calling him 'Mr. Williams,' and he said: 'Cut out that ——. Call me "Tom."'"

Waiting for the actors to get ready, Williams tells Gold that he'll be off in California for a week, visiting a sick friend, and can be reached at the Hollywood Roosevelt. ("It's quite tacky, you know, but it has a big pool.") In Chicago, it turns out, he spends much of his nonwriting time swimming; the columnists duly note that he did 13 laps nonstop at the 25 E. Chestnut pool and 16 laps at the Illinois A.C.

He has brought a rewrite into the rehearsal hall (the original three acts already have been consolidated into two) and the cast gets to work. "I've restored a cut that we made in Key West, Tom," says Keathley.

"I'd like to hear that first," he answers.

One of the new bits of dialog is tested out. "Heh, heh," the playwright laughs. "That's a dirty line."

"Well, I'll make it *so* dirty," Miss Herlie says, "they'll run us out of town."

As the dialog is read, Williams gives suggestions about the proper inflection ("It amplifies the mythic qualities there. . . .") and laughs delightedly at some lines spoken by the actress, "You called me a drunken slut, and told me to —— off."

"Beautiful! Now, I want to hear the lines with the 'lewd, degenerate, leering' business."

He hears them.

"Wonderful."

◠ ◠ ◠

A few days later, Williams is eating lunch at the Ivanhoe. Over a roast beef on sourdough and a half-bottle of Burgundy, he talks about his English agent and close friend, Lady St. Just, and her hopes to produce the play in London with a cast of Margaret Leighton and Paul Scofield. "Scofield said he didn't think that Margaret was right for the part. But then he added, 'Of course, is *anyone*?' Scofield is a wonderful actor, but I think Donald Madden is going to give you quite a performance here. . . .

Eileen's a Scotch-Irish biddie, which is why *she's* so good. You know, I wrote the part originally for Margaret Leighton, who's as thin as picnic lemonade. So you can imagine my surprise when I saw Eileen and her Jayne Mansfield-size boobs."

Aaron Gold shows him a tentative advertising poster for "Out Cry," which is all black and white. "It looks like a funeral announcement," Williams comments. "People won't come to see it. I've always liked red. Or how about something lavender?" He also points out that *Tennessee* is misspelled.

"One more thing. I don't want my name over the title. I never have my name there. That's why I think the title of that autobiography by Frank Capra—'The Name Above the Title'—is so wrong. The *work* is the important thing."

He tells Gold he doesn't want any biographical information listed in the program. "People aren't interested in that. Just say—and this is the honest truth—'Mr. Williams recently received a fan letter, which began as follows: "Dear Mr. Williams: I was very surprised to learn that you are still living. Would you please send me an autographed photo?" Her request was not granted because she did not include her return address.'"

Three days later, less than a week before the opening, "Out Cry" is presented before an audience—members of the cast of another Ivanhoe production, "Another Part of the Forest": John Saxon, Larry Gates, Nancy Coleman and others. Keathley and Williams are discussing the problem of the actors lighting some cigarets in the second act, and Miss Herlie—wearing a tattered, lavender, Blanche DuBois dress, is holding a blonde wig, specially prepared for that ratty look with Linco Bleach.

"How does the 'Dixie Doxie' look?" she asks Williams.

"Very effective."

"Good. My God, they almost didn't let me out of the Ambassador."

She turns to Nancy Coleman. "This afternoon we are giving what is known as a 'rough rehearsal.' So no cracks."

Right near the outset, she blows a line. "Oh, Christ . . . I thought that was the part for the music. . . . Oh ——."

Williams watches the play unfold with great concentration, his left hand occasionally stroking his beard, and his knee balancing a white, flap cap—the kind that Ben Hogan used to wear when he was tearing apart the golf world. He expresses approval of Wrick Paul's cluttered backstage set-up. ("This could be the set for some ponderous Hun drama"), and takes notes and whispers suggestions to Keathley. ("Pause before *sensational* . . . shouldn't she be reacting to his cries? . . . Would *sense* be a better word than *wisdom*?") The air-conditioning is on full blast, and the short-sleeved director makes his own notes, wrapped tightly in Miss Herlie's green cloak.

As the rehearsal moves on, the loudest of the laughter from the dozen spectators comes from Tennessee Williams. At the end of the first act, he agrees it is going very well. "It's a bit discombobulating to have only a few people scattered around the theater," Miss Herlie tells him, and Williams asks Keathley if some university theater students could be invited for subsequent run-thrus. Donald Madden is standing aside, eating another home-made sandwich and drinking from the ubiquitous bottle of Coke.

Larry Gates drops by Williams' seat. "It's lovely. Very moving. I really mean it. I'm glad we have a *writer* again."

"Tom," says George Keathley, "I have a good feeling about the live audience today."

"I don't," says Tennessee Williams.

At the end of the rehearsal, the "Another Part of the Forest" cast again stops by to offer congratulations. Gates says: "It's a beautiful piece of work. It meant much to me. God bless you." The author accepts the praise graciously, but looks as if he doesn't believe it.

He makes more suggestions to Keathley: "There isn't enough time before they go into 'The Two Character Play.' There has to be more of a visual thing to underline it. . . . Shouldn't there be a sound or something—a door bolt perhaps?" The adjustments are noted, and Keathley adds: "Tom, you did it again. You've written a very moving play. They loved it. They all had tears in their eyes."

Williams replies that he felt it was a strange audience.

"Well, you weren't there for the start of the first act," Miss Herlie says. "They laughed a great deal. . . . And later, they were quiet because they were very moved. They just wish *they* had a play like this. . . . I'm glad we had them in."

"I'm not," Williams says. "I didn't like it. They knew what they were doing. They knew they were our first audience. They could have given us more. Did you see me? I snubbed Miss Coleman *cold*."

Five minutes later, an NBC film crew comes in to reshoot a previous interview which had been wrecked by a mechanical foul-up. "I have a great persecution complex," Williams tells the blonde interviewer in what seems to be a light-hearted manner. "You burned all that film. I just wonder what you're up to."

She apologizes, then explains that what they'd like to get is another introductory shot of the actors, director and author in a group. "We have to have you all consulting," she says. "That's the big opening for the segment. . . . I mean, the camera comes in and . . . *Tennessee Williams* . . . wham!"

"Bull——," says Tennessee Williams.

◠ ◠ ◠

It is Monday night, three days before the opening, and the theater is filled with friends and friends of friends who have been asked in to witness the dress rehearsal. "Look at them," points out one Ivanhoe staff member. "No matter what they're passing out—cotton candy or mousetraps or theater tickets—if it's free, they'll come."

Williams attends with Lady St. Just, who has flown in from London, and Audrey Wood, his American agent.

At intermission, a member of the audience gives his opinion: "It's a magnificent play. I'm still trying to figure it out."

On Tuesday, the first of two preview nights, reports filter out that everything is not quite so crushingly cohesive as one lady columnist's purple prose would make it seem. Tempers are flaring, tears are flowing. Williams objects to the Ivanhoe's advertising the Man rather than the Play. He tells a newspaperman to come back with some new questions in 48 hours—because maybe he'll be out of town by then. A column item states that he was "too exhausted" to attend the after-theater party sponsored by the Sarah Siddons Society, but someone says later: "Listen, he was really whacked out. It was awful. Finally, finally, he agreed to make some cuts that George wanted and that were needed.

You know when Eileen and Donald got them? At noon—the day of the opening. And they were still making last-minute cuts up until four hours before the curtain. I mean, isn't that just great for the actors?"

In the early morning hours of Thursday, the day of the opening, a violent thunderstorm crashes across Chicago—providing a possible omen of things to come, for those who are into the Julius-stay-home-from-the-Senate-today school of Calpurnian clairvoyance.

Williams' brother, Dakin, is in the audience for the opening. An attorney from downstate Collinsville, he has made a couple of unsuccessful attempts to get the Democratic nomination for United States Senator. Despite his rather conspicuous black-and-white checkerboard-like sports coat, he is unnoticed by the celebrity-chompers in the audience, many of whom haven't bothered to show up at the Ivanhoe since the dramatic debut—that is, the debut into drama—of Lee Radziwill. At intermission, they and other members of the audience toss out Comments: "This reminds me of 'The Taming of the Shrew' . . . I heard they cut it about 15 minutes; well, they needn't have stopped there. . . . There sure are a lot of blondes here tonight."

The second act begins. There is a line in the play about "the hatchet-man critic snoring in the front row," but this evening the only discernible dozer of prominence is a TV talk-show host.

At the final curtain, at 10:20, there is a modest applause and one faint cry for "Author," which is muffled in the surrounding indifference. "The audience was not a friendly one," Williams is to say later. "They weren't with us."

The crowd drifts into a room at the Ivanhoe called The Keep for the opening-night party; it is the usual Zoo Story, with the crowd blasting up to the freebie bar as if it were the lingerie counter at Goldblatt's in January. Williams and Lady St. Just and Miss Herlie and Madden retreat behind a rectangular table, where they endure hurried interviews, well-wishes and unabashed stares.

"Where the hell does one go in Chicago to wait for the reviews?" someone asks. "The Steak 'N Egger? The Tip Top Tap?"

Keathley says he doesn't know about the others, but *he* is going home. "I thought it went very well tonight. We did everything we could. It's over. I'm just going to bed and we'll see what happens." Williams and his party also decide to thumbs-down the Sardi's-squealing tradition. The next morning, the playwright will get up at 9 o'clock, go down to the hotel lobby, read the morning papers and say to himself, "Oh well."

William Leonard of THE TRIBUNE talks about the "turgidity" of the writing. "The author's old drive has faded, his characters are not so sharply etched, there is seldom the immediacy or the impact one recalls from some of his earlier works."

"What you want to know is whether or not Tennessee Williams has made a successful comeback," Glenna Syse writes in the Sun-Times. "And the answer for the moment will have to be no. . . . 'Out Cry' is so intensely autobiographical that it asks an audience to come into the theater with a knowledge of its playwright that it cannot possibly be expected to have."

That afternoon, Sydney J. Harris states in the Daily News: " 'Out Cry' far more resembles the underpainting of a craftsman than the finished work itself. . . . Williams is not Pirandello, nor Pinter, nor should try to be. . . ." And Roger Dettmer in Chicago Today calls the play "a serio-comedy leaning in the direction of comic elegy that ultimately reminds one of a vine-melon left too long in the sun to ripen."

And a New York-based publication, Women's Wear Daily, thinks so much of an American premiere of a Tennessee Williams play that it sends its regular Chicago bureau reporter to serve as a drama critic. She first describes the Ivanhoe as "a place to see dated melodramas"—a rather peculiar way to describe a theater that has produced "Lemon Sky," "Man-in-the-Moon Marigolds" and "Virginia Woolf"—then goes on to call the play "very talky."

But the radio critics are generous in their praise. Jerome Landfield on WBBM, for example, says, "If you dig poetry, Pirandello, Pinter and Albee, I think you'll dig *this* play." And, three nights after the opening over WMFT, Claudia Cassidy says: "It proves beyond a doubt that Tennessee Williams can still write a beautiful, terrible, magical haunting play. . . . I only know that the play slowly took possession of me as I watched it, that it came home with me, and that it is not likely to leave. . . . There is in 'Out Cry' the terrible, wrenching impact of the compassionate and the implacable so often found in Tennessee

Williams' best plays. . . . I found at the Ivanhoe an extraordinary play staged and acted, I should think, about as well as it can or will be. And I found Tennessee Williams, who can do something not many men can do. He can write a powerful, implacable, compassionate and mesmeric play."

The play which will be presented at the Ivanhoe tonight is not the same play that opened six weeks ago; there have been major rewrites, there have been cuts. Whether it is enough, maybe only Clive Barnes knows for sure.

A strange business, playwrighting. How many Pulitzers and New York Drama Critics awards does one have to win in a lifetime? Whatever the number, it seems, it isn't enough; people demand more, and perhaps so does the playwright. Some might think it would be easy just to put the cover on the typewriter and cry, "—— it," but as Williams has pointed out, the artist cannot turn it on and off and retire at 65 like the businessman.

In "A Look at Tennessee Williams," a book by Mike Steen, William Inge says: "We never made playwrighting a real profession in this country because it's never been a profession that a man can grow old in. We have never appreciated any of our playwrights' more mature work."

And, in the same book, a comment from Maureen Stapleton, "If you don't walk on the water every time, they take potshots at you."

On the shores of Lake Michigan, there is at least one Tennessee Williams fan who is waiting for the shooting to end and the walk to resume: "Maybe he *has* had a string of misses, but I have the feeling that he still is going to write another major play."

"Tennessee says repeatedly that this will be his last full-length play," George Keathley had said just before the start of rehearsals. "I think he's very serious when he says that. It's my personal hunch—and it's only a hunch—that if the play is a very big success, he'll write more. He's said he has lost a certain energy, which is true. If it's a hit, he may become reenergized.

"I think he's also lost a certain *heart*. Who wants to write plays if the critics are going to keep killing them? You can do that once, twice, three times. If you've never been successful, you can do it eight times until you hit it. But when you've had the astounding, phenomenal, national acclaim of a Tennessee Williams and you read, 'What's happened to him?' or 'He's a dead playwright,' or whatever, a lot of steam goes out of you. I'd guess there's a pride involved there, a desire to be back again where he belongs. Because there's no playwright in the English language who has put words together the way he has. O'Neill perhaps had more grandiose themes, Albee perhaps is bitchier, but nobody has the soul, the lyricism, the sense of words and of character Tennessee Williams has."

Maybe "Out Cry" itself gives a clue to the future, there in the second act (unless it's been changed by now), when the sister says of her playwright-actor brother: "When he read it aloud I said to myself: 'This is his last one, there's nothing more after this. The punctuation marks in life include periods which include one that's final. . . .

"'But it wasn't always all lost. There are things to remember when we were—artists!—with power! Events of—great occasions for—celebrations! It doesn't all cancel out to the flat sum of nothing!'"

This fascinating, gossipy, behind-the-scenes story, featuring Tennessee Williams eating roast-beef sandwiches and drinking bourbon on Chicago's North Side while sweating over his play "Out Cry" (a variant title for "The Two-Character Play"), and his relationships with Chicago drama critics, especially Claudia Cassidy, was written by Clifford Terry, a longtime features writer at the *Tribune*. It is a mostly unknown yet startlingly revealing picture of Williams in action, 25 years after writing "A Streetcar Named Desire." Deep into the story, the relationship between Terry and Williams clearly deteriorates as pressure comes to bear on Williams, a writer constantly expected to repeat his past triumphs.

By now, of course, Cassidy was no longer reviewing for the *Tribune*. This latest Williams drama at the Ivanhoe Theatre (the play had been seen in London, but this was its American premiere) had been reviewed, quite briefly, by William Leonard, who had begun his piece with the sentence "There is a hollow ring to Tennessee Williams' new play" and ended it by describing the work as a "a ponderously symbolic undrama." Along the way, Leonard, who did not have Cassidy's affinity for Williams, had made reference to "remnants and reminiscences of the Tennessee William style."

Despite this reaction after the premiere at the Ivanhoe, "Out Cry" did make it to New York, although it reverted to the title "The Two-Character Play," starred Michael York and featured a different cast and director. It played on Broadway for only 10 days, although it showed up off Broadway at various points in the 1970s and 1980s. Williams scholars such as William Prosser regard the play as having "no definitive version."

Terry pulls a lot of revealing material from Williams and George Keathley, the play's director (who did not know at this point that he would be replaced). The picture of opening night is especially fulsome: Williams's brother, Dakin, showed up at the Ivanhoe that night. So did Williams's famous agent, Audrey Wood. But the most poignant section of this article comes at the end, when Terry starts to probe what's it like to be a writer in apparent creative decline.

Terry, though, prints a generous excerpt of Cassidy's radio review for WFMT-FM–this is one way to get one more Cassidy review of Williams into this book, just as Terry was trying to get one more Cassidy review into the *Tribune*–signaling, presumably, to her many remaining fans among *Tribune* readers that if she had still been in her job, the future for "Out Cry" might have been very different.

Meanwhile, Leonard was taking on "Warp."

69

WARP

ZAP! GReech! ZOT! over on Lincoln Av.

Body Politic

BY WILLIAM LEONARD

DECEMBER 17, 1971. Upstairs and down, there's a great deal of action and excitement, even a degree of artistry, at the Body Politic on Lincoln Avenue. The Organic Theater presenting an insane stage version of a futuristic comic strip named "Warp." Overhead, the Dream Theater is portraying dreams submitted by its friends and neighbors.

This is Chapter 1 of "Warp," entitled "My Battlefield—My Body," and it's so good that I don't like it. That's right. It is so like those wild comic books, set in some outrageous land sometime in the far future, that it reminds me of how those cartoons repel me.

Stuart Gordon has mounted a wildly imaginative, colorful and violent melodrama filled with costuming and comedy as well as zap guns and half-dressed beautiful women, and calls it "the world's first science fiction epic adventure play in serial form." It well may be for we've never seen anything like it around here.

It certainly moves rapidly and in all directions, with characters named Symax and Valaria and Sargon and Chaos and Desi Arnaz. Desi Arnaz? How did he get in here? And what difference does it make?

They utter lines like "By the seven moons of Mitra, Cumulus, kill her now!"

Will David kill his sweetheart, Mary Louise? Tune in next month and see. For, yep, the second chapter will be staged in January, both episodes alternating thereafter, Wednesdays thru Sundays. Gordon doesn't say how many chapters there will be. Perhaps he doesn't know.

Dream Theater, upstairs, is less exciting and less theatrical. It presents onstage dreams that actually were dreamed by members of the audience, the company, and others, using the acting and narrating technique developed by Paul Sills at the Body Politic with his Story Theater before it went on to New York and fame.

It's too simple and episodic to become very fascinating. Outside of a Franz Kafka story, "The Country Doctor," there is no continuity, one more or less irrational interlude following another in a presentation that is interesting but not quite entertaining,

The dream of Jacob wrestling with the angel is just that. The water dream is two men in the lake being scooped up by a boat, end of dream. The egg dream is a man breaking out of a carton, end of dream. And so it goes.

The actors are having fun and they certainly are capable, under the direction of Jim Shiflett who has managed to put some vitality into a skeletal scheme.

In this second of two reviews of Organic Theater shows, William Leonard opines on "Warp," one of the most famous Organic projects and a show that would, remarkably enough, move to Broadway the following February. He does so under what's possibly the best *Tribune* headline in this book. Leonard gets tied up in some knots here: he actually writes that the show was "so good that I don't like it," apparently because it reminded him of how much he disliked comic books. Stuart Gordon's coauthor for this play was Lenny Kleinfeld, a.k.a. Bury St. Edmund, who would write some of the most scathing theater reviews the *Chicago Reader* would ever publish.

This show was based, of course, on Marvel comics, although since Gordon and his pals could not get the rights to any of those characters, they just made up their own. And although it marked the Broadway debut of John Heard, "Warp" lasted for just eight performances there.

Organic would have many different incarnations over the years. It would merge with the Touchstone Theatre in 1996, becoming Organic-Touchstone, only in 2006 to become affiliated, as just Organic, with Northern Illinois University and produce very different work. All in all, the Organic never was the same after Gordon moved to Hollywood. But it had a very famous follow-up in the works to "Warp."

Leonard soon would encounter "Boss" in the boss town of America.

70

BOSS

'BOSS': A FARCE THAT'S HALF FUN AND HALF DULL

Forum Theatre

BY WILLIAM LEONARD

CAST

Daley	Dick O'Neill
Sis	Dolores Rothenberger
Quinn	Roy Gioconda
Kennelly	Bill Koza
Michael Richard	James Harms
Lloyd	Joe Bratcher
Sister Mary	Constance Cooper
Alderman Gozchitski	Marty Zagon
Richard Michael	William McCauley
Frieda Toke	Iris Lieberman
Stan Yutu	Bruce Taylor
Betty Jonelle	Julie Jourdan
Cindina Mae	Nancy Irvine
Al	Ed Krieger

MAY 25, 1973. When a show is half fun and half dull, the dull half is the portion that's likely to influence your final opinion. "Boss," the musical satire about Mayor Richard J. Daley and the rogues who surround him, is rollicking and high-spirited for the first half of the way, then gets serious and a little sinister, and, worse than that, simply runs out of steam.

It is a farce only loosely inspired by Mike Royko's book, "Boss," and it can't make up its mind whether it is about the universality of corruption on a parochial scale, or whether it is a lot of snide little jokes perpetrated by burlesque characters in corny costumes and funny hats.

Daley, it tells us, is a clown spouting malaprops and mispronunciations, and tripping the light fantastic while boasting about "the greatest city in the world," but he also is out of sight, out there in the wings somewhere, when there are ghetto riots and policemen whacking hippies over their long-haired heads.

What started out to be fun ends rather sadly. Maybe that is the real story of Mayor Daley. The St. Patrick's Day parade and the green river on the one hand, and the building inspectors shaking down the little guys on the other hand. It does not make for a balanced book for a musical.

"Boss" is a disconnected series of skits and blackouts, with no characters excepting the mayor and his wife sketched in more than one dimension. It is brightly staged, it moves with celerity, and a few times it sparkles brilliantly—but too often it forces its way, heavyhandedly and predictably.

Dick O'Neill, a non-Chicagoan who hasn't lived with the Daley legend, portrays the mayor with a contagious good humor, making him a likable lug but giving us no indication of the imperiousness of his power nor the canniness this highly professional politician possesses.

Dolores Rothenberger sings and tap dances creditably as Sis Daley, tho the mayor's wife is written as a simpleton devoid of warmth.

William Pullinsi produced and directed earnestly and with thoroness. Nick Venden's music often is beguiling, and Frank Galati's lyrics are far more clever than his book, which bogs down too frequently in banality.

One of the brightest aspects of the show is the nimble and precise dancing, beautifully staged by Lou Conte.

The whole thing adds up to less than the sum of its several worthy parts. It's fun and it's jaundice, but it's not convincingly enough of either one.

By 1971, William Pullinsi's Candlelight Dinner Playhouse had been going full blast in the Chicago suburb of Summit for close to a decade (Cassidy was not, in general, a great fan). On the same site in 1972, Pullinsi opened the Forum Theatre, mostly for producing light comedies. "Boss" was a true Chicago curiosity–a musical, commissioned by Pullinsi, based on the book by legendary Chicago newspaper columnist Mike Royko, who had worked, over a 30-year career, at the *Chicago Daily News*, the *Chicago Sun-Times* and the *Tribune* (he died in 1997). As we've seen, this was hardly the first piece of writing by a Chicago journalist to become a show.

In a preview article, Leonard had noted that Mayor Richard J. Daley (the elder of Chicago's two Mayor Daleys) was perfect fodder for a musical, given his style, scale and "the rogues who surround[ed] him." Nonetheless, *Boss* is a serious book; "Boss" the show is a musical farce–aiming, its creators said, to capture "the tackiness" of Daley, who let it be known that he was not pleased with Pullinsi's decision to turn the book into a stage production.

Royko told Leonard that while writing the book (the subject of which had refused to sit for an interview), he had indeed envisioned it as a musical comedy–though he allowed, unsurprisingly, that he was not a theatergoer himself. One of the writers here was Frank Galati, who would go on to become one of the leading figures in Chicago theater and beyond. Royko wasn't directly involved in the adaptation, but he had veto power, which he declined to use.

"Boss" did not do well, as this rather clunky review anticipates. In a later *Tribune* article, Galati told Linda Winer that he wanted to open the show with "a gigantic face of Daley like Aladdin's Castle at Riverview, with a huge tongue hanging into the orchestra pit." That was the style of "Boss." Galati, musing on his early failure, also suggested that "Boss" had not worked because the only really interesting character in Royko's book was Royko himself.

In the meantime, David Mamet was making his mark.

71

THE NIGHT THEY SHOT HARRY LINDSEY WITH A 155 MM. HOWITZER AND BLAMED IT ON ZEBRAS

A FARCE OF A DIFFERENT STRIPE!

Body Politic

BY WILLIAM LEONARD

CAST

Ludwig .... Byrne Piven
Amy Keester .... Mina Kolb
Myron Goldlabel .... Richard Kurtzman
Father Casseltari .... David Mamet
Joseph .... Val Bettin
Harry Lindsey .... Mike Nussbaum

OCTOBER 20, 1973. Now, you're going to find it hard to believe, but "The Night They Shot Harry Lindsey with a 155 MM. Howitzer and Blamed It on Zebras" really is about the night they shot Harry Lindsey with a 145 MM. howitzer and blamed it on Zebras. If that sounds to you as if something crazy is going on at the Body Politic, then your instincts are good.

"Harry Lindsey" is a wild farce that seems straining, somewhere under the surface, to say something cogent about militarism and corruption in high places and the ruthlessness of those in power. But it would rather have fun than concentrate on anything serious, even for a moment.

It is peopled with munitions vendors, revolutionists, spies, foreign agents, one deputy assistant secretary of defense, and one sweet little old lady who lives in her quiet, lovely old home in Southampton, apparently minding her own business, but actually doing nothing of the kind.

Mrs. Keester has in her beautiful parlor the polished howitzer which fired the very last shot on the western front in World War I. She also has Harry Lindsey, who has millions of dollars worth of weapons stored in warehouses all over the world, and sells them to both sides in any and all wars, just because he doesn't like to see things go to waste.

A young activist, whose girl friend heads an integrated revolutionary movement called the Zebras, arrives on the patio by parachute, and Mrs. Keester helps him photograph the entire contents of Lindsey's little book with the list of warehouse locations.

Lindsey's aide attempts to assassinate Mrs. Keester. Representatives of Middle Eastern nations charge Lindsey with double crossing them. They and the young man haul Lindsey and the howitzer offstage and—BOOM! No more Howard.

The zany plot becomes a very complicated scramble that overdoes its insanity and gets a little out of hand before they manage to wind things up, with Mrs. Keester (who else?) holding the fort after the dust has settled.

Mina Kolb, the darling of the early days of Second City, makes her first Chicago appearance in half a dozen years as this heroine, both insipid and extremely canny, and plays her with a relish. Mrs. Keester is a lady to love and to remember, floating serenely thru a boisterous madhouse.

Del Close, who has directed countless reviews, staged this, his first script play, with an emphasis on all the right spots, so these caricatures approximate characters. A company including some of Chicago's numerous skillful professionals gives the play a nice polish.

Mike Nussbaum, doubling as Lindsey and as the captain of a passing vessel sunk by the howitzer shot, has a ball. Richard Kurtzman plays the young revolutionist with telling concentration, while others, too numerous for mention in a period of newsprint shortage, deserve praise.

Dick Cusack, the author, has a lot of funny ideas and some mighty flighty dialog, but he has overloaded his play. It tries to do too many things, all for the sake of fun, and some of them get lost. It's a fine couple of hours of fun, it looks good on Lincoln Avenue, and that's as far as it goes.

Not only did "The Night They Shot Harry Lindsey With a 155 MM. Howitzer and Blamed It on Zebras" come with quite a title, this famously flawed Body Politic production, produced by Byrne Piven and directed by improv guru Del Close, also featured the acting talents of Mina Kolb of the Second City, Mike Nussbaum (who would become a star in Chicago) and a very young David Mamet, playing a priest. The writer, Richard "Dick" Cusack (who died in 2003), was the father of the actors Joan Cusack and John Cusack.

Leonard pretty much damns the proceedings with faint praise. But many involved here would go on to have enormous influence. Especially Mamet.

72

SEXUAL PERVERSITY IN CHICAGO

'SEXUAL PERVERSITY IN CHICAGO': IS THAT ALL THERE IS?

Organic Theater Company

BY LINDA WINER

JUNE 21, 1974. With a name like "Sexual Perversity in Chicago" and a devilish reputation like Stuart Gordon's, the Organic Theater Company's new "x-rated" production sets up its Uptown Center Hull House audience for anything. Or almost anything. Audience intimidation, live cartoons, naked Peter Pans, simulated tortures and bloody swordfights—Gordon has directed them all these past few years, along with Carolyn Gordon and a changing cast of characters to carry out his cavalcade of enterprising young fantasies. For this one, you even have to be over 18 to watch.

Perhaps the only thing an audience would never expect to find inside the splendid little theater at 4520 N. Beacon St. is David Mamet's traditional, uneven, extraordinarily normal, and abnormally ordinary play that opened there Wednesday. It's a new road for the Organic, but a fairly familiar rut for theater.

Like Mamet's earlier play, "The Duck Variations," this one deals intelligently with everyday people dealing helplessly with everyday emptiness. Four Chicago singles—a frustrated kindergarten teacher, a pretty commercial artist, one aging defensive macho, and a hipper young fellow—go thru the standard sexual rituals of a New Townish existence.

Eric Loeb (the hipper) and Carolyn Gordon (the pretty) find their affair has a finite shelf life, while Roberta Custer hooks tiny children onto her hang-ups and Warren Casey spins pathetic stories about last night's deviants. Cliches get courted around as if the words are printed on the singles bar's fake Bauhaus chrome and real sexual perversity lurks in the loneliness behind shallow obsessions, the worries about early ejaculations and proper measurements, plus the seemingly inevitable review after each sexual performance. The bed rolls right out from the bar.

The play is constructed as a series of blackout skits—sketches, really, that do or do not get colored funny before another one begins. The resulting picture is hardly new, but it has frequent vivid sections as Mamet and Gordon catch the contemporary corner on lines like "I'm a lesbian." "Oh, for physical or political reasons?"

It's hard to argue the conclusions, but the play could use an overhaul in the first half hour. It seems difficult enough to say anything profound about the overanalyzed singles lifestyle, but it's disastrous when so much of the play's early sociology sounds like a slow day on "Love American Style." By the time Casey (coauthor of "Grease"), C. Gordon (surely by now the most famous naked body in theatrical Chicago), Custer, and Loeb get deftly beyond sexual stereotypes in Chicago, "Sexual Perversity in Chicago" has almost played itself out.

By 1974, the *Tribune* had a new critic in its stable: Linda Winer (1946–). Hired in 1969 as a music critic following an apprenticeship with the Rockefeller Foundation Music Critics Project, Winer would ascend to the post of chief drama critic in 1974. She was young and female, and Claudia Cassidy took an interest in her work. Indeed, we can see much of Cassidy's influence in Winer's writing, which was notably more progressive than Leonard's.

Winer, who wrote several of the reviews that follow here, would stay at the *Tribune* until 1980, when she left to write reviews for the *New York Daily News*. She worked for that paper for two years, and then was theater critic at *USA Today* from 1982 to 1987. She is best known for her long tenure in the theater critic's seat at *Newsday*, a newspaper she joined in 1987 and where she remains to this day.

Winer is not easily shocked, as her reaction to "Sexual Perversity in Chicago" makes clear: she found it overly tame. For this review, she had shown up at the Organic Theater to see the play, written by one of Chicago's hotshots: David Mamet, a young kid who had hung around with Bob Sickinger's crowd and at the Second City. Winer did not know it, but she was watching the very early work of one of the city's most important writers. If playwright Sam Shepard came to represent the rural aspects of American drama–with works evoking wide-open spaces, domestic dysfunction and long, brooding silences on the prairie, Mamet, by contrast, invented the dramatic language of urban Middle America. His subsequent work would reflect his identity as a provocateur, a satirist. An outsider. A typical product, really, of the Second City.

Mamet was born in Chicago in 1947. The son of a teacher (Lenore June Silver) and an attorney (Bernard Morris Mamet), he attended Francis W. Parker School on the city's North Side. By various accounts (including Mamet's own), it was not an easy childhood. Then, while still in high school, he discovered the Second City.

"As a kid in high school, I hung around Second City quite a bit," Mamet wrote in the *Chicago Tribune Magazine* in 1991. "I was friendly with the owners and their families and was permitted to frequent the joint. Later I worked there as a busboy, and, occasionally, I played piano for the kids' shows on the weekend."

The Second City was in Old Town. It was an introduction to what passed in Chicago for *la vie bohème*. As Mamet recounted in his reminiscence, its denizens hung out at the Hotel Lincoln (where Mamet would later live) and shot craps in the men's room.

The influence of this improvisational comedy club on Mamet is most obvious, perhaps, in "Sexual Perversity." It is very much structured in a scene-blackout-scene fashion, just like a Second City revue. Organic's artistic director, Stuart Gordon, had helped Mamet shape the play into a coherent narrative set against a backdrop of the singles' bars located on Division Street (just south of the Hotel Lincoln). Like so much of the material associated with the Second City, "Sexual Perversity" is an impressionistic look at failed relationships, set in an archetypical Second City locale (the Chicago pickup bar). It follows the travails of two Jewish couples who are unable to keep their relationships together. The piece opens with a guy bragging about his sexual exploits and ends with an expression of desperate loneliness. "Sexual Perversity" is full of profanity, setting both a Mametian tone–a Mametian tone born in Chicago–and an expectation that would haunt this writer for his entire career.

Despite Winer's dashed hopes, "Sexual Perversity" was not a catalog of erotic misbehavior. The titular perversity was, fundamentally, emotional.

When this play was penned, the Second City was already in transition, backing away from its former role as a countercultural critic and becoming part of the mainstream comedy scene. Its sketches would increasingly avoid politics and ideology, focusing instead on love, sex and urban life. Mamet's

"Sexual Perversity" both took advantage of that change in focus and commented darkly on it.

Mamet may have been a child of the Second City, but in the cynical tone and sad, downbeat ending of this play, we can already see his ability both to profit from the shallowness of life and, at the same time, to indict it. The movie version of "Sexual Perversity" (retitled *About Last Night . . .*) was set in Chicago, but its characters were made younger and their mistakes thus more easily forgivable.

73

BEYOND THE HORIZON

A TRAGIC REVIVAL OF AN O'NEILL SOAPER

St. Nicholas Theater Company

BY ROGER DETTMER

CAST

James Mayo	Byrne Piven
Kate Mayo	Penelope Court
Robert Mayo	Matthew Elkin
Ruth	Mary Frances Farrell
Capt. Dick Scott	Gibson Glass
Andrew Mayo	William H. Macy
Dr. Fawcett	David Mamet
Ben	David Wirth

FEBRUARY 14, 1975. Eugene O'Neill waited two years for a Broadway production—at a February matinee in 1920—of his first full-length play, "Beyond the Horizon," portentously described as "An American Tragedy in Three Acts." It didn't star John Barrymore, whom he'd hoped would create the role of a book-loving dreamer with tubercular lungs, trapped on a family farm in New England by a neighbor girl who claimed to love him but didn't.

Richard Bennett—father of Constance and Joan and Barbara—found the script in his producer's office and insisted upon playing it, as a consequence of which O'Neill won his first Pulitzer Prize. It was revived (no, disinterred is the verb) Thursday night by the St. Nicholas

Theater Company, in Grace Lutheran Church on West Belden Avenue, and what is there to say of this misguided enterprise after the fact?

Well . . . for starters, they don't write plays like this today. Not even for installment performances on afternoon television. By any contemporary measure, it is soap opera and melodrama, with line after line like "O Ruth, our love is sweeter than any distant dream." Before his death in 1953, O'Neill was to write timeless tragedies for the stage; and after his death to be judged our greatest playwright to date.

But the early works do not sustain. Not "The Emperor Jones," nor "Anna Christie," nor "Desire Under the Elms," nor "Strange Interlude" (except as a showcase for a tour-de-force company such as the Actors Studio presented on Broadway in 1963). "Beyond the Horizon" predated all of these.

Had he written nothing other than "The Iceman Cometh" and "Long Day's Journey Into Night," O'Neill's reputation as a titan would be secure. But to write these, he had to write other plays.

Out of respect for the man's indelible achievements, his earliest plays ought to be allowed their eternal rest. Occasionally in "Beyond the Horizon," like flashes of lightning, a future landscape is momentarily illuminated. But even with editing by director David Mamet (including a child of the visionary and his fickle wife who really loved a brother gone to sea, tho he was truly the man of the land), this relic of 1920 is turgid, awkward to speak, humorless, and gesticular.

The St. Nicholas Players are nowhere nearly ready to attempt O'Neill—at any stage of his development. The performance was amateurish, this said more in sadness than exasperation. Yes, Mary Frances Farrell (as the wife) and William H. Macy (as the farmboy who goes to sea) have promise, but not yet control of technique, or the craft to externalize internal moments credibly. Byrne Piven in one scene belonged with his own—elder and better—elsewhere than we found him to be.

Besides writing plays, David Mamet was also directing them in Chicago—and, according to critic Roger Dettmer, not directing them very well. This review of "Beyond the Horizon" is the first in the book by Dettmer (1927–2011), who served as the *Tribune*'s freelance theater critic from 1974 to 1976 after stints at the *New York Herald Tribune* and the *Chicago American*, although he primarily was a music writer throughout his career.

Mamet had quite a cast here, including William H. Macy and Byrne Piven, the father of the Evanston family famous for training young actors. Not content with only directing such a difficult classic drama, Mamet also cast himself. And as if that were not enough, he appears to have taken it upon himself to edit the play, if Dettmer is to be believed.

This show was produced by the St. Nicholas Theater Company, which Mamet had started the previous year. As Dettmer points out, along with many of the other critics in town, it was not yet ready to take on O'Neill.

Mamet got back to writing plays—his next one would be a masterpiece.

74

AMERICAN BUFFALO

'BUFFALO' ONLY FRAGMENTS OF THE INTENDED

Goodman Theatre

BY ROGER DETTMER

CAST

Donny Dubrow .... J. J. Johnston
Walter ("Teacher") Cole .... Bernard Erhard
Bobby .... William H. Macy

OCTOBER 25, 1975. If Second City is currently shopping for local pretentions to parody in some future revue, a place to case on weekends through Nov. 9 is the Ruth Page Auditorium at 1016 N. Dearborn St. The target there is "American Buffalo" (as in yesteryear's nickels), which the Goodman Theater's Stage 2 series produced as a play-in-progress on Thursday.

Whether the author, young David Mamet, can organize almost two hours of bleep-rated dialog into a beginning, a middle, and an end is altogether more problematical. His Chicago setting for this undone essay on alienation is an Uptown resale shop owned by Donny Dubrow.

A sad dummy of a kid called Bobby, hooked on drugs, hangs around whenever he needs money, or Donny needs someone to burgle an unguarded house. A second-story maggot nicknamed "Teacher" also hangs around, to play cards after closing hours, and maybe to muscle in on a heist.

GREG MOSHER (*LEFT*), ASSOCIATE ARTISTIC DIRECTOR OF THE GOODMAN THEATRE, WAS AN EARLY SUPPORTER OF THE WORKS OF THE YOUNG DAVID MAMET. HERE, THEY'RE ON THE SET OF "AMERICAN BUFFALO."

In one of Donny's showcases, a coin collector spotted a Buffalo nickel and paid $90 for it. Figuring the guy for an easy mark, Donny has had Bobby bird-dog him until the fellow leaves his place "just around the corner" for a weekend.

When "Teacher" ("Teach" for short) gets wind of the action, he muscles out Bobby for a larger piece of the action. But Donny wants someone named Fletcher included over the protestations of "Teach." Fletcher doesn't show, though, at the appointed hour. In comes Bobby to say Fletcher got mugged; he heard about it from two dykes who sometimes play cards at Donny's. And win, which emasculates "Teach," in any case a bad loser.

Bobby has gotten the name of the hospital wrong. "Teach" begins an irrational interrogation, then hits the kid with a revolver butt. While Bobby bleeds, the phone rings and Donny learns that he was telling the truth. "Teach" is sent to get his car so that Bobby can be hospitalized. And the lights dim.

One can sense the direction in which Mamet wanted to go, although he hasn't yet finished or polished his play. From a precocious philosopher in "The Duck Variations," he has gone the inferential route of Harold Pinter. But "American Buffalo" suggests that Mamet listens in on conversations, like a fledgling Paddy Chayefsky. Pinter and Chayefsky, though, are irreconcilable. Polar opposites, in fact. And we come away with the feeling that Mamet writes dialog first, the characters to fit it, and lastly tries to relate them coherently and meaningfully.

But this hasn't worked. Yet. William H. Macy as Bobby is the only winner in this production. Bernard Erhard is onto "Teach" but the role holds too many contradictions for any consistency of characterization. Since Mamet hasn't even begun to solve Donny, J. J. Johnston is booby-trapped.

The machismo epithets of Uptown become tediously dirty (which they are in real life). But drama is a distillation of life, not mere eavesdropping. "American Buffalo" right now is about 20 usable minutes of a play that Mamet needs to edit, expand, enliven, and point in some direction.

Roger Dettmer was not an especially insightful theater critic, his skills in the music field notwithstanding. This first review of the world premiere of "American Buffalo"—a short two-act, three-character play whose famous plot involves three interdependent men hatching a hapless plot to steal a coin collection from a former customer's house—joins that undistinguished group of opening-night reviews of great plays by critics who completely missed the point. Mamet had taken "American Buffalo," which would go on to win the Pulitzer Prize and earn a reputation as one of great contemporary American plays, to the Goodman Theatre, where Greg Mosher was directing its "Stage 2" series and was hungry for new scripts. William H. Macy was in the cast.

Dettmer writes a pedestrian review, hung up on Mamet's language and the play's apparent resistance to a linear structure. About all he adequately captures of Mamet's skills is his felicity with language. He certainly smells no greatness in the air, no sense of how well the play captures the North Side of Chicago. He did not understand that this is a colorful and famously profane attack on the ethics of American business, as seen from the bottom of its food chain.

The racy dialogue in "American Buffalo" certainly suggests that the Second City was still a strong influence on Mamet. But—not that you would have known it from this review—he also had carefully constructed a kind of surrogate family. Donny and Teach fight for the soul of young Bobby, who will do anything to please and who receives a mixture of placating dollar bills and admonishing blows to the head. In the character of Teach, Mamet had forged a recognizably American, even a recognizably Chicago type, a nasty fellow who smashes up his world, hurling junk, treasures and souls alike into some great slag heap of personal paranoia. But Teach is hardly an urban revolutionary, rather a low-grade loser whose tantrums will never amount to anything more than self-defeating deals and schemes. This is a work very much on a long Chicago trajectory. But Dettmer either couldn't or wouldn't make the link.

Glenna Syse, who was writing for the *Sun-Times*, didn't like "American Buffalo" either. Only one critic loved the play and hailed it as a thrilling new work: Richard Christiansen, then writing for the *Chicago Daily News*. Soon he would move to the *Tribune*, where he would become the champion of the Steppenwolf Theatre Company.

But it would be Larry Kart who first trekked to the players' famous Highland Park basement.

75

THE LOVELIEST AFTERNOON OF THE YEAR *AND* THE DUMB WAITER

STEPPENWOLF'S TWIN BILL SHOWS FLASHES OF ARTISTRY

Steppenwolf Theatre in Highland Park

BY LAWRENCE KART

DECEMBER 17, 1976. The Steppenwolf Theater's location in the basement of a Highland Park school speaks of financial shoestrings. Their current double bill of John Guare's "The Loveliest Afternoon of the Year" and Harold Pinter's "The Dumb Waiter" indicates growing artistic wealth.

Steppenwolf is a young company of former Illinois State University students. Together for less than a year, they have already done works by Eugene Ionesco, Harold Pinter, Hugh Wheeler, and Israel Horovitz, and their ambitious plans include a spring production of Brian Friel's "Philadelphia, Here I Come" and an adaptation of Don DeLillo's novel about a reclusive rock star, "Great Jones Street."

The opening one-acter last Saturday night, Guare's "Loveliest Afternoon," was a stand-in for John Mortimer's "The Dock Brief," which had been previously announced. The substitution was doubly unfortunate. Mortimer's humanistic comedy about a barrister's jail cell interview with his guilty client would have made a fine foil for "The Dumb Waiter," and Guare's sentimental absurdist farce, which may have had some charm back in 1966, now seems as stale and sticky as a decade-old jujube.

A girl (Moira Harris) sits on a park bench feeding the pigeons. A scruffy young man (Terry Kinney) hurtles into the scene, barraging her with inventive paranoia—he's just seen a bunch of pigeons "foaming at the beaks"—and tales about his fearsome wife who shoots at him with a blue rifle. He works as "a seeing-eye person for blind dogs." And so it cutely goes until the inevitable "ironic" reversal.

Kinney did have some amusing moments with his spiels, but the best that can be said about "The Loveliest Afternoon of the Year" is that it was brief. Jeff Perry directed.

"The Dumb Waiter" is 1957 vintage Pinter, melodramatic compared to his later work but an undeniably effective theater piece.

Ben (H. E. Baccus) and Gus (John Malkovich), two gunmen working for a nameless organization, wait in a seedy room for their nameless victim. Gus, the slow-witted underling, has doubts about their situation and surroundings. He and Ben clash over whether one says "light the kettle" or "light the gas," whether the local football club is playing at home or away, and Gus grows more sullen.

Enter the *deus ex machina*. An envelope containing 12 matches is slipped under the door. A sudden clatter in the wall reveals the existence of a dumbwaiter. On it is an order for food. Ben decides to send up Gus' packet of snacks. More orders arrive, requesting increasingly exotic dishes, and soon the play becomes a nightmare—a cat's dream of how it feels to be a mouse.

Under Nancy Chris Evans' direction, this performance may have been a bit short on suspense. But she had Baccus and Malkovich cut right to the heart of the play—the theme of dominance and subservience.

Malkovich dresses Gus in a Mick Jagger-like accent, expressively slumped shoulders, and a pouty mouth. He's perfectly matched with Baccus' Ben, whose air of tense irritation is almost palpable.

Their fine work is showcased by Kevin Rigdon's marvelous dingy set, which takes advantage of the theater's smallness. The audience is just about where the missing walls of Ben's and Gus' room would be. From now through Jan. 16 it will be a room worth visiting.

If everyone who has claimed to have been present in the Highland Park church basement that spawned the Steppenwolf Theatre Company was actually there, it must have been a church basement with a remarkable capacity. But Larry Kart—a veteran *Tribune* jazz critic and editor who would occasionally write theater reviews in this era—*was* there. Kart (1942–) would have a long career at the paper.

And thus here is the very first *Tribune* review of a production from a group that would go on to become arguably the most famous and venerated theater company in Chicago history.

As with the beginning of the Second City, though, the review doesn't reflect the importance of the moment. How could it? For Kart, this was an unknown and very young troupe working in inauspicious surroundings. But he did see the promise of this group called Steppenwolf. There were some soon-to-be-famous names in the show, including Moira Harris, Terry Kinney and John Malkovich (H. E. Baccus would be one of the very few Steppenwolf actors to actually leave the famous ensemble). Kart adroitly compares Malkovich, making the first of many appearances in the *Tribune*, to Mick Jagger.

Highland Park had been home for Gary Sinise and Jeff Perry, two of the other cofounders of the theater company. Both had come back to the Chicago area after attending Illinois State University in Normal (as had Kinney). Most of the actors they recruited were from central Illinois towns.

The actual name Steppenwolf (taken, somewhat randomly, from the novel by Hermann Hesse) had been coined just about a year before Kart's review. Malkovich was new to the company in 1976. And so with this show, it had arrived in the 88-seat basement of the Immaculate Conception School and was duly reviewed by the *Tribune*. This double bill, which became a different bill, Kart reports, very close to opening, was far from the most successful Steppenwolf production. Not too many years later, the *Tribune* would be covering Steppenwolf shows on Broadway.

About 18 months later, Kart would write a feature article charting the company's brief history. In it, he talks with Joan Allen, who says that her father would rather she were working at Caterpillar. He talks with Perry, who speaks of how the group wants to do the same kind of work as Ingmar Bergman and John Cassavetes, who secluded themselves with the same group of actors:

"If you share enough values and stay together over the years, you can create something that can't be done by a one-time collection of individuals." From a man so young, it suggests a remarkably savvy understanding of the meaning of the theatrical ensemble.

Kart's later piece, even more than this first review, offers a prescient analysis of what these youngsters achieved in that basement, and the obstacles they seemed to surmount so quickly. Here's how he begins:

> The trip out to Highland Park puts you in a condescending mood. The Second City syndrome and a suburb to boot. The oldest actor in the company is 24. Probably a group of actors having harmless fun. You spot the sign that says Steppenwolf Theatre, park the car and descend a flight of steps to a basement that looks like what it is–the basement of a grade school. Rows of seats crowd the stage on three sides. The space left open hardly seems big enough for a game of shuffleboard. Then the play begins and preconceptions vanish. The acting is thoughtful, intense. Afterwards, you're hard put to recall another theater experience that worked that well.

And that's why Steppenwolf became Steppenwolf. It didn't take Kart long to understand, just as Linda Winer quickly grasped what "Bleacher Bums" was all about.

76

BLEACHER BUMS

'BLEACHER BUMS' ENDEARING

Organic Theater Company

Leo Lerner Theater

BY LINDA WINER

AUGUST 3, 1977. There are hot dogs, bottled beer, popcorn, baseball, gambling compulsions, winner-loser obsessions, and team fanaticisms for all in "Bleacher Bums," an extended Organic Theater sketch which opened Tuesday at the Leo Lerner Theater in Uptown.

Since I don't care about any of the above, except maybe popcorn and I wouldn't cross a wide alley for that, and since the national pastime has never been mine, and since all Wrigley Field ever symbolized to me was traffic congestion on Addison Street, consider: If I like "Bleacher Bums," anybody could.

And I liked it a lot. Eight virtually topnotch Organic character actors have improvised an endearing "nine-inning comedy," conceived from within by the cast's Joe Mantegna; directed by Stuart Gordon, with additional dialogue by Dennis Paoli, and additional atmosphere by the audience, munching with ballpark dedication around three sides of the theater's shifted arena.

The whole thing takes 90 minutes, with no intermission but a real seventh-inning stretch. The messages are hardly profound, but the caricatures have moments of truth beneath their role playing.

This is an emotional push-over of a play, as much about faith, enthusiasm, fantasy, and ritual as about Cubs fans at the game.

The maligned wife gets vindicated—and a bit patronized?—as a baseball sharpie. The likable blind man with the transistor radio gets the busty blond. The slow-witted fellow gets defended, and everybody comes out to protect the hyperkinetic kid bouncing ethics for team frenzy. The comedy almost gets serious about problem gambling, then, perhaps unfortunately, shies away from dampening the opportunity for baseball bonanza.

A cram course in last week's Tribune series by Bob Logan tells us that the original Bleacher Bums started as pitcher Dick Selma's cheering squad during the team's last winning streak in 1969, then turned sour, and distinguished itself by burning down Chief Nok-A-Homa's tepee during a trip to Atlanta for a game.

The authenticity of the Organic's current view of rabid Cubs fans escapes my innocence. But Gordon has directed the ensemble with even more of his usual high energy, deftly controlled in the limited space of the bleacher benches.

The cast, which apparently costumed itself in ideal clothing details, has turned out a script with none of the problems the Organic often has with its texts. Forget Kurt Vonnegut. It works when the Organic writes itself.

Michael Saad is especially wonderful as the blind fellow with more than terrific hearing, though one should not single out any one in such a tuned ensemble that includes Mantegna, Carolyn Purdy-Gordon,

Dennis Franz, Ian Williams, Richard Fire, Keith Szarabajka, and Roberta Custer. They make—and are—the show.

The Organic, no dummy, has itself a perfect little summer show that capitalizes on the current baseball fever while Gordon wrestles with fund raising and remodeling of their new, bigger Buckingham Theater further south on Clark Street. Their only danger now is a flub from the Cubs.

Linda Winer is quite the stylist here, managing to parse her confessed lack of interest in baseball into a primary qualification for reviewing the show: "If I like 'Bleacher Bums,' anybody could."

And like it they did. "Bleacher Bums" was one of the most famous productions at the Organic Theater, ideal for a company always composed of real actors rather than pretty faces. It was, in essence, an attempt to cash in on the loyal fans of the Chicago Cubs; the populists at the Organic were trying to get some of the hordes populating the bleachers at Wrigley Field to actually walk into the theater, and they figured that the best way to tempt these fans was to show them characters just like them. "I lived right by Wrigley Field back then," Joe Mantegna recalled in an interview years later. "I used to watch the people stream out of the ballpark and I'd try and figure out how we could possibly get all of those people into our theater."

"Our homework," noted Dennis Franz in that same *Tribune* story, "was to go to Wrigley and search the stands for interesting people. We infiltrated them. We took pictures without their knowing it. We befriended them. Then we headed back to the theater, listened to the tape and looked at the photographs, and created a fictitious identity surrounding their lives. We had to alter the names slightly. The aim was to represent the heart of the Cubs fans, the poor souls whose one thing in common is to root for this unfortunate team that breaks their hearts year after year after year."

"Bleacher Bums" ran for about 2 years and subsequently played all over the country, including a whopping 13 years in Los Angeles.

The show was revived in 1978 and again in 1989, with the later production directed by Mantegna himself. A movie was made for the Showtime cable network in 2001, but Major League Baseball wouldn't allow the script to mention either Wrigley Field or the Cubs (Mantegna has said that the baseball league did not approve of the play's copious references to gambling in the bleachers).

In 2004, during a brief period of resurgence for the Chicago Cubs, a new commercial production of "Bleacher Bums" was staged at the Royal George Theatre, with Gary Sandy playing the role originated by Mantegna (who was an investor in the show). This "Bleacher Bums" was modestly successful, but the material proved dated, even though Carolyn Purdy-Gordon and the others had "updated" the show to reflect the current Cubs roster.

Winer nailed the show in 1977, essentially calling it an "extended sketch" with a bleeding heart. It has caught what it is to be a Cubs fan better than any other show before or since.

But what of the South Side of Chicago? By 1977, it, too, had a hefty piece of the theatrical action.

77

THESMO

'THESMO' CHILLS SUPPLE FUNNYBONE

Court Theatre

BY LARRY KART

AUGUST 12, 1977. Perhaps Thursday night's chilly lakefront temperatures froze my normally supply funnybone, but Court Theater's production of Aristophanes' comedy "Thesmophoriazousae" (referred to hereafter as "Thesmo") left me almost totally cold. I can think, though, of three reasons other than the weather for my failure to join in the general guffaws—the intractability of this particular work of Aristophanes to modern adaptation, the University of Chicago, and Tom Mula.

"Thesmo," written in 411 B.C., generally is regarded as the playwright's lightest work. Essentially it serves as a vehicle for parodying the tragic poet Euripides, although the treatment he gets here is gentle compared to the drubbing he receives in "The Frogs."

As the play begins, Euripides has learned that the women of Athens, ticked off by the unsavory picture of femininity in the poet's work, are plotting his death at this year's festival to Demeter and Persephone (the Thesmophoria). He tries to persuade an effeminate fellow playwright to go there in drag to plead his case. When that fails, he gleefully accepts the offer of his nephew Mnesilochus to be the wolf in lady's clothing, and the fun supposedly commences.

The problem in bringing "Thesmo" across to a modern audience is simple. A good part of the play revolves around the literary parody of an author whom next to no one in the audience knows in the original. The solution of director-translator Nicholas Rudall is to substitute lampoons of more familiar figures—Tennessee Williams, the author of the last Court Theater production, Federico Garcia Lorca, Shakespeare, Sigmund Romberg, the creators of "Sesame Street," and what have you.

Most of the time, though, the solution was no solution at all because the parodies bore little relation to the situation on stage. One that did work showed what was awry, as Mnesilochus, trying the get away from a cloddish cop, impersonated Blanche Dubois. There was real humor here—partly because Tennessee Williams' own dialog, wrenched out of context, can sound absurd, and party because in Aristophanes' original the policeman *is* a Stanley Kowalski type.

My indifference to the rest of Rudall's literally yocks, which was not shared by the majority of the audience, probably has a lot to do with Court Theater's home—the University of Chicago. For reasons too complicated to go into here, academic tastes in comedy seem to be satisfied by the mere intention of making a joke. The same situation undoubtedly prevails in a monastery.

So the Court Theater crowd was breaking up at what might be called "recognition comedy." The simple fact that someone would try to get a laugh out of an author as "sacred" as Garcia Lorca was a thigh-slapper. In some ways, the audience at the Blue Max is more sophisticated—it takes more than a label to make them laugh.

In "Thesmo," Mnesilochus (played by Tom Mula) is supposed to be master of the revels. But having seen Mula perform several times this year, I find his unvaryingly cartoon-like acting a style that pales with familiarity. He has begun to smirk with his whole body, as though he were applauding himself. It's hard not to admire his professional sheen but increasingly easy to resist comic business that tries to chuck you under the chin.

Don't let me dissuade you from taking in "Thesmo" at the Court if you think its brand of humor is yours—at the very least it's a slick, fast-moving show. But if you find yourself sitting there without a smile on your face, I'm with you.

The Court Theatre, which would become an artistic anchor in the Chicago neighborhood of Hyde Park, was born in 1955 as an amateur summer operation outdoors on the University of Chicago campus. By the mid-1970s, with a university classics professor named Nicholas Rudall at the helm, it had become a professional theater. This review of "Thesmo" dates to before the Court opened its own home on the campus, which happened in 1981, and before it became independent from the university, a development in 1983.

Larry Kart is certainly in tune here with Court's perennially wonkish identity. Few other Chicago theaters, before or since, would relish the production of obscure Aristophanic comedy. Kart offers a delicious and aptly caustic sketch of the unique Hyde Park milieu. The Court would serve that audience well over the years and earn its long-term support in return.

78

THE WOODS

CLICKETY-CLACK OF DAVID MAMET'S TYPEWRITER IS HEARD THROUGH 'WOODS'

St. Nicholas Theater Company

BY LINDA WINER

NOVEMBER 17, 1977. It is time for a moment of worried impatience, while David Mamet works his way out of "The Woods."

Chicago's most accomplished New Work playwright opened his latest verbal style show at the St. Nicholas Theater Wednesday night and, for people not familiar with the Mamet output, "The Woods"—graced with Patti LuPone—may well have been a dazzling affair.

At closer look, however, this slim two-actor love story is planted with dramatic fertilizer in a lingual and thematic rut.

It lifts its back-to-earth zoological nostalgia from Mamet's earlier two-man "Duck Variations," takes its hip-troubled romantic oversimplifications from "Sexual Perversity in Chicago," and, most problematic of all, progresses almost nowhere in the reconciliation of poetic-fantasy dialogue with dramatic action.

I've been fascinated by the Mamet verbal acrobatics and wacko intensity shifts for years. Still am. I also hate to jump into the "language-defines-action" controversy just as the concerned bandwagon begins in New York.

"The Woods," however, is overly amused by the sound of Mamet's typewriter. It's a lovely sound, admittedly, one of the loveliest. But the words have begun [to] tell us more about Mamet than they reveal about his characters. One yearns for a reason to care about their trivial traumas, hopes for a suspenseful climax that does not seem trumped up for the sake of one, and wishes the words self-conscious and affected wouldn't creep even once into the mind.

LuPone and Peter Weller play Ruth and Nick—a city couple roughing it in his family's summer house. Over a long evening and morning, boy gets girl, boy loses girl, boy gets girl (and vice versa) alongside the supposed ancestral memories of woods, bears, and grandmothers long gone.

Mamet directed "The Woods" himself, his first since a reportedly forgettable attempt at O'Neill's "Beyond the Horizon" in the years before anybody cared whether the "t" was silent in his name. It's a revelation to watch how he lets LuPone stretch and animate his rhythmic lyricism; as though, up to now, other directors have been a little afraid to tamper.

LuPone—sister to Robert LuPone, late of "Nefertiti"—is as compelling as she seemed when she was John Houseman's prodege in the original Juilliard-bred Acting Company. The talent is palpable, if anything, a little too large for the small stage. Her Ruth is all hyped up for the tranquility of the countryside, looking for epiphanies in every frog croak, making cosmic generalizations while showing off for her male audience of one.

For a while, it seemed that Mamet had written a one-character play for two people. We didn't know much about Ruth beyond her theatricality, but we knew nothing at all about Nick. Weller plays him as the still point, the vacuum for Ruth's energies, with children-of-the-damned eyes and a serenity we eventually learn sits somewhere between terror and boredom.

She wants a commitment. (Playwrights always think it's the woman.) He has less in mind. They bring their citified singles-bar mentality to rub against the intoxification of the country, leaving room for romance versus freedom, intimacy versus possession, too few of the fictions in modern coupling, plus some disconcertingly redundant hogwash where pastoral cliches try passing as ageless profundities.

Michael Merritt's plain porch isn't pretty—as though Mamet wanted a neutral set in which the characters can see what they want. They fill it with Mamet's patter poetry, the funny way he twists a formal rep[e]tition with childhood candor, the sputters of emotion, couched in some of his lesser images of dreams, fantasies, and naturalistic-cum-stylized people who inexplicable refuse to use grammatical conjunctions in normal speech. It helps to remember that lesser Mamet's still the best around. And that the best is obviously yet to come.

By 1977 Linda Winer, now the chief drama critic at the *Tribune*, was back on the Mamet trail, although with the success of "American Buffalo" he now was officially a New York playwright.

This superb review is of the world premiere of "The Woods," a famously intense production that featured Patti LuPone in its cast. A keen analyst, Winer was very much aware of, and willing to spar with, Mamet's complex sexual politics. Here, she is already discerning a new direction for this playwright, who would reinvent himself (both politically and aesthetically) many more times in the years that followed. It's also striking how well she assesses LuPone's outsized scale, which later would be put to better use in big Broadway musicals, which Winer would watch from the orchestra. Other Chicago critics were generally more laudatory of this production.

As LuPone recounts in her autobiography, she and Mamet knew each other from their time at Yale University. By the time of "The Woods," LuPone had moved into the Hotel Lincoln, which she describes as "squalid" and a "flea-bitten dive." She also paints a picture of a traumatic rehearsal process, which had her in crisis with her actual lover, Kevin Kline, and falling instead for Peter Weller, her costar in a play that Mamet described as "a celebration of heterosexual love"–bizarre words, perhaps, for a play with so much violence. "David left Chicago after we opened," LuPone writes. "I was stuck in a run of this extraordinary, difficult, devastating play, depressed as hell in freezing Chicago–not what I bargained for."

When "The Woods" went to New York, where it played at the New York Public Theatre, LuPone was replaced by Christine Lahti. She continued her relationship with Mamet, though. In 2012, she appeared on Broadway in his new play, "The Anarchist," which opened and closed with rapidity.

79

WORKING

'WORKING' IS LONG, LOOSE BUT CLEVER LOOK AT U.S. LABOR

Goodman Theatre

BY LINDA WINER

JANUARY 6, 1978. Forty-two remarkable people got up on the Goodman Theater's stage Thursday night to talk about the way they feel about their jobs. By the time they finished, it was clear that working isn't the blessing one third-grade teacher claimed, but that "Working" certainly is.

The musical adaptation of Studs Terkel's "Working," which had its Broadway-bound world premiere at the Goodman, is too long and still uncertain about how to tie up its structural loose ends. But the material and concept are splendid, the performances mostly topnotch, and—considering the range of experiences—the three hour-plus evening could almost be called economical.

After the awful collection of new musicals that have passed through Chicago this season, this latest one was approached with modest expectations. Stephen Schwartz, who adapted and directed Terkel's 1974 oral history, downplayed the premiere as a work-in-progress kind of workshop production. If that weren't uneasy enough, the invitations arrived in a brown paper bag—and proletariat chic foreshadowed the night.

But this is a clever and touching overview of American work, sensitively selected and lifted almost verbatim from the 100 interviews in Terkel's bestseller. To add special meaning to the evening, 14 of the real-life workers were in the opening-night audience.

Terkel's interviews zeroed in on one of the basic themes, one of the basic needs, of modern man. Work in the 1970's is an approach-avoidance affair, from corporate top to the supposedly menial bottom. The culture encourages the concept of individuals, but the economy doesn't want them. Pride of workmanship battles the boredom, bitterness fights the confusion. Status and material goods somehow don't counter the recurring message: nobody's indispensable.

If "A Chorus Line" delves into the motivations behind one specific kind of worker—the show dancer—then "Working" could be considered a Son-of-Chorus Line—"Assembly Line," perhaps, or "Corporate Line," or, more universally, "Life Line." Like "Chorus Line," this one is a documentary confessional that takes its '70s who-am-I? self analyses back onto the stage once more.

While I have not been overly fond of such other Schwartz efforts as "Pippin" and "Godspell," the composer overcomes much of his impulse toward inventively-structured sappy sentiments in this one. In addition, he has wisely recognized the vast diversities of the book's characters and hired five other composers to contribute songs. Schwartz' own songs, in fact, are still the most amiably faceless of the group—but his concept and direction are extraordinary.

"Working" tells us that each laborer has an intelligent, individual need to identify with his work. And this is the kind of show that makes you want to list each cast member's contribution to the whole.

There are 14 actors portraying the 40-odd characters, which makes itemization impossible. Highlights, however, are David Patrick Kelly in two treasured monologues—one about a flower-child copyboy at a Chicago newspaper and one as a salesman spouting the American dream. Rex Everhart can make you ache as Joe, the retired shipping clerk, or as the seaman who has a happy marriage with the terrific Bobo Lewis.

Jay Flash Riley brings a jivy life to "Lovin' Al," a veteran parking lot attendant who finds glamor—thanks to music and lyrics by Micki Grant, best known for her musical, "Don't Bother Me, I Can't Cope."

Schwartz has organized the multiple stories around the story of a family who quits the rat race and tries to find a way to control their existence. Despite the work of Joe Ponazzecki, Jo Henderson, and 12-year-old Jay Footlik, this device does not yet successfully hold the thing together. But, with some work, it will.

Other prize songs among the many are "Millwork," one of the several lovely ones by pop composer James Taylor, and just about everything by Craig Carnelia.

David Mitchell, who did the sets for "Annie," has created a multiplicity of scenery that slides in different worlds with a handful of props—many of them hard-hat orange. Marjorie Slaim's mime-white costumes fit in with the more-mime-than-dance numbers, adding the perfect detail to change the uniform.

The show must certainly be trimmed, considerably, though I wouldn't want to be the one who has to do it. As one of the characters says, people's jobs are too small for their spirit these days. Jobs are not big enough for people. Maybe the theater isn't quite big enough, either. But it's doing a wonderful job trying.

Here, Linda Winer reviews what must have been a remarkable night in Chicago—the original production of "Working," based on the book by famous Chicago actor, oral historian and radio personality Studs Terkel. As Winer recounts, many of the actual workers on whom the show was based were in the audience that night at the Goodman Theatre.

For his 1974 book, *Working: People Talk about What They Do All Day and How They Feel about What They Do*, Terkel had transcribed (among others) the words of a gravedigger, a firefighter, a bookbinder, a skycap, a manager of a business, a waitress and a jockey. Many were Chicagoans. Most proved to be philosophers. All were familiar with the daily grind. The musical version of "Working" essentially sets Terkel's interviews to music and draws from a distinctive musical palette of pop, blues, roots and other populist musical forms to underscore the testimony of these mostly blue-collar, real-life characters.

Of all the Terkel interviewees who are interpreted in song, Kate Rushton, a homemaker before the term was in the lexicon, probably gets the best song of all. Set to music by Craig Carnelia, her interview encapsulates the tone of the show: our most essential workers are the most invisible and the most unaware of their importance. "All I am is just a housewife, nothing special, nothing great," go the formidable lyric to her song, which quickly became an unusually quotidian staple of the cabaret room and motivated a succession of Broadway divas to tap into their sense of inner anonymity. "What I do is kinda boring, if you'd rather, it can wait."

Less than three months after it closed at the Goodman, "Working" reopened on Broadway at the 46th Street Theatre (the unlikely combination of Patti LuPone, playing a call girl, and Joe Mantegna, playing a Mexican migrant worker, were part of the cast). The show did not do well in New York—it ran for just 24 performances. And although many people associate "Working" with a small, Chicago-style ensemble cast, that was far from the reality of that original Broadway production, which got reviews very different from the one published here.

But "Working" had a powerful afterlife in regional theaters, colleges and community theaters. In 2011, a new, updated production was staged in

Chicago at the Broadway Playhouse, a commercial venue just off Michigan Avenue. It was moderately successful, and subsequently was seen in New York. Terkel did not live to see that production, although he saw his most famous work performed in the theater across several decades. Embraced as an iconic Chicagoan for decades, he died in 2008 at the age of 96.

80

CHICAGO

'CHICAGO'–BUMPS BECOME A GRIND IN A BRASSY AND CYNICAL LEG SHOW

Blackstone Theatre

BY LINDA WINER

FEBRUARY 25, 1978. If the Lord or something didn't already create the pelvis, Bob Fosse would have had to invent it. Invent it, back it with neon, surround it with feathers, and star it in musicals like "Chicago," the brassy, cynical, fairly mindless but entertaining enough leg show that suggests, however, that too many bumps can become a grind.

When normal kids were going to Amundsen High in the '40s, Bob Fosse was sneaking over to the Chicago Theater to see vaudeville and running off to Rockford to emcee in burlesque. The biographical details are everywhere in "Chicago," which was subtitled a "musical vaudeville" on Broadway—and still should have been when it opened Thursday for 11 fleshy, razzle-dazzle weeks at the Blackstone Theater.

This is another weak plot, like "Pippin," which the director has shot up with flashy dance, scant dialog, and enough scantier chorus costumes to keep the convention trade in their seats through Fred Ebb and John Kander's 20-or-so painless songs. Unlike "Pippin," however, where the stage gimmicks clashed with the earnest message, the coarse stagecraft is now appropriate to the story of greed and corruption in '20s Chicago. Form *is* function—and that's nice.

As you have probably guessed by now, I am having an approach-avoidance reaction to "Chicago." The story, based on Maurine Dallas Watkins' 1926 play about murdering floozies, is not really much of a story at all. We have already seen Fosse deliver better decadence in his movie version of "Cabaret." His choreography keeps suggesting Liza Minnelli (or vice versa?), and the skin show does get tedious.

Yet, there is a cleverness in the concept that keeps commenting on exploitation while it exploits. As the show's best song says, "Give 'em the old razzle dazzle and they will make you a star." Fosse laughs at himself as well as at us—and they make "Chicago" shine, too.

The adaptation, which he wrote with Ebb, exposes the legal system and the press as their own kinds of vaudeville. Emcees announce the various numbers, most of which take place in a women's prison. There, women who have murdered their men pay a theatrical mouthpiece $5,000 to save their lives—and, in the process, turn them into celebrities.

Everyone, including the matron, is on the take. The orchestra is part of the show, playing the short, upbeat, torchy songs from the second floor of Tony Walton's double-decker set. The Kit Kat Klub meets "The Act," with its own bitter, almost Brechtian results.

Penny Worth is Roxie Hart, a dopey blond would-be singer who casually shoots one of her lovers. Carolyn Kirsch plays Velma, the jailed brunet, whose bid for criminal celebrity gets overshadowed by Roxie. They're both short on voices and aren't helped by uneven miking, but they can certainly dance.

Fosse's choreography continues his liking for the slow dream ooze of decadence, the twisting wrists, piston shoulders, and general piston everything else. Jerry Orbach, the only member of the original Broadway cast, is perfect as the sleazy lawyer who has no illusions about love, and Haskell Gordon, likewise, is an apt sad sack as Roxie's virtually nonexistent husband.

The vaudeville emphasis includes takeoffs on female impersonators with falsetto voices, feather fan dances, a Roxie ventriloquist act, plus Jimmy Durante and Helen Morgan imitations. Patricia Zipprodt, who put breasts on the breast plates in "Pippin," costumed this one with rhinestone beauty marks, androgynous male chorus, rolled hose, garters, plus the aforementioned bare business. You can contemplate the navel all evening, but eventually it's just a bellybutton.

By 1978, the famous musical that had begun in the reporter's notebook of Maurine Dallas Watkins had arrived in Chicago. Linda Winer, in her unusual and intriguing review, focuses on Bob Fosse's early years in the city. She's not especially impressed.

"Chicago," though, would prove unstoppable. A 1996 Broadway revival directed by Walter Bobbie would run on Broadway for 16 years (and counting), play Chicago many times and sprout productions all over the world: rat-a-tat-tat eight nights a week.

And then came Richard Christiansen to the *Tribune*.

81

THE GLASS MENAGERIE

THE POETRY OF 'MENAGERIE' GETS IMPRESSIVE ILLUMINATION

Steppenwolf Theatre in Highland Park

BY RICHARD CHRISTIANSEN

MAY 18, 1979. Steppenwolf Theater's new production of "The Glass Menagerie" has the effect of turning this American classic into a fresh, jolting, completely unexpected experience.

Memories of Tennessee Williams' 35-year-old drama tend to be shrouded in mists of romanticism; but the Steppenwolf troupe, made up of youngsters who hadn't been born when the play made its debut in Chicago, gives the text a thorough shaking and turns it into a play full of surprises.

Some of the freshness comes from obeying the playwright's original instructions for his memory play. In his first manuscript, Williams had called for slide projections bearing images and titles that would accent the values of each scene, but this device was abandoned in the Broadway production and has rarely been used since. At Steppenwolf, the return to slides of photos, paintings, and titles that are projected on a rear wall of the set do indeed emphasize and highlight the moods of each segment without becoming obtrusive or distracting.

What really shakes up the play, however, is the interpretation of the four characters that inhabit Williams' world.

John Malkovich, an amazing young actor whose performances always seem to teeter on the edge of danger, portrays Tom, the narrator

CRITIC RICHARD CHRISTIANSEN, IN A *TRIBUNE* PROMOTIONAL SHOT.

who gives us "truth in the pleasant disguise of illusion," as if he were Williams himself. In the opening minutes, when Tom sets the scene, Malkovich, appearing behind a skrim curtain, actually sounds like Williams in every cadence and tone of voice.

Malkovich's Tom is a dreamer and a wanderer, but he is also a spoiled mama's boy, bored out of his skull by being trapped in a stifling tenement apartment with his flighty mother and strange sister.

As Amanda Wingfield, Anne Edwards gives the most traditional performance. She is still the faded belle reduced to selling magazine subscriptions over the phone, and she still fusses over the arrival of a gentleman caller for her daughter. Even here, however, Edwards emphasizes the woman's despair over her situation by making her a tired, nagging, irritating, and near-frantic mother anxious to get a little peace for herself.

She and Malkovich have at least two scenes that slap the son-mother relationship into sharp focus. In one bit, performed mostly offstage, we hear her peppering him with pellets of anger while he howls back in yelps and barks. In the other scene, he flops into a chair and pouts while she furiously brushes his hair, as a mother would fuss with a baby.

Laurie Metcalf's Laura is not the sweet, sad innocent of many productions, but rather a disturbed young cripple close to catatonia. She rushes for her old phonograph records with eerie compulsion, and she actually seems to be on the verge of physical illness in times of stress.

When Terry Kinney's soft-voiced, easygoing, soothing, and pleasantly ordinary gentleman caller finally does draw her out of her shell, his feat seems the triumph of a psychiatrist or hypnotist over a very sick patient.

H. E. Baccus, the play's director, has inserted soft music and an occasional tinkle of glass to heighten the mood of haunted memories in the play; and Kevin Rigdon's lighting is completely faithful to Williams' request for "shafts of light . . . focused on selected areas or actors, sometimes in contradiction to what is the apparent center."

This is not a gentle, wispy interpretation. It is jagged and harsh in many scenes, spooky and quirky in others. Yet it strikingly illuminates the poetry of the play by casting it in a different light, re-examining its humanity, and dispelling some of the false illusions that have surrounded it in past presentations.

The play is scheduled to run through June 24, with performances set for 8 p.m. Thursdays, 8:30 p.m. Fridays and Saturdays, and 7 p.m. Sundays.

I saw the show on a Sunday evening (Mother's Day) when there were only 20 customers in the troupe's 90-seat basement space at 770 Deerfield Rd. in Highland Park.

It's amazing, and depressing, that this gifted troupe, consistently interesting in its work, was able to pull so few people into so fascinating a production.

With this review of the famous Steppenwolf Theatre production of "The Glass Menagerie," the Richard Christiansen era began at the *Tribune*. Christiansen (1931–) would arguably do as much as anyone to support the growth of Chicago theater, and with the 2004 publication of *A Theater of Our Own*, he wrote its first single-volume history-memoir. He also produced an enormous number of theater reviews before he retired from the *Tribune* in 2002, but like Claudia Cassidy he remained a private person. He did not often reference his own life in his writing, and although he did not share Cassidy's hatred for being photographed or interviewed, he was not frequently written about.

This wasn't Christiansen's first review for the *Tribune*, and certainly not his first review of Chicago theater. Born in the suburb of Oak Park, he began his journalistic career in 1956 at the famous City News Bureau in Chicago, moving a year later to the *Chicago Daily News* and taking a job on the night shift. Two days after the *Daily News* folded, he joined the *Tribune* in 1978 as a so-called critic at large. In 1980, Linda Winer left the paper for the *New York Daily News*, leaving Christiansen as the chief drama critic. He would hold that post for the next 22 years, a period, not incidentally, of enormous growth for Chicago theater.

After the demise of the *Daily News*, Chicago was left with two daily newspapers: the *Tribune* and the *Chicago Sun-Times*, meaning that two main critics held sway in the city. However, the *Chicago Reader*, an alternative weekly cofounded by Robert A. Roth in 1971, also was becoming well known for its extensive theater coverage, often publishing far longer reviews than either of the two dailies. *Reader* critics made it to shows that Christiansen never saw. But the *Tribune*, with its huge subscription base, had the most powerful voice.

Christiansen attended shows in small theaters, which could not be said of Cassidy with any regularity. As Rick Kogan would write in the *Tribune* shortly after Christiansen's retirement, he went to shows "in storefronts, attics, lofts, suburbs and city, and even someone's living room." He was known as a courteous, gentlemanly critic who accentuated the constructive and who, unlike Cassidy, was rarely mean or caustic. He was and is—again, unlike Cassidy—widely beloved by those he covered. Although extensively credited with never being arrogant, Christiansen also was no shrinking violet; much of the growth in Chicago theater came not just from his reviews but from what he could accomplish at the paper due to his enjoying so much political clout within its halls.

Christiansen's reviews were carefully reported; they never were screeds, and he rarely conceptualized or experimented with bravura style. He was not a free-form writer, nor was he a self-regarding critic in the mode of Kenneth Tynan. He was a Chicago newspaperman of the old school. And he never left before the end of the second act. "All my life," Christiansen wrote in his book, "I've been eager to go to the theater," which is clear from the reviews that follow here.

If Christiansen and Cassidy represented the polarities of newspaper criticism when it came to the critics' reputations for benevolence or the lack thereof, the two of them shared the dominant role in arts criticism at the *Tribune* of the 20th century. They held their posts for a cumulative half century, albeit not consecutively. Interestingly, both had an affinity for Tennessee Williams.

This review, written before Winer left, helped bolster the reputation of the Steppenwolf Theatre, a company Christiansen supported with notable passion and success. It has the kind of lead paragraph that sells tickets. And it ends with the writer's lament that only 20 people shared the theater with him on the night of his review. It was as close as Christiansen would let himself come to demanding that his readers head to Highland Park and see what John Malkovich, Laurie Metcalf and Terry Kinney were doing.

Malkovich was clearly not yet the box-office draw he would become, but there's no question that Christiansen saw his talent. The young actor was on a roll.

82

TRUE WEST

STEPPENWOLF'S 'TRUE WEST' A ROMPIN', STOMPIN' SUCCESS

Steppenwolf Theatre

BY RICHARD CHRISTIANSEN

CAST

Austin .... Jeff Perry
Lee .... John Malkovich
Saul Kimmer .... Francis Guinan
Mom .... Laurie Metcalf

APRIL 22, 1982. Steppenwolf Theater Wednesday night tackled—and I mean *tackled*—Sam Shepard's "True West" in a knockdown, slam-bang, all-out battle to the finish. It was a great fight; both Steppenwolf and Shepard won; and the audience, amazingly unscarred from two hours of being slapped around, emerged happily punchdrunk.

JEFF PERRY (*LEFT*) AND JOHN MALKOVICH IN "TRUE WEST," AMONG THE MOST FAMOUS OF CHICAGO THEATER PRODUCTIONS.

"True West" is the most recent leg of Shepard's continuing odyssey into the withered myths and ugly realities of contemporary America. By comparison with his earlier masterwork, "The Tooth of Crime" (currently in a sensational performance by the Remains Ensemble in the Theater Building), it is a spare, taut, tightly crafted piece of work. But it has many of the author's same images and themes—the wasted landscape of the American West, the failure of communication, the mysteriously fragmented family ties, the ridiculous junk society of today and the drying up or corruption of our history and heritage. It has touches of Shepard's surrealistic poetry, particularly in a long, bizarre monologue about a demented old man and his false teeth. And it has, as Steppenwolf's production makes clear with cyclonic force, Shepard's great, inimitable gusher of theatrical imagination.

The story, about two brothers locked in fierce combat in an isolated, realistic setting, is almost Pinteresque in outline; but at Steppenwolf, it's as if "The Caretaker" or "The Homecoming" had been given a rocket shot of speed and sent flying into outer space.

One brother, Austin, is a civilized, married, respectable writer. The other, Lee, is a primitive, thieving, drunken slob of a desert rat who has slithered into a Southern California suburb to hover menacingly about while his younger sibling faithfully housesits for their half-daft mother and tries to finish up a love story for the movies.

Lee, aspiring to his brother's style and talent, forces Austin to write the draft of an incredibly corny Western movie. Amazingly, Lee's glib, phony movie producer thinks it's a highly original work and tries to persuade the polished writer to translate his nearly illiterate brother's Western into a finished, commercial product.

The clash of the two personalities produces an improbable, impossible jumble of words in the movie script and a fantastic reversal of roles. Austin savagely reverts to Lee's crazed, drunken state, while Lee hopelessly tries to cope with the mechanics and accoutrements of urbanity. At the end, the brothers stand facing [each] other in spooky twilight zone, opposite selves irrevocably bound in a bruising, hateful alliance.

The play's contrast of the primitive and the civilized, of reality and art and of truth and illusion is, on paper, full of pregnant pauses, evocative sound effects and significant symbols. There's some of that here, but, under Gary Sinise's direction, this version is more a megaton explosion of the famed Steppenwolf energy.

John Malkovich, his jaw thrust out in simian style, storms the role of Lee with wild-eyed bursts of intensity, mixed with howling, screaming flights of boorish glee.

Jeff Perry, as clever an actor in shaping his softness and silence as Malkovich is in turning on his force and fury, brilliantly transforms the once-gentle Austin into his brother's image, descending from man to beast. He and Malkovich make a great team, two different persons who, at last, become one being.

Francis Guinan has a sly time satirizing the artificial, two-faced Hollywood producer, and Laurie Metcalf dodders on stage briefly near play's end for a hilarious turn as the brothers' loony mother.

I'm not sure at all that this kind of romping, stomping guerilla attack on Shepard's script is what the author had in mind. I'm certain, however, that the play can sustain the interpretation and that Steppenwolf has turned "True West" into one of the funniest, scariest evenings of theater we're likely to see this year.

If there is one show that came to signify Chicago-style theater–in-your-face, macho, aggressive, terrifying acting–then the Steppenwolf production of "True West" surely is that show. This also is the production that launched the Steppenwolf brand on a global scale. It is one of the most famous theatrical productions in Chicago history.

At this juncture, Steppenwolf was performing at 3212 N. Broadway, the same venue wherein Bob Sickinger failed to impress Claudia Cassidy. But Richard Christiansen was behind the company from the beginning. He wrote the kind of review ("a megaton explosion of the famed Steppenwolf energy") that attracted a slew of off-Broadway producers to Chicago, even though the two leading actors, Jeff Perry and John Malkovich, were not yet stars by any means.

Interestingly enough, Shepard was not involved at all with this production (the play had premiered at the Magic Theatre in San Francisco in 1980), nor did he pay much attention to Steppenwolf in its early days. And as Christiansen rightly notes here, this take on "True West" was not necessarily what the author had in mind.

Gary Sinise was determined to get the production to New York, and so he did–though some other members of the Steppenwolf troupe were uneasy about the decision, since the company was trying to move into its own new theater space at 2851 N. Halsted St. (now demolished). But Sinise clearly made the right decision. He took over the role of Austin from Jeff Perry (who decided not to go to New York with the show) and played opposite Malkovich. "True West" opened on November 17, 1982, and ran for 762 performances at the Cherry Lane Theatre in New York. Many different actors played the roles during the New York run (including Jim Belushi and Randy Quaid), but the production would be forever associated with Malkovich and Sinise. Neither they nor their company ever looked back.

Many people think it was Sinise who played the role in Chicago. But it was Perry whom Christiansen admired in Lakeview as he sent Chicago's most famous theater company on its way. He was about to do the same for William L. Petersen.

83

IN THE BELLY OF THE BEAST: LETTERS FROM PRISON

UNFORGETTABLE ACTING POWERS 'BEAST'

Wisdom Bridge Theater

BY RICHARD CHRISTIANSEN

CAST

Jack Henry Abbott .... William L. Petersen

With Tim Halligan and Peter Aylward

SEPTEMBER 30, 1983. The work of William L. Petersen in "In the Belly of the Beast: Letters from Prison" is such an extraordinary achievement, and of such heroic stature, that it crosses the usual boundaries of "acting" into an area of experience I found staggering.

As Jack Henry Abbott, the subject of the book and murder trial on which "Beast" is based, Petersen is called upon to portray a paranoid killer who is also a maimed victim and a gifted artist.

This he does, from the moment he steps on stage at Wisdom Bridge Theater, barefoot and clad in prison issue, and fixes the audience with a ferocious stare of anger and conviction.

Petersen works with his mind and from his gut—and from what I can only call his soul.

He gives us Abbott's Southern accent, his stutter, his physical appearance in letter-perfect detail. And, though he howls in pain and shouts in rage with raw intensity, he is also an expert craftsman in the modulation of his voice and in the movement of his body. Notice, for example, how Abbott's stutter disappears when he is caught up in the rush of his descriptive powers. Or watch how Petersen injects an involuntary shudder into a crucial phrase of vivid dialogue.

These qualities are admirable in acting, and can be accounted for, but how do I account for the fact that minutes after leaving the theater Thursday night, I had to pull my car over to the side of the street so that I could clear the tears from my eyes?

Such shocking power comes only, I suspect, when an actor gives himself to the life of a character with deep inner strength and commitment. Not many actors have the character or intelligence or skill

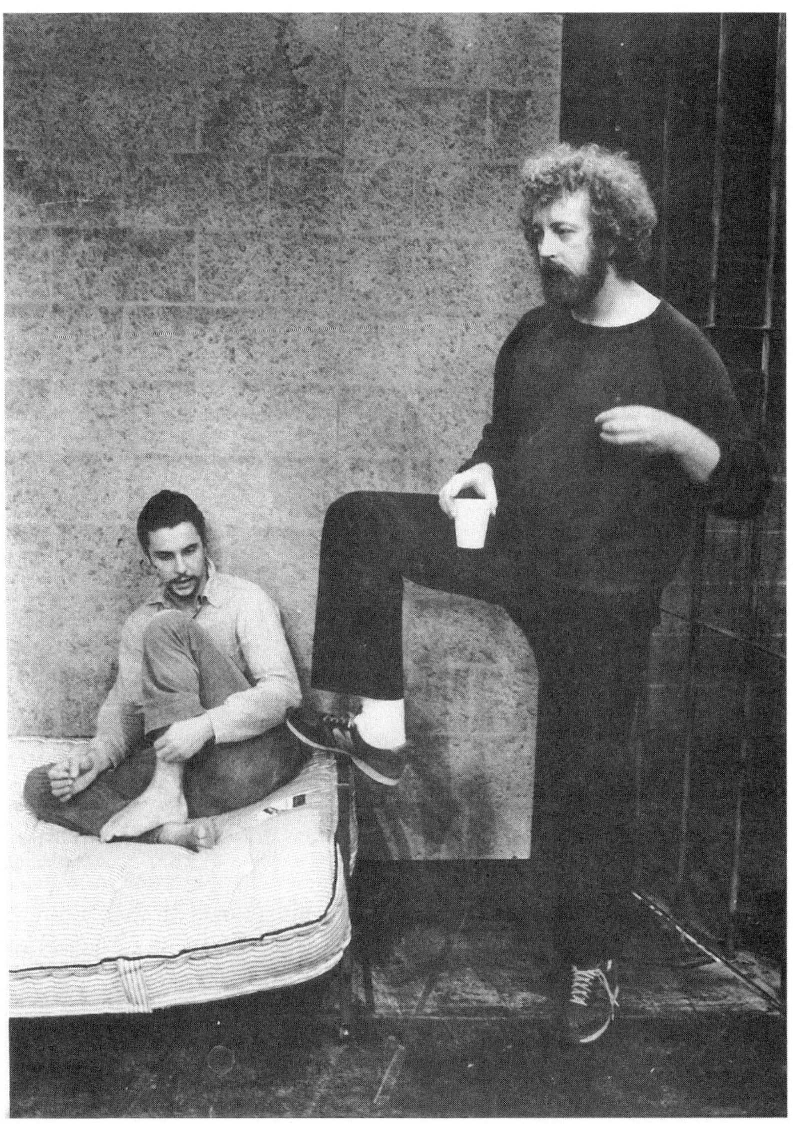

ROBERT FALLS (*RIGHT*) AND WILLIAM L. PETERSEN ON THE SET OF "IN THE BELLY OF THE BEAST" IN 1983. THIS IS THE FAMOUS PRODUCTION THAT MADE CRITIC RICHARD CHRISTIANSEN "PULL OVER." PHOTOGRAPH BY RON BAILEY FOR THE *CHICAGO TRIBUNE*.

to reach that far within themselves, and not many are given roles that seem so right for them, but when they make it, as Petersen has on this occasion, it's breathtaking.

The play containing this young actor's incredible work has been taken from Abbott's now-famous book of vivid letters from prison to novelist Norman Mailer and from the documentation of Abbott's trial for the murder of a waiter in New York City in 1981, soon after Abbott, a literary celebrity, had been paroled from prison.

Robert Falls, who re-arranged the material from an earlier, original adaptation by director Adrian Hall of the Trinity Square Repertory Company in Providence, R.I., has staged the drama with searing force, aided immeasurably by the brilliant lighting design of Michael S. Philippi.

Petersen's portrayal is so riveting and the material is so sensational that the play's stark presentation—with Tim Halligan and Peter Aylward providing flat, stoney-faced narration and acting as occasional secondary characters—is highly effective. It is only when Falls pushes too hard, with Brechtian banners and background music, that his otherwise tough, inventive direction slackens.

One can and should question the veracity of Abbott's melodramatic stories, but "In the Belly of the Beast" nevertheless provokes thought about important social issues and individual crises as few contemporary American dramas have.

And, even in the intermissionless play's most florid moments, there is always Petersen's utterly true, completely real presence to arrest the mind and capture the heart.

If he can sustain that work, and if he can survive the punishment it is putting him through, he will give you—as he did me—a life in the theater you will not forget.

Richard Christiansen's review of the Wisdom Bridge Theater production of "In the Belly of the Beast" starring William L. Petersen is famous for a number of reasons. In the first instance, this review helped establish the career of Robert Falls, who would go on to become artistic director of the Goodman Theatre. In the second, it brought fame to Petersen, who would go on to become a successful television star; on several subsequent occasions, he credited this review with changing his life.

At the dedication of the Richard Christiansen Theater in 2010, Petersen told a story of drinking all night and then running down to the loading dock of the Tribune Tower printing press at four in the morning to snag a copy of Christiansen's review of his solo performance as an incarcerated killer.

He was not disappointed. There is no comparably ecstatic review of an actor anywhere in this book. Indeed, it is hard to imagine that another comparably ecstatic review of an actor was ever written in Chicago; even the Joseph Jefferson appreciation earlier in this book doesn't come close.

The most famous line in Christiansen's review—indeed, in any review he wrote in his 40 years of writing them—is this one: "minutes after leaving the theater Thursday night, I had to pull my car over to the side of the street so that I could clear the tears from my eyes." Since Christiansen lived downtown and the Wisdom Bridge Theater was on Howard Street on the Far North Side, he likely pulled over on either Sheridan Road or Lake Shore Drive.

Thereafter, the "pull-over review" became legendary as the ultimate critical accolade in Chicago theater. One common usage goes like this: "Did Christiansen like it?" "He did." "Ah, but did he pull over?"

At least in print, Christiansen would never pull over again. Petersen had that one all for himself. But David Mamet now had a huge supporter at the *Tribune*.

84

GLENGARRY GLEN ROSS

'GLENGARRY' REFINES MAP OF EXPLORED TERRAIN

Goodman Theatre Studio

BY RICHARD CHRISTIANSEN

CAST

Levene .... Robert Prosky
Williamson .... J. T. Walsh
Moss .... James Tolkan
Aaronow .... Mike Nussbaum
Roma .... Joe Mantegna
Lingk .... William L. Petersen
Baylen .... Jack Wallace

FEBRUARY 7, 1984. With his new play, "Glengarry Glen Ross," David Mamet is returning to the chilling scene and themes that he first pierced in "American Buffalo."

The theme here, as in “Buffalo,” is that of the folly of getting and spending, of the frantic drive for the quick deal and the fast buck that leads men to lie, cheat and steal out of some cockeyed vision of their own manliness and worth in society.

“Buffalo” featured small-time crooks in a Chicago junk shop planning a two-bit, botched-up robbery. “Glengarry Glen Ross” concerns minor-league real estate salesmen enmeshed in the burglary of their Chicago office.

Both plays concern petty crimes; both involve duplicity among friends; both have a surprise, ironic ending; and both are filled with enraged, foul-mouthed confrontations.

But “Glengarry Glen Ross” (which gets its title from the fancy names tagged on the packets of land the salesmen are hustling) is the more classic and elaborate play in structure and in dialogue, and it stands as an impressive sharpening of the amazing skills Mamet exhibited so strikingly in “Buffalo.”

In the American premiere production at the Goodman Theatre Studio, it is also a well-produced, consummately well-acted drama, its actors so tuned to the rhythms of Mamet’s speeches and so perfectly shaped in every detail of their stage life, right down to the rings on their fingers, that they seem to have been born and bred in the low end of the selling game.

Except for one customer who wanders into their net, all of the men in “Glengarry” are salesmen. Their lives are spent in pursuing the “good leads” that will help them close a sale and “get up on the board.” To achieve that goal, they will do anything.

In the first act, a series of three scenes set in a Chinese restaurant and featuring the man-to-man dialogues of which Mamet is a master, the salesmen are introduced as they gripe, bitch, connive and maneuver.

Shelly “The Machine” Levene is a warped, 1980s version of Willy Loman (as in “Death of a Salesman”), a once-hot huckster who has hit what he calls “a bad streak” and is trying to hang on to his job by making a deal with the cold-fish office manager Williamson (J. T. Walsh).

Moss is a furious nobody, a vengeful underling who believes his poor standing in the office is caused by bad breaks and favoritism.

Aaronow is a poor schlemiel who never has and never will have any flair for his job.

Lastly there is Ricky Roma, who sports a winter tan, an expensive suit and a spiel so compelling he can sell real estate to a total stranger he meets in the restaurant.

The second act takes place in the real estate office, after the burglary that had been discussed in the restaurant has taken place. Here, after a slight sag in the action, the loose ends are startlingly tied up and, following a flurry of double-deals and back-stabbings, the play ends with a final, devastating whimper.

Throughout the play, Mamet's poetic gutter language is brilliantly displayed, as he reveals the nature of his characters through their convoluted repetitions, aborted sentences and rushed phrasing.

When Levene rhapsodizes on the moment of truth in closing a deal, when Roma lures a customer with a mesmerizing existentialist rap, when Moss explodes in tongue-tied rage over the injustice of his job, the play surges with vitality, sings with a dark beauty.

Under Gregory Mosher's direction and working in a seamlessly designed production, the cast of seven men plunges into Mamet's evocative world as if to the real estate office born.

The brilliance of the acting often is expressed in nonverbal ways: in the hangdog look plastered on Mike Nussbaum's hapless Aaronow, in the sweaty nervousness of James Tolkan's infuriated Moss, and in the sick dread that crosses the face of William L. Petersen's bamboozled customer.

Robert Prosky as the sagging, aging "Machine" Levene and Joe Mantegna as the slick Rick Roma tear into the long, flashy speeches that Mamet has set before them with virtuoso style and gusto, tossing off each complex twist of phrase and trickily curved turn of expression without a hitch.

Already acclaimed in its London premiere last year and headed for Broadway under the banner of producer Elliot Martin after its engagement here, "Glengarry Glen Ross" has a realistic aura and a carefully plotted story that probably will appeal to a much larger audience than Mamet enjoyed with his last (and more ambitious) play, "Edmond."

Unlike "Edmond," "Glengarry" doesn't open any frontiers for

Mamet, but it does powerfully re-explore and consolidate those dark territories of the American sensibility that this profoundly gifted playwright has made his own.

By 1984, David Mamet was gone from Chicago. But his "Glengarry Glen Ross," both a savage indictment of the inhumanity of American business and a tightly focused exploration of the vulgar rites and dangerous rituals of selfish and amoral men scrambling for their souls at the lower rungs of the corporate ladder, is set back in his home city. It also had its American premiere there, at the Goodman Theatre.

During his Chicago days, Mamet had found a job churning out leads for salesmen selling nonexistent land to retirees. It had proved to be a window into the city's dead-end lives. Even though "Glengarry" had premiered in London, Richard Christiansen immediately recognized it as a Chicago play. "What did I learn as a kid on Western [Avenue]?" says the character of Moss, specifically locating the play in its milieu. "Don't sell a guy one car. Sell him five cars over 15 years."

Christiansen reviews some fine actors here, including Joe Mantegna and William L. Petersen (of "pull-over" fame; see the previous review). But he also was able to put this play in the context of the early Mamet. We could argue, actually, that "Sexual Perversity in Chicago," "American Buffalo" and "Glengarry Glen Ross" all are taking place on different sections of Lincoln Avenue, a thoroughfare Mamet once traversed by bus every day during his time at the Hotel Lincoln. Christiansen knew and understood this better than any other critic, because he'd watched Mamet from his start.

He'd also watched Robert Falls.

HAMLET

MODERN "HAMLET" RAISES LIVELY SPARKS IN A FLASHY SCENARIO

Wisdom Bridge Theatre

BY RICHARD CHRISTIANSEN

CAST

Bernardo .... Mike Wise
Horatio .... John Copeland

Ghost/Player King	Byrne Piven
Claudius	Peter Burnell
Gertrude	Deanna Dunagan
Osric	Tom Benich
Polonius	Del Close
Laertes/Player Queen	Kevin Gudahl
Hamlet	Aidan Quinn
Bodyguard	Neil Flynn
Maid to Gertrude	Melody Rae
Ophelia	Lisa A. Dodson
Rosencrantz	Mike Dempsey
Guildenstern	Chuck Hall
First grave digger	John Marshall Jones
Second grave digger	Don Mayo

FEBRUARY 1, 1985. Pocked with flaws, streaked with invention and emblazoned with daring, Wisdom Bridge Theatre's new production of "Hamlet" is blessed and cursed by its passionate desire to throw fresh, startling light on Shakespeare's tragedy.

Director Robert Falls' interpretation is nominally a "modern dress" version, though it aspires to—and sometimes achieves—something more than merely putting contemporary clothes on its characters.

In Michael Merritt's consistently brilliant setting, lighting and costumes, the design shows us a state of Denmark where darkness, duplicity and corruption are never too far from the surface.

Claudius' first entrance is ingeniously treated as a media event, television monitors showing us the new king and his new bride enjoying the applause of their sycophants, while on stage in the foreground the dark, mourning figure of young Hamlet is shown in shadow.

The court and its inhabitants are vividly sketched. A wall of doors through which aides pop in and out backs Polonius' office; and, after the despair following Ophelia's madness and death, the courtyard is shown as a shambles of old furniture, clothes lines and items in disrepair.

In this atmosphere, a hulking bodyguard always hovers behind Claudius, and the courtier Osric becomes a punkish toady in wraparound dark glasses.

Some of Falls' directorial touches are absolutely on target. It's clever indeed to have Polonius slip his son Laertes a few dollars after the old man has given him his words of advice; and it's most poignant to see the maddened Ophelia splatter her face with rouge and lipstick, parodying an earlier time when she was carefully made up and glamorized to appeal to Hamlet.

One stunning scene of light and sound, when Hamlet goes into a jubilant victory dance to high-volume rock and roll music, supremely captures Hamlet's triumph and the court's confusion after the players' scene has caught the conscience of the king. The gravediggers' scene gets a good, funny kick from a neat bit of casting and performance; and the play's concluding bloodbath is staged with rousing swordplay and suspense.

In his effort to kick the audience into a reawakened awareness of the play, however, Falls' invention sometimes trips him up. His device of giving a different edge to the "To be or not to be . . ." soliloquy is simply a stunt that doesn't achieve its goal. And though the production runs over four hours, including two intermissions, some of the editing that has been done seems curious, to say the least. Why, for example, cut out the key (and short) speech that begins, "So oft it chances in particular men . . ."?

In casting this version, Falls has hit home with one exemplary character concept, and, in Del Close, he has a shrewd, seasoned actor who can make it work. Polonius, as Close plays him, has wonderful little bits to emphasize his petty, devious nature. He fiddles absentmindedly with a calculator, records his daughter's conversations, without her knowledge, on a tape recorder, and he officiously shushes Hamlet when the young prince begins to get unruly in a court scene. Close really does freshen and reinforce his lines with remarkable variation of cadence and change of pitch.

At first, it seems that Aidan Quinn, the gifted young actor playing his first Hamlet, is going to ride home in triumph, too. His first, numbed expressions of grief are superb, and when he zeroes in on a soliloquy with his quiet intensity, the results are riveting. As he moves on, however, he seems to lose power, though his instincts are frequently daring and right. His voice strains, and his unvarying rise in pitch at moments of passion becomes monotonous. There's not enough variety in emotion or register in his line readings.

The rest of the cast is erratic. Peter Burnell's portrayal of Claudius is little more than earnest declamation, while Deanna Dunagan's Gertrude marvelously suggests a well-dressed, poised and handsome hostess who too easily can slip into being a lush.

Kevin Gudahl is a straightforward, strong Laertes, and Lisa A. Dodson is a frightened and crushed Ophelia in her boisterous mad scene. Byrne Piven's ghost, dressed in a gray El Supremo general's uniform, is imposing and sonorous.

Among Hamlet's friends, John Copeland's Horatio is a touchingly timid little preppie pal, and the Rosencrantz and Guildenstern of Mike Dempsey and Chuck Hall are deftly etched as two former frat rats, one a blunderer and the other much more in control.

When Quinn is focused, when Falls' bold imagination punches the right note and when Merritt's design suddenly illuminates the text, this "Hamlet" sparks with excitement. It does not hold together as a consistent piece of work, but some of its fireworks are memorable, and it passes the crucial test of reminding us once again of what a great play this is.

Another very famous Chicago production, Robert Falls's take on "Hamlet" at the Wisdom Bridge Theater is best remembered for the scene in which Aidan Quinn spray-painted "To be or not to be . . ." onto the wall of the set. Even more than "In the Belly of the Beast," this is the show that helped persuade the Goodman Theatre board to take a risk with the maverick young director, and this is the review that brought that show to everyone's attention.

Even before the opening, Christiansen had written extensively about the production in a preview story, noting its $150,000 budget—a small fortune for the tiny Wisdom Bridge Theater. Falls, he wrote, had attended one of the sessions of the Chicago Shakespeare Workshop conducted for Chicago actors by actress Barbara Gaines at a North Side rehearsal hall. There he'd seen Quinn, who would go on to become a famous actor, perform a short scene from "Hamlet." Falls knew that he had found the actor he wanted for his production.

In the preview story, Falls described his conception of the play: "I saw it initially as a very political, contemporary image, as a young man who had been trained for leadership who wants to talk about the state of the world. Then he comes back from college to find his father dead and his mother married to this man he can't stand, and he goes wild."

Christiansen also asked Quinn what he thought of his Hamlet, and got this reply: "Hamlet at the beginning is crushed by what his mother has done. He has been away at school trying to become enlightened. He probably is a bit of a prankster and not a philosopher. His time with his parents has been spent mostly on idyllic summer holidays, so perhaps his father is more a subject of hero worship than a real father to him. He's deeply depressed by the events at home, but he's excited by being depressed, too. And he has this fascination with darkness."

Other notables in this cast were Deanna Dunagan, who would go on to win a Tony Award for her work in "August: Osage County," and Del Close, who would bequeath his actual skull to Falls and the Goodman, for use in future productions of this very tragedy. Alas, state medical regulations meant that Close's actual head was replaced by his friends with a fake skull, as used by medical students.

In the end, Christiansen gave the show a mixed review. But it nonetheless had a way of making his readers want to see the show. "Hamlet" sold out every performance.

And so did a play by a young writer named John Logan.

86

NEVER THE SINNER

'SINNER' RECALLS A SHOCKING CRIME

Stormfield Theatre

BY RICHARD CHRISTIANSEN

CAST

Nathan Leopold Jr. .... Denis O'Hare
Richard Loeb....................................... Bryan Stillman
State's Atty. Crowe .... Jerry Bloom
Clarence Darrow .... Richard Burton Brown

With Mitch Webb, Thomas Carroll, Donna Powers.

SEPTEMBER 11, 1985. The "crime of the century," committed 61 years ago in Chicago, once more unfolded its high drama Tuesday night at Stormfield Theatre in "Never the Sinner," a new play about the "thrill killers" case of Nathan Leopold Jr. and Richard Loeb.

Already chronicled in many novels, plays and films, the crime and its subsequent trial continue to keep their hold on us. The brutality of the murder—the bludgeoning to death of 14-year-old Bobby Franks by two wealthy and intelligent boys, ages 19 and 18—and the sensation of the subsequent trial—in which Clarence Darrow, the confessed killers' famous lawyer, was successful in keeping them from the hangman—have lost none of their horror or fascination through repetition.

John Logan, the young author who has retold the story in "Sinner," does not present his work as either a journalistic document or as strictly a trial drama. His play—which gets its title from a remark attributed to Darrow, that "I may hate the sin, but never the sinner"—leaves out large parts of the trial's long story; and though parts of the summaries to the jury by State's Atty. Robert Crowe, demanding the death penalty, and by Darrow, pleading for mercy, are included, they are not big, flamboyant showpieces, such as Orson Welles' hambone orations in the movie version of Meyer Levin's "Compulsion."

Using court transcripts, newspaper accounts and imagined dialogue, and with a 1980s sensibility that deals directly with the two boys' homosexuality, Logan instead concentrates on the nature of the relationship between the brilliant "Babe" Leopold and his mesmerizing lover "Dickie" Loeb.

The play, confined to a courtroom pen in Russ Borski's varnished wood set, begins with Leopold, a devoted ornithologist, giving a lecture on birds of prey. Then, with the lighting of Borski and Mary Quinlan helping to make the transitions, the drama moves between the courtroom and flashbacks of the defendants' boyhood and the immediate events surrounding their decision to kill as "an intellectual-emotional experience."

Three actors on the periphery act as reporters, psychiatrists and witnesses, filling in the continuity between courtroom scenes.

At the end of the play, Logan intercuts the final arguments of Crowe and Darrow, so that they, in effect, form a debate on capital punishment. Jerry Bloom, as a dapper, dogged Crowe, and Richard Burton Brown, as a kindly, homespun Darrow, bring off this counterpoint effectively.

But it is on the two boys that this play rests, and, under Terry McCabe's direction, two young actors new to Chicago—Denis O'Hare, as Leopold, and Bryan Stillman, as Loeb—carry the show.

Some of the play's pacing is off, bits of its impressionistic reportage misfire, and the two principals occasionally rush or swallow their lines. But the big scenes, including the abduction and murder of Franks, play thrillingly; and Stillman and O'Hare make the intimacy and the sickness of their affair both tender and horrifying.

With his good looks and dazzling smile, Stillman aptly personifies the golden boy gone wrong in a nervous little laugh or sudden burst of violence.

O'Hare, already an actor of finesse and power, gives us a white-faced and high-strung Leopold, polite and correct in manner but portrayed with white-knuckle intensity. Whether breaking down in tears when he realizes he is not a "superman" or holding his elusive lover in a desperate embrace, he is a character actor of riveting force.

John Logan, the writer of the play Richard Christiansen reviews here in rather clinical style, would become the highest-paid writer in Hollywood, responsible for the screenplays to *Gladiator*, *Hugo*, *The Aviator*, *Sweeney Todd* and several movies in the James Bond franchise. He would also go on to write such plays as "Red." But first Logan would spend a decade living in Evanston and writing plays in Chicago, greatly supported by Christiansen's reviews.

"Never the Sinner" is among his best plays and a consummate Chicago drama, probing the lives of two of the city's most notorious citizens, so-called thrill killers Nathan Leopold and Richard Loeb, who were saved from the electric chair by the stirring oratory of their attorney, Clarence Darrow.

At the time of this review, Logan was just 22 years old; the play began as a writing project when he was a student at Northwestern University. The Stormfield Theatre was a non-Equity company; none of Chicago's other Equity companies had wanted to put on Logan's play. Terry McCabe, the director of "Never the Sinner," would later become artistic director of the City Lit Theatre, a small but long-lived company on the city's North Side.

In an interview some years later with the *Tribune*'s Sid Smith, Logan said he had written the play in two weeks. After nine months of research.

"Chicago theater in the '80s was my Paris in the '20s," Logan told Smith as the men sat in Logan's Malibu home. "But it's a difficult life, difficult to earn a living. I've been infinitely more successful as a screenwriter, and, don't get me wrong, I have a good life. But does it give me as much personal satisfaction? No."

Denis O'Hare also would go on to an illustrious acting and writing career. And in Chicago, a new theater company would appear behind a pub.

87

KING HENRY V

SOUNDS OF THE CITY FAIL TO SPOIL THE CHARM OF "KING HENRY V"

Chicago Shakespeare Workshop

BY SID SMITH

AUGUST 5, 1986. A labor of love is bearing rich fruit in the form of a stunning, full-length production of William Shakespeare's "King Henry V" on the outdoor terrace behind the Red Lion Pub, 2446 N. Lincoln Ave.

Overcoming the clank of "L" trains, the thunder of overflying jets and even the occasional odors from a nearby back-yard fish fry, 17 performers enact 45 parts and serve up the heroic sweep of a major chapter in English history. Their tiny platform space plays home to battlefield carnage and coy royal courtship, to knavish fooleries and kingly crises, to senseless bloodshed and to lusty victory, all in a production that's as economic as it is well-spoken and affecting.

The project is part of a quixotic effort to forge a professional Shakespearean troupe here. Called the Chicago Shakespeare Workshop, the group consists of professional actors who make their livings in commercial films and theater and even through the occasional television voiceover. They're donating their time here as part of a short-lived Actors Equity Showcase. Their performances are sometimes a little hammy, but they're never amateurish. The language is richly delivered, the cadences are hypnotic and the scenes are not struggled through or survived—they're enjoyed.

Heading the list in the title role is Si Osborne, a dashing young actor who has worked mostly in regional theater elsewhere. He explodes right away with ferocious emotionalism, too soon, maybe, but it's so grabbing it doesn't matter. Later, he literally flies onstage to deliver Henry's famous "Once more unto the breach" rallying cry with romantic abandon, a right touch for Henry. He manages anguish, growth in leadership, clumsiness in romance and overall imposing presence, and while he overacts a bit, that's a quibble—he's a terrific find.

Bruce A. Young, a towering black actor, at first plays the chorus with sly relish, almost as if narrating "Kismet" or "Cabaret." But in a key later speech, he crouches in a patio tree and croons with lush poetic eloquence, making the moment memorable and spine tingling. Bernie Landis captures the Welsh nonsense and the grandfatherly sweetness of Fluellen. But they're all good, including Ernest Perry Jr.'s Bardolph, Tony Mockus Jr.'s unctuous Dolphin, Katherine Lynch's quietly real Boy, Robert Scogin's creepy cleric and high-flying Pistol.

Like Shakespeare's text, director Barbara Gaines celebrates her spatial limitations. She gives the actors free rein, which makes for a sweep in styles that's sometimes as kaleidoscopic as the production's inventive costuming, a rainbow of military garb from Elizabethan fancy to Vietnam-era khaki.

But she uses other technical elements with firm, poetic control, employing the tightness of the space to underscore the vast expanse of the subject. Through careful lighting, a modest but evocative sound system, some use of the audience aisles and even an occasional fog machine, the tiny space takes an amazing journey through the centuries to Agincourt and finally into the complex soul of a king and his people.

From this inauspicious workshop on the terrace of a Chicago pub frequented by Anglophiles would grow one of the city's most important theater organizations: the Chicago Shakespeare Theater, formerly the Shakespeare Repertory Theatre, previously known as the Chicago Shakespeare Workshop. In 1999, it took up residence on Navy Pier in a theater building that cost $22 million. Barbara Gaines would remain its founding artistic director.

In many ways, Chicago Shakespeare Theater would become the city's great classical repertory company (both as a presenter and a producer) for which Claudia Cassidy had longed in all those columns of hers. But as this review by Sid Smith—arts reporter, Richard Christiansen's longtime backup and, later, the *Tribune*'s longtime dance critic—recounts, it had begun in classic Chicago ragtag fashion, centered entirely on the actors and the raw text. The observant, droll Smith (1950–), who hails from Mobile, Alabama, saw something remarkable amid the pint glasses and fish and chips. The acting, he allows, was a little hammy, but filled with passion and a need for attention.

And as with so many Chicago companies that came before them, buoyed by similar reviews, these nascent Shakespeareans never really looked back.

88

THE GRAPES OF WRATH

SLUGGISH ROAD SPOILS 'GRAPES'

Steppenwolf Theatre at the Royal George Theatre

BY RICHARD CHRISTIANSEN

CAST

Jim Casy	Terry Kinney
Tom Joad	Gary Sinise
Pa Joad	Robert Breuler
Ma Joad	Lois Smith
Grandma	Lucina Paquet
Grampa	Nathan Davis
Ruthie	Dana Lubotsky
Winfield	Christian Robinson
Noah	John C. Reilly
Uncle John	James Noah
Rose of Sharon	Yvonne Suhor
Al	Jim True
Connie Rivers	Tim Hopper
Floyd Knowles	Ramsay Midwood
Mrs. Wainwright	Rondi Reed
Aggie Wainwright	Elizabeth K. Austin
The starving man	Darryl D. Davis
His son	Relioues DeVar

SEPTEMBER 19, 1988. It takes a very long time for Steppenwolf Theatre's "The Grapes of Wrath" to finish, and when it is all over, in director Frank Galati's reverent and ambitious adaptation of John Steinbeck's novel, admiration for its effort must give way to disappointment in its results.

Filled with 37 actors, and faithful in minute detail to Steinbeck's celebrated 1939 story of Dust Bowl migrants, the $500,000 production on stage at the Royal-George Theatre has a stirring live musical score, repeated special effects of fire and rain, and several examples of Galati's abundant gifts for sculpting striking stage pictures.

Occasionally, and crucially in the play's final scene, a moment arrives when the actors and the carefully plotted stagecraft combine to create a strong surge of emotion. More often, however, the sluggish flow of action breaks down into a hushed, sometimes inaudible exchange between two glum characters placed in a dim spotlight on the front of the stage.

The play's failure to take on life does not come for lack of trying. Galati's great admiration for Steinbeck's key work of the Depression era is immediately evident in the production's attention to the minutiae of costumes and stage directions, all taken directly from the book. The members of the Joad family, the poor and good folk whose journey from their ruined farm to the promised land of California forms the novel's central story, are dressed precisely and move exactly the way Steinbeck described them.

Scenes have been telescoped or transplanted, characters have been deleted, and some of the novel's most distinctive passages, including the painstakingly naturalistic account of a land turtle's progress across a dirt road, have necessarily been dropped.

But the adaptation also has kept traces of Steinbeck's pseudo-biblical narrative through the voices of a "Brother" and "Sister" who set the scene, and through a lively four-man band that, using Michael Smith's original score and Steinbeck's words as lyrics, creates much of whatever vitality the production enjoys. The brief musical segment adapted from the novel's chapter on conniving used-car salesmen is one of the show's few unalloyed joys.

On the plain, deep wooden stage designed and lighted by Kevin Rigdon, the large cast sometimes is formed into stunning group portraits, from a shadow army of helpless migrants, shuffling along on their way West, to an angry crowd of striking workers, shouting cries of defiance at the ruthless orchard owners who have cheated them.

Yet for most of its three hours, the production simply slogs along, earnestly droning on in drawn-out conversations and clunkily prolonging stage business such as the Joads' loading up of their battered truck. The special effects of fire and water, moreover, are more distracting gimmicks than necessary storytelling elements. Some techniques, such as projecting the opening paragraphs of the book's Chapter 28 onto a blanket, are irrelevant touches, of no help at all in clarifying the action.

For a production graced with some of Steppenwolf's best actors, "Grapes of Wrath" has amazingly little to offer in strong performances.

As Tom Joad, the angry young man whose journey to militant social action parallels the Joads' sorrowful trip West, Gary Sinise seems merely dejected, his acting fires banked by the show's dour solemnity.

Terry Kinney, as the scraggly, fallen preacher Jim Casy, dutifully assumes a folksy accent, but like many other good actors in the cast, he cannot conjure up a real character from the dialogue.

Lois Smith, as the forever wise and saintly Ma Joad, does convey the weight and dignity of this admirable woman; but she has problems projecting her voice in the theater, and in Saturday's early performance, she dropped or mangled some important Steinbeck lines.

In a much smaller role, John C. Reilly is remarkably effective as Noah Joad, the strange, simple brother who slips away from the family early in their travels.

Perhaps adaptor-director Galati loved "The Grapes of Wrath" too well. A little less love might have created a livelier play.

Here is a rare thing: a seminal Chicago production by the Steppenwolf Theatre Company that Richard Christiansen did not like (Frank Rich, writing for the *New York Times*, was far more enthusiastic). Christiansen came around in time—he reported on the huge success of this production, a Frank Galati adaptation of the John Steinbeck novel, when it subsequently played the National Theatre in London to rapturous reviews from the British press. By then, the show had changed greatly from the production Christiansen reviews here: the cast shrank from 41 to 35 actors and musicians, and the script was extensively restructured with an eye to removing the "sluggishness."

"The play now moves more smoothly, and its performances are uniformly better," Christiansen would write. "In some cases, they're superb." But this review of the Chicago production of "The Grapes of Wrath" is a useful reminder that Christiansen, in contrast with the common perception, did not always play the role of chief enthusiast of Chicago deeds of daring, even if he shades his comments with the disappointment of one who fervently wished the show had been better and saw the aim as well as the result. Christiansen did not write pans like Cassidy. He encouraged even in disaffection.

After London, which was preceded by a dry run at the La Jolla Playhouse in California, "The Grapes of Wrath" moved to Broadway ("an epic achievement," wrote Rich in the *New York Times*), further cementing the Steppenwolf brand. This was the company's first full-on Broadway show, soon to be followed by "The Song of Jacob Zulu," "The Rise and Fall of Little Voice," "My Thing of Love," "Buried Child," "One Flew Over the Cuckoo's Nest," and, in 2012, "August: Osage County" and "Who's Afraid of Virginia Woolf?"

89

MARVIN'S ROOM

'MARVIN'S ROOM' OFFERS UP A BREATHTAKING VIEW

Goodman Theatre

BY RICHARD CHRISTIANSEN

CAST

Bessie .... Laura Esterman
Dr. Wally.. Tim Monsion
Ruth .... Jane MacIver
Bob.. Peter Rybolt

FEBRUARY 20, 1990. "Marvin's Room" is a beautifully written, deeply moving new play that has been given a superbly acted, near-perfect production in its premiere at the Goodman Theatre Studio. It's a major step forward for playwright Scott McPherson and director David Petrarca, and it's a stunning acting triumph for its leading lady, Laura Esterman.

Like his first play, "Till the Fat Lady Sings," McPherson's new work is a story of an eccentric, divided family seeking reconciliation. Now the promise he demonstrated in that 1986 drama has been abundantly fulfilled with an assured balance between sorrow and joy, rage and laughter, piercing pain and utter hilarity.

This is the story of Bessie, a shy, drab spinster who at the outset learns—from an incompetent doctor in a scene of deadpan comic genius—that she has leukemia. The chief support for her invalid father Marvin and Aunt Ruth in their Florida home, Bessie also has an estranged sister, Lee, an aspiring beautician who, somewhat reluctantly after learning of her sister's plight, journeys to Florida with her two sons, one of them a bitter and disturbed young man, on the chance that they might provide the bone marrow that could save Bessie's life.

The rest of the play deals with how these strange, often loony people cope with the basic issues of life and death within their family.

There are many rapturously theatrical scenes in "Marvin's Room," climaxed by a moment of transcendent beauty at play's end. Typical is the heart-rending scene in which Bessie, having collapsed while on a family outing at the Magic Kingdom of Walt Disney World, wakes up in the children's rest area, her crumpled body squeezed into a cute little toddler bed marked "Baby Bear."

McPherson's almost breathtaking ability to combine the ridiculous and bizarre with the poignant and profound in an illuminating juxtaposition is strengthened in every instance by Petrarca's spare, sensitive production, which is consistently inventive, never intrusive.

The play's exquisite modulation loosens a little in its second act, when it slips close to sentimentality, but the performances, so finely tuned by Petrarca, never fail. These include the work of Lee Guthrie as the gruff, battered Lee; Mark Rosenthal as her hostile, anguished son; Karl Maschek as his bookish little brother; Tim Monsion, in a small gem of a performance, as the befuddled physician Dr. Wally; and Jane MacIver as the pixilated Aunt Ruth, oblivious to her family's tragedy but deeply involved in the soap opera characters she faithfully follows.

Most of all there is Esterman, an actress whose slight figure and sad eyes are energized by an acting passion of sure and true aim. There's not a false move in this extraordinary portrayal; when she comes to the devastating moment in which she proclaims how lucky she has been in the love of her life, she will break your heart.

"Marvin's Room" was a very unusual night in Chicago theater. For one thing, the play is about dying. For another, its author, Scott McPherson, was a 30-year-old Chicago playwright who'd moved to the city after growing up in Columbus, Ohio. He'd worked in the Goodman Theatre box office and for the Bozo the Clown TV show as a script writer. He'd written only one previous play, and that was while he was in college.

With this rapturous review full of emotional praise, Christiansen changed McPherson's life—to mention that of the young director, David Petrarca, and the leading actress, Laura Esterman. When he loved a show as he loved this one, he had a knack of writing in such a way that sent people to the theater.

Christiansen liked the show so much that he took in another performance, this time at the Hartford Stage, and wrote a column about his return visit. The word *AIDS* now entered his review; in the playbill, McPherson had written about how his lover had grown sick. By 1991, the play had opened at Playwrights Horizons in New York, and Christiansen was there to write yet another positive review. He wasn't alone in his praise—in the *New York Times*, Frank Rich called the piece "one of the funniest plays of this year as well as one of the wisest and most moving." By the New York opening, McPherson himself had full-blown AIDS and had been hospitalized in Chicago. But he made it to opening night, Christiansen reported. He also reported that McPherson was full of new plans—for a movie version of the play; for a big new commission from the Goodman Theatre.

"Marvin's Room" now seemed more like a metaphoric drama about a modern-day plague. Scott McPherson died on November 7, 1992. "Mr. McPherson's death," Sid Smith wrote in the *Tribune*, "robs Chicago's theater scene of one of its brightest hopes."

"Marvin's Room" would not be the only Chicago production of its era to deal with a health crisis.

90

WINGS

'WINGS' SOARS TO ARTISTIC HEIGHTS

Goodman Studio Theatre

BY SID SMITH

OCTOBER 27, 1992. In his 1978 "Wings," playwright Arthur Kopit elevated the visceral suffering of the stroke victim from the made-for-television movie to the realm of serious drama.

In the new "Wings," composer Jeffrey Lunden and writer-lyricist Arthur Perlman transpose the story to contemporary opera. Now getting its world premiere at the Goodman Studio Theatre, "Wings" is actually billed as a musical theater piece, though it's without a complete song, and it defies classification, distilling its spartan presentation from a number of art forms.

But labels prove irrelevant. From its brief opening, ushering in Emily Stilson's stroke, with a crash into darkness and the shutdown of a gramophone, to its lonely, piercing, unforgettably sustained final note, "Wings" is a journey to cherish, an inspiring story of frailty and grit, encased in an artwork uncompromising in integrity and gilded with lean, spine-tingling magic.

Lunden and Perlman effectively musicalize Kopit's script with tinkling, meandering melodies, at times suggestive of modern Stephen Sondheim, more often heir to the dissonant Americana of Samuel Barber. Whatever their influences, their score hypnotically mirrors

Emily's damaged state of mind, while alternately evoking the chilling cohesion of her emotions. She's a born-again fetus struggling to escape darkness and return to the triumph of her youth in the 1920s, when, as daredevil acrobat, she would climb aboard the wings of an airborne plane. (Kopit's play is inspired by the actual experiences—and stroke—of air-show actress Laura Kilian.)

Director Michael Maggio brings marvelous, gingerly realism to sessions with fellow patients (one marvelous cheesecake "song" is the closest the production steers toward musical comedy shenanigans) and Emily's struggles to break through the gibberish. A set of sliding doors, shadowy lighting effects and sculptural stretches of rope rest in abstract relief to an all-too-real world of humor and exploding, tiny truth.

Holding it remarkably together is the uncanny Linda Stephens as Emily. Serving up her aging vibrato as if a glass of priceless wine, she's brilliant, rarely pausing in her stream of sung utterances, and yet somehow never letting you forget she's a woman forever robbed of her speech. That key paradox ignites "Wings," a battlefield of words, both poetic and nonsensical, in a somehow uplifting work about people who've forgotten how to use them and must struggle valiantly to remember until they die.

"Wings" was another highly esoteric Chicago hit. This play, too, is about illness–and a musical to boot. The piece originated in the experience of the playwright, Arthur Kopit, whose father had suffered a stroke and was a patient at the same rehabilitation center as Laura Kilian, the basis for the character of Emily Stilson. Interestingly, Kilian's son, Michael, was on the writing staff of the *Tribune*. Sid Smith, who gave this beautifully written review, caught its central achievement: the musicalization of Emily's struggles to communicate.

Smith's support buoyed the show, which was picked up by the New York Public Theatre. Linda Winer, at this point writing for *USA Today*, also came back to Chicago to see it.

91

METAMORPHOSES

TREATMENT OF OVID'S 'METAMORPHOSES' A SERIES OF CAPTIVATING CHANGES OF HEART

Lookingglass Theatre Company at the Ivanhoe Theater

BY RICHARD CHRISTIANSEN

OCTOBER 27, 1998. The entrancing "Metamorphoses" is indeed a play about transformations. It is an evening of almost magical changes, wrought through the unique imagery of theater; and, finally, after 90 minutes of storytelling that ranges from the reverent to the cockeyed, it is, most movingly, a play about the transforming power of love.

Adaptor-director Mary Zimmerman's latest work for Lookingglass Theatre is in many ways similar to their earlier spinning of ancient fables, "The Arabian Nights." Again, the actors unfold a series of folk tales illustrating the tragedy, comedy, laughter and despair of mankind. And again, Zimmerman and her designers have brought a splendid imagination to their vision, trading the rich Arabian atmosphere of "Nights" for the spare elegance of the classic myths related by the Roman poet Ovid.

At the Ivanhoe Theatre, the setting for the stories is simple, striking: an oblong wading pool, backed by a painted panel of the heavens and what looks like the door to a Chicago three-flat. Above, a small crystal chandelier. Like almost everything else in the production, it's a perfect match, mixing contemporary urban objects with timeless elements.

Some of the language is directly from Ovid, as translated by David Slavitt; a small segment, giving a modern shade of darkness to the myth of Orpheus and Eurydice, is from the German poet Rainer Maria Rilke. Most of it, however, comes from Zimmerman and her 10 actors, giving a sharp, often playful edge to the tales of gods and men. One of the highlights of the play, for example, is Doug Hara's hilarious turn as the impudent Phaeton, in shades and swimming trunks, lolling on a raft while telling his therapist about his father fixation and his disastrous attempt to drive the old man's chariot of the sun.

At times, this antic twist to the ancients is in danger of trivializing the material. But more often than not, despite poor sightlines and tricky acoustics, the imagery of both language and movement is ingenious or beautiful or both: A slow shower of large white paper Z's drifts down from the heavens during a dream sequence; Aphrodite, the goddess of love, appears in a strapless red gown, a cigarette dangling from her lips, like a '40s sex goddess; Halcyone and Ceyx, a mourning wife and her dead husband, are transformed into birds with the simple gesture of two actors gradually, calmly spreading their arms like wings.

The play begins and ends with the tale of Midas, the king who wished everything he touched would turn to gold. Given a sharp satiric twist by Raymond Fox as the ultimate capitalist pig, Midas disappears from view at the sad end of his story; but, in a stroke of genius that brings these tales of transformations full circle, he reappears at water's edge to give the show a happy ending and a final embrace of love.

To create such an astonishing moment of beauty requires technical mastery, mental agility and theatrical inspiration. It also requires—and "Metamorphoses" has this in abundance—a great heart.

One way of looking at modern Chicago theater is to picture it as a three-legged stool. One leg was carved from the improv tradition forged by such groups as the Compass Players and the Second City. One was crafted by the in-your-face tradition that ran through Bob Sickinger's Hull House Theatre and was writ large by the actors of the Steppenwolf Theatre Company. And the third? Well, that can be traced through the story-theater tradition developed at Northwestern University by Robert Breen and Frank Galati, which then exploded into life at the hands of the Lookingglass Theatre Company, a group of Northwestern University graduates who did more for the forgotten visual component of Chicago theater than any other theater company before or since.

"Metamorphoses," which Richard Christiansen reviews here with his typical descriptive detail, was in its very first incarnation at the Ivanhoe Theatre (which is now a liquor store); it is the most famous, and most acclaimed, of the Lookingglass productions to date. Structured chronologically and spanning a time period moving from the creation of the world through the reign of Julius Caesar, "Metamorphoses" is Mary Zimmerman's adaptation of Ovid's mythologically based collection of stories about characters who change shape. As Christiansen notes approvingly, Zimmerman had decided that a pool of water would be the ideal metaphor for a story of transformation.

A huge success, the show moved to New York's Second Stage, where it opened just days after the September 11, 2001, attack on the World Trade Center. It was widely credited with helping New Yorkers channel their terrible sense of loss: in the *New York Times*, critic Ben Brantley described the piece as "opening the emotional floodgates." Beginning in 2002, "Metamorphoses" played for a year on Broadway. It also became a staple of the college and regional-theater circuit, produced with and without its trademark pool.

In 2012, many of the original cast members Christiansen reviews here (including the pivotal Raymond Fox) returned for a restaging of the production at the new Lookingglass Theater inside the Water Tower Water Works on Michigan Avenue. The revival was a triumph: the characters' ages were indistinct, and the landscape was timeless in orientation. It was rapturously received once again.

More than any other show, this was the production that launched Zimmerman's career as a director of international acclaim, including her tenure at the Metropolitan Opera in New York.

92

THE PRODUCERS

'PRODUCERS' PRODUCES; THOUGH IT WAS A GREAT FILM, IT SEEMS TO HAVE BEEN DESTINED FOR THE STAGE ALL ALONG

Cadillac Palace Theatre

BY RICHARD CHRISTIANSEN

FEBRUARY 19, 2001. Endless in its invention, relentless in its energy, extravagant in its design, witty in its silliness and shameless in its show bizziness, the stage musical of "The Producers" is an absolutely socko monster hit.

It is based, of course, on the classic 1967 film, written and directed by Mel Brooks, in which a bellicose, washed-up producer named Max Bialystock ("I was the biggest name on Broadway! Thirteen Letters!") who has been reduced to playing sex games with 85-year-old women (who have such rude nicknames as "Hold-me Touch-me" and "Yank-me Spank-me") in order to finance his shows, teams up with a meek, nebbishy accountant named Leopold Bloom in a plot to make a fortune by staging "Springtime for Hitler," the world's worst musical.

In the musical "Producers," here through Sunday in its pre-Broadway run at the Cadillac Palace, the story remains the same, more or less, as that of the old movie, with major plot additions and variations coming mostly in the second act.

Amazingly, the jokes and gags repeated from the movie are still funny, and sometimes funnier, probably because they are given ferocious, vivid new delivery by the stars Nathan Lane and Matthew Broderick as Bialystock and Bloom.

And, though the show started out as a movie, it now seems clear, in director/choreographer Susan Stroman's buoyant transformation, that this story about a Broadway musical was destined all along to be a Broadway musical.

Instead of two big numbers, "Springtime for Hitler" and "Prisoners of Love," in the movie, the stage musical has more than a dozen new, ingeniously generic Broadway show tunes composed by Brooks.

Everything that was hilarious and/or outrageous in the movie has been punched up to the nth degree in the musical.

No detail to add to the vulgar fun is overlooked. The posters on Bialystock's office walls bear the titles of such ridiculous shows as "The Breaking Wind" and "This Too Shall Pass." In Brooks' loony vision of Broadway's future, plays are called "A Streetcar Named Murray" and "South Passaic."

When Bialystock and Bloom first ascend to a rooftop aviary to visit the nutty playwright Franz Liebkind (Brad Oscar, filling in for the injured Ron Orbach on the Friday night performance I saw), the author of the "new neo-Nazi musical" even gets his pet pigeons into the act.

And when the producers go to meet with the preening, cross-dressing director Roger DeBris (Gary Beach, in high heels and resplendent in the glittering gown fashioned by designer William Ivey Long), his townhouse, in designer Robin Wagner's giddy setting, is a rhapsody of lavender and cream. DeBris' "common-law assistant" Carmen Ghia (Roger Bart) doesn't just flounce; he flies. And besides Carmen, DeBris introduces a whole new household of zanies, an over-the-top gay and lesbian design team, plus a Village People-type vocal group.

The musical doesn't have some of the movie's best scenes. Bialystock and Bloom seal their pact in the producer's office, not, as in the film, at the orgasmically gushing fountain of New York's Lincoln Center (although there is a neat homage to that movie scene at the end of their big stage duet "We Can Do It"). And, again unlike the movie, we do not get to see the audience's initial appalled reaction to "Springtime for Hitler."

But the production number itself is to plotz over, staged to the max by Stroman with one preposterous and dazzling excess piled on top of another and climaxing with the singing-dancing entrance of Adolf Hitler himself. ("I'm the kraut who's out to change our history!")

Brooks, working with co-librettist Thomas Meehan, is naturally all over the production, infusing it with his own view of entertainment. His idea of show business culture stems from a love of an older, glamorous Broadway (or maybe one that never was), a Broadway when every show had a line of statuesque chorus girls, when customers got dressed up to go to the theater, and when critics, instead of attending previews, actually went to an opening night—wearing tuxedos.

Brooks' affection for this fabled cityscape is immense, and it is accompanied by a vital vein of burlesque humor, replete with ethnic and gay jokes.

You can't miss that influence. Brooks' face appears on one of the theater posters ("When Cousins Marry") in Bialystock's office, and, in a sweet salute to the master that repeats a trick from the movie, his recorded voice can be heard in song in the "Springtime" extravaganza.

His basic ebullience, wit and good cheer have been everywhere strengthened by his associates in the musical. Chief among them is Stroman, whose cleverness with handling props and staging mini-spectacles has never been better. Satirizing her own Tony Award-winning work in the musical "Contact" and drawing on everything from "Fiddler on the Roof" and "42nd Street" to "Les Miserables" and "Singin' in the Rain," she has created a cavalcade of sensational song-and-dance numbers.

She gives her regards to old Broadway with all the strengths of the new Broadway. Her cast of 22 people is small for a big musical, but, top to bottom, they're the best, with most of the chorus members playing choice small comic roles too.

Sometimes, Stroman doesn't give enough. One would like to have seen more use of those tap-dancing walkers in the wonderful first act finale with Bialystock and his chorus of little old lady investors. And sometimes Stroman pours on too much. The frenetic "Der Gutten Tag Hop Clop" for Bialystock, Bloom and Liebkind is at this stage a little sloppy, and unfunny, in execution.

The second act, which is unsteady or rushed in parts, still needs polishing. But for the most part, as in Bloom's marvelous transformation from office drudge to Broadway playboy in the "I Wanna Be A Producer" chorus line, the show is unstoppable and Stroman is unbeatable.

Not the least of the show's virtues is the fact that Lane as Bialystock and Broderick as Bloom newly create their own marvelous images of roles that had been indelibly originated by Zero Mostel and Gene Wilder in the movie.

They're a deliciously matched pair, Lane with his big, brazen asides and takes, and Broderick with his furtive, awkward moves and looks. They deliver the laughs, and the schmaltz, in their gloriously odd couple relationship.

His shoulders pulled back and his chest stuck out in nerdy fashion, Broderick is lovable in his portrayal and incredible in his singing and dancing. In his love duet with the blond sex bomb Ulla (Cady Huffman), he's a geek's vision of Fred Astaire. "There's a lot more to you than there is to you," Bialystock tells Bloom as they embark on their show business odyssey; and Broderick makes that fact abundantly clear in his joyous performance.

As for Lane, he is in paradise here, effortlessly tossing off one-liners and mercilessly nailing down punch lines. For all the imagination poured into its everybody-on-stage numbers, this musical has no better scene than "Betrayed," the second-act virtuoso solo in which Lane recaps the entire musical, including intermission, from the confines of his jail cell.

The show he celebrates is more a triumphant reassertion than a landmark innovation in Broadway musicals. But until the next "Oklahoma!" or "My Fair Lady" or "A Chorus Line" comes along to thrill and excite us, "The Producers" will very nicely keep us happy.

Richard Christiansen immediately saw that "The Producers" was totally unlike any other out-of-town tryout that had ever tried its luck in Chicago. This was a near-perfect musical comedy, capable of sending its audience into nonstop fits of laughter. It would, of course, become a monster hit on Broadway—at least for as long as Matthew Broderick and Nathan Lane were willing to stay in the show. As Christiansen clearly realizes here, this was a show that proved to be dependent on its two stars. That was the only bloom on the rose.

As reflected in his writing, Christiansen had a soft spot for vaudevillians (and a famous love for Mickey Rooney). He also had long written admiringly of Mel Brooks. But this show was a phenomenon right from the start—tickets flew out the door. In various subsequent interviews over the years, Lane, Brooks and others from "The Producers" all would describe a blissful Chicago experience: they discovered, to their constant amazement, just how much audiences, night after night, loved their new show. They would change virtually nothing before enjoying a repeat of this success in New York.

Another Chicago director would be heading in that direction.

93

PACIFIC OVERTURES

LESS IS MORE IN SONDHEIM'S MUSICAL OF EAST MEETS WEST

Chicago Shakespeare Theater

BY RICHARD CHRISTIANSEN

OCTOBER 19, 2001. A daring extravaganza and a financial failure when it first appeared on Broadway a quarter-century ago, "Pacific Overtures" still holds a very special place in the pantheon of Stephen Sondheim musicals.

Intended by director Harold Prince as a kind of American Kabuki, the show had a book, by the young writer John Weidman, that in episodic scenes traced the opening of Japan to the West, from the arrival of Admiral Matthew Perry in 1853 to the highly westernized nation of the present.

Like almost everything else these days, this tale of a clash of cultures has extra relevance in the here and now of America; but the principal, compelling reason for seeing the show remains, as in the past, the chance to catch the extraordinary Sondheim score.

Today, the corruption of Japanese culture by America is much less an issue than it was 25 years ago, but the Sondheim songs are as stimulating as they ever were.

The dazzling revival staged by director Gary Griffin in the upstairs auditorium of Chicago Shakespeare Theater has only 10 actors in its diverse all-male cast playing the musical's 61 roles, instead of the 19 all-Asian men used in the Broadway production; and in place of the original elaborate scenery and costumes, this arena-style staging has a simple wooden floor and plain black clothes decorated with bits of atmospheric accessories.

This simplicity in the stage settings of Daniel Ostling is stunning, however. The props, though few, are used to striking theatrical effect. All that the stage needs for scenery for the song "Someone in a Tree" is a plain ladder with an actor perched on its top. The costumes of Mara Blumenfeld quickly identify shogun, admiral, fisherman and emperor through the use of a few well-chosen details of headdress and sash added to the basic black.

Every step of the staging by Griffin and choreographer Marc Robin is carefully, elegantly placed so that nothing is extraneous.

Above all, this imaginative production offers big, strong voices and a superb four-man orchestra giving Sondheim's music and lyrics their full due.

To prepare himself for this assignment, Sondheim immersed himself in a study of Asian music so such songs as "Four Black Dragons" and "There Is No Other Way" would show their roots in a non-Western mode. Yet even in these exotic exercises, the style is distinctly Sondheim, their words and notes clustered in brilliant progressions.

A song such as "Please Hello," which finds gunboat diplomats of the United States, Britain, Holland, Russia and France arriving in Japan, gives the composer a chance to show off his versatility as he satirizes musical forms of all five nations. But an even more impressive feat is the song "A Bowler Hat," which in a few verses encapsulates the entire westernization of Japan.

Joseph Anthony Foronda is the commanding reciter who narrates the show's history and brings the action to an abrupt conclusion in modern-day (1976) Japan. The other ensemble members, all splendid, are: Kevin Gudahl, Neil Friedman, Michael Hagiwara, Roderick Peeples, Anthony Hite, Jeff Dumas, Richard Manera, Nathaniel Stampley and Christopher Mark Peterson, whose song delivery, among his equals, is outstanding.

This important Richard Christiansen review helped take the career of a major Chicago director, Gary Griffin, to its next level, on Broadway. Griffin would go on to direct "The Color Purple," a musical based on the Alice Walker novel that eventually would gross some $300 million.

More important for Chicago, perhaps, this also was the first of what would become a suite of well-known and widely admired Griffin interpretations of works by composer-lyricist Stephen Sondheim, including hugely successful productions of "Follies" in 2011 at the Chicago Shakespeare Theater and "Sunday in the Park with George" in 2012. Sondheim became interested in Griffin's work.

For Griffin, it all started with this review of "Pacific Overtures," a notable attempt to create a new, intimate version of one of Sondheim's most complex musicals. Christiansen saw and admired what Griffin was trying to do, ushering in what we might call a new era of Chicago-style interpretations of great Sondheim musicals.

By 2002, Christiansen had turned 70 and had announced his departure from the *Tribune*. His timing was shrewd. His beloved newspaper was about to be hit by the crises of an upended industry.

94

LONG DAY'S JOURNEY INTO NIGHT

GOODMAN'S 'JOURNEY' FLASHES BRILLIANCE

Goodman Theatre

BY RICHARD CHRISTIANSEN

MARCH 6, 2002. Like the great play itself, Goodman Theatre's revival of Eugene O'Neill's "Long Day's Journey Into Night" is a melding of the awesome and the gauche, the supremely right and the awkwardly wrong. It has moments that will break your heart, and, then again, it has bits that will leave you scratching your head.

Written in 1939–'40 and not produced until 1956, three years after the author's death, "Journey" is O'Neill's masterpiece, its strengths rooted in the American tradition of family drama. Its story "of old sorrow" (as the playwright described it) is all the more realistic because it is based on the history of O'Neill's own family.

Robert Falls' production, extremely sensitive to the author's every wish in stage direction, keeps the play solidly anchored as a realistic work, building its tension through the progress of one crucial day in the life of the four members of the Tyrone family in the summer of 1912.

There's no attempt here to reinvent the drama in its physical or emotional focus. The play's repetition, while maddening at times, is also essential. Its hammering effect is necessary for the story's grueling long day. Any severe editing or reworking would take away from the work's power.

Although there is no sense of the oppressive heat of the day in the play's setting, there is a telling atmospheric touch in the mournful foghorn that blankets the drama in its final segment; and Santo Loquasto's setting on the Goodman's large main stage meticulously reproduces the second-hand furniture and borrowed look of the Tyrones' New England summer home.

Similarly, the production's casting faithfully follows the playwright's intent.

As O'Neill stipulated, the wastrel son Jamie (Steve Pickering) bears a strong physical resemblance to his father, the imposing actor James Tyrone (Brian Dennehy). Falls plays on this by having Pickering and Dennehy stand toe-to-toe as they square away against each other in familial battle, their burly physiques and defiant faces in profile.

At the same time, the slight and consumptive younger son Edmund (David Cromer) resembles his frail and aesthetic mother Mary (Pamela Payton-Wright), as you can see when they come together in desperate embrace. He is clearly a "mama's boy," as his older brother so contemptuously describes him.

The key event in this family's story is Mary Tyrone's descent into drug-addled delusion. Starting with a mild nervous play of the hands in the first act's morning scene, she gradually and then precipitously falls into her old drug habit of the past, reaching bottom in the dead of night.

Around this calamity the play painfully, passionately and at times laboriously explores the characters of the family members.

Each one, as they reveal in some of the play's most remarkable, introspective passages, is a victim of the past, their characters trapped in a pattern they cannot escape, whether it be the father's miserliness, Jamie's drunkenness, Mary's frightened insecurity, or Edmund's brooding darkness.

When her husband begs Mary to "forget the past," she responds with her (and O'Neill's) searing statement: "Why? How can I? The past is the present, isn't it? It's the future too. We all try to lie out of that but life won't let us."

Though she is absent for most of the play's climactic fourth act of father-and-sons confrontations, Mary Tyrone is the central figure of the drama. It is her loneliness and grief that permeate the play, and her final scene, when she is a ghostly wraith retreating into the past, while her exhausted husband and sons look on helplessly, is the great, tragic peak of the drama.

At least it should be. But in her sincere efforts to portray Mary Tyrone's volatile state, Payton-Wright pitches her performance too high and on the border of shrillness, so that her drug-induced ramblings become more comic than tragic. Consequently, her final appearance, instead of being shocking, is cause for laughter, and it takes all of her considerable skills to get the audience back on track to the play's last, powerful moment.

You can blame some of this drop-off on O'Neill's dialogue, which can be stiff and stilted. But Payton-Wright's high-intensity portrayal, while rightly aimed, sometimes misses the mark in its eagerness to make a strong impression, and it sets the drama off balance. Whatever the cause, the production teeters between brilliance and blurriness.

When it clicks, however, it's staggering in its impact. Dennehy, white-bearded and white-maned and speaking with the slightest Irish brogue, is a magnificent physical presence as the elder Tyrone, a tired old lion still able to roar. In parts of the play he seems slightly detached from the action; but in others, he shows all the shrewd instincts, good humor and great heart of his bedeviled character. And when he rises to his feet with a sudden cry of triumph to recall his glory days as a gifted young actor in Shakespeare, there's majesty in the work.

Cromer's Edmund, bookish and intense at the start and barefoot and wracked with spasms of coughing at the last, is an ideal Eugene O'Neill doppelganger, an embittered and yet innocent poetic soul.

The production's most consistent and finally most powerful portrayal comes from Pickering's Jamie, whose outburst of love-hate for his brother near the end of the play is as terrifying, as pitiful and as overwhelming as O'Neill ever could have imagined. Though his character is blunt and rough, Pickering's portrayal is subtle and sharp.

It's long, it's erratic, it's dotted with pitfalls; and, in the end, with all its quirks, "Long Day's Journey Into Night" towers above as a landmark of theater. In its flashes of brilliance, and in the fierce blaze of its passionate moments, Goodman's production confirms the beauty of this great American drama.

This is Richard Christiansen's last review for the *Tribune*, handed in and published without any fanfare or overt self-reference to a critic who was coming to the end of a 40-year career writing about Chicago theater. That was not Christiansen's way; here, as previously, he prefers to keep the focus on the work at hand. He wrote little or nothing about himself. Even to his friends, he would remain a very private man, especially in retirement.

Yet it is hard to overstate Christiansen's public influence on Chicago theater. Unlike Claudia Cassidy, his focus was not on subpar touring shows but on the nascent theater scene on the city's North Side. He was a crucial early supporter of many people now numbered among American theater's most important artists: David Mamet, John Logan, Robert Falls, the entire Steppenwolf Theatre Company and, of course, William L. Petersen. He wrote reviews that actually prompted people to go to the theater. He also was an important editor at the *Tribune*, so he could elevate the amount and prominence of its theater coverage to a level and scope unequaled at any other newspaper, with the notable exception of the *New York Times*. But more important than all that was what was inarguably one of the main reasons for Christiansen's beloved status among those he covered: he went to theater, and seemed to enjoy doing so, virtually every night. Like his longtime competitor Hedy Weiss at the *Chicago Sun-Times*, Christiansen was, by his own admission, always ready to take his aisle seat.

This enthusiasm is a rare quality in a critic of such an extraordinarily long tenure. Certainly, there were those who found his notices too generous (although, as we have seen, he wrote many negative reviews). There were also those who thought his support for the theater to be too much or overly boosterish. For sure, Christiansen would never be unkind, as would Cassidy, in the service of a withering line in a review. We could read his entire body of work and conclude that cattiness is nowhere to be found.

This gentleman's self-effacing dignity was exactly what endeared Christiansen to artists who felt, almost without exception, that he was a critic who both respected them and could be relied on to show up, and a little early. And they respected him right back.

When it comes to Christiansen's history (fused with memoir) of Chicago theater, its title, *A Theater of Our Own*, is telling. We might note well the use of the word *our*. Though very much an old-school newspaperman, as resistant to "being written about" as Cassidy was before him, Christiansen did not write about "a theater of *their* own." He felt he had become a crucial part of his own story about Chicago theater, even if he did not quite come out and say so.

There were many celebrations of Christiansen's work at his retirement, and many moving tributes paid (Cassidy's retirement did not get the same response, not that she have wanted it). At one of these gatherings, a playwright and screenwriter named Rick Cleveland held up a picture of his wife and children in the family's nice house in Southern California. He pointed to Christiansen, who was crying. "Without this man, I would have none of this," Cleveland said. "I never felt like I had a home. Richard Christiansen gave me a home in the theater."

Many Chicago theater artists felt the same way. For a generation or two of them, it was never quite the same after Christiansen retired. The man who had helped them build "a theater of our own" was no longer in the aisle seat, leaning into the show and willing everyone involved to do their best.

The *Tribune* set about trying to fill his shoes.

95

GEM OF THE OCEAN

WILSON'S 'GEM' A DIAMOND IN THE ROUGH

Goodman Theatre

BY MICHAEL PHILLIPS

APRIL 30, 2003. In a good production of an August Wilson play, it's not uncommon for his theatrically charged language to beget language of another kind. Wilson's characters can spark something even in a predominantly white, predominantly restrained non-profit regional theater subscription audience. That something is simple: a true, spontaneous vocal response.

In his fledgling new work, "Gem of the Ocean," Wilson writes a terrific, sharp-tongued encounter between washerwoman Black Mary (Yvette Ganier) and Citizen Barlow (Kenny Leon), in the kitchen of the house belonging to the ancient Aunt Ester (Greta Oglesby). Like so many careworn female characters in the Wilson canon, Black Mary has had her share of wastrels and users.

"Take it all," she says to Citizen, an Alabama country boy new to Pittsburgh. "You got a woman in your hands. Now what? What you got? What you gonna do? Time ain't long, Mr. Citizen. A woman ain't but so many times filled up. What you gonna do? What you gonna fill me up with? Love? Happiness? Peace? What you got, Mr. Citizen?" Ganier plays this bitter, powerful taunt like a fast, furious fiddle solo. The Sunday night Goodman Theatre audience, not immune to the arid and slack patches of Wilson's latest, was suddenly beside itself.

The superbly acted Goodman production of "Gem of the Ocean," directed by Marion McClinton, marks the first step for what is, at present, a wobbly mixture of spiritual and melodramatic concerns. The play is a long way from finished; Wilson's better, truer dramatic instincts are frequently shoved aside by a less compelling brand of on- and offstage incident.

But when those instincts are on, they're on. At one point Wilson's most vivid creation, the ex-slave and Underground Railroad worker Solly Two Kings (Anthony Chisholm), plunks down a piece of chain on a table. The way Chisholm does it, the smack of metal on wood reverberates throughout the theater. "That's my good-luck piece," he says. "That piece of chain used to be around my ankle. They tried to chain me down but I beat them on that one. I say I'm gonna keep this to remember by. I been lucky ever since." At the word "ankle," Sunday's audience uttered a quick gasp of realization. Wilson can concretize a man's past in five sentences and a single gesture.

Even in its current, somewhat muddled form "Gem" is more interesting than Wilson's previous drama, the 1980s-set "King Hedley II." "Gem of the Ocean" is the most overtly allegorical and Bible-soaked of all of Wilson's major works. It takes place in 1904, earliest among Wilson's decade-by-decade chronicles of African-American life in the 20th Century.

We're in the cavernous Pittsburgh Hill District home of Aunt Ester, who is a full, magical 287 years old—as old as the oldest African in America. This iconic figure's house is a place of sanctuary, shared by Black Mary (Ganier) and by Eli (splendidly low-key Paul Butler, whose rumbling voice carries its own Sensurround speaker). Up from Alabama, Citizen Barlow (Leon) has a splotch on his conscience, rela[t]ing to the death of a millhand accused of stealing a bucket of nails. (We hear an awful lot about that offstage mill across the three-hour, five-minute running time of "Gem.") He seeks a soul-cleansing from Ester.

Wilson first introduced Ester, healer of the dispossessed and grieving, as an offstage figure in "Two Trains Running." Here he treats her as the soul of African-American history, albeit a soul whose toenails still need clipping.

LACKS DRAMATIC ENERGY. Despite the fine efforts of actress Oglesby, Wilson has yet to energize this character in dramatic terms. Icons are tough that way. Wilson gives her a wonderful, deceptively brief entrance and, later, some strong arias about God and the waters she has crossed. But she's a bit windy.

"Gem" springs out of one of Wilson's peak achievements, "Joe Turner's Come and Gone," which was set in 1911 and is a close cousin in every respect. (The plays share one of Wilson's rare white characters, the so-called people finder Rutherford Selig played by easygoing, droopy-eyed Raynor Scheine.) In "Joe Turner," fiery-eyed Herald Loomis is stricken by a vision of bones rising up out of the ocean. They are the bones of Middle Passage casualities, enslaved Africans who never made it across to America.

A LEAP INTO THE SUPERNATURAL. In "Gem" Wilson expands upon that spellbinding passage, making it a central and splashy element.

Aided by Eli and Black Mary, Ester takes Citizen to the City of Bones by way of a trancelike seance, complete with multicolor lights—the sole misstep in an otherwise gorgeously designed production—and a leap into the supernatural.

This aspect of "Gem" bumps uncomfortably against its more prosaic passages. The Hill District's toadying Little Caesar of a sheriff, who is in fact named Caesar (Peter Jay Fernandez), is not much of an antagonist. Straight out of an "Uncle Tom's Cabin"-brand melodrama, Caesar is not just a venal man of the law; he's a venal landlord, too, the kind who might actually spend his wee hours rehearsing the line, "You must pay the rent!" The character gets some laughs, but they're not really the right ones. It's a testament to Wilson's intuitive skill that he doesn't make Caesar a fire-breathing villain every second. But in the end he's dramatically ineffectual, wandering in and out of a play that, despite its proximity to and overlap with "Joe Turner," is a more stilted affair, its characters isolated in separate, lonesome orbits.

No one can blame Wilson, who has written several of the best American plays of the last couple of decades, for wanting to explore Ester more fully. No one can blame him for revisiting the Middle Passage horrors, albeit in a more literal and less mysterious way than in "Joe Turner." (In "Gem," there's a lot of talk of death, dismemberment, violence of all kinds.) But by literalizing the slave-ship experience and taking Citizen Barlow and the audience to the City of Bones, Wilson may have robbed his own metaphor of its theatrical punch.

There's a larger question nagging at this play. Was Wilson better off as a dramatist before he started looping back on himself, linking his plays' characters in terms of lineage or, in the case of Aunt Ester, bringing an offstage character into the spotlight? (Hedley in "King Hedley" is the son of a character in "Seven Guitars," and so on.) I wonder.

In a more joyous sense, however, I wonder at the authority and skill of McClinton's ensemble. The pacing is on the languid side, but that'll improve naturally with a few more performances.

LOOKING GOOD. The show looks just right, thanks to David Gallo's shadowy scenic design, dominated by a splendid staircase off to one side, and to Constanza Romero's shrewdly characterful costumes, and to Donald Holder's silvery-blue lighting. (Caveat: Those cheesy effects for the City of Bones scene.)

Famous for his shaggy first-drafts, Wilson hasn't yet resolved his extremes between magical-realism and turn-of-the-century corn. As always, though, when his characters hit on just the right memory or image, you know you're listening to a front-rank writer.

The playwright's still cutting this particular stone, but "Gem" may yet shine.

After Richard Christiansen's much-feted retirement in 2002, Michael Phillips (1961–) took over the position of chief theater critic at the

Tribune. He came from the same job at the *Los Angeles Times*; prior to that, he'd been the theater critic at the *St. Paul Pioneer Press*, the *San Diego Union Tribune* and the *Dallas Times-Herald*. Phillips would be a very different kind of critic from Christiansen: a writer with great sharpness, exacting standards and an occasionally withering wit. He would remain in the post through 2006, at which point he replaced Michael Wilmington as the *Tribune*'s film critic; Chris Jones (1963–), the British-born author of this book and a longtime freelance critic by now on staff as Phillips's second-string reviewer, took the theater seat. Both Phillips and Jones were hired by the paper in 2002–it took two writers to replace Christiansen. After that year, when resources at the *Tribune* began to diminish in the face of declining advertising revenues and print circulation, it was difficult to imagine that such a decision had been made.

This Phillips review is of the world premiere of August Wilson's "Gem of the Ocean," one of two Wilson plays to premiere in Chicago ("Seven Guitars" was the other). Premiers notwithstanding, all Wilson's plays have long enjoyed a warm reception in Chicago, where the Goodman Theatre is one of the only theaters in the country to have produced them all. Although written toward the end of Wilson's famous 10-play cycle, "Gem of the Ocean" is the first, chronologically speaking. As had long been his practice, Wilson was traveling with his play on a circuit of regional theaters–he typically revised, and frequently cut, his dramas on their way to Broadway. So Phillips here attempts to help the great African American playwright shape his work.

Wilson was writing quickly at this point. His last play, "Radio Golf" (set in the 1990s), was rushed into completion while the playwright battled cancer (he died in 2005). Many are of the opinion that "Gem," which Phillips endorses here, is Wilson's last great play. Nonetheless, he struggled to raise the necessary funds to take the production to New York. As the *Tribune* reported at the time, he had to keep taking breaks from his writing to schmooze potential backers.

Like Wilson, Stephen Sondheim still had to work for his success.

96

BOUNCE

SONDHEIM DOESN'T 'BOUNCE' HIGH ENOUGH

Goodman Theatre

BY MICHAEL PHILLIPS

JULY 2, 2003. The problem with world-class talents is more our problem than theirs. We expect the world of them, every time. Stephen Sondheim is a world-class talent. He has the right to do a modest, unpretentious show whenever he likes.

But the wit, melodic spice and stylistic brinksmanship distinguishing Sondheim's music theater career, across hugely important shows and minor ones, leaves you unprepared for the dispiriting mildness of "Bounce," Sondheim's first new show since "Passion" nine years ago.

There's a lovely, casual quality to a host of Sondheim tunes past, ranging from the best of his first full-length score, "Saturday Night," to the Jule Styne inflections of "Merrily We Roll Along" to the most fetching songs he wrote for the film "Dick Tracy." So the straightforward, 32-bar world of "Bounce" isn't so un-Sondheimian, really.

Yet the show lacks its titular ingredient. It's not edgy enough in its love/hate brotherly dynamics and exploration in American rapaciousness, and it's not funny enough to be a full-bodied musical comedy. It's eh. And if there's one reaction I thought I'd never have to a new Sondheim musical, it's eh.

In one song, "Addison's City," Sondheim refers to architect Addison Mizner's Spanish-Moorish-Xanadu aesthetic as "everything too much." Despite flashes of inspiration, in "Bounce" everything is not quite enough.

The Goodman Theatre world premiere, which opened Monday, marks the reunion project of composer/lyricist Sondheim and director Harold Prince, their first since "Merrily" in 1981. "Bounce" also reunites Sondheim with librettist John Weidman, his man on "Assassins," as well as "Pacific Overtures," which Prince directed. New as "Bounce" is, a half-century has passed since Sondheim first noodled with a musical about the early 20th Century chameleons known as Addison and Wilson Mizner.

An oft-quoted Broadway wag, Wilson Mizner's resume spanned a hundred professions—from prospector to boxing manager to screenwriter—and a thousand more entrepreneurial scams disguised as professions. Addison Mizner joined his brother in many of these. (He was one of several Mizner children in real life; in the musical, which like most musicals is only a little bit factual, there's only the two of them.) He found his niche as an architect, and in 1920s Florida, he put a giddy grin on the face of Boca Raton with his brother's help, before the boom went flooey.

In scale and spirit, "Bounce" clearly heads in the direction of an old George Abbott show—fast, medium-budget, loud and funny. The song titles bespeak a stripped-down, blunt-edged quality: "Bounce," "Opportunity," "Gold!" (which, for a time, was the show's title, after "Wise Guys"), "Alaska," "The Game," "Talent," "You."

MEETING MADE IN HEAVEN. The show begins with two deaths. Addison, played with unexpected force by Richard Kind, passes on in Florida, creditors at his door. Wilson, played by a strenuously jolly Howard McGillin, dies a screenwriter's dream death in Hollywood: on his back, underneath a would-be starlet. The Mizner brothers meet in heaven and immediately begin fighting, just like old times. "Bounce" unfolds as an extended flashback, its picaresque structure detailing the boys' ups and downs and near-constant rancor.

The Mizners' life "wasn't exactly a Horatio Alger story," as one of the brothers puts it. From Papa Mizner (Herndon Lackey), the boys early on learned to grab opportunity by the nearest available metaphor, especially if the metaphors are of the gambling or pioneering or bouncing variety.

From Mama, portrayed by screen legend Jane Powell with the kind of authority only a screen legend can provide, Wilson and Addison learned that their sibling rivalry was justified. Mama always liked the "fun" brother, Willie, better.

A GENTLE WALTZ. In a deceptively gentle waltz, "Isn't He Something?" Mama lauds him for leaving her "drunk with laughter," crediting Addie more offhandedly with leaving her "sober after."

The closeted homosexual Addison finds fulfillment with young

Hollis Bessemer (Gavin Creel, who has a terrific low-keyed way about him). The other, deeply unsympathetic Mizner, Wilson, is the "bad" one, the disreputable drug addict and thrill junkie.

Early on, in the Yukon, he and Addison meet up with dance hall gal Nellie (Michele Pawk). Years later, in New York, Wilson runs into the newly married and divorced Nellie, now worth millions. They marry; he drags her down with what she calls "the gambling and the cocaine and the chaos."

Too many of Weidman's book scenes plain don't work. In the stridently wacky "New York Sequence," a succession of Wilson's business partners—a prizefighter, playwright—are shot dead in the nuptial bed shared by Wilson and Nellie. The door-slamming antics fall flat. In the Yukon, memories of Hope and Crosby in "Road to Utopia" are plundered, half-heartedly.

Twice, glimmers of the "Bounce" that could've been—though preferably with a different title—shine through the disappointment.

Addison's transformation from lost soul to architect seems to have pulled the best out of Sondheim. In the segment called "Addison's Trip Around the World," which rides on a pleasing, "Paint Your Wagon"-y melody called "I'm On My Way," Addison's taste for collecting whatnots from Guatemala, Hawaii, Hong Kong and elsewhere leads him to realize he needs a place for everything. Why not design one?

This segment goes somewhere and forwards the narrative, elegantly.

When Act 2 takes the action to Florida, "Talent" (Hollis' dream of building an artist's colony) and "You" (an expression of love, both sweet and funny) make you wonder if the real show here—the show lost in the wings, while Sondheim and Weidman focus on an increasingly sour brotherly-love/hate relationship—is the one about how Addison Mizner designed his dream of Jazz Age sunshine. But then, I suppose, comparisons to "Sunday in the Park With George" would run rampant.

FAILS TO MESH. Prince and scenic designer Eugene Lee rely on roll-drop sets to visually propel the story. The drop curtain, which acts as a prelude to orchestrator Jonathan Tunick's mellow "Bounce" overture, depicts a laminated-placement style map of the U.S. It is framed by blow-ups of picture postcards from the show's many locations. The two visual notions don't jibe. And in that regard, they jibe with the rest of the show all too well.

The cast works hard. Kind, who always worked a little too hard on "Spin City," comes through here with a canny, heartfelt performance.

McGillin tries, too, but he's essentially miscast; he doesn't come naturally to seedy, larger-than-life bombast, and he oversells comic and dramatic material that doesn't have enough comedy or drama going for it.

Pawk insinuates her way through the show with ease. But the ups and downs of these constantly reinventing folk aren't much in the end.

In the mid-'50s, Irving Berlin tried and failed to musicalize the Mizner brothers. A handful of tunes written for two different versions survived, and were recorded for the "Unsung Irving Berlin" album. "You're a Sucker for a Dame" and "You're a Sentimental Guy" may sound like the titles of good Berlin, but they're not; they're a little flat, too on-the-nose.

Astonishingly, given the gulf in artistic temperament between Berlin and Sondheim, the same goes for the bulk of the "Bounce" tunes. On first hearing—and I plan on a second—I'd say that something in the Mizner story appears destined to lead legendary Broadway songwriters down a garden path to trouble, like greenhorns being led to a poker table.

For Stephen Sondheim, the Chicago world premiere of "Bounce," his first new musical since "Passion" in 1994, proved to be a rather vexing occasion.

Sondheim first pondered creating a musical about the Mizner brothers back in 1952, when he was just out of college. But as he would tell *New York* magazine many years later, David Merrick had beaten him to the rights to Alva Johnston's book about the Mizners. And so it took 51 years before "Bounce" premiered, to mixed reviews like this one, at the Goodman Theatre in Chicago. Phillips calls the show "eh" here, damning it in two letters.

The musical's creative team had been at pains to downplay the gravitas of the show, describing it before the opening as a kind of romp or unpretentious vaudevillian lark. But a new Sondheim musical premiering in Chicago was big news nonetheless.

Phillips actually went back to the show a few days later and published another notice, essentially saying that he had seen nothing on a second viewing that made him change his mind. He then reviewed it a third time the following November at the John F. Kennedy Center for the Performing Arts in Washington, DC, where he declared the piece "better," if still "vexing." Actually, the show had been intended for the Kennedy Center's twenty-fifth anniversary celebration, but had taken longer to write than Sondheim anticipated.

Thanks in part to this review, it would take until 2008 for Sondheim to get his show to New York—even then, the destination was not Broadway but the New York Public Theatre. By that time, "Bounce" was on its fourth title, "Road Show" (the other two were "Wise Guys" and "Gold!"). Gone were the vaudevillian gestalt, the woman stuck between the brothers, the second act and many of the songs, including what was once the title number. In their place were many deeper individual moments, a newer emphasis on personal relationship, and a minimalist concept. Still, the core of the Mizner brothers' story remained elusive. Perhaps John Weidman and Sondheim had been attracted to a pair of overly amorphous and contradictory human beasts.

In his 2011 autobiography and lyric collection, *Look I Made a Hat* (the follow-up to *Finishing the Hat*), Sondheim devotes a huge amount of space to discussing all the different versions of "Bounce" over a 14-year span, noting that it should offer the interested reader some insight into the tortured development of a musical. "It would be a more effective demonstration if the show had eventually been a hit and the songs familiar," Sondheim wrote, a tad ruefully, "but you'll get the drift."

97

AUGUST: OSAGE COUNTY

'OSAGE COUNTY' A BLAST OF TRUTH AND SIN

Steppenwolf Theatre Company

BY CHRIS JONES

JULY 9, 2007. Given his lip-smacking relish for the agonizing unpeeling of familial pain, it's doubtful that Tracy Letts will be declared the official playwright of the state of Oklahoma any time soon. The Sooners already gave their hearts to that romantic 1943 musical set within their nascent borders, and nobody will want to see "August: Osage County" performed in the Tulsa schools.

But with this staggeringly ambitious—and, for my money, staggeringly successful—three-act domestic opus for the Steppenwolf Theatre Company, Letts has penned a major, not-to-be-missed new American work that eulogizes the perversely nurturing dysfunction of family life on the Plains as surely as it skewers the arid absurdities of its underpinning.

And with the help of director Anna D. Shapiro, Letts has built a vehicle for the great Chicago actress Deanna Dunagan, who plays the caustic Weston family matriarch, presiding over a grown trio of sisters who've rushed home to Pawhuska to find out why their father, a sometime writer and constant drinker, has suddenly disappeared. Popping pills, telling truths and exploding her kids' inadequate defenses, Dunagan spits out the kind of brilliantly acidic performance that will be remembered in this town for years to come.

If you'll pardon the inherent overstatement and reductionism, "August" is like an Oklahoman "Long Day's Journey Into Night" shoved into a blender with Quentin Tarantino (with added Lillian Hellman and Jonathan Franzen syrups). Remarkably, the strangely sweet resultant milkshake re-energizes the great American tradition of the pseudo-memoir about growing up among the parental crazies, because it flavors its recognizable home truths with enough sin, lies and black comedy to keep your eyes popped out on stalks for nearly 3 1/2 hours.

Until now, Letts ("Bug," "Killer Joe") was best known for the comic-gothic thriller. And "August" has recognizably cheeky parentage. Murder is always on the cards. Letts' actual father, Dennis Letts, plays the father who causes all this trouble. And to make the point that his signature Weston family lives on purloined land, Letts brazenly includes a Native American character, deliciously played by Kimberly Guerrero, who literally lives in the attic and comes down to do the white man's cooking.

Despite the inside jokes, the most impressive aspect of this unexpectedly compassionate play is its hubristic but immensely appealing attempt to explain the paradoxes of life that make people go bananas in the oft-forgotten middle of the country. Letts captures the dangerous paradoxes of educated, pseudo-academic lives led in the shade of flyover State U's wholly unfriendly to the growth of ivy. "This is not the Midwest," asserts Barb Weston (Amy Morton, scintillating as the chief sister), as she walks reluctantly through the door of her childhood home. "Michigan is the Midwest, God knows why. This is the Plains: a state of mind, right, some spiritual affliction, like the blues?"

God knows, that's a question that runs to the core of the Steppenwolf aesthetic as Chicago has been led to understand it these past 30 years. And perhaps that's why this remarkable show—more than any other production at this theater in quite some time—so powerfully energizes and centers the acting ensemble. Many of Chicago's artists are refugees from points west. Clearly, Letts knew for whom he was writing. And they're more than happy to unleash their demons for him.

Except for briefly inorganic sections of the third act, when revelations pile up too fast and the play's very few false notes emerge, director Shapiro gets complete truth throughout. So when Morton falls in agony on the stairs after her character gets shocking news, it's the kind of personal collapse that's instantly recognizable as the one that terrifies and awaits us all.

The constantly shifting plot is best experienced rather than spoiled in advance summation, but know that "August" is chock-full of such riveting scenes. Sally Murphy, who plays the least confident of the three sisters, was so moving Saturday afternoon, one deeply invested in her character's quest for a perverse piece of happiness. And as the variously inept, or floundering, or morally questionable spouses, lovers and relatives who inhabit Letts' mostly matriarchal universe, Francis Guinan, Ian Barford, Rick Snyder and (especially) Jeff Perry, make a memorable collection of impotent post-colonists with nothing left to conquer.

The main point, of course, is that there's no escape from Osage County. Mariann Mayberry totally nails the third and final Weston sister: a lost soul who first claims personal salvation in Florida (Florida!) with a crummy man. "Everything lives," she cries, when finally forced to face some truths about her family and herself, "somewhere in the middle."

No critic can offer useful self-analysis. But this first review of the author's tenure as the *Tribune*'s lead theater critic surely is indicative of a new trend in the first decade of the 21st century, when Chicago productions seemed to transfer to New York with greatly increased frequency. By now, the city not only had a theater of its own; it had a creative product for which there clearly was an export market.

To some extent, that was helped by the new ease with which *Tribune* reviews now could be read in New York thanks to Internet access. Even as the changing face of the media roiled the newspaper economically, paving the way for a disastrous deal with real-estate tycoon Sam Zell that would send the once-proud Tribune Company into bankruptcy in December 2008 (it would emerge only at the end of 2012), *Tribune* arts criticism could be more easily read by producers from out of town. As a result, more producers were getting on planes to Chicago to see hit productions like "August: Osage County." The new play by Tracy Letts moved quickly to Broadway, where it outgrossed more than half the musicals on the Great White Way, and then traveled to both London's National Theatre and Sydney, Australia.

"August: Osage County" won the Pulitzer Prize for drama in 2008, making Letts the first Chicago recipient in living memory (David Mamet had already left Chicago when he was afforded the same honor). Without question, the play is one of the most important ever written in the city. It would be reviewed in the *Tribune* several times; the notice here is only the first. Anna D. Shapiro, Letts and Steppenwolf actresses Deanna Dunagan and Rondi Reed would all go on to win Tony Awards. Amy Morton would score a Tony nomination and widespread acclaim for her emotionally intense performance. The script would become the fastest-selling title in the history of its publisher, the Theatre Communications Group. And "August" would also set off a feeding frenzy of sorts, attracting a slew of A-list actresses interested in snagging the lead roles in the movie version, scheduled for release in the fall of 2013, with Meryl Streep and Julia Roberts in the two lead roles.

To a large extent, "August" rebranded the Steppenwolf Theatre for a new generation while continuing to showcase its ensemble-driven aesthetic. The New York reviews would be very positive, especially when it came to the production. But when it came to the question of whether this is a truly great American play—an heir to, if not a peer to, the O'Neill model—a split emerged. Some critics took the same position as the review here, arguing that the play is the first great American drama of the 21st century. Others thought it to be an enjoyable but terribly overpraised melodrama in the Lillian Hellman rather than the Eugene O'Neill tradition. Various critics' impressions depended on whether they regarded the characters as sufficiently weighty in metaphor and magnitude, and the narrative in theme and truth. And these depended on whether they thought the great American play could (or should) be updated for an era when audiences require a little more free-flowing, self-aware juice with their traditional steak.

We could argue with foundation that "August: Osage County" cheapened the form. Or we could argue with even firmer foundation that it revitalized it like no other drama in decades. Either way, audiences flocked to see the play, which would become one of the most famous of the Chicago productions.

98

A STEADY RAIN

'A STEADY RAIN' POURS FORTH FLOOD OF COP ATMOSPHERICS

Chicago Dramatists

BY CHRIS JONES

SEPTEMBER 29, 2007. Whenever your spirit gets weary, the Chicago theater pops out a new play like Keith Huff's "A Steady Rain," a gritty, rich, thick, poetic and entirely gripping noir tale of two Chicago police officers whose inner need to serve and protect both consumes them and rips them apart.

But a stellar new Chicago play's emergence is rarely accompanied by a production with the raw guts of Russ Tutterow's simple but nonetheless powerful world premiere at the diminutive Chicago Dramatists studio.

Sweating nervously under the lights and both fighting to tell their side of the duologue from the other side of a table, actors Randy Steinmeyer and Peter DeFaria look, feel and sound exactly like what they claim to be. Cops rather than actors. Flawed humans rather than archetypes. Lifelong Chicagoans whose childhood playground was a Dan Ryan overpass and whose core values aren't up for debate or subject to the conclusions of a sensitivity seminar.

It's not that we haven't seen these kinds of characters on a stage before—any police drama has to navigate its way around an overcooked genre. It's just that Huff creates a pair of frontline workers who manage to be intensely sympathetic and, on occasion, thoroughly repellent. Better yet, their inner conflicts are expressed with such articulate humanity that your throat gets constricted as you watch them.

Steinmeyer and DeFaria are willing to go to some very tough places here for your artistic stimulation, and I surely wouldn't miss the chance to watch them make that journey. This is far and away the best show I've ever seen at Chicago Dramatists, and I've been going there regularly for 15 years.

As professions go, theater critic and police officer aren't close cousins. But I reckon most real Chicago cops would admire this 95-minute show. For sure, the core story deals with an officer whose domestic turmoil intrudes inappropriately on his duties. You can see echoes here of the police brutality scandals that have roiled this and other police departments at darker moments in their histories. But even as he makes no excuses, Huff also makes you see why. The play seems to understand all sides. And for its backdrop, we have the very streets outside this theater.

Huff needs to work on (and shorten) the last 15 overwritten minutes, which are the only moments when a mental comparison with Hollywood genre intrudes and pulls you away from the reality of the Chicago moment. But the storytelling skills of this Iowa-trained playwright are truly remarkable.

In many ways, "A Steady Rain" reminds me of "Hizzoner," the long-running theater piece about the first Mayor Daley. Both shows seem to understand the human toll of keeping order in Chicago.

"A Steady Rain" would travel all the way from the tiny Chicago Dramatists, the scene of this review of the world premiere, to Broadway, where the two Chicago actors reviewed here would be replaced by two megastars: Daniel Craig and Hugh Jackman. Along the way, the success of this simple drama about two Chicago cops would change the life of its 48-year-old playwright, Keith Huff (unknown at the time of its premiere), but also lose its specificity and its Chicago soul.

Several of the city's theaters had rejected the play before it finally got produced at Dramatists. After this review, it was picked up by two commercial producers, Frank Gero and Raymond L. Gaspar, who first restaged the show with its original cast and directors at Chicago's Royal George Theatre Cabaret. Then both Craig and Jackman became attached to the project, which made Broadway a natural locale. When "A Steady Rain" moved to Broadway in the fall of 2009, the presence of these stars sold virtually every ticket of its limited 12-week run. Bizarrely that summer, two plays set (at least partly) in the Uptown neighborhood of Chicago were both playing at the same time on Broadway, virtually across the street from each other (Tracy Letts' "Superior Donuts" was the other show). They were part of a rush of Chicago shows to Broadway.

Craig and Jackman came to Chicago to research their roles, causing a small riot at a courthouse building, but neither was as convincing as Peter DeFaria and Randy Steinmeyer had seemed on the night of this review. Sometimes celebrity can get in the way. The design of the Broadway production was especially irritating. Everyone, it seemed, had confused the three-flats of Uptown, the actual Chicago neighborhood, with the brooding towers of Harlem—or what New Yorkers think of when they hear the word *uptown*.

New York critics were not kind to Huff or his play. Nonetheless, writing offers poured in from Hollywood, and he ended up writing for the hit cable-TV series "Mad Men." Eventually, he came back to Chicago, but he no longer needed a day job.

99

OUR TOWN

'OUR TOWN' ASTOUNDS! THAT'S RIGHT, 'OUR TOWN'

Chopin Theatre

BY CHRIS JONES

MAY 3, 2008. David Cromer has directed some distinguished Chicago productions in his career, including Next Theatre's "The Adding Machine," for which he just snagged a bucket-load of award nominations. But I think his brilliantly revisionist and astounding new production of Thornton Wilder's "Our Town" by The Hypocrites is his masterwork to date. And it takes place in a Wicker Park basement for 20 bucks a ticket.

In the jaw-dropping third act, which makes some truly shocking and inspired conceptual choices that are best experienced without foreknowledge, I found myself speaking the words "Oh, my God" to no one. And despite eccentricities, I'm not that given to inappropriate interjections. It's just that this "Our Town" hit me that hard.

If your tastes run to shows that make you stare right in the face of your own mortality and inability to prioritize what and who really matters in life, your own petty obsessions and jealousies, then cancel whatever you're doing tonight and go and see this show. And, to save you an e-mail after, you're welcome.

"He's going on like this about Thornton Wilder's 'Our Town?'" you must be thinking. "That hoary small-town staple of the high school repertory?" Ah, but you've never seen it done like this before.

Here is what Cromer (who plays the stage manager along with directing) does: He removes every last shred of sentimentality from the piece, replacing it with a blend of cynicism and simple human truth. But—and here's the rub—he does so without removing the vitality and sincerity. Like many great revivals (the current "South Pacific" at Lincoln Center is in my mind), it's neither archly conceptual nor a subversion of a great American play, but an explication for the modern age.

I'm telling you, it's that revelatory a show.

Wilder, of course, deserves much of the credit. I kept thinking of the last episode of "Six Feet Under," when Alan Ball whisked us forward to learn the mostly undignified fates of the characters we'd come to love. Wilder did much the same in 1938, and he was smart enough to do so in the middle of the play.

In Cromer's hands, it's as if you're being whisked in and out of your own grave. His modern-dress "Our Town" is staged in and around the audience. You spend two hours thinking about communities and what we've done to them, as well as about how parents in small towns risk imbuing their children with the tyranny of low expectations.

The performances aren't flashy, or the work of hugely experienced actors, but most of them are pitch perfect nonetheless. Tim Curtis does superb work as Mr. Webb; Stacy Stoltz is a deeply emotional Mrs. Gibbs; Jennifer Grace is a yearning, believable Emily. In the third act, the actors seem to come out of the floor and surround you with their sadness and stoicism.

Cromer calibrates "Our Town" with clear-eyed intelligence. You see the beauties of small-town America and its limitations, laid out before you as directly and powerfully as the Chicago theater can muster.

This remarkable production of "Our Town" by the Chicago company known as the Hypocrites, staged in the basement of the Chopin Theatre, made director David Cromer's career. Moreover, it would turn into a longer New York run for the iconic drama than it had received even when first written.

The review here—another, of a 1939 production, appears earlier in this collection—was almost never written. The *Tribune* was pondering taking a pass on the show; nobody was expecting much from yet another version of the overexposed Thornton Wilder classic, long associated with earnest but sanitized high school productions. The Hypocrites were using non-Equity actors. The show was to be performed in the basement of the Chopin Theatre–a cramped space with notably intrusive pillars. But from that sort of thing in Chicago, remarkable results can emerge.

As the review notes, Cromer had excised all shreds of sentimentality from the play and forced his audience to confront its own mortality as surely as if he'd delivered the news that everyone was suffering from a collective terminal disease. Not only did Cromer direct this conceptual wonder, he leveraged his own complicated personality into the central role of the narrator. It was a performance that (somehow) combined compassion, intelligence and the kind of earnest bluntness that we always want from a physician delivering tough news. The show was a huge hit, selling out and returning for an encore run the following autumn.

This wasn't the first time Cromer has dazzled Chicago audiences in intimate surroundings. His 2006 production of "Come Back, Little Sheba" for Shattered Globe was a brilliant piece of direction. So was his take on Austin Pendleton's "Orson's Shadow" in 2000 at the Steppenwolf Theatre. These shows used different levels of actors, ranging from big New York names and the likes of Tracy Letts to the mostly youthful, non-Equity crew making up the cast of "Our Town." But Cromer's productions have all had a brilliant conceptual core, rooted in the most powerful kinds of human truths. Truth, precision and revelation form his collective calling card.

In 2009, Cromer's "Our Town" moved to the Barrow Street Theatre in New York, where it ran for more than a year (though there were fewer bodies in the graveyard). After being awarded a so-called genius grants from the MacArthur Foundation, Cromer became a Broadway director, and was profiled in the *New York Times Magazine*.

"Our Town" played other theaters. Cromer did other shows, in Chicago, New York and elsewhere. But that magical Chicago night in the basement of the Chopin Theatre was never replicated.

100

CLYBOURNE PARK

PLAY ON HOUSING, RACE OFFERS NEW WRINKLES TO 'RAISIN'

Steppenwolf Theatre Company

BY CHRIS JONES

SEPTEMBER 19, 2011. If you question whether the discussion of Chicago's racist history can still cause shivers among modern-day Chicago theatergoers, you need only watch what happens at the Steppenwolf Theatre in the first act of Bruce Norris' searing play "Clybourne Park." Quite often there are moments in theater when an audience, suddenly brought to attention, falls quiet. But the silence that suddenly descends at Steppenwolf when a white seller of a house in 1959 asks the simple question, "Well, what sort of people are they?" is something else entirely. It is the silence that comes only with fear and recognition.

You hear sharp intakes of breath, see a few heads spin around to discreetly check the racial composition of the audience, and then there's a kind of palpable dread of what's coming, even though the tawdry history of race, real estate and Chicago—the stories of "turned neighborhoods," violence, expressways constructed as lines of racial demarcation, rapid flights to Glen this or Elm that—has been amply recounted in numerous volumes.

We're still less than a life span removed from the issues that the late Lorraine Hansberry wrote of in 1959 with her seminal Chicago drama "A Raisin in the Sun." When revealed, or re-revealed, with the skill that Norris re-reveals them in "Clybourne Park"—both a riff on and a chronological expansion of "Raisin"—they still are raw. Superficially, the dilemma of the Youngers, a black family that wants nothing more than the right to live where it wants, has been solved. The Youngers could likely do that now. But you only have to drive down one of the streets around Steppenwolf, perhaps one of the streets that, strangely, is not a through street but dead-ends on a certain block, to see how little, as well as how much, has changed.

Even though Steppenwolf has premiered almost all of Norris' work—he would not have a career as a writer without this theater—

"Clybourne Park" arrives belatedly in Chicago, with a past in New York and London. (It opened Sunday night under Amy Morton's restrained and carefully wrought direction and featured unstinting performances from John Judd and Karen Aldridge.) It comes with a formidable reputation, having won this year's Pulitzer Prize for drama. Another, separate production is headed to Broadway later this season. "Clybourne Park" is everywhere, but, mark, nowhere else is it playing within a few steps of Clybourn Avenue. The aspirational white neighborhood in "Raisin" was fictional, but that one word, "Clybourne," was a pretty good indication of the locale in Hansberry's mind. And the play is being performed right there. Designer Todd Rosenthal's house is, to say the least, recognizable, although a bit too nice to knock down.

"Clybourne Park" is a masterful work for various reasons. Its referents back to the Hansberry play are as inspired as they are logical. Act 1 of the Norris play is set, at precisely the same moment, in the very house where Hansberry's Youngers want to move. Norris focuses on the white family (a couple, played by Judd and Kirsten Fitzgerald) moving out to the suburbs, and the attempts of those in their neighborhood to prevent the sale of the house to a black family. Norris' conceit is that no one realized the race of the buyers until the eleventh hour, which, given the well-documented tactics of some of the fear-mongering real estate agents of the era, is entirely credible.

Karl Lindner (Cliff Chamberlain), the notorious representative of the "residents association" who shows up at the South Side door of the buyers in the Hansberry play only to be rebuffed, has now come to dissuade the sellers from making the sale, which also makes perfect sense. Norris proffers a couple of equally inspired solutions to the issues that "Raisin" raises but does not really explore. He suggests that the white sellers didn't care about selling to a black family because they had their own reasons to hate their community—and maybe they weren't alone, and maybe that's why communities like the one they lived in fractured—and he comes up with a reason as to how Lena Younger got the cheaper house that made her move possible.

Act 2 is set in 2009 in the same Clybourne Park. Now a white family wants to move into what has become a predominantly black neighborhood. Well, "move in" isn't the best expression. It wants to tear down the house and build a McMansion (in 2009, Norris just got in under the recessionary wire for that to be credible). This time, the black residents aren't pleased. Echoes of the past—descendants of the previous generations, victims of race wars from one side or another—are everywhere, despite new language and carefully negotiated intimacies. Double-casting reveals many resonances. And yet at the heart of the play is another American agony that perhaps has nothing to do with the color of anyone's skin.

And that's why this is Norris' best play. Steppenwolf audiences are familiar with his satirical skills, his ease with lampooning urban liberals with kids and SUVs and revealing the hypocrisy behind their trips to Whole Foods—their raw ambition, their fevered, dysfunctional souls. But "Clybourne Park" goes a great deal further. Simply put, it understands and explicates the roots of hate in fear. There is nothing smug or distant or cheap about the authorial voice: It is compassionate and it takes responsibility, even as it is relentless in its peeling of the racial onion, down to its fetid core.

Morton's cast doesn't immediately kick into gear. Fitzgerald and Chamberlain offer relatively broad characterizations—Fitzgerald layers her work with a kind of 1950s gauze—that take time to grab hold, but they surely wield some power (Fitzgerald is best in the second act; Chamberlain in the first). Stephanie Childers, who plays Karl's wife, and then a buyer, is fine throughout. So is Brendan Marshall-Rashid, in both acts a weaselly hanger-on, and the subtly self-effacing James Vincent Meredith, who plays two African-American men who seem to have very different stations in life and yet find themselves constantly having to calm others down.

But this production is rightly dominated by Judd, who plays the wound-tight seller escaping to the suburbs, where he hopes he can uncoil. Judd paints a formidable picture of a bitter, angry man whose sense of community has been upended and who smells both revenge and misery. And there is no other Chicago actress who can convey the weight of moral authority quite like Aldridge, even when, as the years of the play go by, she finds herself moving from playing a black maid, looking to keep the lid on a white tinderbox, to a richer, more powerful, more assertive woman, stuck on the other side of a still-yawning divide. And probably no happier.

Lorraine Hansberry's "A Raisin in the Sun," reviewed by Claudia Cassidy earlier in this book, was the inspiration for "Clybourne Park," a play by Bruce Norris that would sweep New York and London, winning the Laurence Olivier Award for best new play in London, the Tony Award for best new play and the 2011 Pulitzer Prize for drama.

This drama would become one of the most successful plays ever written about Chicago—and it suggested that the complex relationship between race and real estate in that city remained raw half a century after Hansberry's portrayal.

Norris, a former Chicagoan and Northwestern University graduate known for a caustic writing style, pursued a twin-track career as an actor and a playwright (he appeared in the movie *The Sixth Sense*, among other credits) before emphasizing writing in more recent years. He has had a long relationship with the Steppenwolf Theatre Company, which has premiered almost all his works (including "The Infidel," "We All Went Down to Amsterdam," "The Pain and the Itch," "A Parallelogram") except, it turned out, his most successful play of all. When the play won the Pulitzer, Steppenwolf artistic director Martha Lavey explained that she had decided to premiere "A Parallelogram" instead, on the grounds that she considered "Clybourne" more of a departure from the playwright's usual socioeconomic themes.

But after its triumphs in New York and London, "Clybourne Park" did return home to Chicago, where it received the blistering Steppenwolf production reviewed here. After all, it is set in the Lincoln Park neighborhood immediately surrounding the theater, so it's certainly not hard to imagine Norris basing this brilliant play's white characters on Steppenwolf subscribers, the very people in his audience.

And so "Clybourne Park" landed at Steppenwolf in a way it could not land anywhere else but in Chicago. Yet, had Cassidy not supported "Raisin" at its time of greatest need, probably none of this would have happened.

101

THE ICEMAN COMETH

THE BOTTLE AND THE DAMAGE DONE \ ROBERT FALLS, NATHAN LANE, BRIAN DENNEHY AND ENSEMBLE CAST PLUMB THE FASCINATING DEPTHS OF 'ICEMAN COMETH'

Goodman Theatre

BY CHRIS JONES

MAY 4, 2012. They don't talk the language of chemical addiction in Harry Hope's New York saloon—once a first-class hangout for sports, now a brutal "Bottom of the Sea Rathskeller" where the denizens have fallen as far as anyone can fall in this world, save for that one final tumble. In Eugene O'Neill's day, boozing to mind-numbing excess was seen as a character flaw, a weakness, a psychological consequence, a pastime of men who've left the field for the grandstand and find themselves damned either way.

But despite this great American drama's existential themes—its conclusions about how, when forcibly shorn of our life-enabling, self-delusional pipe dreams and made to confront the tyranny of our own reduced expectations, we're all in danger of jumping off the fire escape—bottles of alcohol are characters as potent as Larry Slade, James "Jimmy Tomorrow" and the rest of the gang. Their end-of-the-line cafe has popped up on the stage of the Goodman Theatre in honor of director Robert Falls' closely detailed, formatively rich and relentless demanding production of "The Iceman Cometh," starring the very complicated duo of Brian Dennehy and Nathan Lane and a formidably intense ensemble of actors whose demons rage before you for close to five hours.

Although never explicitly referenced, there's a clash here between the modern language of addiction—which would argue that without sobriety, all else is just more delusion—and the way O'Neill's flailing clutch of mutually enabling drunks writhe and dance around the insistence of Theodore "Hickey" Hickman, the dark, dangerous angel of this saloon, that they put away their pipe dreams and find peace with their own dismal reality. It's one of the main fascinating aspects of this searing evening of theater. The play, written in 1939 and deeply and

THE CAST OF THE GOODMAN THEATRE'S 2012 PRODUCTION OF "THE ICEMAN COMETH," HAILED BY MANY AS THE FINEST SET OF CHICAGO ACTORS EVER ASSEMBLED IN A SINGLE SHOW. PHOTOGRAPH BY LIZ LAUREN FOR THE *CHICAGO TRIBUNE*.

profoundly understood by this director, paints as brutal a picture of the destructive power of the demon drink as any playwright ever has painted. Yet its action doesn't turn on a comfortingly simplistic drunk-sober axis. To watch "Iceman" today—a production on this level, anyway—is to feel you know more about these characters than they know about themselves, and yet have that surety constantly upended.

You find yourself wanting to tell 'em all to put down the drink first and then make a choice, for God's sake, only to find you actually could use one or two yourself. In this oft-brutal life, who's to say alcohol is not as valid a palliative as any? Not O'Neill, nor Falls, nor Dennehy's Larry, that's for sure. We see what such a view does to Hickey and those who love him.

In the ever-fascinating trajectory of a career indivisible from the city where he has done almost all his work, Falls' third production of this play arrives as he tries to pull away from his huge, high-profile, conceptual spectacles and focus on simpler human detail in the Stanislavskian tradition. You can see both sides of the man on display here—fascinatingly, this latest "Iceman" for Falls is both a fresh walk outdoors, and a comforting retreat to a previous success. That's manifest in Kevin Depinet's powerful set design (inspired by John Conklin's set for the 1990 production), which manages to be at once simple and then suddenly epic. And the inherent duality of Falls' work here—the tension between past and present—is a potent and wholly appropriate echo of what O'Neill's characters are undergoing. It is a show in sync with the text and the times, both reverent and aptly exploratory of a new, nervous moment.

Deep directorial work with fine ensemble actors is the most successful element of this production. When John Hoogenakker's soused Willie gets the heebie-jeebies, you get the shakes yourself. That's just one example. The bar is filled with these rich and haunting individual pictures, be it James Harms' heartbreaking Jimmy (a quietly magnificent turn), John Judd's seething Piet, John Reeger's atrophied old limey, Larry Neumann Jr.'s old circus man or John Douglas Thompson's Joe Mott. Thompson, whose big scene is riveting, offers an endlessly complex fusion of geniality and rage. And then there's Lee Wilkof's Hugo, a darkly comic character who barely lifts his head from the table, and you can't blame him.

The tarts are fulsome souls from Kate Arrington, Lee Stark and Tara Sissom, and the two bartenders, Rocky (Salvatore Inzerillo) and Chuck (Marc Grapey) grouse their way through their amoral (or immoral) jobs pouring from bottles, trying not to get too scared themselves. Although fully realized all the way down the cast list, the detail of these characterizations is most potently on display through Stephen Ouimette's Harry Hope, a character whose personal crisis is so believable and wrenching as to dominate the third act, and a good chunk of the fourth. More than anyone else onstage, the terribly sad Ouimette shows us the warmblooded man that was, or that could still be, if growing old were only easier. It's a stunning performance.

Dennehy is no slouch here either. The veteran actor long has occupied a particular, paternalistic spot in the Falls universe, and you can see here the singular relationship between this huge onstage persona and this director, writ large on the O'Neill canvas. Falls directs his longtime muse as mostly separate from the assemblage, frequently bathing him in his own glow, part of a rich light scape from Natasha Katz. Dennehy, clad in a costume from Merrily Murray-Walsh that hangs from a frame more gaunt than we remember, digs into his increasingly Beckettian self, staring out front on most occasions, a raw picture of a man growing old and not much liking where it has left him. As Dennehy's Larry ruminates, Patrick Andrews' uncompromising Don Parritt, the young, surrogate son who has come to demand the drunk but brilliant old anarchist get back into the game, sits at his shoulder. Gnawing at him like a gnat. Dennehy keeps sinking off into some malaise, only to come roaring back into antagonistic life every few minutes, spitting out confrontational lines and grabbing attention as he sees the high cost of listening to Hickey, a visiting character beloved for his long history of bankrolling booze-ups, so much faster than everyone else.

Lane, a star name with the guts to challenge himself, has yet to find all the requisite sides of his doomed salesman. Hickey is a charmer with money, and when Lane first enters smiling, throwing dollar bills into the air, he embodies that side of his man. You believe he can sell anything, even himself. And, to his further credit, Lane doesn't hesitate to reveal the deep personal pain underneath, including one scintillating moment of personal collapse. His performance does not lack for poignancy or a dark side. One has flashes of Oliver Hardy, and then a gut-wrenching glimpse of the loneliness of the man on the road.

But this most crucial performance, at this juncture, does lack for menace and malevolence—crucial persuasive qualities that, I think, Lane could yet find within himself. These drinkers are instantly scared of Hickey, who they want to believe will care for their needs but who they feel brings danger and the scars of death. One might think of him as the dark doppelganger of the angelic Czech woman in the musical "Once." Here, we don't see what scares them so much. Lane's Hickey is too separate from the whole. It is as if he has forged a complex, intense performance all by himself but has yet to plug it into the network. Such a connection is the ongoing challenge for this gifted actor, especially if this show is to move to Broadway. "Iceman" relies on Hickey not just to be things, but to do things to others, as life and the bottle have done to him.

With Chicago theater an ongoing entity and the fiscally diminished *Tribune* nonetheless publishing daily theater reviews, any ending to this collection of reviews risks seeming arbitrary. But the Goodman Theatre's 2012 production of "The Iceman Cometh," a singular feast of Chicago acting, seems as apt a production as any with which to close this book.

Nathan Lane, the star of this show, has said in numerous interviews that Chicago is the only city in which he would want to take such a risk. The resultant production was not perfect, but it nonetheless embodied so many of the qualities for which *Tribune* critics such as Percy Hammond, Claudia Cassidy, Linda Winer and Richard Christiansen, in their different ways and styles, had campaigned: a world-class, homegrown theater putting on a classic, consummately American play—the very play, actually, that so vexed Cassidy when it was not honored with a critic's award—better than any other city in the world.

"The Iceman Cometh" had Chicago-style intensity, Chicago-style truth, a Chicago-style disdain for profitability, a Chicago-style focus on actors who understood the working, drinking stiff. Its director understood scale and magnitude and his home city's inherent and long-standing aesthetic relationship with the Daniel Burnham creed "Make no small plans." This was a show with brawn and a bleeding heart. If any production could be said to be a culmination of the issues discussed in all these reviews across so many decades, this is that show.

Here was a production embodying a Chicago theater that had—some 150 years after the *Tribune* started reviewing shows—matured, cemented its own brand, developed its art. It no longer needed to define itself entirely in relation to New York—which is not to say it would ever get over its Second City complex entirely, as this was such an essential part of the city's artistic identity. Even so, it's no longer likely that some successor to Hammond will overhear a New York director or producer telling his or her cast to "make it loud for Chicago." Our Town may be younger than New York, but it wasn't born yesterday.

More likely, that director or producer will be overheard worrying about making the show good enough for a theater city that has come so very far. May there always be a critic from the *Chicago Tribune*, regardless of ownership or platform of publication, cajoling, kvetching, encouraging and, above all, watching the work, night after night.

--30--

ACKNOWLEDGMENTS

This book would not have been possible without the kind help of many people. I'd like to thank Gerould Kern, current editor of the *Chicago Tribune*, and Jane Hirt, its managing editor, for making these reviews and illustrations available and for opening up the newspaper's morgue and library for use. Three other editors at the *Tribune*, Geoff Brown, Doug George and Scott Powers, were also crucial in helping this project come to fruition.

My patient, supportive editor at the University of Chicago Press, Paul E. Schellinger, and his assistant, Jenny Gavacs, deserve much of the credit for the final shape of the book. Arvid Sponberg and Frank Rich, who read and commented on drafts of the manuscript and suggested some of the reviews that appear here, also provided enormous help, as did Jeffrey Eric Jenkins.

I could not have finished this work without the help of Sarah August Hecht, my editorial assistant, who shared my love of these old reviews and retyped so many of those from the predigital era. The errors and questionable judgments herein, however, are all my own.

My wife, Gillian Darlow, and my two sons, Peter and Evan, were just as supportive as they are when I leave them to go to the theater. My parents, Arnold and Jacqueline Jones, were great sounding boards, as on all else in my life.

I'd also like to thank the several living *Tribune* critics, who greeted this project with enthusiasm.

This book is for Peter and Evan, who came to the theater young and, I hope, will love its successes for a lifetime while tolerating its failures. And it's dedicated to the oft-beleaguered, hardworking men and women of American newspapers who go to the theater, or the movies, or the concert hall, or the nightclub, night-in, night-out, and tell us what they find there.

BIBLIOGRAPHY

Bryer, Jackson R., and Robin Gibbs Wilder, eds. *The Selected Letters of Thornton Wilder.* New York: HarperCollins, 2008.

Christiansen, Richard. *A Theater of Our Own: A History and a Memoir of 1,001 Nights in Chicago.* Evanston: Northwestern University Press, 2004.

Gitlin, Martin. *Audrey Hepburn: A Biography*. Westport, CT: Greenwood Press, 2009.

Grossman, James R., Ann Durkin Keating, and Janice L. Reiff, eds. *The Encyclopedia of Chicago.* Chicago: University of Chicago Press, 2004.

Gussow, Mel. *Edward Albee: A Singular Journey.* New York: Applause Theatre Books, 2001.

Hecht, Ben. *A Child of the Century.* New York: Plume, 1954.

Hughes, Langston. *The Big Sea*. New York: Alfred A. Knopf, 1940.

Kipling, Rudyard. *American Notes*. Boston: Brown, 1899.

Kolin, Philip. *Tennessee Williams: A Guide to Research and Performance.* Westport, CT: Greenwood Press, 1998.

Linn, James Weber. *Jane Addams: A Biography.* Champaign: University of Illinois Press.

LuPone, Patti. *A Memoir.* New York: Three Rivers Press, 2010.

Niven, Penelope. *Thornton Wilder: A Life.* New York: HarperCollins, 2012.

Rose, Philip. *You Can't Do That on Broadway!* New York: Proscenium, 2001.

Sweet, Jeffrey. *Something Wonderful Right Away*. New York: Limelight Editions, 1987.

Walker, Alexander. *Vivien: A Life.* London: George Weidenfeld and Nicolson, 1987.

Wendt, Lloyd. *Chicago Tribune: The Rise of a Great American Newspaper.* Chicago: Rand McNally, 1979.

Wilde, Oscar. *Essays and Lectures by Oscar Wilde,* London: Methuen, 1908.

. . . and the pages of the *Chicago Tribune*

INDEX